Campbell's Collection

Over 800 Stories,
Observations,
Personal Experiences,
and Minority Opinions

by Thomas D. Campbell

Illustrations by Dudley Condron

2012

Third Printing

Cumberland Presbyterian Resources
8207 Traditional Place
Cordova, Tennessee 38016-7414

Campbell's Collection

Entire contents ©2009 by Thomas D. Campbell. World rights reserved. This book may not be reproduced in whole or in part, or transmitted in any form, or by any means electronic, mechanical, photocopying, recording, or others, without written permission of the publisher, except by a reviewer who may quote brief passages in a review.

Third printing, April 2012.

ISBN: 978-0615625645

Cumberland Presbyterian Resource Distribution
  8207 Traditional Place, Cordova (Memphis),
  Tennessee 38016-7414

About the Author

THOMAS D. CAMPBELL was born in Decatur, Texas, on March 31, 1939. He grew up in McKenzie, Tennessee, and earned degrees from Bethel College and the Cumberland Presbyterian Theological Seminary in that town, and later a pair of degrees at Brite Divinity School at Texas Christian University in Fort Worth. He has been Director of the Program of Alternate Studies for the denomination since August 1, 1994. In the years prior to that he was pastor of churches in Texas, Arkansas, Kentucky, and Tennessee. He was weekend pastor of three churches in Arkansas from 1995 to 1997. Since that time he has been serving in the same capacity with two Presbyterian congregations in Northern Mississippi. While a pastor in Knoxville, Tennessee, he and Dudley Condron traveled to Colombia, South America, for a two-week visit to churches and mission points in February, 1988. Tom and Dudley traded puns going and coming, which exhibited gradual but certain deterioration in quality and taste. Dudley's dentist in Memphis, Dr. Herbert Blumenthal, is a lifelong friend of Tom Campbell's. Herb and Tom were members of the Class of 1957 of McKenzie High School. Tom and Dudley go way back, too, but Tom did not know that Herb and Dudley knew each other until a few years ago.

About the Illustrator

DUDLEY CONDRON is a native of Muskogee, Oklahoma. He has degrees from Bethel College and the Cumberland Presbyterian Theological Seminary, both in McKenzie, Tennessee. He was pastor of churches in Oklahoma and Tennessee. For two decades he was Editor of <u>The Missionary Messenger</u> for the Board of Missions of the Cumberland Presbyterian Church. After retirement Dudley attended the University of Memphis and earned a degree in art, an area of interest he had cultivated throughout the years. His dentist friend, Herbert Blumenthal, encouraged him to go and get an art degree. That spurred him on and he reached another pinnacle in his life with that achievement. There have been many occasions when Dudley has had opportunities to exhibit his art work in the Memphis area. He and his wife Joyce attend the Cumberland Presbyterian Church in Germantown, Tennessee.

Topical Index

Listed By Story Number

Animals and Other Creatures of God

29	90	91	203	254	255	267	292	742

Christian Life

48	62	65	70	73	76	86	115	122	141
144	167	178	179	186	198	200	206	229	240
242	250	278	293	317	319	341	358	364	365
371	372	413	444	454	456	464	472	477	493
501	548	555	616	656	790	818	821	827	837
860	866	881							

Church

13	18	19	33	41	42	43	47	49	52
54	64	66	71	72	104	106	114	119	120
138	143	152	173	190	205	230	248	258	274
284	308	336	337	348	369	379	380	391	392
425	450	457	458	465	466	467	478	484	495
504	522	527	534	541	567	589	609	611	624
626	632	636	639	648	659	673	674	675	718
739	747	777	778	783	805	829	846	859	879
885	888	889	895						

Church Signs

28	84	94	163	183	294	349	357	366	415
441	470	473	480	481	488	492	517	519	536
539	544	558	559	583	595	602	612	617	620
640	672	676	689	690	693	696	705	729	735
743	755	760	774	780	791	819	848	855	861
864									

Cumberland Presbyterian Church

157	264	265	291	304	311	318	367	411	461
474	526	568	571	572	642	649	671	677	680
681	798	804	810	820	822	878			

Driving

4	7	8	10	12	24	36	38	724	782

Family

56	57	98	168	169	170	171	208	209	210
216	227	231	232	249	257	268	270	302	303
329	340	360	385	386	613	661	662	663	664
665	709	715	716	781	784	826	863	875	880
891	896								

Marriage

103	192	193	285	396	482	529	530	543	545
614	703	768	831						

McKenzie, Tennessee

67	80	134	135	136	140	162	212	224	416
435	479	494	532	580	641	643	654	751	858

Ministerial Blunders

5	6	59	95	96	118	137	142	166	191
194	266	310	333	350	351	352	359	538	540
566	569	610	771	853					

The Ministry

14	30	32	45	46	81	113	116	125	158
161	195	196	201	236	273	286	305	314	331
335	343	347	353	362	368	489	533	542	547
573	607	628	629	669	711	752	754	757	773
794	807	809	815	823	824	834	838	845	847
869	872	884							

Other Signs (Besides Church Signs)

1	127	128	164	176	181	182	239	260	261
281	283	295	296	354	423	424	442	459	471
490	491	511	513	546	564	600	618	631	634
645	660	697	710	713	722	727	728	737	738
740	764	779	792	795	799	873	894		

Personal Experiences

2	3	15	20	21	22	23	25	26	31
35	37	39	44	50	51	60	61	69	79
83	99	100	105	107	108	132	148	172	211
238	252	256	263	287	306	320	339	356	375
378	387	389	390	399	402	403	409	410	412
436	447	475	550	556	562	563	570	578	579
586	587	594	596	603	605	606	635	638	679
686	687	698	699	701	717	734	736	811	812
830	836	851	854	856	867	868	883	887	890
893	897								

Politics

147	197	215	316	338	344	345	406	432	448
455	463	485	515	520	554	560	561	565	575
576	582	585	623	630	666	683	685	700	708
731	749	750	758	765	766	767	775	793	817
833									

Prayer

11	110	111	123	126	145	146	246	300	521
608	621	650	668	814					

Preaching

16	17	85	92	93	109	117	149	151	175
177	185	188	189	207	226	269	271	307	309
397	401	404	419	420	421	449	460	497	502
505	506	508	510	516	525	531	574	584	590
591	592	593	597	644	651	652	653	655	657
684	695	712	723	744	745	748	759	786	787
789	800	801	803	813	835	840	841	842	843
844	850	857							

Program of Alternate Studies

438	439	552	625	682	730	797

Scriptures

53	97	102	112	130	131	150	155	156	159
160	214	219	220	221	222	233	237	241	251
262	276	277	279	321	322	323	332	342	346
370	393	400	407	408	414	418	422	426	431
434	437	446	451	462	468	476	498	499	500
557	601	604	622	667	678	746	761	762	769
770	788	839	849	852	892				

Seminary

174	213	324	325	326	327	328	483	598	692
870	874	876							

Stories and Observations

9	27	34	40	55	58	63	68	82	87
88	89	101	121	124	133	165	180	184	187
199	202	204	217	218	223	225	228	235	244
247	253	259	272	280	282	297	298	299	301
312	313	315	330	334	355	374	376	377	381
382	383	384	388	394	395	398	405	417	427
428	429	430	433	440	443	445	453	469	486
487	496	503	507	509	512	523	524	528	535
537	549	553	577	581	588	615	619	627	633
637	646	647	658	670	688	691	694	702	704
706	707	714	719	720	733	741	753	756	763
776	785	796	802	806	808	816	825	828	865
877	882	886							

Worship

74	75	77	78	129	139	153	154	234	243
245	275	288	289	290	361	363	373	452	514
518	551	599	721	725	726	732	772	832	862
871									

Introduction

Sooner or later, a person decides it is time to put some thoughts on paper. Large and important reasons are not required. A person just wants - or needs - to do it. Here is my "collection." The items found herein are not in any order at all. They emerge from years in the ministry and more in life. They consist of stories told and untold - sometimes from the pulpit, sometimes not - as well as church signs, billboards, TV and radio commercials, deep thoughts, shallow thoughts - very shallow thoughts - first-hand experiences of one kind or another, personal biases, diatribes - right, left, and center - as well as happenings from the near and distant past. Occasional notations on certain scriptures appear as well, if for no other reason than to try to give this publication some legitimacy.

When I decided on this project, I began to carry a little notebook around, the very one Dr. Ernest Campbell (no relation), former pastor of the Riverside Church in New York City, advised us Cumberland Presbyterian preachers to have with us at all times when he was the guest preacher at the 1981 Ministers' Conference at Bethel College in McKenzie, Tennessee. I did not take his advice then. Dr. Campbell had said in 1981, that, if we did not make it our constant companion, "May it go ill with you!" For two decades, I neglected to abide by his counsel. I would think of a lot of good things but did not write them down. This inaction flew in the face of every wise teaching of every wise professor of preaching I ever heard of and it had an adverse effect on my sermons: I could have used such helps, believe me. One day in 2000 I wrote Ernest Campbell to say that I was not doing a good job of following his instructions. I had done the things I ought not to have done, and had not done those things I ought to have done. In the next mail he sent me one of the little notebooks he had recommended along with a note, dated October 27, 2000, that said in part, "Should the Rapture come and you be found without your notebook I would feel terribly responsible! Use the enclosed in good health, and let me know when you will need a replacement." Even with his encouragement, I did not start writing in it for a few more years.

I have not filled the notebook up yet, but I have written in it (and on various scraps of paper, envelopes, receipts, and old bulletins) many times. Sometimes, though, I did not make it to my desk in time. I would think of a story or an experience and would promise myself to put it in print soon. It would slip my mind and later I would sit at the computer, racking my brain, trying to remember, and usually to no avail. So out of my many apologies that come from the writing of this book, the major one is to those "stories, observations, personal experiences, and minority opinions" that left my mind from the time I thought of them to the time I started to jot them down. This edition leaves out many pretty good items that were forgotten "in transition."

One feature that will redeem this book and bring it up almost to a level of respectability is the series of sketches provided by my friend, colleague, and fellow Cumberland Presbyterian minister, the Reverend Dudley Condron. After he consented to help in this way, as bunches of items were written, I would see that he got copies. We met at Danver's Restaurant on Union Avenue in Memphis, Tennessee, (same booth every time) on numerous occasions to make the exchanges. He would take them home and read them and create drawings as commentary on some of the written items. His great work brings spice and visual relief to the book while also providing some respite from the written stuff. Dudley's creative mind and heart have blessed the world and the church these many years. He is certainly not to blame for the written stuff but is to be praised for the visual relief.

I have attempted valiantly to give credit where credit is due on quotations and stories. Where I have no idea of the source, I give credit by at least acknowledging I did not make it up myself. Where real names of personal acquaintances and colleagues are used, permission has been requested and granted in each case, where possible. Any omission is sadly regretted. If, by chance, I have repeated myself by telling the same story twice or otherwise have duplicated something earlier told, please pass that off as bad proof reading on my part and move on. It is of some consolation that the Book of Proverbs also contains some repetition.

I appreciate the efforts of those who became "readers" of the proposed book in the weeks and months prior to publication - Matthew Gore, Susan Gore, Barry Baker, Judy Baker, Tom Johnson, Roberta Johnson, Linda Campbell, Scott Coleman, and Dudley Condron. My special thanks to Matthew Gore for expert assistance in its publication and publicity. Karen Wilson, my administrative assistant in the office of the Program of Alternate Studies (PAS) for the past fourteen years, provided the format and added to the design that got it ready to send out on the road to publication. My work and hers came in our "spare time" and did not interfere with our responsibilities at PAS. I am grateful to Kerry Wilson for scanning the sketches when our scanner failed to cooperate. Reverend Eugene Norris of The King's Press in Southaven, Mississippi, provided the final touch in printing and publication.

I didn't know when to stop. First there was the goal of 100 items. Then it continued to rise. I fully realize that a little fewer than 900 items is definitely too much. A word of caution: Do not attempt to read this through and expect it to have a plot. More wisely, read items at random (and still you will not find a plot).

Thomas D. Campbell
September 2009

Chapter 1: 1-50

"Welcome, No Vacancy"

1

My wife Linda and I spent a weekend in Gatlinburg, Tennessee, a few years ago and as we walked around we came upon a motel whose permanent sign at the top said "Welcome," but whose changeable sign below read, "No Vacancy." I wonder if some churches convey two different messages, whether written or not.

2

Our family took a vacation in 1980 and traveled from our home in Texas to Arkansas, Tennessee, Virginia, and Washington, D.C. Near Nashville, Tennessee, we visited The Hermitage, the home of President Andrew Jackson. Outside was a tent where visitors were shown a video, then we stood in line to tour the house. While standing there I noticed the front corner of the house. There was a beautiful, red down spout. It had the initials "AJ" carved on it and the year "1823." It was clean, untarnished by the elements. It also was closed at the bottom and at the top. Evidently no water had ever flowed through. Right behind this was another down spout: old, rusty, broken in spots. Obviously much water had flowed through this one. A little later, just before we went into the house, the tour guide talked about the mansion, and called our attention to the two down spouts. The guide informed us that one was for show, the other for work.

3

After preaching as a guest minister, I was invited to the home of one of the families in the church. The time came for the meal to be served. I went to the bathroom to wash my hands, which I did, but when I looked for a towel I could not find one. I was getting desperate until I saw hanging there about seven or eight little towels sort of placed beside and a little on top of each other. One was blue, another yellow, another red, another green, another purple, and still another orange. They looked so neat and beautiful. I started to reach for one to dry my hands, and all of them, in unison, said, "Don't even think about it." I was startled and stood back. I still thought about drying my hands on one of them and trying to fold it neatly back in its place so no one would know, but decided against that. Just then, I noticed another towel, over there by itself, an older, less attractive towel, and I dried my hands on that towel. The pretty ones were for show, this one for work.

4

I do not ordinarily feel Pharisaical, though there is some secret joy in that. But it has happened occasionally as I have driven along the interstate or even in the city. I see a patrol car and immediately look down at my speedometer. Lo and behold, surprise!! I am driving within the speed limit. And I pray, "Lord, I thank thee that I am not like other people, those speeding and about to be pulled over."

5

It is not wise to take oneself too seriously, although one is wise to take one's work seriously. This goes for preachers, too. Otherwise, how would I have been able to make it through the last remaining steps of a worship service and get out of there as swiftly as I did after offering this benediction: "May the grace of our Lord and Savior Jesus Christ, the love of God the Feather, and the fellowship of the Holy Spirit be with you all. Amen."

6

A fellow student at Brite Divinity School back in 1969, in a discussion of ministerial blunders, told us this one. One minister tried to give the benediction. It came out this way: "Mace, Grease, and Percy go with you always. Amen."

7

One's sense of justice may not coincide with that of others. Driving on the interstate, at or a little above the speed limit, one is passed by a car going exceedingly fast, perhaps something like 90 or 100, and can only hope that the police will see and apprehend this reckless driver. Sure enough, one tops a hill a few miles later and there at the side of the road, just up ahead, is a trooper's car with blue lights flashing nestled behind a car it has stopped. A sigh of relief and a feeling of satisfaction, however, are followed by disillusionment, for the car the trooper stopped is not the right one.

8

I was in danger of being late for a meeting at a church in downtown Dallas and my drive from Fort Worth was filled with anxiety. I finally found the street where the church was located but turned and went the wrong direction. Right street, correct lane, but wrong direction, and getting farther and farther away from my destination. What to do? Traffic to the left, traffic to the right on this one-way street. Time was of the essence and I was moving away from the downtown area. Then, up ahead, I saw one of the most beautiful signs I have ever seen. Yes, it was old, and slightly tarnished by weather and time. But it was still one of the most beautiful signs ever. Why? Because of its message: "U-Turns Permitted."

9

Our eldest daughter owned and directed a day care center and employed several young women as assistants. The parents of one of the employees dropped by the center and the employee brought them to meet the director saying to her parents, "I want you to meet my friend, Kelly Shanton." After a brief visit the parents left. When they had gone, Kelly said to the young woman, "I'm not your friend; I'm your boss." I need to remember that when I think of God. It's so tempting to get cozy with and about God.

10

In 1980 our family vacationed from our Texas home into Arkansas, Tennessee, and Virginia and back, a total of 3,400 miles. Two parents and three daughters for ten days practically lived in a car and somehow got along with each other. In fact, it was easier than we thought it would be. It took some work but we did it. No arguments. No fussing. No extensive whining. A few games as we traveled probably helped, as did a group song or two. However, when we returned home, a difference of opinion between husband and wife, long forgotten now, arose and quickly erupted into an intense argument. We handled the hard part, the 3,400 mile journey. We muffed the easy part, the part where the family lives the ideal life at home.

11

We were in a committee meeting involving four churches in northern Mississippi. Two of the churches were those where I have been preaching for over ten years. One of our members had her six-year-old granddaughter, whom she had pretty much taken to raise, with her. Seven of us were on the front porch of a house used by one of the churches as a fellowship and Christian education center. The granddaughter had brought a blanket and some dolls, and with her grandmother's help had spread the blanket on the porch a few feet away. As the meeting went on, the granddaughter would periodically leave her blanket and dolls and come over to her grandmother and give and get a great big hug. Then she would return to her spot. That may be part of what prayer is all about: leaving our place to go to God and then, being reassured that all is well, returning to our activities.

12

While driving the nation's highways I notice little white crosses at the side of the road usually draped with flowers marking where a loved one had an auto accident and was killed. One would think they are placed mostly at dangerous curves and hills, but just as many if not more are placed beside level and straight roads where the vision is unhampered. Strange isn't it: we do well in the dangerous times and places but are less observant and careful in the easy times.

13

What makes a church a "Bible" church? Many congregations and groups advertise themselves as "Bible" churches. I may be wrong, but I think in many of their worship services not much Bible is read. Perhaps a short text for the sermon. In more liturgical congregations and groups, though they may not advertise their tradition as being a "Bible" church they do in fact read the Bible in worship a great deal more: the call to worship, the call to confession, the prayer of confession (often from scripture), the assurance of pardon, the offertory sentence, the Lord's Prayer, the responsive reading (always from scripture), the creed (often from scripture), the benediction, not to mention the scripture reading or readings relating to the sermon. I'm not sure here which one is the "Bible" church.

14

He called in mid-afternoon and asked to meet me in the church office. Upon his arrival he said he and his wife were leaving our church. He said the church was not spiritual enough. This young couple had been members for two years and had participated quite regularly in worship, study, and fellowship activities. Now they were leaving because the church was not spiritual enough. I spoke in defense of the people of the people of the congregation, but to no avail. There was possibly one person in the church, and he named her, who might just possibly be spiritual enough, but the rest were not, and he was not so sure about her. After he got through with that indictment he said, "And what's more, you are not spiritual enough." I hemmed and hawed and cleared my throat and coughed and sputtered my way through some sort of self-justification, also to no avail.

I think I learned something from that. A year or two later another family decided to leave the church for similar reasons. We were not spiritual enough. By this time I was better prepared. "That's just fine," I said to them. "We will miss you. I hope you enjoy your new church wherever that might be. I'm afraid we are not going to get any better here. What you see is what you get. I know we are not spiritual enough. I know I am not, but I'm afraid this is about as good as we are going to get. I hope you find the church that fits your requirements." We are, after all, pretty much what we will be. God can change us, but most of the time it is subtle, over a period of time. Besides, I wonder if his definition of "spiritual" stands up under intense scrutiny. I wonder if mine does.

15

Where we lived in Texas, six miles out of town, the trash man came by once a week. We would leave our dumpster out by the street and he and his men would empty it into his big truck and move on. We had this old waste basket, bent, scratched up, even a hole or two in the side. It was time to get rid of it. We put trash in it and left it with the dumpster out by the street, counting on the trash man to take it away. When we got home from work and school, the empty container was there and alongside it was the old waste basket. So the next week, I decided I would wait until the truck arrived before taking the old thing out, again full of trash, so they would see me and get my message: take this thing away! In full view of the workers, I took it to the street, stood it beside the big can, and walked back to the house. I didn't make it to door before I heard a voice, "Mister, you left your waste basket out here." It's not easy getting rid of unwanted things and habits.

16

I preached on "When Temptations Knock on Your Door." Splendid sermon. Triumphant. Simple solutions to conquer temptation. You can overcome. Happy day! At the door one person asked, "But what do you do if you do not conquer temptation?" That brought my feet down to the ground where the people were. The next Sunday the sermon was "What Happens When We Don't Resist

Temptation?" Something about God's forgiveness, encouragement, support, and saving grace.

17

The sermon was about sheep and how we are like sheep: stubborn, wandering, following the slightest whim and curiosity, easily swayed by passing interests. Afterward, a woman said, "I used to own some sheep. You left out one other. Sheep are cuddly." This helped a lot and I was certain to list it with the others when I went to preach to inmates in a state prison.

18

Out of the mouths of children

I have learned pretty well what not to do in the so-called Children's Sermon, or Time for Children during worship. I was absent and the church had a guest speaker. One of the women of the church had volunteered to do the children's moment. I knew she would do well. When I returned I asked her how it went. She said it went fine and described what she did, an elaborate thing with a board and a hammer and nails and making holes in the board and something on sin and forgiveness. "But then," she said, "I made a big mistake. I asked, 'Now what have you learned from this?'" One little boy said, 'Nuthin.'"

19

If you're the leader, don't go into the children's moment too confident. It was Christian Family Week and I talked about that famous Old Testament couple, Isaac and Rachel. If I said "Isaac and Rachel" once I said it ten times. In the midst of this sweet story a hand was raised, and the hand belonged to a little eight-year-old girl whose face looked familiar. "Daddy," our middle daughter Kim said with a clear voice heard by everyone in the sanctuary, "It's Rebekah."

20

It's different strokes for different folks. I had a late-night breakfast in a restaurant in Oklahoma City, and the food was good. As I was eating, a young couple came in and went through the same buffet line I did. Before long I heard the young man's voice getting louder and louder, complaining about the food. The manager came out and the volume from the customer got higher as he described how terrible everything was. I heard the manager say he would not charge them anything, but this did not calm the irate, profanity-spouting customer. He and the young woman stormed out, and as I walked by a little later I noticed their plates still there. They had eaten about half of everything on their plates, and it looked very similar to what I had. I thought my breakfast was pretty good. They didn't like their meal, which was similar to mine. It's different tastes for different folks.

21

I have seen great movies and some very bad ones. One of the worst ever was "Xanadu" with Gene Kelly and Olivia Newton John. I think it was bad because it was supposed to be good, and it wasn't. I mentioned that to my assistant one time and she said it was one of her favorites. I mentioned it to a congregation in a sermon one time and five people came up later and said it was one of the very best films they ever saw. Then when I got outside I saw that there were different colors and shapes and brands of automobiles in the parking lot. Yes, it's different strokes for different folks.

22

I was a college student and preaching at a little church in a very small community. Sunday dinner was with a husband and wife who were members of the small congregation. After a delicious meal, we sat in the living room and visited. Making conversation, I asked how long they had been married. "Fifty years," said the wife. "Oh?" I responded. "When is the date?" "Today," said the husband. "It's fifty years today." I asked if there had been or would be a reception or other type of observance. "No," said the wife. "This is the way we wanted it." The husband added, "Even though our children wanted to do something, we asked them not to plan anything." So there we were, the three of us, quietly observing their golden wedding anniversary.

23

Being a Good Samaritan is not easy. I went to Arkansas to bring my mother back to East Tennessee to stay with us over the holidays. While I was at her place a heavy rain and high winds hit the area. On our drive eastward later we rounded a curve and there up ahead was a tree that had been blown down and now it lay halfway across the highway. It seemed we might have been among the early ones to see this. I slowed down and my mother and I talked about what to do. There seemed to be three options: First, get out of the car and warn oncoming traffic, waving them around the tree. Second, find a farm house and ask to borrow their phone to call, or request that someone in the house call, the nearest police or state trooper so they could get somebody out there to move the tree. Third, get back in the car, drive on to the next town, find the police station and inform authorities. I opted for the third plan and five or six miles on up the road there was a small town. Victory! The very first turn was to the State Highway Patrol office. I turned in, stopped the motor, and jumped out, half running to the building. I was a few feet from the front door when a trooper came out headed to his car. He saw me and asked, "Are you here about the tree?" "Yes," "We heard about it already. A truck is on the way." What a wonderful opportunity to be a Good Samaritan, but somebody had already filled that role. That was all right.

24

Being a pessimist is a full time job. I am in a hurry and up ahead is a signal light. It is red. I say, "Oh no, the light is red. I'll have to stop." Or, I am in a hurry and up ahead is a signal light and it is green. I say, "Oh no, by the time I get there it will be red and I'll have to stop."

25

In Kentucky I had opportunity to visit in several prisons, meet some of the inmates, and conduct worship occasionally. I talked with many men who had been locked up for a time. I stayed in touch with a few who were released. One ex-inmate said, "There is only one thing more scary than the day you go to prison; it is the day you get out."

26

Patience is a Christian virtue. I wonder if one is supposed to employ patience all the time, such as at Express Lines of grocery stores where the sign says "12 Items or Less." A cartoon I saw said there should be an Express Line for English majors reading, "12 Items or Fewer." More times than one can count, I have been in those lines and could not help but notice that persons in front of me obviously had more than 12 items, and my patience ran thin. However, it may not be so much what they have as what I feel. If I am really, really impatient and in a hurry, I might look ahead of me and be critical, if only silently, of a person with a dozen eggs and a six-pack of Dr. Pepper, for, after all, that is 18 items! A cartoon in the newspaper brought on this comment.

27

In a newspaper many years ago, I read one of those "fillers," a short paragraph. It said that a man was killed while working on a bridge in Canada. Then the article reported that, on the average, one person dies for every bridge that is built. Jesus built a bridge from God to humanity, and died. Martin Luther King built a bridge connecting humankind and breaking down barriers, and died. Others have built bridges bringing people together, and died during construction.

28

Traveling in Arkansas, I would drive by a place of worship of the Church of God tradition. Its sign read like this: CALVARY CHURCH OF GOD. One time a big storm came and caused damage in the area. The last letter on the sign was blown off. For several weeks the name of the church was CALVARY CHURCH OF GO. We need more churches named Go. There may be enough named Rest, or Stay, or Wait. We need more named Go.

29

For more than twelve years we had a dog named Ginger. She was a mixture, sort of a Dashacockerpeekapoo. Her body was low on the ground. Her ears were too long and when she drank water, they often got wet. She stayed in the house most of the time. When we came home in the afternoon she would be at the top of the stairs, tail wagging, body twisting and dancing, so happy, so glad we were home, so overjoyed to see us. Unless, and this is a big one: unless she had gotten into the trash and scattered it all over the kitchen floor, in which case, when we got home she would not be at the top of the stairs wiggling and dancing. In fact, she was practically nowhere to be found. We would look and look and look some more. Finally, we would find her under a bed, all the way back in the corner, curled up, hiding. We came to realize that if she is at the top of the stairs, all is well. If she is not at the top of the stairs, the worst has happened: the trash has been tipped over and there is a mess in the kitchen and Ginger, realizing her guilt, has hidden herself. I don't know how far down the creature chain the concept of sin goes. I thought I knew, but Ginger brought about some rethinking among some of us humans.

30

I was reading a book on leadership, but that was interrupted when Linda walked into the house, having purchased a rather large suitcase. We were getting ready for the annual vacation and she wisely decided that instead of multiple bags we could put just about everything in one. It was a good buy, and just about everything did fit in. Trouble was, it was truly a large suitcase. How to get it to the car and to the airport and to the check-in station? I first tried to push the thing and it wouldn't budge. Then I picked it up, thinking I might carry it, but it was too heavy. Finally, I thought of a third way. I noticed that this bag, like others, had a handle you could pull up, and it also had wheels. You could pull the handle up, place the bag on its wheels, and PULL the bag easily. That done, I went back to my reading on leadership, desperately hoping to find some good ideas.

31

In Fort Worth I went by and picked up a ministerial colleague. He was holding a revival in the city, but there was no service on this Saturday night so we were going to the baseball stadium to see the

Texas Rangers in action. The interstate was only a few blocks from the house and it would get us there pretty fast, but I knew a shorter route, a more excellent way, and we started out. Twenty-five minutes later, after this short cut and that one, and this turn and that one, we came upon the house where I had picked him up. We had made a complete circle and ended up where we started. But we made good time!

32

When I go into a store and need to find an item I sometimes ask a nearby clerk. One of two things will happen: Either the clerk says, "That's over on Aisle 9," and goes on with other things, or, "Follow me. I'll take you there." The latter is better, because usually, after finally finding Aisle 9 I am unable to locate the desired item. Once a man with an out-of-state license drove into the parking lot of Memphis Theological Seminary asking how to get to the bridge crossing the Mississippi River. I could have told him. It would have been complicated. He would have had to stop once or twice more for an update. I had the time. I said, "Follow me. It's easier to show you." I still like it when clerks say, "Follow me. I'll take you there." Jesus said, "Follow me; I'll take you there."

33

Sometimes religious words and terms are hard to understand or to put in everyday language. I was wondering about the word "redemption," in fact trying to learn more so I could try to preach about it. This was back in the days of S & H Green Stamps and Quality Stamps. You traded at a grocery store and at a service station that gave the brand of stamps you were collecting. Family discussions and debates occurred as the stamps accumulated: keep collecting, or go and buy something with these stamps that are taking up space in the house? Finally, one day we put all ours in the back seat of the car and drove to the stamp place in Fort Worth. Turning onto the street where it was located, we saw the sign on the front of the building: "S & H Green Stamps Redemption Center." Those stamps were doing nobody any good at home. They were of great value when they were redeemed. This helped me understand "redemption" a little better. The church is a "redemption center."

34

A fellow worker at Memphis Theological Seminary told about her father, who was in the hospital. He had been in great pain and, she said, used the "pain pump" - a dose of morphine or some other soothing drug that he could control with a push of the button - quite often to bring some ease and comfort. To this somebody else said, "I wish we had pain pumps in everyday life." Sometimes there is nothing around to make the pain go away. But we do know our Lord suffers with us.

35

I was asked to be the director of a five-day junior camp (ages 9-11) at a campsite where we would stay the night in cabins. I tried to make the evening recreation strenuous so the children would be tired enough to go right to bed at the designated time. This was not completely successful. In fact, it was not successful at all, at least in my cabin where about a dozen boys stayed. On the first night I finally got them quiet enough to have our evening devotional. And I told them it was now time for lights out and sleep. The lights were turned off, but the noise resumed. The boys, all excited, were not ready for sleep or for staying in their own beds. They instead hopped from one to another and tussled with each other while yelling and laughing really loud. Although I had specifically told them it was time for quiet and rest, they seemed to ignore my calm but clear call for peace and quiet. With the lights out, I turned in, but the voices seemed to get louder and louder. There seemed to be no end to this. I let it go a few minutes longer. Then, there in the darkness, I sat up in my bed and let out the most horrible, blood-curdling scream you could imagine. Immediately, everything was quiet, and within five or ten minutes they were all asleep. I did this on the second night and the third night as well as the fourth. On the fifth and last night, I happened to be in the cabin early in the evening. The kids were outside engaged in some directed activity. One little boy came into the cabin, walked to his bed, and said to me, "Mr. Campbell, I'm tired. Can you go ahead and scream at us early tonight so I can go on to bed?"

36

You're about to pull out onto a highway from a county road out in the open country. You stop and look both ways. To the left you can see at least a mile and a half and there is nothing coming. To the right you can see that far and there is nothing coming. You look to the left again, then to the right again, then to the left and the right a third time. Then you pull onto the highway and turn left. Fifty feet down the highway you happen to look into your rearview mirror and a big truck is barreling down on you, and you ask, "Where did that truck come from?" This is the way it is. We make preparations, we plan ahead, we look both ways, then go forward, and something is always there that we did not plan on.

37

"It's not fair, he's too big!"

When I was ten years old the hometown newspaper and posters around town announced that Santa Claus would be in the town square two Saturdays before Christmas. Those who were invited to meet him were children ten years old and under. I arrived in plenty of time on that afternoon and immediately saw Bill C. I was bothered by that because I knew Bill was a grade ahead of me and had failed a grade, which would make him at least twelve, if not older, and the announcement was clear: "Children ten and under." Santa had not arrived yet, so perhaps Bill would leave before starting time. However, upon Santa's entrance into the town square Bill was still there, milling around with other kids, head and shoulders above the others, even getting close to Santa. This upset me greatly. The announcement specifically said, "Children ten and under," and here was someone who was at least twelve, if not older, who acted like he belonged in this crowd. Bill showed no inclination toward leaving and, worse, this seemed to bother no one else. Here was somebody disobeying the rules, ignoring the announcements on age requirements, walking around like he belonged there! I could not enjoy Santa's hearty greetings and laughter; I was too angry. This should not be! It isn't right! I was still bothered by this and when I got home I told my mother, broke into tears, laid my head on her lap and cried some more. It just was not right! He should not have been there! He knew better! Luke 19 tells of when Jesus invited himself to the home of the hated Zacchaeus after Zacchaeus had climbed a tree to catch a glimpse of Jesus. Luke 19:7 says, "All who saw it began to grumble." They knew Zacchaeus did not belong and should not have been there.

38

Getting out of a crowded parking lot after a football game or concert is not easy. I inch along carefully, and after a long while I am close to the road leading out to the highway, but nobody seems inclined to let me in. I flash my lights, wave at other drivers, and hope beyond hope I can get into the flow of traffic going out; otherwise I might be here all night. Why doesn't somebody have the decency to let me in? Finally, somebody stops to make room for me to pull out in front of them and I move quickly into place. What a relief! I'm home free! Life is good. Now what are those cars doing trying to squeeze in from the side? Who are those characters? Who do they think they are? I was here first! And don't bring up Matthew 18:23-35, the Parable of the Unforgiving Servant. Wait until I get out of this parking lot.

39

I boarded a plane to somewhere and found my seat. Shortly after, a young college-age man also came aboard and sat down by a middle-age gentlemen who was reading a book. I was directly across the aisle from them. Immediately the younger man began to "witness" to his seat mate. No introductions. No casual talk. No moments of getting acquainted. Not even an inquiry as to whether the other man was "saved" or not. He just charged ahead, making some typical statements, quoting some typical scripture, and, all along, assuming, I suppose, the older man was not a Christian. Otherwise, why this full-court-press type of witnessing? I felt for the older fellow who had been ambushed, cornered, and confronted by an in-your-face speech in such a discourteous manner. I could not hear what the man with the book said to the overzealous disciple, but very soon he was back to reading his book. I thought, Jesus did not say, "Go ye into all the world and be obnoxious."

40

We often think we should have words of wisdom for every occasion, but I feel a particular inadequacy in hospitals. It seems that when I walk through the front door into the lobby my mouth goes dry. Then when I visit a patient I am ill at ease, probably worrying more about what I should do next instead of thinking about the person in the bed. I have been just a little encouraged by a story an uncle of mine told while he was in the armed services. At one show for the troops the actress Lana Turner appeared with Bob Hope but was unable to sing or speak. She whispered in the microphone, "I have laryngitis." To which a private shouted, "Just stand there." I have learned that ministers and lay people can "just stand there." It's not the words; it's the presence.

Just being there can be enough

41

Alex and June (not their real names) were longtime members of the church and busy workers. They were not Sunday School teachers, nor did they sing in the choir. He was an elder through several rotations and she helped keep Sunday School records. They never took the opportunity to address a large group of people, nor were they in any way accomplished in public prayer. In fact, I never had occasion to hear either one of them pray. Furthermore, they were not always in agreement with me or my ideas and said so occasionally. Yet with every funeral of a person in the church, they were there. They were present in the church, in the funeral chapel, and at the grave. They said no words but were present. They stood in respectful reverence for these friends in the church, known or not so well known. Occasionally they were the only members of the congregation present. They could always be counted on. They never uttered a word. But they were there. What a mighty witness!

42

One time a woman came to my office. I did not know her, had never met her before. She said she lived next door to Alex and

June, the couple mentioned above, and they were terrible neighbors. She listed several complaints and went on and on. I sensed that this person had issues (in some casual questioning with two people in the know, without revealing the subject, I learned she had many, many issues) and the couple she was talking about had very little to do with her problem. But she kept on talking about them. While Alex and I had disagreed on a couple of things over the previous eight years as pastor and member, this was ridiculous. I interrupted her (that was the only way I could get a word in) and told her I was not going to hear anything else she had to say and would she please leave. She kept talking, asking why I as their pastor did not do something. I told her I was going to do something if she did not leave and that was escort her out of the building. I told her that both he and she were dedicated workers in the church and performed one of the most important ministries in our church (though they would not consider it a ministry) by attending funerals and grave side services representing our church and I was not going to sit there and listen to anything else she had to say. It was a chore getting her to get up and leave my office. I never told Alex and June, but as this woman finally departed, I breathed a prayer of thanks for such a dedicated couple in our church.

43

There was another couple. They lived on the other side of Alex and June, a few houses down. They had been longtime members of the church but had never attended in the six or so years I had been there and probably not for a few years before that. In fact, like so many inactive members, they were overlooked by me; I just had not gotten around to visiting with them. Alex said one day, "You might want to drop by their house sometime; they'd be glad to see you." It was obvious Alex had stayed in touch all these years. They welcomed me warmly. We never talked about church, but the visit was so genuine and so friendly I made it a point a few weeks later to visit them again. And again no talk about church but I did learn more about them as they told about their life together, their family, their children and grandchildren. One day they came to church and were there every Sunday after that until I left and I hear they still attend every week, usually sitting right behind my oldest daughter and her family so they can see and visit with our grandsons. I attribute that to their neighbor and his wife who simply kept in touch... and cared.

44

On a Sunday morning in February 2009 we were on our way to our two churches in Mississippi. About ten minutes from the first one a deer streaked out and we hit it. I was driving and saw only a blur. Linda was not looking out at the time and she said she saw nothing. I did not slow down. The car was heavily damaged but we managed to complete our journey to the churches and back home. Some weeks later a man in one of the churches was visiting with his elderly and ailing father, who was having symptoms of Alzheimer's. Gordon casually mentioned that his pastor hit a deer the other day. His dad said, "Did he cuss?" The answer is no, but that was certainly a viable option at the time.

45

I was pastor of a church where my grandmother (on my mother's side) was a member. She lived in the same house with my aunt and her daughter (my cousin). In sending out church newsletters, I sent one and only one to that address, until my grandmother said she would like a newsletter for herself, one she would not have to share with anybody else. That taught me a lesson: Where there are more than the usual generations in a household, one newsletter won't do. I never made that mistake again. My grandmother might have been living in somebody else's house, but she was still, for newsletter purposes, a separate family unit. We pastors make the mistake of forgetting what folks give up when they go to live with their children.

46

Pete was a city policeman and taught our second grade class in Sunday School. He and his family had neighbors across the road out there in the country. That family had a lot of dogs and one time the father and the teenage son came down with a terrible sickness that the doctors had trouble diagnosing. By the time they had it pegged, it was too late. John, the father, was dying of Rocky Mountain Spotted Fever, acquired from ticks. His wife Shirley was there by his side and rotated between being with him and with their son who was in the children's hospital some miles away, also with Rocky Mountain Spotted Fever. He would survive, but his father died. As John lay dying with Shirley by his side, Pete and his wife were present, too, as good neighbors and friends. Shirley asked something like, "Why does God let this happen? Why did God do this?" something almost anybody in anguish would say. I was proud of Pete before, but even more proud after what he said next: "Shirley, God did not do this. And God does not like this any more than you do. He grieves with you. He is sad, too. His heart is broken." I was over by the door standing in awe of the feeling and the depth of Pete's theology, and wanted to say but didn't: "A wonderful ministry you have here, Pete!" He would not have thought of it that way, but it was true.

47

The little congregation had an average attendance of about twenty. We had a bulletin and a rather formal service including lighting the candles. Max was about seven years old and was our acolyte every Sunday morning. His mother told us that one Sunday Max was not feeling well and she suggested they stay home from church that day. Max would not hear of it. "They need me," he said. "We've got to go." Max and his little four-year-old brother were the only children in the church and therefore the only children in Sunday School. They missed out on a lot of big-church activities and did not have the opportunities to be involved in a busy church life. Yet Max and his little brother knew they were loved, and Max knew he was needed. Sounds like a church to me!

48

There is the idea that once a person becomes a Christian, no instruction is needed in anything, because the fact of becoming a Christian turns one completely around. You might call it an "instinctual thing." Therefore, according to this way of thinking, all people need is to come to Christ and all other matters - stewardship, human relationships, prejudices, hatreds, bad habits - will disappear and the new Christian can immediately start making right decisions and do good things. It has been compared to the instincts of animals. Before the Tsunami in and around Indonesia right after Christmas a few years ago it is said that animals were getting out of there by the droves. They sensed something was wrong. Our dog Desi, may she rest in peace, could tell a storm was coming long before the weather man on TV announced it. She would shake and shake and we had to hold her to try to settle her down. But my faith in the instinctual nature was shaken somewhat when I saw a public television special on penguins. The parent penguins were trying to prepare the baby penguins to face the world and be prepared for adult life. But first they had to get used to the icy water. The film showed parents leading their kids to the water and trying to get them to step in.

The children put their feet in and immediately ran back up the hill. Then the parents would lead them again to the water and again the little ones would stick one foot in only to run away from it as fast as possible. So much for instinct. I always thought penguins took to icy water by nature. There are some features of the Christian life that may need instruction, nurture, and cultivation before the new disciple begins to make progress. That's why we need Sunday School, Bible study, mission and evangelism seminars, workshops on race relations, and inner city experiences in ministry with the poor.

49

In Kentucky a young woman attended our church and she said she lived in a nearby apartment complex. As soon as possible, I called to see if I could visit her. That evening we had coffee and cake in her kitchen and I asked how long she had lived here. She said a few months and then told me she used to live elsewhere but friends had recommended her present residence. When she came and talked to the manager about the possibility of moving she was asked her name, present address, and other information, including, "And what is your disability?" The young lady was a bit taken aback by this question. She replied, "Well, I have epilepsy, but I did not know it showed." Her friends obviously knew and wanted the best for her. Then the manager explained that every person in the apartment complex had some sort of disability. That's how a person qualified. Then the young lady told me that next door to her was a woman with Parkinson's disease, and down the hall was a woman with MS, and one floor below was a man with cancer. Everyone living there had some sort of disability. I thought how it would be if, when a person joined the church and the church secretary or membership chairman interviewed that person, one of the routine questions might be, "And what is your disability?" "Well," the new member might say, "I do have anger issues." And another might reply, "Jealousy. That's it. Jealousy." Still another might whisper, "I'm an alcoholic." And another might answer, "I am easily depressed." Is that not what the church is? Are we not all people of some disabilities? Look only to the Apostle Paul with his thorn in the flesh plus his weak prayer life (2 Corinthians 12:1-10) and you can know that we all bring our weaknesses to Christ and the church. It might be said this way: Weak Christians, Strong Church.

50

Luke 15 has three parables from Jesus, each about being lost and being found, as George Buttrick so eloquently tells it in his classic book on the parables written back in the first half of the twentieth century: the parable of the Lost Sheep, the Parable of the Lost Coin, and the Parable of the Lost Son. Lost and found. We know the feeling of being lost - in a department store, on a tangled web of highways, on the residential streets of towns or cities looking for a certain address, wandering in life without a purpose or goal. But being found! That has mixed blessings. Sometimes we do not want to be found, whether it is by God or anybody else. However, it is wonderful to be found when you did not even know anybody was looking for you. We had moved from Texas to Kentucky and then on to Tennessee, and thus had been gone from the Lone Star State for several years, when some friends sent us a notice out of a local newspaper: The State Treasurer of Texas was looking for us, and for a few hundred other people, too. I had some money coming to me, if only I could prove I was alive and I was who I said I was.

It all started when our first child was born. Somebody came by selling Mutual Funds. I had never heard of Mutual Funds, but it sure sounded good. It would cost only $25 a month. Somebody else would decide on investments and the other complicated stuff. We could sit back and let them make those decisions, while watching our money grow. Only trouble was, we could not pay the $25 a month like we thought we could. We lasted about three months. We never notified the company, figuring they would know we dropped out. That was the only thing we could figure was the basis for any money coming our way after all these years. Having contributed $25 a month for only three months, I felt there would not be much coming. Yet when one figured the interest over almost thirty years, the numbers could well be astronomical. I got greedy, thinking in the thousands, maybe even the hundreds of thousands. And I was wishing we had stayed with the program for all these years! A check came and it was for $1,200. Taxes had already been taken out. It was not what my greed wanted, but it was a blessing anyway. It was good to be "found" even if I had to help myself be found. It was good news. From Adam on, God has been searching for us, wanting to find us and give good gifts.

Chapter II: 51-100

"The Check Is In the Mail"

51

When we lived in Texas I attended a youth conference in Arkansas. Before the trip, I paid some bills, including Sears, a $50 check, I recall distinctly. I do not remember whether the bill was long overdue or whether it was just overdue. It must have been one or the other, for at the youth conference, where you had to park your car, then carry your luggage a half a mile or more to the camp site, and where there was one phone and one phone only, and that was a pay phone, I got a telephone call. While eating lunch with all the others, I was tapped on the shoulder: "You have a telephone call," and the outside pay phone was where I was to take the call. And so I am saying hello and it is Sears. "Have you sent a check for $50 lately?" "Yes, I have." Then I said the immortal words: "The check is in the mail." I think just as I said those words forty seven people were walking by, lunch now being over, and heard me utter those lines. Oh, the embarrassment. The humiliation. The shame. And oh, the persistence and tracking abilities of Sears, too! Whom did Sears call to find me? And who would have known? Others in my family were visiting relatives in another part of Arkansas. What process did Sears have to go through to track me down? I was found. I was not happy being found. Adam was not happy being found of God. Sometimes being found is not good news.

ℰᏇℭᏇℰᏇℭᏇℰᏇℭᏇℰᏇℭᏇℰᏇℭᏇℰᏇℭᏇℰᏇℭᏇℰᏇℭ

52

In Burleson, Texas, in the late 1970s there would be several church buses driving around on a Sunday morning, making their appointed rounds, picking up children who said goodbye to relieved and sleepy parents. The buses came from different areas, not all representing Burleson area churches. It is interesting to read the signs on different church buses. One I remember was: "Come with us and we will do you good," and gave the biblical reference, Numbers, Chapter 10. That was a clear, sincere, definite invitation. Only trouble is, it is only the first part of the passage, for the other half says, "I will not go." I wonder about the promises churches make; "Come with us and we will do you good." That does not always work out well. Besides the invitation appeals to the selfish interests of the people being invited. Perhaps that is why Hobab said, "I will not go." So the invitation was re-worked and Plan B was put in place: "Come with us and you will be eyes for us." Hobab accepted the invitation. What if churches appealed, not to the selfish interests of people and their families, but to their missionary spirit and willing hearts and their hunger for challenging discipleship. Membership might be lower than desired, but the folks there would likely be more mature Christians.

53

First John, Chapter 4, talks about the need to "test the spirits to see whether they are of God." A ministerial colleague was a highly effective pastor for his people. I admired him and his ministry. In the early 1970s, several forms of religious practice were bursting onto the scene, each clamoring for attention. Such new or old practices as healing, different methods of evangelism, and the underground church were being publicized and practiced. He reached for them all, trying frantically to be involved in them. Once I ran into a mutual friend, also a minister, and asked, "Have you seen our friend lately?" To my surprise he informed me that he was in the psychiatric ward of one of the city's hospitals and had been there for about two months. After trying all of the other movements, he began to employ the tongues approach, reading, studying, trying to learn everything about it. His mind was becoming so confused; there were so many ways, and so many approaches. The explanation he had for those involvements was, "If it is of the Lord, I want to be a part of it." In his frantic attempts to be a part of everything that was of the Lord, he had strung himself out and was of no use to anyone. He needed to test the spirits and to apply some sort of measuring rod in order to determine whether or not he should participate. Instead, he had plunged headlong into every new movement that had the name of Jesus attached to it. Just because it is good and is in the name of Jesus does not mean everyone needs to participate in it. We need to test the spirits.

54

When an ice storm comes through, churches have to cancel their services. People stay home and some of them watch television and catch a worship service from one of the downtown churches in the city. We did that one time and I made a list of some of the advantages of television church:

1. You don't have to dress up; I'm talking bathrobe and slippers here.

2. You can get up and walk around anytime during the service- make yourself a sandwich, get yourself a handful of chips and chew on them to your heart's content, not having to worry about how loud you are.

3. Your view and your seating are better than being there. Usually you can count the warts on the preacher's nose - and you're not having to sit in one of those uncomfortable church pews pretending to be comfortable... and interested.

4. You can switch to another service at any time. You attend worship at some church and you are stuck with your choice. But with television religion you can try to find a church with music you like or with a preacher worth hearing. If the sermon is second-rate, switch to the other channels.

But there are a few disadvantages to television religion. Nobody at that church knows I'm watching. They don't know my name. It was difficult to join in on the singing. At the end of the service the preacher did not ask me how my mother was doing or how my new job was going, nor did the minister discuss coming to see me sometime. Actually with television religion, I was an observer, not a participant. An observer can keep a safe distance. A participant gets involved. The next Sunday the weather was fine and it was good to see our church folks again.

ഈ೧ഇഈ೧ഇഈ೧ഇഈ೧ഇഈ೧ഇഈ೧ഇഈ೧ഇഈ೧ഇഈ೧ഇ

♪♪

This quotation cannot be traced and I do not know who said it: "When one first joins the ranks of management, there is zero experience and 100% enthusiasm. By the time of retirement or death, the mixture is 100% experience and zero enthusiasm. In between the extremes, there is a relatively short time in one's career, when there is the optimum combination of both experience and enthusiasm." I wonder how that works out for long-time Christians and church members. The work can get to you. The unhappiest man I ever met never came to church but his wife did. I decided to visit them in their home. That was my first time ever to see him. From the very opening of the conversation, he was angry, grumpy, highly critical of others. Evidently nothing made him happy. His wife, sitting patiently by, was silent, head down most of the time. Then I asked, "What is your occupation?" "I work in the Complaint Department at the United States Post Office." I wondered: Did the job make the man, or did the man make the job? And I wondered: What do we bring to the life and work of the church?

56

Special-day cards can get too mushy and sugary. To balance that out, along may come a Father's Day card like the one I got from one of my daughters: On the outside, these words: "Dad, there is no way I can repay you for all you have done for me... helping me in so many ways... getting me out of jams... supporting and encouraging me..." And then you go inside and read: "So please quit billing me."

57

An aunt of mine was the court reporter for Judge Eva Barnes, a family court judge in Fort Worth, Texas. My aunt Olive quoted Judge Barnes many times. One of her jewels of wisdom was this: "If you don't learn about life at your mother's knee, you won't learn it at any other joint."

58

Phillip Workman, after more than twenty years on death row in Tennessee, was executed by lethal injection. His last request was for pizza, but not for himself. He wanted the warden to give it to a poor family, which the warden refused to do. When this news got out, hundreds of people provided pizzas for hundreds of poor families in the Nashville area.

On making your life count

59

I had this very important meeting. I wanted to be well-dressed and make a good impression. I wore my best suit and a nice, new blue shirt with a button-down collar. I think the tie looked pretty good, too. Overall, I was well pleased with my appearance as well as the meeting. Later in the day I had occasion to look in the mirror. The right button of the button-down collar was buttoned, and the left one was not. It had been that way all day. Sometimes you think you "have it" when you don't.

60

I was part of a two-man team to go to Korea and teach classes to ministers under the auspices of the Cumberland Presbyterian Church. A bunch of us would meet at a donut shop every morning before class. You got your donut or cinnamon roll or bagel and then you went to the counter and ordered your coffee. Then, and not until then, would the workers make the coffee, pour it for you, and bring it to your table. In America - at least in the places where I have been - you get your own. In Korea they wait until you need it and then make it. That's not poor planning; it's great service.

61

One morning recently I decided to ingest the following into my body: "Corn Syrup Solids; Partially Hydrogenated Soybean Oil; Sodium Casseinate (a milk derivative); Dipotassium Phosphate; Mono and Diglycerides; Sodium Silicaluminate; Sodium Tripolyphosphate; Diacetyl Tartaric Acid Esters of Mono and Diglycerides; Artificial Flavors, Beta Carotene; Riboflavin and Titanium Dioxide (artificial colors). Contains Milk." No, I was not trying to commit suicide, but pouring some "Non-Dairy Creamer" into my morning cup of coffee. Sometimes it is better not to know the details.

62

Bruce Harnell was a United Methodist student at Brite Divinity School in Fort Worth. He was pastor of the church in Rio Vista, Texas, where he lived with his wife and children, and was a member of that community's volunteer fire department. One of those sudden Texas rainstorms came and flooded the streets of Rio Vista. Bruce and other firemen went to work trying to rescue people from their homes. He got tangled up in some branches, brush, and debris that sucked him under and he drowned. Although he was preparing for ministry, he was already doing ministry and he gave his life for others. Sometimes when we think we are preparing for something in the future, we find ourselves doing that service in the present.

63

On a plane to Korea, I saw several young Korean families with small children. One of the children dropped something and said, "UH, oh!" I thought: That expression crosses language boundaries easily. As does another word: I have heard several languages spoken, in addition to English. Some things heard are prayers. It seems that no matter the language, the prayers end with "Amen." And we are drawn together even more.

64

When a college or professional baseball game is completed, the winning team goes out on the field and players, manager, and coaches high-five one another while celebrating another victory. The losing team slinks away into the dark tunnel leading to the clubhouse, unhappy, perhaps angry, already looking to the next game and a better outcome. I see a resemblance in a worship service when people greet one another gladly as though celebrating a victory. In fact, they are celebrating God's victory over sin and death. Church folks know they are on the winning team.

65

Has this ever happened to you? You are almost late as you drive into a parking lot. You see a car ready to back out and you position your car to move right into that spot. Just as that car leaves and before you have a chance, still another car, coming from another direction, zooms in and takes what you had your eye on. Later you are sitting in the same doctor's office across from the villain. How do you act? When you find that out, let me know.

66

I had a conference to attend in a hotel and as I stood in the lobby I heard the loudest, strangest racket ever. Band instruments were being played, and while they may have been played well, they were not together. In fact, it was obvious each instrumentalist was doing his or her own thing. In fact, everyone was warming up. It was terrible. You never heard such an awful racket coming out of that room one floor up from the lobby. However, within minutes, the room was quiet, and then, what a contrast, the most beautiful music ever heard wafted from that place. Just then I walked by on the way to my meeting. Standing before the players was the director, leading them. They were on the same page, playing the same tune. It was great. What a difference the director made.

67

Civic pride is a wonderful thing. We were on vacation in Charleston, South Carolina, and riding a horse-drawn carriage as we toured the city. Our guide, a college-age young woman, provided a narrative as we made the journey. I remember she talked about the fact that Charleston is a peninsula reaching out into the ocean and that two rivers, the Ashley and the Cooper, "come together to form the Atlantic Ocean." Isn't that great! This reminds me of a citizen of the town where I grew up saying that the combined circulation of the <u>New York Times</u> and the <u>McKenzie Banner</u> was over a million.

68

My nephew worked in St. Joseph, Missouri. His family lived in Platte City, thirty miles south. One day he and I went to St. Joseph and saw some historic places, including the Pony Express Museum at the place where the Pony Express started. That method of delivering the mail lasted only about six months because the railroads came along. On the walls were old posters and advertisements. One item was a call for riders. It said "Orphans Preferred." Young men under 21 were especially invited. Also, "Must Be Willing to Risk Death Daily."

69

On a day in Korea when I did some sightseeing with others, our translator was a young Korean woman who did a great job of communicating in both the Korean and English languages. She said she also could speak Chinese. Late in the day I asked her if she planned to take on a fourth. She said she was going to learn Japanese "after I graduate from high school next year." "How old are you?" "I'm seventeen." Well, I'm sixty-eight and I can barely speak one language, English, although I can remain silent in thirteen languages, and I'm working on my fourteenth. Somebody, maybe Mutt or Jeff in the comics, said he could speak every language but Greek. "Say something in German," to which Mutt or Jeff replied, "That's Greek to me." "Well, say something in French," and the same reply came: "That's Greek to me." My admiration for the talents of this young woman is understandably great.

70

Someone sent me directions on how to get someplace. It was one of those Yahoo maps. The small print said, "When using any driving directions or map, it's a good idea to do a reality check and make sure the road still exists, watch out for construction, and follow all traffic safety precautions." "Make sure the road still exists." This sounds like good advice for life itself.

71

I worked part-time in a McKenzie grocery for Mr. Clifford Bateman, as did my two brothers. There I learned to "candle" eggs. Farmers would bring eggs into town and Mr. Bateman would purchase them, put them in those containers that hold a dozen, and place them on display for sale. But first we had to "candle" the eggs to make sure they were all right for sale. This, by the way, was the only time a worker got to sit down. You sat on a box and held the egg up to a hole in another box from which a light shone. You would turn the egg this way and that and if no spot showed up you knew it was a good egg. One of my self-esteem moments came when I was doing this task and an egg I was "candling" showed a spot. I told Mr. Bateman, who was at first skeptical. Then he said, "Well, let's just see." Lo, and behold, when it was cracked open, it was noticeably bad. Then he said, "You're right." I felt good. I had done my job well. It is satisfying to do a job well and to be affirmed by others. There may not be enough of that in our churches.

72

While working at the grocery store in my youth I learned much from the manager/owner, and not all of it was grocery store-related. On a late Saturday night, after closing, he would take us workers home. To get to his car we walked back behind the store, far behind the main parking area in almost complete darkness, and farther away from the town square. Why did he park that far away? It is simple. He did not want to use up a space that a potential customer might need. It took awhile in my different pastorates to consent to park where it said "Pastor" because that was a choice spot, right near the front door. Especially on Sunday mornings I really wanted to be at the farthest area from the church so visitors and others would have a chance at it. I smile in gratitude when I notice church members parking farther away so visitors can experience more convenience and comfort as they become acquainted with the people and facilities.

73

I talked with a young man recently who is a new Christian. He said he has some forgiveness issues. He remarked that he hasn't begun to work on that yet. He has not needed to, he informed me: He's into martial arts.

74

Our five-year-old granddaughter was into T-ball and played for the church where she attended Mothers' Day Out. The field was near the church building. One day during a game she had to go to the bathroom and her grandmother took her into the building and down the hall. Just then they walked by the sanctuary and little Paige put her finger to her lips to signal quiet.

75

Paige, our granddaughter, age five at this writing, comes often to visit in our home. Her grandmother, instead of turning on the television, may play music, many kinds and styles. Once Paige was walking through the house when organ music started. She quickly went and sat down on the couch and was very still and quiet. Her parents undoubtedly have helped her well regarding reverence in the sanctuary.

76

In the spring of the year I was in Memphis for a church task force meeting of some sort and we all went to lunch afterwards. At the restaurant I noticed several people walking out with a black mark on their head and I thought they might belong to some middle eastern religion or something. A few more walked by and I then figured these were patients at a nearby cancer research hospital. Finally, and it took time to sink in, I realized those were ashes on their forehead, and that this was Ash Wednesday. They would wear this mark the rest of the day. It was the beginning of Lent.

77

Reverence in the sanctuary is an ongoing issue in the church. On the one hand, when people gather just before worship they may not have seen each other for a week so they want to visit. But on the other hand this is a time for preparation for worship and a reverential quietness should prevail. One visitor complained to the pastor at the door following the service about how loud it was until right at the start of worship. The pastor responded, "Yes, isn't it wonderful how much our people love each other." I heard of one church where the people were visiting like that. When the organist played softly they whispered or talked very softly. When the organist played loudly the people talked louder and almost had to shout to be heard by someone next to them. So as the music softened, so did the people, and when it swelled, the talking got louder. Once the organist revved up the pipes to a high volume, then all of a sudden stopped, and you heard a woman say, loudly and clearly, "Well, I fry mine."

78

I do not have mixed emotions about applause in a worship service. I am not undecided. I do not like it, do not think it appropriate, and do not participate in it. I realize I am in a minority on this. However, being in the minority has never really bothered me. I once felt applause was not a very good thing until I attended a worship service as a visitor a few summers ago and emerged from that service convinced applause is a terrible thing. The children sang and the congregation applauded. Later the adult choir sang an anthem and the congregation applauded. Somehow I managed to survive that, but not what happened at the conclusion. After the sermon and the closing hymn and the benediction, the adult choir sang a choral response. Then the congregation applauded. We all need some re-orientation on this, something now missing from many sanctuaries, something old fashioned, something we call reverence.

79

I did not get a cell phone until the summer of 2001. I said I didn't need one, but on the first day I made ten calls. I always noticed when in a restaurant, for example, a customer would get a call on their cell phone. How impressive! That person must really be important. Once in Memphis I was talking on my office phone to another minister who was in Birmingham. Then I had this idea: Could we hang up and could she call me on my cell phone in twenty minutes? I was going to lunch and she could get back to me then. Thus, it came to pass that I went to Burger King and at the prescribed moment my phone rang and we continued the conversation. I looked around to see if others noticed how important I was. Most did not pay any mind at all, but some did. I was well pleased.

80

Mrs. Mary Lou Grenade was the children's director in the First Cumberland Presbyterian Church of McKenzie, Tennessee, during our childhood years in the 1940s and 1950s. Whenever a child in the Sunday School had a birthday we all gathered after classes and before worship. "Miss Mary Lou" had a wooden cake that used to be white but so many hands had handled it there were blotches and spots and finger prints permanently emblazoned on it. In the middle was a place for one candle. She would light the candle and we would stand around that cake with the honoree especially close to it, and we would say this prayer. I still remember it:

> "Many happy returns on the day of thy birth,
> May sunshine and gladness be given.
> And may the dear Father prepare thee on earth
> For a beautiful birthday in heaven."

Such a beautiful prayer it is. I guess that is one reason I still remember those moments.

81

Many years ago I read an article by a pastor that began, "When I completed my education at..." No one should be able to say, "When I completed my education..." We should never quit learning and should never, ever "complete" our education. However, as I understand that particular pastor's ministry, he may have been right. I think he quit learning, quit reading, quit attending ministers' conferences, quit attending seminars and ministerial learning opportunities. The few books in his study were published during his years of formal education; he had purchased none since then. Education should create a hunger for more. The Ph.D. may be tired of going to school, but knows there is much more to learn and will usually take the necessary steps to keep on learning.

82

In Batesville, Arkansas, back in the 1960s I invited the pastor of the local First United Methodist Church, Reverend J. Albert Gatlin, to speak to a regional gathering of Cumberland Presbyterian young people. Early in his talk he told what was probably an old story, but it was the first time I had heard it. A seventh grade boy was to be in a play and had one line. It was, "It is I; be not afraid." All month he rehearsed this line at school and at home: "It is I; be not afraid. It is I; be not afraid. It is I; be not afraid." But on the day of the performance he was very nervous and when his time came he stood on the stage, knees shaking, voice cracking, and said, "It's me, and I'm scared to death."

It's me and I'm scared to death!

83

As a sixth-grader I played on the elementary boys basketball team. We practiced in the gymnasium at the school. Once during practice a Bethel College student came to watch us. He was not just any college student; he was a professional baseball player who attended Bethel in the off-season and would eventually coach junior high and high school teams. We were running laps and I was leading the pack. I wanted to impress him so I accelerated and got farther ahead. I was hoping as I made each lap and passed by that he might say something like, "Way to go," or "Good work." Instead, even as I ran faster and stretched the lead, the only thing he said to me was, "You can do better than that," with heavy emphasis on the first and last words. Where was the praise?

Where was the amazement on how fast I was running? No, all he said was, "You can do better than that." Trouble was, he was right.

84

Church signs abound wherever one travels. Here are a few seen over the years:

BE YOUR FAMILY'S SOUL SUPPORT

COME HOME, ALL IS FORGIVEN

SIGN BROKEN:
MESSAGE INSIDE

And an unintended message:
CALVARY CHURCH (on one sign)
DEAD END STREET
(on another right beside it)

85

I have problems with the wandering preacher. I don't mean wandering from one part of the country to another, but away from the pulpit, the sacred desk, the place from which the sermon should be preached. Call me unrealistic. Call me uncompromising. Call me to dinner. It doesn't matter. The preacher's place is behind the pulpit. I hear several excuses, I mean reasons, why preachers stray. Somebody said, "I want my sermon to be personal, and I believe this helps." Somebody else spoke up: "I preach without notes and I want people to see that so they'll know I'm speaking from my heart." And so it goes. If I am in the congregation I want to know where the preacher is at all times. If I happen to look down and then look up and the preacher is not there, I must search the sanctuary for the long lost prophet. And I do not want the preacher in my face, down where we are sitting. If the preacher stays behind the pulpit at all times, the personal, informal, without-notes kind of preaching can still take place, and listeners know at all times where the preacher is. The pulpit is the sacred desk, the place for preaching. In the book <u>Moby Dick</u> the whalers' church is near the sea. The pulpit is shaped like a boat and the minister ascends to the pulpit by means of a rope ladder, then pulls it up. Now the preacher cannot come down and the people cannot go up. A perfect picture. I once heard a Cumberland Presbyterian minister tell a story about another minister who was at the pulpit ranting and raving, stomping and Bible-thumping. A little boy said to his mother, "Mommy, what are we going to do if he gets out of there?" I rest my case.

86

Darrell Pickett is a bi-vocational minister in Glasgow, Kentucky. He has been on the local police force, was later elected police chief, and then mayor of the town, all this while serving as pastor of the Clear Point Cumberland Presbyterian Church in Horse Cave, Kentucky. When he was a police officer I was in town to conduct some classes in the Program of Alternate Studies, of which he was a student, and on one of those days he picked me up at the hotel to go to lunch. He was wearing his police uniform. After we had sat down at the table in the restaurant the young woman assigned to take our order came over and, before we could order anything, said, "You saved my life," looking at Officer Pickett. He sat there, like I did, silent and a bit taken aback. She said it again, "You saved my life." Then, this: "Six years ago you came to the local high school and talked about the DARE program (a nationwide drug prevention effort). What you said saved my life. I want to thank you for putting me on the right track in life." We may never know whose life we touch. We may never know when words said reach another person. In the occasional moments when we do know, we praise God for the opportunity to help.

87

A 911 call came in and the message was frantic and desperate... and mixed: "Bring help. My mother is hurt. She's bleeding. By the way, how are the Red Wings doing?"

88

A country song tells quite a story. A woman is singing and she remembers that during the courtship stage, her boy friend said, "Marry me, and I'll take you to Rome, Athens, and Paris." The song goes on and ends this way: "Sure enough. We married. And we have lived in Rome, Georgia; Athens, Texas; and Paris, Tennessee."

89

A young man, 26 years old, said he started keeping a diary at age 16. One page per day for ten years, and ongoing. He commented, "Some days sad, some days happy. But there's always another page."

90

Our dog Dutch loved to ride in the car. He was quite comfortable with it. He was a Schnoodle, something between a Schnauzer and a Poodle. He died and we got another dog, Ginger, a Dashacocker-peekapoo, sort of a mix of several breeds. Long ears that almost dragged on the floor and got wet when she drank water. A body that almost touched the floor when she walked. Whereas Dutch loved to ride in the car, Ginger just thought she did. She would beg and beg to get in the car and upon entering would immediately cry and whine and cry some more. And the ignition key had not even turned the motor on! Before the car got out of the driveway Ginger was a basket case. She bounced all over the car on trips, front to back, back to front, up, down, all around, even on trips to the grocery store. What she thought she wanted, she did not want once she got it.

91

We lived out in the country from the town of Burleson, Texas. The drive into town took us by farms and fields and cattle. Rounding one bend in the road on a hot summer day, we saw cattle grazing, and on their backs were these little white birds. Egrets, they are called. The work of the cattle and the egrets was a cooperative effort. The cattle ate the grass and the egrets ate the bugs and flies and gnats that tried to make their home on the backs of the cattle. The four-legged animals were happy with this arrangement. They swished their tails, not to keep the flies and gnats away, but out of happiness. The egrets had a feast. This went on day after day. The living arrangements were perfect. Cooperation is always a good thing.

92

I once lost a family from the church before we ever had them. I was going to preach on that text, "Put on the whole armor of God," Ephesians 6:10-17, and talk about the "belt of truth," "the breastplate of righteousness," "as shoes for your feet put on whatever will make you ready to proclaim the gospel of peace," "the shield of faith," "the helmet of salvation," and "the sword of the Spirit, which is the word of God." My sermon title, printed in the bulletin, was "How to Dress Like a Christian." I believe it was a father, mother, and one child who walked in just before the worship service, were handed a bulletin, glanced at it (including the title of the sermon, no doubt) and promptly turned around and left the building. I never saw them again. They must have gotten the wrong idea, thinking that the preacher would advocate strict dress such as some religious groups might demand. As they left, I wanted to cry out, "Come back! It's not what you think! Give us a chance!" The sermon title scared them away, I am convinced.

93

Sermon titles do send messages. Sometimes they promise more than they give. I was on vacation in a large city right after Christmas and noticed in the Saturday newspaper a long list of churches. Some had the title of the pastor's message. One was this: "Jesus' Answer to 'It's a Wonderful Life.'" "It's a Wonderful Life" is that classic film starring James Stewart in which he comes to doubt whether his life means anything. During the course of the movie he is persuaded that he is important to many people. I attended that church the next day. Outside of an opening sentence or two about the film, the pastor never again mentioned the movie in his sermon, which had very little to do with the inviting title. The sermon title helped to get me there, but the sermon itself did not follow up as promised.

94

A church in the area has a neon sign that flashes different messages. One is, "We're Here for You." A ministerial colleague and I would wonder aloud: Why not say, "We're There for You"? After all, is the church not called on to go out into the world and not wait for people to come to its facilities? I know what they mean when they say, "We're Here for You," but that other message is important, too.

95

We often make life harder than it needs to be. As a young minister I was with another preacher who was holding a revival in the rural community. When we visited in different homes, he drove. Once we came to a farmhouse and there was a gate. I got out, opened the gate, he drove through, I closed the gate, and then got back into the car for the drive up the hill to the house. After the visit, we got back into the car, he drove down the hill and we arrived at the gate. I got out of the car and opened the gate. He drove through. I closed the gate in front of me and climbed over the gate, which, incidentally, had barbed wire over the top. When I got back into the car, the preacher said, "I saw what you did." Then and only then did I appreciate the fact that I made an easy task harder than necessary.

96

More often than we would like to admit, we make things more difficult than necessary. Once while I was doing the "time for children" in worship, always a dangerous moment, the children and I stood around the table where the two altar candles were burning. I had placed several other unlit candles on the table in order to tell a story, but now I could not find a match, did not have a lighter, and thus was looking around for some way to light these candles. One of the younger children came to the rescue: "You have two candles there on the table already burning; take one of those and light the other candles," was the substance of his message, as I recall. I think he actually said, "Use one of these!" pointing to one of the altar candles there within easy reach and in full view. The congregation enjoyed that moment.

97

The Genesis account of the first sin is well known, but the second sin is often overlooked. It is intriguing, showing how the desire to blame others for our misdeeds has been around a long time. After the disobedience occurred, God talked to Adam about it, but Adam said, "This woman you gave me" is the problem. It's her fault. So God turned to Eve, who promptly pointed to the serpent. She said, "It's not my fault; it's the serpent's fault." And, of course, when

God turned to the serpent, the serpent didn't have a leg to stand on...

98

The Bible is important for many reasons, not the least of which is its honesty. Take families, for example. While the Bible talks at different places about what a family should be, when it narrates actual stories of real families, it spares no one but tells it like it is. Adam and Eve, in their first bunch of children, had Cain and Abel. Cain killed Abel. Joseph was the spoiled, arrogant, obnoxious little brother that his older brothers could not stand, and they thought about killing him, but instead sold him into slavery. There is old Eli with his troublesome sons. We see Isaac and Rebekah and their terrible twins, Esau and Jacob, the latter favored by Rebekah; David had a son named Absalom who caused David many sleepless nights. David stole Bathsheba, somebody else's wife. Seldom if ever, in both the Old and New Testaments, do we find very many good examples of what a family should be, but there are plenty of examples of ordinary people having some ordinary, and extra-ordinary problems. There are no ideal families. Once there was the young man who set out to find the perfect woman to marry. After years of searching, he found her. Only trouble was, she was looking for the perfect man.

99

When I traveled to Colombia, South America, in 1988 with Dudley Condron, a ministerial colleague, I carried a borrowed camera, volunteered and provided by a husband and wife in the congregation I served. We visited several churches and schools and other interesting places, giving speeches and chatting with the people. During a program at a school, I placed the camera under the chair where I was sitting. Hours after the program was over and we had been to some other locations, I suddenly missed the camera and, tracing my steps in my mind, remembered where I had left it. A phone call to the school, followed by a long wait while somebody went to the auditorium to look for it, followed by a voice back on the phone reassured us: The camera was right where I had left it, and we could pick it up at the principal's office. What's this world coming to? Nobody stole the camera! Was it lack of opportunity, or nobody saw it, or what?

100

One time I left a store and headed back to my office. Just before I drove into the parking lot, I realized I did not have my billfold with me. I always take it out before sitting down to drive and put it in the front seat beside me, and it was not there. I stopped the car immediately and searched the car. Nothing. Then I hurriedly turned around and headed back to the store. I drove into the parking lot of the store. My old parking place was empty and as I drove toward it, I saw the billfold, there on the pavement, right beside where my car was. I had obviously dropped it while climbing in. What's this world coming to? Nobody stole my billfold! Was it lack of opportunity, or nobody saw it, or what?

Chapter III: 101-150

"The Lost Billfold"

101

Once my wife lost her billfold, possibly at a service station while filling up with gas, possibly somewhere else. A few hours later she got a phone call. A man had found it and everything was intact. He would bring it by. Not much later, he did so. We were very fortunate.

102

I had a biblical experience recently. In a café within a hotel in Hot Springs, Arkansas, I ordered crab cake, and when it was delivered, I asked the server if they had tartar sauce. She asked, "Tartar sauce?" I said, "Tartar sauce." "I'll get it for you." Many minutes passed. I decided to nibble on my crab cake, hoping to get some tartar sauce before too long. But the time passed and my server had apparently disappeared. Suddenly there she was, with an ample supply in a bowl. She said, "I had to go downtown to get it." "What?" I replied. "You did not have to do that; you could have told me you did not have any tartar sauce. Thank you very much for your extra effort." The biblical experience? David, thirsty, expressed a desire for water from an old familiar place which happened to be on the other side of where the enemy was camped. One of his servants risked his life to go and get some water from that special place and when he returned with it, David was so overcome with gratitude and humility, he poured it on the ground. I know now sort of how David felt But I did not turn over the bowl full of tartar sauce.

103

Weddings can be happy events... and chaotic. Things do not always go well. One time the groom fainted in a wedding I was trying to conduct. The bride and I saw it coming and we caught him before he landed on the floor and then he revived. In the rehearsal for another wedding, I noticed that the air coming through the vents made the candles flicker and I knew it would be bad if any of them went out. So the next day, just before the wedding, I slipped back and turned the air-conditioning off. After all, it was going to be only a fifteen-minute, or so, wedding. We almost sweltered in that brief time. So much for good intentions. I had a few weddings with a colleague, who was a former pastor of the congregation. I would have the early part, up to and including, "Who gives this woman to be married to this man?" Then we would walk up the steps where he would have the vows and rings and pronounce them husband and wife. Then I would introduce them as Mr. and Mrs. _____. All went well most of the time, but once I forgot to ask, "Who gives this woman... ?" and walked up the steps anyway, with no one following. When I reached the top step, I realized what I had done, or not done. From there I asked, melodically, dramatically, with great feeling, "Who gives... this woman... to be married... to this man?" Several people later said that was the most powerful part of the ceremony. A church member got married in a United Methodist Church in Florida, where she was teaching at a university. The wedding cake got there late, very late. First the caterers took the cake to Trinity Episcopal, then to Trinity Presbyterian, then to Trinity Lutheran. By the time they found Trinity United Methodist, the reception was over. The bride said to give the cake to the young people. We have this consolation: At a wedding Jesus attended, they ran out of wine at the reception. Something always goes wrong at a wedding.

104

So many things depend on "where you're coming from." For example, if you study the history of Texas, you'll read a lot about the Alamo, but if you study the history of Mexico, the Alamo gets about two paragraphs. Our Old Testament authors made a big thing of the Exodus, with page after page after page about that event. I'm guessing Egyptian historians gave the whole thing short shrift. And what about American history and the Revolution and 1776? Our history books contain much, while one would surmise that history books in England would be more restrained. In the Cumberland Presbyterian Church we still hurt from the 1906 attempted union with the Presbyterian Church (USA); yet their histories and others on American church history barely mention it, and usually cite another date, 1907. I'm leafing through a book entitled <u>Christianity Through the Centuries: A History of the Christian Church</u>, by Earle E. Cairns. It covers the subject well, but in regard to the Cumberland Presbyterian Church there are two occasions when it is mentioned: page 418 when he tells that the denomination started with the formation of Cumberland Presbytery, the main cause being education of ministers, and page 427 when he mentions that the denomination experienced union with the Presbyterian Church USA in 1906. That's it.

Nothing else. The General Assembly of the Presbyterian Church in America met in Memphis in June of 2007. There was nothing in the local paper, yet to that church the actions of the body were important. The same could be said about the General Assembly of the Cumberland Presbyterian Church that met in Hot Springs, Arkansas, the next week. To my knowledge, there was nothing in the Hot Springs newspaper about it. I recall that, at this writing, there is a war raging in Iraq, with hundreds of people killed every day. And I seem to recall that the biggest news was the release of young heiress Paris Hilton from jail after twenty three days, her stay resulting from drunk driving charges. The well known story of an early nineteenth century occurrence may say it well. In a small village in Kentucky, folks are visiting at the general store as usual. Someone asks, "Anything special happen today?" Someone else gives this answer: "No. Tom Lincoln's wife had a baby boy. That's about it."

105

I resist change. I am usually the last to acknowledge or admit change has occurred. I am a creature of habit. Same routine every morning. Same routine every night. Therefore it is a shock, and I hesitate even to mention it, that I have made a change. When I fill out those many forms and my Social Security number or checking account number might be needed, I use the dash or hyphen between sections, like this: 123-45-6789. But lately I have altered my style of living. Exercising my freedom to change, I have decided to omit the dash or hyphen. Thus, my numbers might read like this: 123 45 6789. Call me a rebel, call me reckless, call me wild, but I have made that tumultuous decision. From now on, I am going to omit the dash or hyphen... most of the time... or at least some of the time. There, I've told you. I feel better already.

106

In a church in Texas a new family walked in a few minutes before worship time, a mother and two children. "What kind of church are you?" she asked. "Are you a fundamentalist church?" I said, "Well, we do believe in the fundamentals of the faith..." "I don't like fundamentalists." A week later another new family appeared: "Is this a liberal church?" "We are not arch-conservatives or fundamentalists, I can say that," I answered. "I don't like liberals." Two weeks later, I got a phone call fifteen minutes before worship.

"What kind of church are you?" I was ready: "What kind of church do you want us to be?" I forget the answer.

107

We lived in Lexington, Kentucky, a few years in the early 1980s. One Saturday morning we met two other ministerial couples at Shakertown, near Harrodsburg, for breakfast. This tourist area attracted people from across the nation. I was chosen to go to the hostess and give our names. A man was in front of me and he stepped forward and said, "Ter Horst." After the hostess had taken his name and he stepped away, I approached him and asked, "Are you Gerald Ter Horst?" He replied, "Yes." I said, "I want to say how proud I am of your actions. I know it was a hard thing to do. Many people salute you for your courage." I saw tears in his eyes and he said, "Thank you." Who is Gerald Ter Horst and what did he do? When Gerald Ford succeeded Richard Nixon as President of the United States, Ford asked Gerald Ter Horst, who was then editor of the Detroit Free Press, as I recall, to be his press spokesman. But a few weeks later, when Ford pardoned Nixon, Ter Horst resigned out of conscience. He forsook fame, public recognition, the glamorous Washington life in a presidential administration, to speak his conscience. He did indeed settle into national obscurity. But he could undoubtedly live with himself quite freely after that. And, years later, he and his family were at Shakertown. I'm glad I met him.

108

We just saw a wonderful movie, "Evan Almighty." A TV news anchor is elected to congress. He and his family move to Virginia. He ran on a promise to "change the world." God intervenes and tells him he can change the world, all right, but not quite like the new congressman thought. On God's instructions, he builds an ark. Other interesting things happen before, during, and after its construction. We left the theater inspired. There was no profanity or nudity or even any innuendos that might make one nervous if one's mother were watching the film, too. Linda and I agreed it would be a wonderful movie to show to a church group. Several good messages are in it. It's lighthearted and fun, too. We left with spirits high.

We had only hurriedly read the Memphis paper that morning and did not read the movie reviews. So when we got home, we resumed our reading and were shocked to read the review of "Evan Almighty." Four stars sit out beside each movie title. A movie's worth, according to the reviewer, is evidenced by how many stars are filled in. All four stars darkened means "great." Three stars darkened means "very good." We were surprised to see only half of just the first star darkened beside the title of "Evan Almighty." The reviewer's first sentence called the movie "claptrap," and subsequent words and sentences were not any friendlier. We thought, "Would we have gone to see this production if we had read the review earlier in the day?" Perhaps not, but we would have missed a wonderful experience.

Once a few weeks earlier, while we were in Baltimore on vacation, I read a review of the second or third "Pirates of the Caribbean" movie starring Johnny Depp. The writer for the <u>Baltimore Sun</u> could not say enough bad things about this piece of junk. On the same day I picked up a copy of the <u>Washington Post</u>, whose movie guy said it was probably one of the top ten movies of all time and would go down in history as a classic. Once more, different tastes for different folks. By the way, I just read in a church newsletter that the youth of a church were going to go see "Evan Almighty" at a local theater and then eat together at a nearby restaurant. I guess they did not read the reviews.

109

After worship one Sunday morning in the church where I grew up we were greeting the pastor and he was greeting us. "I enjoyed your sermon," said one. "Good message," said another. A woman came through and said, "I enjoyed your message. Oh, I forgot! I didn't hear you; I was keeping the nursery." So many such compliments are routine and habitual. What if we were more honest? "Maybe it will be better next week, pastor," or "You just didn't have it today, did you?" or "Nice talk," or "Nice try, preacher." I remember in one church a woman walked through and confessed, "I'm sorry. I was just not able to listen to you today." I tried to tell her that the lack of communication was my fault, not hers. She did not hear much because I did not say much and what I said I did not say well.

110

Public prayer is a heavy responsibility because the one praying aloud is supposedly praying on behalf of all others in the congregation at that moment. All the more reason, then, to pray (as Jesus suggested, by the way) "Our" Father, and say "we" instead of "I" and continue to make the prayer first person plural, not first person singular. I am sure God understands and even takes everything into account when a person praying, again on behalf of all others there, says, "Lord, I just thank you..." and "God, I just pray ." although it may get on God's nerves. First, it's about more than the one person who is praying aloud. Second, no need to say "just" so many times, or any at all. That's like the young man saying to his girl friend, "Mary, pardon me, but if I could just have a moment of your time, I just want to ask you just to marry me." Or, the baseball manager starting an argument with an umpire: "Excuse me, sir, but I just want to say I disagree with you..." Using "just" seems to be saying, "I just want to apologize for bringing this up and I just know you are really busy and I am truly sorry for interrupting your busy day, but I just want to ask... ." Lord, deliver us from such prayers that seek to cozy up to you as if you do not welcome a forthright, straightforward, first person plural prayer on behalf of all.

111

Another problem in prayer is the much-addressed God to whom we pray. It usually goes something like this: "Father, I thank you for this beautiful day, and Father, I pray for our church, and Father, bless all families.... "Do we talk to family members or others like that. Husband to wife: "Mary, I just bought a new set of tires for our car, and, Mary, I'll be home a little after five, and Mary, what's for supper?" No, once is enough. Jesus, in the Lord's Prayer, did not say, "Our Father, which art in heaven, and Dear Heavenly Father, hallowed be thy name, and Dear Heavenly Father, thy kingdom come, and Father, thy will be done..." It's like if we don't keep addressing God, God might lose interest and go away. Father, forgive us for, Father, we know not what we do, Father. I felt that somewhat when someone called me on the phone and said, "Mr. Campbell, this, and Mr. Campbell that, and Mr. Campbell, this and Mr. Campbell, and Mr. Campbell" again and again. Hey! I'm here! I'm not going anywhere. I'm listening. No need to call my name twenty-seven times in this conversation.

112

In his Letter to the Galatians and other letters the Apostle Paul uses the word "justify" many times. I have tried to understand, using everyday thinking, what "justify" means for us. How about this? When a government cuts taxes for the very wealthy and places more hardship on the middle class and the poor, one might ask, "How can they justify that policy?" Suppose a football team is ahead of another team 70-0 and the coach of the team that is far ahead keeps his first team in all the time. One might ask, "How can the coach justify that decision?" An example could be when the University of Florida defeated the University of Kentucky in football in October of 2008, something like 65 to 5, leaving the star quarterback and many other first-team players in the game an unreasonable amount of time. Do those examples help us understand what it means to be justified? By the death of Christ on the cross, we are justified. We are justified by faith. What is wrong between us and God is made right, justified, by these drastic actions. We are justified.

113

I had been pastor of a certain Texas church for seven years. A committee from another church attended one Sunday morning. They were on the search for a pastor for their church. These people are easily spotted by local folks. While they try to sit in separate sections in the sanctuary and attempt to mingle with the crowd, they are usually identifiable by their early arrival, as well as their usual arrival in the same automobile. This Sunday was the Sunday after Easter. Now Easter was a great crowd, over 130 in this relatively new congregation and thirty in a choir that did a great job on the anthem. But on this, the Sunday after Easter, Low Sunday in the official church year, we had maybe 50 in the service, and eight in the choir that didn't even try to sing an anthem because of so few there. The sermon, too, went along with the general spirit of the day, a rather ho-hum, tedious message soon forgotten by all, no doubt. After the service I was standing in the hallway with one of the search committee members who, in fact was from the same home town where I grew up. A wise, discerning woman of the congregation came by, shook my hand and his, and said, "And that's the best he can do, too."

114

A song director or soloist will sometimes say before the next selection, "Listen to the words." I have thought that suggestion to be unnecessary. Of course, we will listen to the words. Somebody will be singing them and we cannot shut our ears. We might just turn our minds to something else entirely, yet the sound will penetrate and something will seep in regardless of our efforts to shut out the words. It might help sometime if the soloist sang so that the congregation could understand what was being sung. So, sometimes, when I hear someone say, "Listen to the words," I want to shout out, "I WILL NOT!" But as of yet I have not done that.

115

Being "spiritual" is important. Lord knows, I have tried. Once I thought I saw a spiritual man. He had changed since the last time. He seemed to walk with a different walk, had a different air about him, lifted his head higher. I thought, "That man is very spiritual." Then one day, I, too, had to get bifocals. Then I understood what I had seen. I, just as he did, had to learn to walk again.

116

I was with a group of ministers for a morning gathering at a church. It happens that the pastor and I ended up in his study while others were elsewhere in the building. The pastor, head of a large congregation, spoke highly of me. He said, "I especially appreciate your piety." I knew then he knew nothing about me. I assure you, I showed restraint and did not laugh when he said that, well not out loud anyway.

117

Some ministers were talking about their work. I said my hardest times are when I visit in hospitals. I don't know what to say most of the time. I stand there. I don't have any words of wisdom. Then one of my colleagues said, "But they've heard you preach." What a wonderful thing to say! What a terrific load off my shoulders! What wonderful counsel from a wise, loving colleague! It's not that what he said was true about me, you understand, but I know what he was talking about. A pastor's sermons should exhibit a love for the people, indicate an openness to them, and help create a sense of concern, empathy, and accessibility. So that, even if the minister is tongue-tied at the hospital bed, the patient knows how the minister feels. I was ministered unto by my colleague.

118

It is important while in a funeral processional to keep your mind on the present. I had a funeral on the north side of Fort Worth and the grave side service would be on the south side of the city. After the service we started driving. Leading the way was the hearse. Then the car carrying the pallbearers. Then my little Ford Fairlane. It was a hot August afternoon in 1968. The caravan turned onto a familiar road, for it was the direction one went to get to the church. Ah, the church. It was a young, growing congregation with many activities during the week. In fact, that night there was something going on and I would be there. I remembered some things I had to do at the church before the afternoon turned to evening, and time was passing. It didn't help that the traffic in front of me was slow as Christmas. I was getting more and more impatient. I eased barely across the center line and noticed there was nothing hindering those cars in front me. Why weren't they going faster? Then I did it: I looked once, then twice, then I pulled out and passed the first car and as I did I noticed the driver looking back at me. Then I came even with the next car and this driver also gave me a look. Then, and only then, did I remember I was in a funeral processional and had better get back in line. I slowed down and let the first car move on, then the second, and then I moved in behind that car. We eased on into the cemetery, our vehicles in single file, and twenty or thirty others coming in behind us. To my benefit, no one standing around the grave said anything about my adventures in driving or attempting to pass the hearse and the pallbearers.

119

Walking down the halls of a church one time, I came to the nursery. Over the entrance was this passage: "We shall not all sleep, but we shall all be changed" (1 Corinthians 15:51).

120

Signs like "Entrance" and "Exit" grace many places and buildings. I've often wondered why, in churches, we do not have, instead of "Exit," the word "Exodus."

121

The elements of nature are both friendly and fearsome. Take water, for example. Water to drink quenches the thirst, cools off a person, brings relief. Water puts out fires, provides fun in the summer for swimmers, floats boats and ships traveling to distant shores taking food to the world. But water, when floods come, can become contaminated and not fit to drink. Flooding ruins homes and drowns people. Or consider fire. It has its good qualities: It provides warmth in the cold weather and light in darkness. But fire also destroys and kills. We live with the friendly and the fearsome.

122

Religion brings out good and bad qualities in people. It can cause people to show compassion and mercy, hope and help. But, unchecked and over-zealous, it coerces, kills, imprisons, executes, and persecutes. This has been true because of the many ways people live their faith, including Christianity. I was pastor of a church that bought property in a new subdivision. The developer saw no reason to sign anything because, he said, "I am a Christian." Wisely, the leaders of the new church had other thoughts and compelled him to sign on the dotted line. Sure enough, months later, when he saw how valuable the property he sold us was becoming, he tried to back out. Our leaders stood their ground and he had to keep his word. The "I'm a Christian" ploy was just that, an attempt to skirt an agreement and to camouflage dishonesty with the cloak of Christianity. It may be that we should beware of those who have to "tell" us they are Christians.

123

Prayer is at its best when it is balanced with service. A conscientious, faithful Christian I know said she was not spending three hours in prayer as she would like, and she regretted it. The reason: She was tending to the needs of others. I thought: There should be no regrets. What a wonderful combination - prayer and service. Prayer leads us to service, and service leads us back to prayer.

124

I have been reading the three-volume set of books entitled Power At Sea, by Lisle Rose (2007, University of Missouri Press), a narrative of the advancement of naval war since the late nineteenth century. In a restaurant a server, after inquiring and then hearing my description of what I was reading, said he had read that the controversy was not finished about the Titanic (not a battleship) and how it was sent to the bottom of the sea. Some still suspect sabotage. And then he said, that other ships beside the Titanic sank in that era (1912), but the Titanic got the most attention because it was touted as "unsinkable." Had its builders and owners not boasted, its demise might not have occurred nor would it have received as much press. "Pride goeth before a fall," or something like that, said one Old Testament sage. No one, no nation, no ship, can boast of invincibility. And the more pride there is in supposed strength, the greater the fall. People, nations, and ships would do well to take notice.

125

We sat in the waiting room of the hospital. A cousin of Linda's was close to death from leukemia. With us was his wife. His brother, a minister, was at his bedside when he died. The minister-brother came into the waiting room and said, "It's over. He's gone." We sat in silence. In a few moments a young hospital chaplain entered. He didn't know any of us. He didn't know our church affiliation or our spiritual condition or our real needs. Without hesitation he started talking as if none of us were Christians and as if we didn't know anything about the scriptures. The minister-brother, wisely, I suppose, said nothing, although he could have told the chaplain a thing or two. We let the chaplain give his prepared speech, have a prayer, then leave. Then our mourning resumed. I don't think he had a clue as to our situation. I suppose he thought he had done his job.

126

It has been about twenty years now since the Berlin Wall came tumbling down and Communism lost its zip. I credit Mikael Gorbachev for much of the thawing of the Cold War, as well as American presidents, including Ronald Reagan, for steering our nation toward that great moment. Many people can get at least part of the credit. Some say the whole thing started when a small Lutheran congregation in the Berlin area started praying for the wall to come down in their midweek services. That has encouraged me about this Iraq fiasco America has gotten itself into. Almost every Sunday, in the two small congregations where I preach, I pray "that all bombs fail to detonate, and that all guns shoot crooked, and that no one gets hurt and that everybody get discouraged and goes home." Just a week ago two car bombs in London failed and were found before any damage could be done. God may just be in the bomb and gun failure business. I'm going

to keep praying that these weapons fail and the makers of wars give up and go (or come) home.

127

I saw this sign on a store years ago:

> WE BUY JUNK. WE SELL ANTIQUES.

128

How often have we noticed this sign on different business establishments: UNDER NEW MANAGEMENT. You might say that is a description of one who has become a Christian recently.

129

I attended a service where a man was ordained to the gospel ministry. After his ordination, toward the end of the service, he presided over Holy Communion. We walked to the table and he and another minister served us the elements. I was three or four people behind the one taking the elements and after she walked away I saw the newly-ordained minister disappear. He was stooping down to serve a little girl. Then he reappeared. Her mother had moved on, and as she finished partaking, she went to her mother. She did not walk. She sort of ran and skipped. My first thought was: "Should we not all run and skip after such a glorious experience at the Lord's table?"

130

Exodus 13:17 tells us: "When Pharaoh let the people go, God did not lead them by way of the land of the Philistines, although that was nearer..." You look at the maps in the back of your Bible and you will see one that traces the wanderings of the children of Israel. It looks like the work of a three-year old. Markings all over the place. Doubling back. Retracing steps. Going miles out of the way, it seems. Some surmise that had they gone along the seashore straight to the Promised Land, it would have taken a few months at most. Instead, God led them by "the roundabout way (verse 18)" and it took them forty years. Bad direction? A divine mistake? No. Think of what they would have missed: Sinai, the Ten Commandments not once but twice, the Ark of the Covenant, the Red Sea, manna from heaven, and a dozen other monumental events. Some who are called to preach want to get on with it. Since

God has called there is no reason to travel the "roundabout way" of education with all its wanderings. Yet to take the short cut would be to miss out on so many challenging experiences, so many times of biblical awakenings, so many life-changing moments. Besides, in life, it's the trip just as much as the destination that counts.

131

You are eating at a restaurant and ask for another napkin. Is it not surprising that the server brings four or five napkins for you? You ask for some more butter and out comes a bowl full of those little containers. Just about every time I experience something like that in an eating establishment, I am reminded of the passage in Ephesians 3:20-21: "Now to him who by the power at work within us is able to accomplish abundantly <u>far more than all we can ask or think</u>, to him be glory in the church and in Christ Jesus to all generations, forever and ever. Amen." God is ready to provide far more than we ask or think.

132

Linda and I were on our way to California where I would conduct some classes in the Program of Alternate Studies with one of our students. We had flown to Las Vegas for an overnight stay and then would rent a car to make the four-hour trip to Trona, California. In our hotel we waited at an elevator and when it opened, we both said, "Twelve, please." The couple in the elevator immediately said, "You're from the South, aren't you?" We acknowledged that it was so. We later reflected on this. Was our southern accent so pronounced (excuse the term) that it was this obvious? And in just two words? Some years later I was talking with this same California student, now an ordained minister, about this. He immediately gave an explanation I never thought of. "It's not the accent," he said, "It's the 'please.' You said 'please.'" By the way, the husband and wife in the elevator were from Kentucky, on their way to California, as loyal Kentucky Wildcat basketball fans, to see their team play UCLA.

133

It's all a matter of perspective. Knoxville, Tennessee, is on the far-eastern side of the state of Tennessee, a state much longer from west to east than it is wide from north to south. I once met a family from North Carolina that had recently moved to Knoxville. One of them said, "This is the farthest west I have ever been." Here is another one: Our denominational committee that planned the annual ministers' conference asked one of our Cumberland Presbyterian ministers in Louisville, Kentucky, to be in touch with a denomination that was predominantly midwestern in its population as its leaders conducted that church's ministers' conference. He received information in the mail and actually attended the meeting. The brochure advertising the gathering announced it would be in Louisville, "in the heart of the Deep South."

134

Wherever one lives is, to that person, the "center of the universe," where everyone would live if given a choice. That's the way it was when we grew up in McKenzie, Tennessee, a town of some 5,000 in upper West Tennessee. There were many roads leading out of our town - to Paris, Trezevant, Gleason, Greenfield, Huntingdon, for example. So we had the Paris Highway, the Trezevant Highway, the Gleason Highway, the Greenfield Highway, and the Huntingdon Highway. I never heard it to be any different. It was only some fifty years later that it dawned on me that, in those towns, those very same roads were called the McKenzie Highway, the McKenzie Highway, the McKenzie Highway, the McKenzie Highway, and the McKenzie Highway. A ministerial colleague preaches at a church between McKenzie and Greenfield. To him, the church is just off the Greenfield Highway. His first time to mention that at the church was quickly corrected. It's the McKenzie Highway among those folks.

135

As we grow older, we tend to remember with increasing fondness the teachers we had in our childhood and youth. Mrs. Gladys Kelly taught piano in a little room within the facilities of the elementary school. I do not remember expressing a desire to learn to play the piano. However, my parents believed it was a good idea, and I took piano for five or six years. I do not believe much of it "took," however. It was not the fault of Miss Gladys. I did learn a lot about music, but since I was reluctant to practice on my own, I did not make much progress. I appreciate the initiative of my parents that placed me in that learning situation. The most memorable times were the recitals. One year there was to be a little pageant. "Old King Cole" was to be the presentation and a close friend and I were to be the "pages." Everything the king said we repeated. "I am very unhappy." "The king is very unhappy." "I am tired." "The king is tired." On the same evening of "Old King Cole" would be individual recitals of the students of Miss Gladys. Sadly, a few days before the big event, as we were running out the door of the elementary school in a rush to the high school for a rehearsal, the door (with a glass window) slammed quickly on my outstretched hand and cut it severely. Sixteen stitches were needed and at the recital a week later I could not play my selection. However, with my right arm in a sling and my wrist well bandaged, I filled the role of one of the pages in fine fashion.

136

One day Mr. Miller came to town. He was there to sell band instruments. He picked a good target, for, although there was a high school band, there was no program for junior high or elementary kids and, therefore, nothing to "feed" into the high school band over the years. Mr. Miller did well. Several parents purchased instruments for their children. I must have been a sixth-grader. Our purchase was a coronet (similar to a trumpet, but a little smaller). A friend got a clarinet, another a trombone, another a saxophone, still another a trumpet. Soon we were formed into a little band of learners. Our teacher was Mr. Charles Doran, who was the high school band director and at least eighty by that time. He had played in a band directed by John Phillip Sousa. He put us in our chairs according to the different sections and he sat in a chair with a bass drum at his feet. He held a trumpet in his right hand and banged the bass drum with his left. He would play the trumpet and beat the drum at the same time while also teaching us to play the various instruments. He was gruff, demanding, unreasonable, and yelled at us. I learned a lot, including a keen appreciation of the great marches of John Phillip Sousa. Later my younger brother picked up on the trumpet (or coronet) and in our bedroom before going to sleep we would often whistle and hum and otherwise perform marches such as "The Washington Post March," "El Capitan," "Stars and Stripes Forever," "Semper Fidelis," "Gloria," "King Cotton March," and many other Sousa greats. I hold those memories to be priceless. I went on to play the French Horn and then the Baritone in the high school band, leaving my old coronet for my little brother until our parents could purchase a new trumpet for him. Years later when the Broadway play and movie entitled "The Music Man" hit the scene, I remembered Mr. Miller, who must have left our town feeling really good, having sold quite a lot of band instruments.

137

I was presiding over a group of ministers and we were recounting ministerial blunders, both known and experienced. There were major goofs, such as standing at the pulpit behind a live microphone singing "The Gloria Patri" while everybody else was lifting up "The Doxology." One of us heard a minister say that Napoleon discovered America. Still another report was of a pastor who, when someone passed him a glass of water after he and the choir entered the sanctuary for worship - the water being necessary for the empty baptismal fount that someone had forgotten to fill when they cleaned up on Saturday - drank it. One pastor preached a Father's Day sermon - and included other items in the bulletin pertaining to Father's Day - but unfortunately did it all one week early. This went on and on. All of a sudden, I noticed that my watch said it was dinner time and so I hurriedly ended the meeting and just as hurriedly led the closing prayer, which ended this way: "... We pray this in Jesus' name. Bye-Bye."

138

There was an assembly of faculty and staff at Bethel College and I, as student congress president, was invited. The guest speaker was the president of Lambuth College, a neighboring school only forty miles away. He stood and said, early in his address, "There should be no competition among lighthouses."

139

We had a new family visit our church one time. Father, mother, three daughters. They were Baptists, and now were visiting our Cumberland Presbyterian Church. On the way out the door the father asked for some written materials about the denomination and the local church. I gave him some books. By appointment, I visited them some time later. He had a list of questions two pages long. One question was this: What do the two candles on the communion table mean? What do they symbolize? I tried to answer. My reply went something like this: The two lit candles represent the humanity and divinity of Christ. I thought I did pretty well until he said, "I thought they might be there to remind us of the hardships the early Christians endured, as they worshiped in caves and other secret places. The candles provided light for their worship." I liked that very much and told him so. In fact, I have given that explanation as often as I have given mine.

140

Our high school graduating class had another reunion. This time it was the 50th anniversary. McKenzie (Tennessee) High School Class of 1957!! This is the fifth or sixth time we have gotten together. Out of the small class of thirty eight, a few have died. Some others could not be present for the celebration and we missed them. Twenty-three of us showed up. It was great to see one another and to share our stories. We made it a point to call one another by their names used back then. "Jenny" today was "Jenny Lou" back then. "Sue" now was "Molly Sue" back then. "Tom" now was "Tommy" fifty years ago. "Bill" was "Billy" and "Norma" was "Norma Jean." It's "Willa" now but then it was 'Willie Mae." Some left town the day after graduation. One of those did not return for over forty years. Others stayed close by and made our little town and the surrounding area their place of residence and work. Those who left did so either to find work or to go to college, or, if they attended our local college, departed after their years there. It seems we get closer as the years go by. My mother used to say old friends are the best friends. It is getting to be that way. We have the usual mixture of widowhood, divorce, job loss and change, illness, surgery, sadness, and personal loss. These experiences have been balanced by family, job satisfaction, professional advancement, good health, and, all things considered, personal happiness. The memories remain and we rehashed them one evening and the next morning. Our class members have lived in places such as California and Delaware and Kentucky and

Florida and Texas and Arkansas and Georgia as well as many parts of Tennessee. Some have lived in big cities, others in small towns. A good portion, as mentioned, stayed in the McKenzie area." The way we were" was a pretty good way. No matter where we live, we are still a part of the town and school that helped shape us.

141

On the way to our house in the country outside Burleson, Texas, was a Baptist Church. The pastor built a home on the lot next to the church. He built a signpost where he could place different messages, such as "Be Saved Today," or "God Is Love," or "Jesus Saves," or "Prayer Changes Things," as well as others. After a few years he resigned as pastor and left the area. Someone not connected with the church bought the house. I had this question in my mind: To make their Christian witness, should they keep putting messages out on the signpost? I put this question to a group of high schoolers one time, just for general discussion. The reactions were mixed. Some said keep doing it. Others said take the signs down. Some said it sounded like a good way to witness. Others thought the sign cluttered up the front yard and if they owned the house they would remove it. How do we witness? Should all Christians have a sign in their front yard? The new owners eventually took down the signpost.

142

As a pastor in Lexington, Kentucky, I would visit in several hospitals: Central Baptist, The University of Kentucky Medical Center, and two or three others. One time a church member told me he was going into the hospital for surgery the next morning. He later called from the hospital to say he was in Room 527 of the University Hospital. After giving him time to get settled in, I drove over to the hospital, parked my car, and walked into the lobby. Just to make sure all was well, I stopped at the desk to make sure my friend was still in Room 527. The lady checked, and checked again. "We don't have anybody by that name," she said. I replied that I was his pastor, and I knew he was here because he just called and, in fact, said he would be in Room 527. So, if she did not mind, I would go on up. "But sir," she replied, "We do not have him listed as a patient here." I replied with something to this effect: I know visitors are discouraged, and this is a Sunday afternoon and the hospital wants peace and quiet, but I am this man's pastor and I believe I have a right to walk in and see my own church member. Something like that. She said, "Sir, he is not on our list of patients." Then I said, and I quote, "He called me less than two hours ago and said he was in Room 527 of University Hospital and I am here to see him." Then she replied, "Sir, this is Central Baptist Hospital." I stood there, then started edging to the door while still facing the desk. As I walked backwards out of the hospital, she called out, "I won't tell anybody!" I hollered back, "Thanks!" as I slipped out the front door and slinked away, head down, to my car.

143

Pastors know that people in their congregations will sit in the very same pews each Sunday. If a family or individual be not seated at a certain pew there is no need to look elsewhere. The people in question are absent. We are creatures of habit, as they say. While at the summer session of the Program of Alternate Studies of the Cumberland Presbyterian Church, held on the campus of Bethel College in McKenzie, Tennessee, I, like others in the school, would attend a church in town on Sunday morning. The PAS community worships together every day in the week, but on Sundays we scatter to different churches of our choice in the area. In 2006 I decided to go up the hill to the First United Methodist Church of McKenzie. I had attended various functions there as a child growing up in the town, but never a Sunday morning worship service. I sat on the far right side, second row from the back. One year later, I decided to attend there again. I sat on the far right side, second row from the back. Why? I do not know. It just seemed the thing to do. I returned in 2008, third consecutive year. Same pew. No doubt, if I return in 2009, that is where I will sit. If someone else is there, will I say to them, "Pardon me, but you are sitting in my pew"? We shall see.

144

I was reading Volume II of a series by Lisle Rose called <u>Power At Sea</u>, a history of naval warfare around the globe. There was this phrase on page 50 that jumped out. A country built a ship that was designed to "outshoot those ships it could not outrun, and outrun those it could not outshoot." This sounds like good strategy for a basketball team. Given the battles between good and evil that all Christians must fight within their own souls, it might be good strategy there, too.

145

Church folks on a bus tour of Louisville, Kentucky, became friends with the tour guide, especially after she asked all of them to pray for "Mary Jane." How nice of her to ask, and how considerate of her to include us in her thoughts and prayers for Mary Jane, they all agreed. And so they did pray for Mary Jane, each one individually, and just as they were stopping but before they had a chance for a group prayer, the tour guide said, "Thank you for your prayers for Mary Jane. I know they will help a lot. She's running in the sixth race at Churchill Downs today."

A prayer for Mary Jane

146

"Prayer concerns" in worship services are common, and highly valued. They go pretty much like this: Sometime before the Pastoral or Morning Prayer the pastor asks if there are any prayer concerns. One by one, people mention a grandmother, an uncle, a sister, ill or facing surgery or grieving. Someone else has started a new job; we will pray for that person. Another family or church member is looking for work. Still another is moving to another area to take a job and needs the congregation's prayers. I would get just a little uneasy if this were to occur every Sunday. Legitimate concerns they are, but they are all "local" - centered on the congregation or personal and family situations. Forgotten may be the prayers for the lost, for war torn nations, for the oppressed, for those in prison, for the hungry, for peace in the world. I could go on. I have no suggestions. Nor do I have any solutions. By and large, I do not ask for prayer concerns. I should. But I don't. Maybe some of the above is why.

147

National tragedies bring presidents to the scene: Reagan to Houston after the Challenger disaster; Clinton to Oklahoma City following that bombing; George W. Bush to Ground Zero after September 11, and New Orleans after Katrina and Minneapolis after the bridge collapsed over the Mississippi River. Politics aside, the first two mentioned were good, almost "pastoral" in their roles, as they sincerely grieved with the people. Bush, on the other hand, either by instructions from his handlers or out of his own personality, felt the need each time to cheer the people on, to promise that things would get better, to predict that those grieving would overcome. It took a while for me to land on this. Why was Reagan so strong and helpful? Why was Clinton so eloquent and supportive? They were suffering with the people, allowing the time of grieving to play out, not rushing to make promises or even look to better days. The time for grieving was now. They were part of it. This, of course, is wisdom for pastors. In 2 Kings 6:24-30 a king is grieved by the suffering of his people, who do not think he is sensitive to their pain. But the king tore his clothes and "the people could see that he had sackcloth on his body underneath..." He was suffering with his people. I related this to a church audience one time. There was a reception to follow, so I took my robe and Bible to the car first. As I turned to return to the church a man shook my hand, then said, rather forcefully, "Two days after 911, I saw President Bush crying on television." I said, "Thank you very much."

148

Not all cars are the same. That makes it risky to rent a car. At least twice that notion came home to me clearly. I was driving late in the evening on an interstate in Tennessee surrounded by big trucks. I had my lights on, of course. It began to drizzle just a little, then a lot. I reached for the gadget that would turn on the windshield wipers. At least there was where it was on my own car. However, on this one, it was the light switch and, instead of starting the windshield wipers, I turned off the lights. Now I am going up a hill, trucks to my back and front, and to my right (I was trying to pass) and now I can't see that well and, worse, others cannot see me. It seemed an eternity, but I finally managed to find the light switch and survived that scare.

Another time was not so bad. Another rental car was my transportation from Shreveport, Louisiana, to Marshall, Texas. I opened the front left door and pushed a button inside the door to open up the trunk in which to toss my luggage. That's the way it was with the car back home. I heard a click, all right, which told me the trunk was now open, but when I went to deposit my bags, it was locked. Not thinking anything else about it, I used the key to open it. Now I am headed west on I-20 and picking up speed. To my surprise, I see the hood bobbing up and down (fortunately it was held down by its latch, but still had some leeway and was doing a pretty dance). Then it dawns on me that the button I pushed that did not open the trunk did loosen the hood. I slowed down gradually, pulled over, and slammed the hood shut, with no harm done. I was a pastor then and am now, and have learned that things are not automatically the same from one church to the next and one must examine closely where one is and consider the traditions, decisions, experiences, and vision of each church before deciding what buttons to push.

149

We preachers, standing at the door after the service and shaking hands with folks, hear such things as "Nice sermon," or "Good message," or "I enjoyed that message," or similar words of commendation. We like those affirmations, sincere or not. We might not take to "That was a nice talk," as enthusiastically as we should. What really encourages me is when someone walks up and says something like, "That passage means more to me now than it did," or "I never thought about that text in that way," or "I had always assumed this or that about that scripture, but your message helped me to understand it better." If preaching focuses on a text, what better words could a preacher hear than these? This may mean there has been a little bit of instruction and at least a little bit of inspiration.

150

I have never been able to understand, and therefore preach from, Matthew 22:11-14, the parable of the man who showed up at the wedding not dressed for the occasion. But I think I know how he might have felt. In the summer, between my eighth and ninth grades, there were political rallies in the town square. I was an upcoming high school band member and already had my uniform. The director passed the word in town for all band members to be there at a certain time on Saturday. Somebody would be there to speak in behalf of one of the senatorial candidates. I must not have listened, for when I arrived, dressed in blue jeans, tee shirt, and sneakers, every other person in the band was dressed sharply in the blue and white uniform of the day: white pants, white shirt and dark tie, blue coat, blue hat. I stood out like a sore thumb and got some fierce glances from others. After we played a few numbers the main speaker stepped forward. When it was over, I vowed to myself this would never happen again. It was announced there would be another rally one week hence, on the next Saturday, same time in the afternoon. My mother washed my white band pants, starched them stiff, ironed my white shirt, helped me get ready. I was there on time, ready to go. Unknown to me, the director had told everyone to go casual this week. You guessed it: I was the only one dressed in a band uniform. I got it wrong again! Again, I don't know what the message of the parable is in Matthew 22:11-14, but I think I know how that poor fellow felt. It would have helped if I had listened. Maybe that was his problem, too.

Chapter IV: 151-200

"Warm Sermon, Pastor"

151

A ministerial colleague loves to tell about a man who in speaking to the pastor after worship would say, "Warm sermon, pastor, warm sermon." Every Sunday it was the same thing: "Warm sermon, pastor, warm sermon." Several years later, on his last Sunday before retirement, the pastor asked the man what he meant by his weekly assessment, "Warm sermon, pastor, warm sermon." His answer: "Not so hot."

152

As a pastor in rural or small town churches I would experience the honor of having someone in the church come up after the service and say, "You're going with us to Sunday dinner ('lunch' in the big city) today." Like, "This is our Sunday to have you with us." I would know that this is the schedule the church folks outlined. Next Sunday another family would have me over, and the next still another. Since I was a single pastor at the time this certainly was a welcome invitation. But not all invitations are the same. I learned that people sometimes invite you but don't mean it. It's just a courtesy thing. One time a woman in the church invited me to take Sunday dinner at her house. I accepted. Little did I know that she did not really expect me to do so. We walked into her house and she went to the kitchen. At 12:30 she was still in there. At 1:15 she was still working. At 1:45 still no meal, and I was in the living room biding my time. We sat down to eat at around 2:50 or 3:00 in the afternoon. Obviously she had not planned this. I should have politely turned her down when she invited me to dinner at her house. But I didn't know.

153

What is it about the third verse of a four-verse hymn? Why do many churches and their song leaders omit that verse? It must be a time thing; perhaps it is thought the hymn is too long if sung in its entirety. The most flagrant use of this was purely unintentional by good folks at a community-wide Easter sunrise service. We sang "One Day," a hymn that takes us through the complete Jesus story. The first verse was about his birth and life and ministry. The second verse was about his death on the cross. The fourth verse was about his imminent return. What verse did we omit? The third. What was it about? The resurrection. What was the occasion? Easter.

154

Leaving out the third verse in a four-verse hymn can diminish the message, especially if the end of one verse leads into the beginning of another. There is no better example than the end of the third verse in "A Mighty Fortress" and the beginning of the fourth verse. Verse three has this last line: "For lo! His doom is sure: One little word shall fell him." The next starts out: "That word above all earthly powers-No thanks to them-abideth." If we did not sing verse three and began verse four with "That word..." we would have a right to ask, "What word?"

155

Psalm 8 is great: mighty, majestic, powerful. The King James Version says God "hath made man a little lower than the angels," or some such wording. The New Revised Standard Version, pretty much like the Revised Standard Version, says, "You have made (man, us, them) a little lower than God." Well, what happened to the angels? I was confronted after an evening service one time by a couple of people in the church who challenged me for saying that we don't need angels, there is nothing between us and God, and this (the angel thing) was the understood line of authority and responsibility in earlier days, but now we know that we can have direct connections with God and angels are not necessary and are not a part of the chain. They said there are angels and the KJV version is the right interpretation. Later the conversation got into "guardian angels," none of whom I need personally and the absence of whom I believe to be the case. This says nothing about what scholars believe the early manuscripts of Psalm 8 really say, which may be why the NRSV and the RSV (and possibly other translations) exclude angels from this psalm.

156

In a church in Lexington, Kentucky, a young couple attended worship. It was their first time to visit. At the door following the service we met. Pretty much before we got into the innocent and polite courtesies of personal introductions, the young man asked,

"Do you believe there was a Second Isaiah?" I replied, "Well, yes I do." It went down hill from there. They never came back.

157

Like all denominations, ours has had board executives and they all pretty much have worked in one location in our headquarters in Memphis, Tennessee, up until recently, anyway, when some restructure has taken place. One time, while I was serving a church in East Tennessee, a search committee person from a church in another state called to ask if I might be interested in talking with them. But before we got very far on that, she asked, "What do you think about those people who work at the denominational center in Memphis?" I said, unhesitatingly, "I know them well, I like them, and I think they are all doing a good job." That not only slowed the conversation considerably; it helped bring it to a fairly rapid close, and I never heard from that church again. We have this mental picture of denominational executives and other employees as being "bureaucrats" and we envision negative images from that. They are people. They are good people. This is true, I am sure, in all denominations.

158

When I was a pastor in Texas a church in another state called to see if I would be interested in talking with them. I said I would be happy to do so. Since I was scheduled to be in that part of the country soon anyway we arranged for me to be in that city for a couple of days to see the church, meet the people, and sit down with church leaders. All went well: wonderful midweek service, and cheerful and warm reception by all, and then the sit down time with elders and deacons. We gathered in the pastor's study. They asked me to sit in the nice comfortable chair at the pastor's desk. And then came the questions. Well, really, the first question, which was, it really was: "Do you believe Daniel was really in the lions' den?" Without flinching I said, "Yes, I do. I believe the Bible indicates that to be so." The visit continued and then ended. The next morning, on the way to the airport, my host, one of the elders, asked if I would be home on Sunday afternoon, which was about three or four days away. I said I would. He said he would give me a call on Sunday afternoon, no matter what the session decided. That was December of 1980. I am writing this in the year 2007. I am still waiting for that call. I have just about given up on it. In fact, after about six months had elapsed, I wrote to the one who had promised to call me, and said, in effect, that if I had been a younger minister and was seriously interested and needed the consideration by the session, I would have been hurt and greatly offended by the no-call. However, since I, by that time, was a "veteran" (I was all of 41 years old!!) I was not all that bothered, except by the lack of courtesy on his part. I never received a reply to that letter. I guess I was not as enthusiastic as I should have been about Daniel in the lions' den.

159

The Apostles' Creed, in its original form, did not have the line, "He descended into hell." I understand this was added much later. Cumberland Presbyterians generally do not include that line when they recite the Creed. Other Presbyterians usually include it, however. But some Cumberland Presbyterians evidently also believe it should be in there. I tried to preach a Sunday evening series on the Apostles' Creed in a church in Texas several decades ago. Regarding this section, I deemed it necessary to mention that I understood the reference to Jesus' descent into hell was in part at least from 1 Peter 3:19-20 , where he "preached to the spirits in prison, who in former days did not obey..." I mentioned that I believed Jesus experienced hell enough on the cross, with the pain and suffering from the nails in his hands and feet as well as his separation from God ("My God, my God, why hast thou forsaken me?"). Not so, said a few members of the church later in a discussion. But I held my ground fairly well, I thought. The debate was a draw. My reasoning - and faith - on this subject remain as then: the extremes of suffering, both physical and spiritual, came to Jesus on the cross. No more was needed. He paid the price. We do not sing, "Jesus Paid It Partly." We sing "Jesus Paid It All."

160

I was trying to lead a group of junior highs and senior highs in a Bible study. We were sitting in a circle and reading, one by one, from some Old Testament stories. A junior high girl, when it came her time, had a section on Rachel. However, when reading it aloud, she said, "Rascal." That, of course, got corrected; however, it is not at all inaccurate regarding many Bible characters: Jacob, Esau, Aaron, David, Absalom, Rebekah, Judas Iscariot, Simon Peter, Thomas, and Paul. Rascals all.

161

When I was a candidate to become pastor of a larger church than I had ever served - and one of the finest congregations in our denomination - the search and interview process had narrowed down to one, me. I went before the church session for a visit, and, while the elders deliberated later, my wife and I sat in the pastor's study with some of the search committee members. The pastor who had just resigned had been there for a total of about nineteen or twenty years, had done a great job, was a wonderful leader and preacher, and was widely recognized and appreciated in the denomination. Now here we sat, waiting. I said this: "Well, if they call me, I hope I can do as well as (the one who had recently resigned)." The spokesman for the group hardly let me get the sentence out before he said, "We don't want that; we want somebody better." I cannot explain how liberating that statement was. They did call me; I did accept; I did become the pastor of that church, and, of course, they did not get someone better. Nor did they get someone as good. For some strange reason, though, the spokesman's words took absolutely every ounce of pressure and burden off my shoulders. I did not devote one minute of any day of my pastorate in worry or anxiety about the possible comparisons. I learned a lot from what I knew of my predecessor's ministry there, and the church continued in all of the ventures planned when he was there. But I was never stifled or burdened. He was always supportive and encouraging. When I left nine years later, the church got "somebody better." Whenever the day comes that I retire as Director of the Program of Alternate Studies, I hope they get "somebody better."

162

Much to our disappointment, some endeavors take awhile, and gradual progress takes place. When our first child, Kelly, was approaching school-age (pre-kindergarten, maybe), we tried to prepare her all summer. "Soon you will go to school," "It won't be long before you go to school." The day came. She dressed in her finest, took her supplies, maybe even her lunch box, I don't recall, and the day went well. That night, as bedtime approached, we said to her, "It's time to go to bed so you will be rested to go to school tomorrow." She responded, "Again?"

163

Church signs continue to fascinate. Here are some more. I have no comment on their efficacy, theological accuracy, appropriateness, or good taste:

ARE YOU HUMBLY GRATEFUL OR
GRUMBLY HATEFUL?

HELL IS HOT
HEAVEN IS NOT

ASPIRE TO INSPIRE
BEFORE YOU EXPIRE

COME HOME
ALL IS FORGIVEN

CHRIST AROSE
NO BONES ABOUT IT

CHURCH SIGN BROKEN
MESSAGE INSIDE

SEVEN DAYS WITHOUT PRAYER
MAKES ONE WEAK

MOSES WAS A BASKET CASE, TOO

ATM INSIDE
ATONEMENT - TRUTH - MERCY

THE HEAT OF SUMMER IS OVER
BUT HELL IS STILL HOT

164

Speaking of messages, this bumper sticker was on a car on the streets of Tennessee's capital city:

WELCOME TO NASHVILLE
NOW Y'ALL GO HOME

165

A ministerial colleague was in law enforcement prior to becoming a preacher. He told how in the small town where he worked, funds were low, and there was not enough money to buy radar guns. However, he said, in parking the police car in an obvious place, standing out on the side of the road, and holding a hair dryer as if gauging speed by radar, quite a bit was accomplished. The town had more drivers choosing not to speed and a few more dollars for the city treasury as well, thanks to those who occasionally exceeded the speed limit. Sadly, the city council found out about the hair dryers and chose to reprimand the police force for these tactics. I seem to recall that pretty soon there was money available to buy a couple of real radar guns.

166

When we ministers are not what we should be and do not do what we should do, we are often an embarrassment to the faith. One source of embarrassment is those preachers who use funeral services as opportunities to evangelize recklessly, give altar calls, condemn, rant, and rave; in effect, those who mistreat and abuse the pulpit, the family of the deceased, and others in attendance. Just when I am lulled into the notion that all is well in this respect and there is no more of that kind of flagrant ministerial self-righteousness, it happens: some preacher makes an outright fool of himself (it is usually a male, so I'll leave it at that) and abuses grieving families and friends in this egregious way.

I was in one of those states of denial until just the other day when it was reported that a pastor of a mega-church in the Dallas area was preparing to conduct a funeral service for a man in his church. It was going to be a full-fledged service, all the trappings and trimmings, a full pulpit oration in keeping with this pastor's image and status. Then, with less than twenty four hours before the funeral, the pastor announced he was refusing to have anything to do with it. The reason? He learned that the deceased was gay. This minister just had to stand for what he believed was "righteousness," I suppose. Never mind any thought of compassion, support, or love.

A few years ago, I heard from people who had been in attendance at the funeral of a young man who had struggled with a drug problem and was killed in an automobile accident. The victim had in fact been working through his situation. He was much loved by family and friends and fellow college students, and the wreck was unrelated to drugs. The one who preached the sermon, however, thought this was an excellent opportunity to condemn drug use and to let that be the main, if not only, message of the sermon. I heard personally from two enraged people who had been in attendance. They were beside themselves with anger at the audacity, absence of courtesy, obnoxious attitude, and callous nature of the preacher. One of them wrote a letter to the minister protesting his message, but never received a reply.

If ever Ecclesiastes 3:1 applies in modern times, it is at funeral services: "For everything there is a season, and a time for every matter under heaven." Then the chapter continues with a number of statements, all beginning, "a time to... and a time to..." As I ponder the stories above, I note that those ministers violated at least five of the fourteen admonitions. No wonder so many people are turned off by the church.

167

The church emphasis for the month was stewardship and the pastor, in sermons and informal conversations, was encouraging people to raise the percentage of their giving. She was heartened, in spirit if not in results, when one person came forward after a worship service and said, "You will be happy to know that next year I am raising my giving. Now I am giving about 1/20th of my income each month. Next year I plan to raise that to 1/25th."

168

Our three daughters were old enough to stay home by themselves during the summer while their mother and father worked in their respective jobs. On most days I would go out to the house at noon to check on everybody. They were always just fine. Once I entered the house and they were, all three, on the floor, heads propped up on their hands, watching a soap opera. I sat at the kitchen table and observed their intensity. At a commercial break I called to them, "Girls, please come over here; I want to tell you something." Reluctantly, they got up and ambled over to the table and sat down. I was aware that in most soap operas these seem to be recurring themes: marriage, divorce, affairs, kidnappings, amnesia (many cases of amnesia), uncertainty of who is whose mother or father, imprisonment, terminal illnesses, what are thought to be terminal illnesses that are later diagnosed as much less, very bad people, very good people, the apparently good guys ending up being bad, and the apparently bad guys ending up being good, and other episodic situations. After they sat down I said, "Girls, I have waited until now to tell you this. You are old enough to hear this and understand. I have hesitated to bring this up, but I feel it is time. I (clearing of throat), I (brushing back a tear), I am <u>your real father</u>." All three girls groaned, rolled their eyes, and quickly got up and went back to watching television. But I was pleased with myself, and could not wait to tell their mother about this wonderful conversation that was so in keeping with "The Young and the Restless" and "All My Children" and "Days of Our Lives" and the rest. So it was that as she was preparing the evening meal I again was sitting at the kitchen table and said, "Guess what happened at noon today," and then I told the story, which ended, "I am <u>your real father</u>." To which she replied, "That's what <u>you</u> think!" My wife has throughout the years managed to have the last word and the last laugh, this event being a striking example.

169

While our girls were elementary and high school age, they watched a lot of daytime television and not only soap operas. In fact, other shows received their attention more than the daytime soaps. Through the years we have heard lamentations from preachers and churches and self-appointed experts on culture about "what our children are watching on TV" and "the whole world is going down the drain" and "it is a hopeless situation," and similar cries of despair. I was already noticing what our daughters were watching and it was, indeed, shocking. Here was the lineup for one week's watching: reruns of "Gilligan's Island," "I Love Lucy," "The Andy Griffith Show," and "Father Knows Best," and other such corrupting productions. It is a wonder they ever made it through their childhood and youth.

170

When our girls were growing up, I heard our youngest tell a story that went a little beyond the basic facts, probably in order to liven it up a little. I remember turning to her and saying, "Kristen, if I've told you once, I've told you a million times, don't exaggerate."

171

I am the middle of three brothers. All three of us attended Bethel College in McKenzie, Tennessee, for all or part of our college undergraduate work. None of us married anyone we met while at Bethel. We have said this, "We could have married any girls we pleased. Only trouble is, we couldn't please anybody."

172

I do remember one girl at college. She worshiped the ground I walked on. She later went into real estate. (Thanks to the cartoon Frank and Earnest for this one)

173

"They did it for the money." We have heard that familiar sentence many times. In 2007 the controlling family of the Wall Street Journal agreed to sell the paper to Rupert Murdoch's company, despite Murdoch's track record of turning a respectable news organization into a right-wing ideological tool as well as a puppet for his own financial ambitions resulting in a decline in quality and objectivity. Of course, he promised that would not happen this time. It is obvious this family "did it for the money." However, I know of a church located on a prominent site in a town near here that was offered one million dollars by Walgreens drug chain if they would sell them the corner lot of that property. Not once but twice did the company make an offer, the second offer being larger than the first. The church leaders said "No" both times. In fact, I'm told that the elders prefaced the second "No" with a particular word, not appropriate here, that had four letters. The last two were "l," the first was "h," and the second letter was not the first vowel, or the third, or the fourth, or the fifth. That's all I can tell you. Some things are worth more than any amount of money. Words like integrity, character, and mission prevailed where that church was concerned, and the leaders practiced all of these virtues valiantly and boldly.

174

The speaker at the Seminary retreat talked about "informative" learning and "transformative" learning. The former is learning that eventually fills up a person's brain and there is no room for more. The latter is learning that changes the person. That thought came like a breath of fresh air to me because I work with folks who are going to school to become ordained ministers. It certainly fits snugly with the words of Paul in Romans 1:2: "Do not be conformed to this world, but be transformed by the renewing of your minds, so that you may discern the will of God--what is good and acceptable and perfect."

175

I preached a series of sermons one time with the words "Coping With..." at the first of every title: "Coping With Grief," "Coping With Sin," "Coping With Heavy Burdens," "Coping With Disappointment." I had this really good sermon ready called "Coping With Indecision," but never could decide when to preach it.

176

Some signs on stores make you look twice, and then think. Like this one. Read it and go figure.

> EARS PIERCED
> WHILE YOU WAIT

177

The preacher was preaching from a manuscript. As he finished one page, he would place it to the side and go to the next one. He was preaching on Adam and Eve, and along in the message he got to the end of another page that read, "And Adam said to Eve..." but when he turned the page he knew something was wrong. So he turned back and read it again, "And Adam said to Eve..." and turned the page, but again things were not right. A third time he read the last words on the previous page: "And Adam said to Eve..." and when he turned the page and the right one was not there, he mumbled, but too loudly, "There's a leaf missing."

178

The little boy was buttoning his shirt from top to bottom. But he started off wrong and slipped the first button through the second hole. As he went down the row of buttons the shirt did not look right. His mother said, as he continued, "You need to start over." The boy said, "No, it will end up all right." No, it won't. Sunday School helps kids get started off right.

179

Two men were aboard a plane and other people were coming on. A long-haired young man came down the aisle. One whispered to another, "I don't like it when men have long hair." The other said,

"I believe Jesus probably had long hair." 'Yes, but I would love him more if he didn't."

180

Neatness is a virtue but it can be taken too far. I listened to a woman tell about her son that she sent to church camp fifty years ago at age seven or eight. She had everything packed neatly, with all items in their place. When she went to pick him up on the last day and to get his stuff in his cabin, she opened the suitcase and everything was still in its place, as clean and neat as six days earlier. Her son had worn the same clothes all week. After swimming he would put them back on. He slept in these clothes on a mattress with no sheets because he did not take any out of his suitcase. This happened with a boy from a church I was serving, and he and I were in the same cabin, just across the way from each other. I was not observant enough, that is for sure.

181

A billboard in Fort Worth, Texas, had this advertisement for a plumbing company:

> OUR ROYAL FLUSH
> BEATS YOUR FULL HOUSE

182

A billboard in Lexington, Kentucky, had this advertisement for a laundry:

> WE DO DIRTY THINGS

183

A sign on the front door of a United Methodist church in the Memphis, Tennessee, area announced:

> WELCOME HOME

184

Sometimes "new" isn't all it's cracked up to be. While a pastor in Knoxville, Tennessee, I received a phone call saying the mother of one of the men in the church had died of a sudden heart attack, and that the family was in the family waiting room in the emergency ward at a local hospital. We gathered and prayed and visited briefly, then went out to the family home on the edge of the city. It was a simple frame house obviously several decades old. I was sitting in the living room and looking out the window. Just up the hill, in the next lot, was a beautiful brick house. The woman's son saw that I was gazing in that direction and said that, after the couple had lived many, many years in this house, his father had built his mother a brand new house and it was that one up on the hill. They moved in, but every day when her husband got home from work he would find her looking out the kitchen window toward the old house, crying. She missed it. They moved back down the hill to the old house. This was where she wanted to be. "New" was not all that good. The "old and familiar" was what she wanted and needed.

185

I am uneasy with wandering preachers, whether they wander around the pulpit and stand everywhere but behind that sacred desk, or wander all over the scriptures when preaching. A sermon is about a text or passage of scripture. It is that simple. Yet so many entrusted with the proclamation of the gospel employ dozens of chapters and verses in addition to the main one, if it is possible to identify the main one. So many preachers say they bring other passages to "support" the main scripture which is supposedly the basis for the sermon. My argument is that every passage chosen for a sermon can stand on its own legs and needs no support from any other. In fact, to reach out to all those other verses is to acknowledge that the text I have chosen is not strong enough in and of itself to provide a foundation for a sermon. Furthermore, a sermon that lasts, say, twenty minutes seems to me to be at its best when it focuses on one thing, one text, one message. This week, this message; next week, another. But if it wanders all over "kingdom come" and uses scripture quotations from Genesis to Revelation, the listener, I am certain, goes away uncertain as to what the message was or what it was about. The roles of a pastor are many: counselor, visitor, listener, administrator, preacher, teacher, but not "wanderer." Stand at the pulpit. Preach on one passage. Then sit down.

186

"Testimonials" are wonderful. These occur when Christians stand and tell their life stories, or portions of them, as they recount how the Lord has made a difference in their lives. Trouble is, there is a tendency to exaggerate the more one tells the same story. It's almost a case where individuals try to "out testify" others. An old Monty Python skit has three or four of the group recounting their childhoods and how poor they were. With each account, the person talking tries to show how his family was worse off than the previous story teller's. It gets pretty ridiculous before it's over. I just don't understand why people do that. But then I remember one story I have told about getting trapped in a hospital elevator in Fort Worth. The event itself was probably, at most, forty five seconds, but it seemed longer before the maintenance crew got the elevator going again. The first time I told the story the event was less than a minute, then the next time a minute and a half. In the third telling I was trapped for five minutes. I am getting good at this; the tenth or eleventh telling has me in that elevator for forty-five minutes, going on two hours. I am so diligent in trying to make the story as interesting as possible. Have I told you how I fell on some ice and broke my arm and how long I lay there before somebody found me?

187

No doubt you have heard of the conversation two people had that went this way:

"Why is there so much ignorance and apathy in the world?"

"I don't know and I don't care."

188

What to take to the pulpit is a decision every preacher makes every Sunday. Along with the Bible, some take a complete manuscript. Others take an outline. Others take neither. Each approach is worthy. Thousands of ministers employ one of the above. Most are in a routine where they approach the pulpit the same way every Sunday. Here is my suggestion for manuscript preachers: If you are going to use a manuscript, use it, and do not drift over to either of the other two, especially the extemporaneous (without notes) approach. This is especially needful for the happiness and comfort of the listeners. They know you are using a manuscript. They can guess the approximate number of pages you have and therefore the approximate time of completion. But when you wander from the manuscript, no one is certain when you will return, and you may not know, either. Wandering from the manuscript indicates you are not confident in what you have written, or you have thought of something new you want to say, or you want to expand on a thought you have in your manuscript. In all of these, precious time is taken up, people are getting restless, and you are not back to your manuscript yet. To my mind, the choice of manuscript preaching means you give up the right to provide any extemporaneous remarks. Some of the most powerful sermons ever preached have been offered by ministers using a complete manuscript. There is no justification at all for anybody to suggest that a preacher without notes is more inspired than a manuscript preacher. For both, much of the inspiration arrived before pulpit time and they have chosen different ways of proclaiming - after hours of study, prayer, and reflection - what the Lord has given them to say.

189

I am certain that the Lord forgives sin. Even the sins of ministers. The Lord forgives us preachers of many things, maybe even everything. Everything, that is, except "dull and boring." The people of our congregations have gone to great sacrifice of time and energy to get to church and they could be going other places and doing other things. The least we can do is not be "dull and boring" in our sermons. I am not sure what the word "passionate" means in all respects, but I do know that the person in the pulpit needs to be interested and involved and, yes, enthusiastic. There must be a sense of urgency. I don't know where I read it, perhaps in a book or two, but I do know that a pertinent question for us to ask of our sermons is, "So what?" I have tossed in the trash basket more than one sermon idea or complete sermon itself when I have not been able to answer to my satisfaction that probing question. We are, all of us, able to recall sermons that did not seem to matter to the one in the pulpit.

190

As we preachers look out upon our congregations during the Sunday morning worship service, we are prone to forget what some of our people had to go through to get to church, especially if there are little children to get dressed and ready. I heard of one single mother with four small children who got her family to church on time every Sunday. One day the pastor asked her, "How do you do it?" She answered, "I start on Tuesday."

191

Ministers meet a lot of people and try hard to remember names. I have called people by their wrong names and lived with great regret for months, even years, wondering if the relationship could ever be healed. Some preachers are helped by using word association, but even that can backfire. A pastor met a man in town named Lummoch, and since that rhymed with "stomach," he felt all would be well. A few months later Mr. Lummoch attended church for the first time. At the door after worship the pastor's memory kicked in, at least in part. "Good morning, Mr. Kelly, it's great to see you again. Thanks for coming."

192

Ministers find themselves conducting weddings in various settings. A woman in the church was set to marry a rodeo man. The wedding would be in the rodeo arena on the campus of a community college. The groom and the bride and the bride's two teenage daughters would ride in on their respective horses. All went well. That was the problem. That meant I could not say to any of them who might have been in too big a hurry, "Hold your horses!"

193

Love Can Find a Way

A phone call to the church got me involved with a couple who wanted to get married. Trouble was, the bride was in Knoxville (where I lived) and the groom was in Houston and would normally be back in plenty of time for the wedding. However, he was jailed on a traffic violation. I got to the apartment where the groom's mother lived and where the bride had gone for the wedding. The plan was this - and it had the approval of law enforcement in Houston. We would have this wedding by long distance telephone. The apartment had two phones. Soon the groom was connected and the three of us could converse (Colleagues: No need to remind me of the many ministerial traditions and vital elements, such as counseling, that did not happen in this case!! Why I did this, I do not know.) The wedding was conducted by phone with the bride in Knoxville and the groom in Houston. Don't ask me where the license was purchased. I don't know. I do know that there could not be an exchange of rings. Nor could the groom kiss the bride. Having broken every rule of protocol for ministers in this situation, I deserved every headache that came with this experience.

194

At one church her name was Pat and his was Hilton, but, early on, I called him Clint by mistake, and for some reason that name stuck in my mind. I always had trouble calling him by his right name. We joked about it, especially when I started calling her Gladys just to make it worse. When they married they asked an old pastor friend of his to have the ceremony. I told them they did not ask me because I would have said, "Clint, do you take Gladys to be your lawful wedded wife?"

195

In a couple of metropolitan areas where I was a pastor, there arrived on my desk a copy of the "Christian Yellow Pages," a phone book of advertisements from plumbers, barbers, car dealers, pharmacists, department stores, hair dressers, lawyers, grocery stores, restaurants, donut shops, office supply stores, and many others who in their ads announced that they were Christians. The idea here was, obviously, that people should patronize "Christians" who are in business. From Day One I have had problems with this, and once wrote to the company about it, with no reply. First, there was a litmus test for these merchants and business people. Yes, they were Christians, but they were "born-again" Christians, and they met the doctrinal requirements that qualified them to be in the "Christian Yellow Pages." I read the list of requirements. No thank you.

Second, the very idea of trying to persuade Christians to patronize only Christians was repugnant. This approach assumes too much. It seems to assume that only Christian business people deserve your support and non-Christians do not. Nothing here about honesty, integrity, fair-dealing, or even competence, not to mention the laws of the land and the Declaration of Independence and the Constitution. Just, are they Christians? And are they

Christians according to the criteria set by sales people and executives at the "Christian Yellow Pages" corporate offices?

Third, this represented, to me, an attempt to put non-Christian enterprises out of business. Only Christians deserve to make a living. Only Christians deserve your support. I do not believe that is the right "Christian" attitude to have. Christians should not have a business advantage over anybody else, nor should they, by virtue of their faith, seek to eliminate the competition. Furthermore, this is one area where "Christians" should not stick together. It is one thing to support a friend or fellow church member by eating at their restaurant or taking your car to their repair shop, or buying life insurance from them. It is another thing to be a part of an attempt to boycott "non-Christian" businesses entirely.

196

One time a sales person from a "Christian" radio station came by and wanted me to consider having a weekly 15-minute program, paid for, of course, by our church. I had listened to the different programs on the station every so often, usually in passing, never very long. But I knew its approach and its message well enough to know I would not fit in so well. He gave his speech and tried to sell me on the idea. I tried to tell him they did not want me. He was persistent. He wouldn't let go. So I said, "Do you want somebody on your radio station who is pro-choice? Do you want a minister advocating equal rights for all, and I mean all, people, regardless of sexual orientation, for example? Do you want to take a chance and then hear me speak out against capital punishment? Do you want someone on your station that talks about Second Isaiah (I just threw that last one in; I didn't really say it)?" He got up and left quietly. I am sorry the conversation had to go that far.

197

Religious litmus tests in politics have gotten out of hand. Candidates think they are supposed to "out-righteous" the others, act sincere when praying in public, proclaim some sort of faith, and then say, "It is faith that sees me through." Oh, please. I long for the candidate who says, "That's none of your business" when asked about religion. Some of them respond that way when their families are criticized or when reporters ask hard questions about their personal lives. Why not on religion? One of our presidents when campaigning years ago, before he became president, was asked, as were others on the stage, who his hero was. While others said Churchill, or Plato, or Thomas Jefferson, or even Mother Teresa, this guy said "Christ." Well that stopped the conversation. You can't top that. Then he was "elected" president. After almost seven years in office, I ask myself - and anybody else in the range of my voice - "When does the Christian part kick in?" Invasion of another nation, deceiving America on the reasons for that invasion, authorizing torture of suspected terrorists, holding suspected terrorists in prison for years without charges or access to lawyers, unwarranted eavesdropping on American citizens, tax reductions for the rich, cutting funds for the poor. Those are only a few reasons why I am skeptical about this guy's allegiance to Christ. I would ask if having somebody like Christ as your hero should not mean that, eventually, you decide to try to exercise a Christ-like spirit in all your endeavors. Enough of this so-called "Christian-in-office" stuff. Let's have somebody who abides by the Constitution and the laws of the nation and acknowledges that there are three equal branches of government. People wear the wristband that says "WWJD" which means "What Would Jesus Do?" In the operation of the American government, somebody needs to ask "What Would Jefferson Do?" Or Washington? Or Adams? Or Madison?

198

Paul admonishes his readers in Galatians 6:9, "Let us not grow weary in well-doing." Christians get tired. Church leaders grow weary. I think, though, that there is a difference between being tired IN what we do and being tired OF what we do. I've known some church folks who have grown tired OF being in the church, OF dealing with the hassles that go with church involvement, OF the week-in and week-out voices that come from all sides in church matters. But, fortunately, there have been church folks who were simply tired IN what they were doing and needed a rest. They still believed in, and were going to be involved in, the life of the church, but they just needed some rest. They were tired IN what they were doing. A caution here is that if time is not allotted for that kind of rest, for some rotation of leadership and sharing of responsibilities, those tired IN might evolve into those tired OF the church.

199

The late, great George Shearing was a renowned jazz pianist, and blind. One time, in the height of his career, a reporter asked him,

"Have you been blind all your life?" To which Mr. Shearer replied, "Not yet."

200

I chatted with a woman the other day, a native of these parts, who with her husband had returned to the area after twenty years in a western state where, she said, she "came to know the Lord." That, of course, was good news, but then she became harshly critical of her childhood and youth experiences in the church in her community where she now belonged. The preachers then didn't preach "the Word." Her home church then was not the right kind of church. Now it has that spirit and the right kind of pastor. All this was interesting as I heard her testimony. Silently I wondered if she was too judgmental about her early life in the church. While I have no doubt she "came to know the Lord" out west, I have reason to believe that somehow, in spite of the local church's many deficiencies, that congregation planted the seed and opened up the way for her so that she had a sense of readiness for the gospel in her adulthood. I hear this every so often: A person embraces the gospel enthusiastically as an adult after some great spiritual experience. That person's testimony, almost inevitably, turns to negative statements about previous church experiences. But, again I offer the suggestion that the early experiences, now seen negatively, helped pave the way for that great spiritual moment.

Chapter V: 201-250

"Two Views of Evangelism"

201

I visited with one of my ministerial colleagues whose gifts are in evangelism. All of his pastorates have had that as an emphasis. People are saved, lives are changed, the church grows. He indicated amazement that not every minister has that emphasis or "preaches the Word" to spark those results. My response was that pastors have different gifts but that they all contribute to the total kingdom movement. Some are strong in Christian education, others in preaching, others in worship, others in teaching, others in administration, others in pastoral work. But all contribute to the greater good. Further, I noted, the many fine results of this minister's preaching may have come out of earlier nurture and inspiration provided by others, so that the good evangelistic preaching done by my ministerial brother brings to fruition the accumulated work of previous influences. The work would not be complete without the conversion/commitment moments, but what led to those moments - with some individuals - started farther back. I gave the example of Stephen's faithfulness in the face of death as he was being stoned and Saul (Paul) held the coats of those throwing the stones. Later Saul was converted on the Damascus Road. It is possible that God's blinding light and dramatic moment came suddenly; it probably did. But Saul, I believe, was deeply affected by the witness of Stephen's courage and that could have very likely stayed in his mind and worked on his heart. When he fell to the ground hearing, "Saul, Saul, why do you persecute me?" his response was, "Who are you, Lord?" Now what does that say? Does it not imply that Saul had not been able to get Stephen's faithfulness off his mind and heart and when the dramatic moment occurred, he was already moving toward that moment of surrender? So, my colleague's wonderful response was, "Then, previous pastors planted the seed" that finally led to the salvation experience. He said what I was trying to say, and said it better. It is understood and celebrated that God can move people's hearts spontaneously without previous undergirding, and this minister is very good at finding those people and bringing them to Christ. Yet there are others who have grown and gained from earlier nurture that were ready for the conversion type of preaching this and other faithful ministers provide and that all of us other preachers could improve on. Every sermon can have an evangelistic flavor and, of course, different texts help us focus on different areas of life with God.

202

I don't know where I heard this story. I have never seen it in print, so feel free to tell it. A man sang bass in his church choir and was good. Others said he was very good. He knew he was very, very good. In fact, he may have had an inflated opinion about how truly great he was. He was talking to his pastor about a dream he had. "I dreamed I died and went to heaven and sang in this magnificent heavenly choir. There were 1,000 sopranos, 1,000 altos, and 1,000 tenors. It was a wonderful thing." The pastor said, "Wait a minute. You said you dreamed you were in a heavenly choir and there were 1,000 sopranos, 1,000 altos, and 1,000 tenors and that it was a wonderful thing. Weren't there any basses? The man replied, "Oh, I was there."

203

Some things look so innocent but can be so vicious. A few years ago in our condo area there was a little white kitten, friendly (it meowed as you walked by) and pretty (all fluffy white). It roamed around the neighborhood a lot. Obviously somebody nearby was providing food and water. We have several squirrels in the area and lots of trees. They are up and down and all about. One day as I drove out of the area I saw this pretty little kitten chasing a squirrel up a tree. What fun! I thought. They are playing together! Thirty minutes later I returned and I saw on the ground by a tree that pretty white kitten sitting there observing a squirrel lying on its back and breathing heavily, looking like it was at death's door. Later it died. Here was this pretty white, supposedly innocent, kitten that had chased and chased this little squirrel until the bushy-tailed animal could run no more. I do not know if the cat actually bit or clawed or scratched the squirrel, but I do know that the cat overcame the squirrel in a life-or-death struggle. The feline was not as innocent as it appeared.

204

We live in Memphis, a city on the banks of the mighty Mississippi River. Actually it is not the same river it was ten years ago. Or five years ago. Or one day ago. Or one hour ago. In fact, it is not the same river it was a minute ago. It flows southward toward New

Orleans and the gulf. It is constantly flowing. You look at it and then look away and then glance again and you are seeing a different river. I suppose this is a good reminder that things never stay the same.

205

A disgraced professional football player, with a salary in the millions, has admitted he took part in arranging dog fights at his place, financing the enterprise, and killing dogs that did not perform as desired. In a court hearing where he pled guilty, he expressed remorse. In a public statement later he told of his disappointment in himself, and acknowledged lying to the owner of the team, the coach, family members, and friends, when he had previously said he had nothing to do with the horrific matter. In the middle of his statement, he said, "I have found Jesus." I'm sorry, but I am usually skeptical of this kind of statement of faith. I want to believe him and hope and pray that we now have a changed life before us. But I will continue to have doubts. I guess I would have been one of those skeptical Christians that would not have welcomed that so-called newly-converted man named Paul (he had even changed his name from Saul), the same fellow who had aided and abetted in the persecution of my fellow Christians, the same thug that had held the coats of those who stoned Stephen. If I had eventually given in and voted to allow him in my church, I would have continued to doubt if this fellow with the new name of Paul would ever amount to much.

206

The diaries of Mother Teresa have been made public and we see that she sometimes expressed doubts about God and about her call. This admission will no doubt drive some people up the wall who cannot imagine a saint's having any doubts at all. Well, first of all, the true saints (and Mother Teresa was certainly one of them) do not see themselves as saints, and they certainly do not try to "act" like saints, whatever that means. Therefore, to read from this lady's diary that she had her highs and lows, that she sometimes doubted, heightens, not lowers, her status as a saint.

207

I was preaching in Seminary Chapel from John 16:12: "I still have many things to say to you, but you cannot bear them now." Don't ask me how I moved from that to telling about the deaths of pets. A family in our church in Knoxville loved their very old dog and when he became extremely sick the dad took the animal to the veterinarian, one of many trips. This time the vet could not help and the two agreed it was time to let go. The dad called his wife, who worked at the local high school, and both daughters. One was a teacher, the other worked in a day care center. The teacher's husband, an architect, also was notified. They all stood around their loved one for about two hours and smiled, cried, and expressed gratitude for all the good years and watched as the pet drifted slowly away, thanks to the vet's help. A few weeks later our little Dashacockerpeekapoo, Ginger, was having a very rough time. She, too, had made many trips to the vet. This time when I took her he said there was nothing else he could do. I said, "Then it's time." He asked, "Do you want to call your family?" I said, "No." "Do you want to come back here with her?" I said, "No." And I left the building. That night at dinner somebody asked, "Where's Ginger?" I told everyone what I had done. They hit the ceiling. Why? Why do that? But after they settled down and thought about it, they indicated that they understood, and that it had been the right thing to do. Everybody would have had a very hard time standing beside her, telling her goodbye. So I told that story in Seminary Chapel. After the service one of the professors said to me, "Tom, if I ever get sick I don't want you to take me to the doctor; I'll get a ride with somebody else."

208

Parenting was, and is, a joy. At Christmas time we got things for our three girls, and on many occasions they were triplicates: three identical dolls; three identical kitchen sets; three identical baby carriages; three bicycles, almost identical, for the older one got a bike just a little larger than the other two. I, especially, looked for things that did not have those three most dreaded words in the English language for parents: "Some Assembly Required." When those words appeared on a potential gift, I knew I would be up all night working on something, and usually on several items. Being in a family, trying to be one of the parents, can be difficult. After all, those three words are in that picture, too: "Some Assembly Required." That is, making a quality family life doesn't just happen.

209

One time when Kelly, our eldest daughter was five or six I was trying to put something together. It was not Christmas time. Perhaps I was trying to get it ready for a birthday or some other special day. I was having trouble. She said, "Daddy, read the constructions."

210

Those bicycles we got for our three girls one Christmas consisted of two the same size and one a little larger. A year or two went by and our youngest was riding hers with training wheels. She begged. She pleaded. She asked softly for us to take those training wheels off because she wanted to ride her bike without them. We were not ready for her to do that. One time most of us were in the family room and heard a loud clanging in the garage. Bang! Bang! Bang! It wouldn't stop. It seemed to be getting louder. I looked out the kitchen door into the garage. Kristen, our youngest, had a wrench and was beating on those training wheels, trying to get them off. I got the message.

We removed the training wheels. I suppose most parents want to keep the training wheels on just about everything so their kids will not get hurt, but sooner or later they grow into wanting to try life without them. Sometimes it's not a pretty sight; months later Kristen took a big fall from riding the big bicycle. She fell onto some rocks. It was New Year's Day and we took her to a hospital in the next town. She had multiple scratches but that was all. This incident did not dampen her determination. With gratitude from all of us for training wheels, it is accurate to say they must come off some day. Parenting is a joy, but it is never easy.

211

I am often slow to catch on. Sometimes I don't catch on at all. A church member out in Texas told of a man who had a pet snail. He decided to attach four wheels underneath and then it looked sort of like an automobile. He needed to give it a name and he just put the letter "S" (for Snail, I suppose) on each side and on the back. Then he rolled the snail down the hill. Somebody saw that and said, "Look at that 'S' car go." After the church member told the story, he waited for a laugh, a smile, anything. I felt nothing. I did not know, and he had to explain it to me, that the pronunciation of those syllables results in an articulation of a delicacy found in the finest restaurants. O.K.

212

I, along with other juniors in my high school class, made history. Six of us were the first people ever to take what was then called "Driver Training." The local Ford dealer provided the car and the boys' basketball coach did the teaching. The first two weeks were spent under the hood as we learned about the motor, the manifold, the air filter, and other things. Then in the next couple of weeks we sat in the car and talked about driving. Then we started driving. Now understand: I did not need this. When the class started I had already been driving six, eight, even ten weeks, so I did not need any of these classes. I had gotten my driver's license earlier in the summer. I was cool.

And then it was my turn to drive. In starting the car, I forgot to put my foot on the clutch (the car had "straight shift"). In backing up I failed to put my right arm over the back of the seat so I could see better. In driving I failed to maintain the 10 o'clock, 4 o'clock position with my hands. In turning I failed to make the correct kind of signal (this was before all cars had turn signals). In stopping, I was too sudden. In getting out of the car I failed to look in all directions to make sure the coast was clear.

It was obvious that before I learned anything about driving, I had to "unlearn" a lot of bad habits. "Pride goeth before a fall," and I fell. I "knew it all," but needed more help than anybody else in the class.

213

My first year in Seminary, the worship leader at the "beginning-of-the-year" retreat told us that sometimes there are things we need to "unlearn." For us ministers and would-be ministers that was sound advice. Much of my Seminary education was "unlearning." This reminds me of how Jesus taught in the Sermon on the Mount in Matthew 5: "You have heard it said... but I say unto you... "The disciples had to "unlearn" some things before they could "learn" other things.

214

Fear is a human emotion that is often a real concern. According to the Parable of the Talents (Matthew 25:14-30), one man got five

Talents, another, two, still another, one. The fellows that received five and two, respectively, went out and invested their part and came back with double the amount earlier received. The one-talent man reported to his master: "I was afraid and I went and hid your talent in the ground." He was condemned for not producing. I have a hunch the other two were afraid, too, but whereas the one-talent man's fear immobilized him, the other two were mobilized by their fears. I watched part of the New Year's Day Cotton Bowl on television three decades ago. The fullback for the winning team had charged over from the two-yard line in the closing seconds to win the game. When interviewed later, he was asked what happened on that play. Here were his words: "I don't know. I had my eyes closed as I hit the line. I didn't see it." He acknowledged something of a fear that mobilized him. He just went ahead in spite of some reservations about the whole thing.

215

After September 11, 2001, some politicians and office-holders took the opportunity to base just about everything they did on fear. Not so much their fear, as ours. If they could hold the threat of terror over our heads, they believed we as a nation would do just about anything, give up just about any of our constitutional rights, in order to make ourselves and our nation "safe." But someone centuries ago - was it Benjamin Franklin? - said something like this: "If we sacrifice liberty for security, we end up with neither." And now, in a highly politicized culture, that is the main thing some incumbents and candidates are pitching. So far, they seem to have been pretty successful in their attempts at scaring the bejeebers out of us. To paraphrase Franklin D. Roosevelt, in a twisted way: "The only thing we have to campaign on, is fear itself." This is not who we are as a nation. I think of these matters especially every time I jump through the dehumanizing hoops at airports, and every time I see old ladies, young children, and other "least likely" suspects manhandled, hollered at, embarrassed, and belittled in those airport lines.

216

Isn't it true that our reactions to the events in our lives depend more on how we feel than the events themselves? Take a family meal, for example. Father, mother, little children. One child spills her glass of milk. Why is it that, on one occasion when that occurs, the father gets all in a dither, fumes and frets, foams at the mouth, and otherwise hits the ceiling, and on another occasion, the father speaks reassuringly, "Oh, that's all right. We can clean it up. Everything's going to be all right." It's the same amount of milk each time, the same glass, the same little girl, and the same part of the day. But the reactions of the father are completely opposite. The difference is not the milk, nor the girl, nor the glass, nor the time of day. It's what's happening in the mind and heart of the father, whether he has had a good day or bad, whether he's worried about something, whether he is involved in deep thought (No, probably not that).Is it not true that our responses to events, serious and not so serious, depend on what is happening inside our own hearts?

217

I was reading a book on the history of World War I. There jumped out at me this quote: "World War I was unnecessary but inevitable."

218

In the same book on World War I, it was reported that soldiers on both sides carried back packs that weighed in the neighborhood of sixty to eighty pounds. And, as they sloshed around in mud and climbed hills and ran double-time as needed, these burdens no doubt felt even heavier. Somehow that text in Hebrews 12:1-2 applies here as we consider the burden of our sins: "Therefore, since we are surrounded by so great a cloud of witnesses, let us also lay aside every weight and the sin that clings so closely, and let us run with perseverance the race that is set before us, looking to Jesus the pioneer and perfecter of our faith..."

219

Regarding Luke 18:18-25, the story of, as we call him, The Rich Young Ruler, why did the man not follow through on the advice/counsel/admonition of Jesus to "Sell all that you own and distribute the money to the poor... then come, follow me"?

There are three possible barriers that held him back. First, he must sell everything he had. He loved his possessions. He had spent years accumulating them. Was that the item holding him back from eternal life? Could he take that step?

Second, he must take the money from the sale of his possessions and give it to the poor. Ah, that could have been the main problem. It is one thing to sell what you have, but what are you going to do with the money? Invest it in certificates of deposit? Buy another house? Take that around-the-world vacation you always wanted to take? Get a larger yacht? So here is Jesus telling him to give it to the poor. Now that could be a major drawback to this man's project of self-improvement, given his likely disdain for the less fortunate.

Or was it the third demand from Jesus: "Then come, follow me"? Hey, all I wanted was the keys to eternal life. I did not want to get involved in any activities or organizations that would demand a lot of my time and allegiance. I had no intention of working with other people in any way. I was just asking an innocent question about the way to eternal life after I realized that the Ten Commandments were not enough. Based on Jesus' remarks after that conversation, this man's riches were a real barrier to his entrance into the kingdom. He didn't want to sell; he didn't want to give; he didn't want to follow.

220

The Chief Justice of the Alabama Supreme Court wanted to place a concrete monument with the Ten Commandments on it on government property. He lost a court battle and the plaque was removed. He would have incurred much more expense had he tried to list all 613 Old Testament laws. At least he had the wisdom to try to exhibit the Decalogue, which summarizes the 613, we are told. The judge could have been even

The one and only commandment

more economical had he remembered that the Ten were summarized, not by Jesus (according to Luke 10:27) but by a lawyer who had confronted Jesus with questions about eternal life. Jesus asked, "What is written in the law? What do you read there?" The lawyer answered, "You shall love the Lord your God with all your heart, and with all your soul, and with all your strength, and with all your mind (from Deuteronomy); and your neighbor as yourself,"(from Leviticus) summarizing the Ten and shrinking them down to two. But then along came Jesus later (John 13:34) and shortened the Two to One: "I give you a new commandment, that you love one another." What if the good judge had tried to put out a plaque (somewhat smaller, perhaps) that read, "Love One Another"? From 613 to 1. Unfortunately, the one that is left is the hardest, and, of course, it covers the entire law. Whether it is 613 or 10 or 2 or 1, we cannot escape the commandment: Love one another. But this one question: Why did our Lord, in completing the decrease from 613 to 1, decide to keep the hardest commandment of all?

221

What is this reverencing of the Ten Commandments? There is a clamor to exhibit them everywhere. Like the Ten Commandments are the be-all and end-all of life, government, politics, civility, and corporate America. Preachers, do not. I repeat: DO NOT do the following. Do not ask for a show of hands in your congregation on how many think the Ten Commandments, and the Ten Commandments alone, ought to be the Law of the Land, which seems to be the cry of some. "If we would just live by the Ten Commandments, all would be well." While they are worthy and vital commandments for the community of faith and those outside as well, they leave something wanting if they are to be the Law of the Land. Just one example: How are you going to enforce these laws? Take Commandment No. 10, for example (according to Exodus 20:17): "You shall not covet." Now I'll admit covetousness is a bad thing and it is bad to covet. But how in the world could the police and F.B.I. enforce that one? Commandment No. 10 is probably the only one I can be breaking right now and no one (except God) knows it. Or consider Commandment No. 5: "Honor your father and your mother." Notice it does not say "obey." It says "honor." "Obey" might have a possibility of being enforced in a police state, with spies in every home, but "honor" your father and mother? How to enforce that? And, regarding Commandment No. 4, I can picture a Sabbath Enforcement Task Force cracking down on Sabbath violations, that is, after somebody tells us what activities (in this American culture) are "in" and what are "out." I could go on. Some of the Ten are so obvious and flagrant that they might be enforced; in fact, some are on the books now in all states, such as murder and stealing. Again, preachers, don't try this in your own church! Do not ask for a show of hands on whether the Ten Commandments should be the Law of the Land. You don't want to know. Trust me on this.

222

The Ten Commandments are not all they are cracked up to be. They have been viewed as the answer to all our nation's problems, if only the government would allow them to be displayed on government property. Something in Luke 18:18-25 sort of brings matters into perspective. A rich ruler came to Jesus asking about how to inherit eternal life. Jesus mentioned the commandments and the fellow said "I have kept all these since my youth." Hold it right there! Here is someone who has, according to his own testimony, "kept" the commandments all his years, and he comes asking Jesus about how to inherit eternal life? What does this say about the Ten Commandments? It says that, though he has "kept" the commandments since his youth, they are insufficient. They do not bring life. They do not enrich life. They are not enough. Jesus saw this, of course: "There is still one thing lacking. Sell all that you own and distribute the money to the poor, and you will have treasure in heaven; then come, follow me." And, of course, he did not do those things. Besides losing a person who could have been an asset to the kingdom and could have endowed several hospitals, supported several schools, built a few churches, and fed the poor in the deepest wells of poverty in the city, Jesus was saddened because this man's life was built on obedience, not compassion. He grew up obeying the laws of God but had no heart for people. He was fixed on himself, and cared not for others.

223

I was watching a movie on television entitled "Tell Toledo Goodbye." A man trying to explain life to a younger man said, "Life is a fish fry - you gotta expect a few bones."

224

In my high school days two students performed a skit in the school assembly which depicted the following: On a farm the mother was in the kitchen fixing supper. Her teenage daughter came ambling in from the backyard. "Ma," she said slowly, "I need a glass of water," and the mother gave her a glass of water and she went out the back door. A few minutes later she was back: "Ma," again slowly. "Yes, what is it?" "I need another glass of water," and she re-filled the glass, and out the daughter went. A third time, then a fourth time. On her fifth trip, the mother, a bit exasperated, asked, "Why do you need so many re-fills of water in your glass."

"Ma," again slowly, "The barn is on fire." We preachers, with every text, probably need to decide how soon to come forth with its main message. Do we build up to it slowly, gradually, moving toward some sort of emotionally and spiritually strong finish, or do we just burst out in the first sentence and say it, or better yet, shout it? Sometimes the message inside the text will tell us the approach to use.

225

When you watch television movies, most of the time at the bottom of the screen something about the story is provided as well as the "kind" of movie it is. It may say "Horror" or "Science Fiction" or "Drama." A few will say "Comedy." I wish under "Comedy" they had a few categories, such as "Partly Humorous," and "Intended to be a Comedy," "Thinks It Is Funny," and "Contains Some Humorous Moments." Some movies labeled "Comedy" may have some humor in them but they are far from being comedies and probably were not intended to be labeled as such. Sermons can have drama, humor, pathos, emotion, inspiration, instruction, invitation, and encouragement - all in one. But I hope listeners still consider them sermons.

226

Speaking of sermons, the husband went to church and the wife stayed home, not feeling well. He came home after church and the wife asked, "What did the preacher preach about this morning?" Response: "I don't know; he never told us."

227

I was in a grocery store the other day. A woman had two small children with her and they were not adhering to her instructions to stay close to her and not be taking things off the shelf. She yelled at them. Everybody in the store could hear. At a gas station a mother got out of the car yelling at her two little boys and when they got in the convenience store she was yelling again. To hear these mothers you would think their children were hoodlums, bums, good-for-nothings. Now I realize parenting can be exasperating and frustrating, but am convinced that outbursts such as these say more about the parents than about the children. They are unhappy, pressed financially, angry at something or somebody, too hot, too rushed, and wish they could be somewhere else at the moment. But they take it out on their children, who will probably yell at their own children twenty or twenty five years from now.

228

Sometimes when bad things happen to us, we ask, "Why me?" It may be a diagnosis of cancer, a job layoff, a turndown on the house we want, an unfair and unjust court decision, or a series of devastating events that don't make sense. To ask "Why me?" seems natural. Sometimes we even expect to get an answer. A few years ago, the great relief pitcher for the Kansas City Royals, Dan Quisenberry, came down with a brain tumor and it turned out to be inoperable. He had a death sentence hanging over him. He was able to go about life for awhile and was asked for interviews with reporters. He had an unusually healthy attitude about it all. Of course, he was concerned about his family, and of course, he did not want to die, but when he talked about it he would often say, "Some people ask, 'Why me?' But I ask, 'Why NOT me?'" He went on to talk about how he viewed himself as a part of the human race and we are all in it together and how nobody is immune to this terrible tragedy in their lives. It can happen to anybody. Fame, fortune, and status do not matter. His question, "Why not me?" still rings loud and clear. His was a healthy "theology."

229

I listened to two men talk after an important meeting of the General Assembly of the Cumberland Presbyterian Church, held in San Antonio, Texas, in June of 1969, where there were major items before the body. The voting on some matters was close, the discussions lively. Now, one day after the Assembly, in the kitchen of the manse of the First Cumberland Presbyterian Church in Austin, Texas, one was saying to the other, "I guess we were on the wrong side" on a certain issue. "No," said the other, "We were on the LOSING side." The first speaker was my uncle, the second my father. I learned from overhearing that conversation. Accept the vote and move on. Hold on to your convictions.

230

Meetings of church courts are sometimes interesting, sometimes boring, sometimes exciting, occasionally tense. Much of the progression as well as the success of the meeting depends on the one presiding, which in my tradition, is the Moderator. The traditional rules of Robert's Rules of order are "in order" and most of the time all goes well. Yet the Moderator can sometimes do better than the current performance, if only in the "little things." A motion is made and seconded. Then the Moderator asks if there is any discussion. There being none, the one presiding says, "Those in favor of the motion, say 'Aye.'" Then, and here's the hard part, "Those opposed, like sign." Hold it! No, maybe it's this: "Those opposed..." and the Moderator offers no suggestions on what those in the negative should say. Puritanically, here is the correct way: "Those in favor of the motion, say 'Aye.'" "Those opposed, say 'No.'" You might be surprised, or you might not, as to how many persons presiding in church courts do not give clear messages as to what to say for those choosing to vote in the negative.

231

Henry Campbell was my father's father. He lived to be 96. After my grandmother died in about 1952, he moved from Texas to come and live with us in McKenzie, Tennessee. "Mr. Henry," as the neighbor boy called him, had been a farmer and a teacher in one-room schools. He died in 1963. Sometime before that, I somehow came upon a note he had written during the sunset of his life. It contained only three or four sentences. It was his appraisal of his life. In essence it said: "I have not done anything worthwhile in my life. My days on earth have not been spent wisely. I have accomplished nothing." I recall that my parents and I (and probably my siblings) talked about the note. I believe it was an honest assessment. My grandfather really felt that way about himself and his time on earth. He was a humble, self-effacing man. But his assessment was not correct. He did make an impact on many lives for good. He was an avid reader, a student of history, a former school teacher, and a quiet and good person who enjoyed a good story. He was a Christian, an elder in his church, one who stood for goodness and kindness in the world.

232

Henry Campbell, my father's father, was living with us in McKenzie, Tennessee. He moved there following the death of his wife, our grandmother, Bell Kirkpatrick Campbell. On a day in 1954 I got home from school and bent down to pick up the daily paper, The Nashville Banner. There on the front page, was the biggest headline I had ever seen. It said:

SEGREGATION OUT

There followed an article reporting that the United States Supreme Court, in Brown VS. Board of Education, had ruled segregation unconstitutional and that public schools across the country would be de-segregating "with deliberate speed," or something to that effect. When my father got home from work I showed him the headline and his first words were, in almost a whisper, "Don't mention this to Grandfather." I never did. We as a family never did either. Thereafter I was more alert to anything Grandfather would say regarding race. I never heard him talk about the Supreme Court decision, but, now that I was alerted, I did detect, very seldom but very clearly, some prejudice on my grandfather's part. Our parents did not consider themselves radicals or revolutionaries, but they did believe in thinking and doing the right thing. I don't remember if they ever actually said very much about race, but their attitudes were evident in many ways. Older brother Sam, as a youth leader in the Cumberland Presbyterian denomination, was criticized by some because of his articles in the church magazine supporting integration. Regarding Grandfather, who died in 1963, I think we all recognized the generational differences and appreciated what his life experiences had been.

233

The Letter to the Hebrews tells us "Jesus Christ is the same yesterday and today and forever" (Hebrews 13:8). That message is fraught with good news (for us) and bad news (for us). The good news is that Jesus will always be our Savior and Lord. Other good news is that Jesus will always be sufficient for us. That kind of stability is an island of peace and comfort amid an ocean of change. But here may be some of the bad. Jesus will be forever and always bringing a discomfiting message, egging us on, being on our case, never satisfied with our discipleship, not letting us rest on any laurels we may have thought we accumulated in life. There will always be something else to do, another place to go, another person to help, another cause that needs our volunteering. Yes, Jesus is the same. The same Savior and Lord that won't let us go and won't let us assume all is completely right in this world.

234

I attended the funeral of a ministerial colleague recently. The church was packed. We sang three hymns but I did not have access to a hymnal. I could recall the first verses of these hymns and some words from other verses, but mostly I watched other people sing and in trying to read their lips sang along with them. I have done that now and then: watched other folks sing. It is quite a spiritual moment. When I have my nose in the hymnal I am not that aware of others, but when I look around and see others lifting their voices, I think I am more likely to take in the message of the hymn. At that funeral one of the selections was "Praise Him! Praise Him!" In the third line of verse one, these words appear: "Like a shepherd, Jesus will guard His children, In His arms He carries them all day long." I have probably sung that hymn hundreds of times, but at that funeral, and looking around at friends and colleagues, and seeing them and hearing them sing those words, I was moved. I saw fellow ministers joining in, those who have been faithful shepherds to their congregations for years, now joyfully acknowledging that Jesus, the tender shepherd "will guard his children" and "in His arms He carries them all day long." They are not alone in their pastoral work. And Jesus is their shepherd.

235

I knew a young man studying for the ministry who said that before he entered the ministry he was on drugs. He said, "My wife 'drug' me to Sunday school; she 'drug' me to Sunday morning worship; she 'drug' me to Wednesday night prayer meeting."

236

A pastor was attending a wedding reception at the church. A woman in the church came up and said, "You are never in your office. I come by and you are always out." Before she finished a man in the church walked up and said, "You are always in your office. Every time I drop by the church, there you are." The pastor replied, "Here. The two of you work this out," and walked away.

237

No doubt you have heard about the little girl reciting the 23rd Psalm. She got it wrong, but she got it right: "The Lord is my shepherd; that's all I want."

238

I have had the privilege of traveling to and through Death Valley. It was in December. The weather was mild, somewhere in the high 50s and low 60s. Linda and I could have traveled south from

Trona, California, to Barstow, then on to Las Vegas to catch our plane, but this time we traveled the northern route. What a trip! Death Valley was all we imagined. And since the weather was so nice the rental car did not get hot. We did not have to worry about its air-conditioning burning out since we did not use it. The best we could tell, very little plant life exists in Death Valley. A few months later we saw a special television program about that awesome area. It showed people who tried to walk the distance through it, but to no avail: they could not take the unbearable heat that long. But it also showed a couple of surprising items. First, there are little isolated streams running underground that help keep some crawling creatures alive. Second, something amazing occurs on those few occasions when it rains in the Death Valley. Flowers bloom. They almost literally light up the place. People come from all around to witness this. They know this phenomenon occurs for only a few days then the flowers are gone. But for those days that which is haunted by death and desolation is decorated by beautiful flowers. Amid the death and desolation we often see around us there are streams of life and flowers of inestimable beauty. They have been identified. They are God's grace and God's love. We can usually see these in the lives of other people, God's special creation, made in God's image. Made for desert existence.

239

Several possible bumper stickers for these days and times are making the rounds. Here are a few:

IF YOU WANT A NATION RULED BY RELIGION, MOVE TO IRAN

NO, SERIOUSLY, WHY DID WE INVADE IRAQ?

AMERICA: ONE NATION UNDER SURVEILLANCE

240

We won't find anywhere a church named THE CHURCH OF THE CLOSED BIBLE, and understandably so, for we are a people of the Book. Yet that name may suggest a truth not often noticed. Luke 4:16-30 tells us that Jesus went to the synagogue and "stood up to read, and the scroll of the prophet Isaiah was given to him. He unrolled the scroll and found the place where it was written (his first miracle, since there were no chapters and no verses with numbers and scrolls were not so easy to handle while standing). He read the scripture and while he was doing that all was well.

Then, "He rolled up the scroll, gave it back to the attendant, and sat down." So far, so good. "The eyes of all in the synagogue were fixed on him. Then he began to say to them, 'Today this scripture has been fulfilled in your hearing.' All spoke well of him and were amazed at the gracious words that came from his mouth. They said, 'Is not this Joseph's son?'" But it was downhill from there. The words coming from Jesus' mouth after that did not fall on receptive ears. He said things they did not want to hear. At the end, "all in the synagogue were filled with rage. They got up, drove him out of the town, and led him to the brow of the hill on which their town was built, so that they might hurl him off the cliff. But he passed through the midst of them and went on his way." While he was reading from the Bible, all was well. But when he closed it and started telling what it meant, the people were offended. Sometimes we are called on to close the Bible and get on with the mission God sent us to do. Bible study? We need more of it. In-depth Bible study? More of that, too. But, sooner or later, we close the Bible and talk about the meaning and challenge of what we just read. That can be dangerous. The safer way is to keep reading the Bible and never try to put its teachings into action.

241

I am persuaded that First Corinthians 13 - the love chapter - is not about weddings. It is about church life. Yet we quite often read this chapter at weddings. It is, after all, so beautiful. Notice, for example 13:4-7: "Love is patient; love is kind; love is not envious or boastful or arrogant or rude. It does not insist on its own way; it is not irritable or resentful; it does not rejoice in wrongdoing, but rejoices in the truth. It bears all things, believes all things, hopes all things, endures all things." In my conversations with those studying for the ministry I have screamed and hollered not to have this chapter included in the wedding service. It is not about husband-wife relations. It is about a church that had everything - faith, stewardship, service, missions, biblical studies, good teaching, good preaching. Everything, except for the fact that the people did not like each other. So Paul, trying to rescue the congregation from self-destruction, wrote this phase of his letter especially to confront that problem. So far, so good. Just a few days ago I watched the video of my oldest daughter's wedding, held in May of 1992. Guess what! There in the midst of it all was a responsive reading and you can know for sure where it came from. That's right: I Corinthians 13. Trouble is, I helped my daughter plan the service! And I probably have conducted at least a dozen weddings since then where this was read. So much for consistency in teaching and practice!

242

We Christians experience struggles and undergo hardships quite regularly. Becoming a Christian does not make one immune to frustrations or pain. Therefore, it is quite refreshing to see where the Apostle Paul, who himself undoubtedly experienced daily trials and tribulations, acknowledges this. In Romans 8:38-39 he makes a list of common human concerns, items that could "separate us from the love of God in Christ Jesus our Lord." They include, in his words, "death, life, angels, rulers, things present, things to come, powers, height, depth, and anything else in all creation." He says that none of these can separate us from the love of God, but it is uplifting to see that he, also being human and Christian, understands how these things can

"Nor things to come..."

bring a person down. I am thrilled that he included "things present," which in my mind may be the most sinister, the most draining, So many people are troubled about what is happening "right now" in their lives. Contending with the present: the job, the boss, the hours, the unhappiness, the lack of benefits, the price of gas, the price of groceries, the burdens of taking care of family members, the fears about inadequate health insurance if one has any at all, These and other "things present" can drag one down. We rejoice that even "things present" cannot separate us from the love of God in Christ Jesus. This good news is what keeps us going. And if "things present" are a worry, just think of the "things to come." That problem is included in the promise, too.

243

I think most congregations, when they sing "All Hail the Power of Jesus' Name" sing it to the tune called Coronation. This seems to be the most traditional. But there are at least two more tunes, and one of them I really like is the one called Diadem. In Diadem the basses and tenors really go to town on the refrain. It is downright fun the way those two parts go up and down and all around. And when I am in a congregation that sings it, I release all the pipes and heist the bass part to the highest heaven. I really get with it. It is that kind of tune. I attended a "Live Christmas Tree" event one December at another church, and to get us started, the music director led us, accompanied by organ and piano, in "All Hail the Power," Diadem version. We stood for the hymn. I was standing toward the back and right in front of me were a woman and her little boy, who was so young he stood on the pew during the hymn. He was looking straight ahead but when I let loose on the refrain, he turned around and looked me squarely in the eyes, perhaps wondering something like, "Who is this?" His mother did not notice at first, but when she did, she put her arm around him and gently turned him back to face the front. Second verse: same response. As we began the refrain, and I let her rip, he again turned around to stare at me, and again she did not at first notice his about face but when she did she again gently turned him toward the front. Third verse: same thing. Now along comes the fourth verse. And before we get to the refrain, well before, in a nonchalant fashion, as though to protect her child, she puts her arm around him in order not to let him go through the same routine. I'm sorry. That's the way you are supposed to sing that hymn. I always like to try and "bring forth the royal diadem" when we sing this one.

244

A young man set out to run across the country, from the Pacific coast to the Atlantic coast. He braved the heat and the cold, the rain and the snow and the sun, uncooperative drivers, wind, fatigue, and exhaustion. He ran from early morning to early evening, and sometimes into the night. After the adventure of several weeks was over, he sat down to be interviewed by reporters. Somebody asked what the greatest problem was. Was it the snow in the high mountains, the rain, the sun in the western desert, the traffic in the cities? "It was none of those," he said. "The worst, most aggravating, most frustrating part of the trip came when I would get a little pebble in my shoe. That almost brought me down." Is that not the way it is in life sometimes? We can handle the big items. It's those little, bothersome, aggravating rascals that drive us crazy.

৯০৫৪৯০৫৪৯০৫৪৯০৫৪৯০৫৪৯০৫৪৯০৫৪৯০৫৪৯০৫৪

245

Two weekends after "911" I was at a church for special services as their guest speaker. On Friday night, just before the service of worship, the pastor and I were sitting in his study. He is a retired Army chaplain and this was his first pastorate after that career. One of the men in the church walked in and suggested to the pastor that, from now on, in every worship service - not only in this series of services, but every Sunday morning and evening - the congregation should sing at least one patriotic hymn. First I will tell you what my reaction as a pastor would have been. It would have gone something like this, "You know, I hadn't thought of that. That's an idea. Let me dwell on that and give it some thought." And, of course, I most likely would not have gotten around to doing it. Here is what the retired Army chaplain, now a pastor - patriotic to the bone, probably not a single drop of blood critical of the administration in his veins that ran red, white, and blue - said. He said, "No. We are not going to do that." That's what he said. I sat there, shocked and impressed, and thought that I would not have had the boldness to respond to one of my church members that way, although I wish that I did have. The man making the suggestion stood there for a moment somewhat taken aback. He offered a meek response to which the pastor again said, "No," and then the church member left the office and walked back into the sanctuary. Steeped as he was in military-national-patriotic fervor, having only recently left the military, this pastor did the right thing. Call it separation of church and state. Call it not willing to clutter up every service with patriotic hymns. Call it what you will. It was a gutsy response, especially in light of the nationalistic emotions running strong in those days immediately after the destruction of the twin towers and part of the Pentagon, and the fear and anger that followed those events.

246

Bishop Desmond Tutu and I attended a luncheon together one time. Actually there were two hundred other ministers present. He had come to Lexington, Kentucky, to address the graduating class at the University of Kentucky. His daughter would be receiving her degree. This ministerial gathering was at noon the day of the mid-afternoon commencement service. In talking to us, Bishop Tutu told of when white people came to South Africa. He said, "The white people had the Bible and we had the land. Then they said, 'Let us pray.' When we opened our eyes, we had the Bible and they had the land."

247

Years ago I was reading something on the biographies of Confederate generals. The book told of one who, as I recall, was a Presbyterian deacon. An author described the general this way: "He lived by the New Testament and fought by the Old Testament."

248

This young, bright couple visited our church in Lexington, Kentucky. She was a music teacher in local schools. He was a law student at the University of Kentucky. I asked them if I could visit them. They said yes. A few days later I entered their small apartment ready to talk about our church, the many things we were doing and offering, and trying to do and offer, that might be enticing to them. But before I could get started with my list, he asked, "What are you doing in missions?" In my mind, I threw my list away. Their top priority was not what we could offer them, but what was the church doing in the world? I don't know whether I handled that very well. I was happy to talk about the many things our denomination was doing throughout the world and in the United States, and how our small congregation was doing its part financially to support that work, plus what the local church was doing in the community, which was quite a bit considering its small membership. They continued to attend and joined. As with others in that church, they moved to other parts of the country after graduation. But this fine couple reminded me what the real appeal of a church is and should be: What are we doing for others?

249

We were eating out and met up with another couple. As we were visiting, we got into sleeping and waking up and how many hours and such like. The question was asked to the wife of the other couple: "Do you wake up grumpy every morning?" Her answer was, "No, sometimes I let him sleep."

250

A friend, a native of Mississippi, came to the annual Old Monroe Homecoming near Algoma. Her husband is Chief of the Division of Infectious Diseases at Johns Hopkins University School of Medicine. She said he was not able to come down from Baltimore for this special occasion because he was revising his book on infectious diseases. She said he revises it every year. When she gave that report, I thought: How awesome! Continuing to add to and take from as new information comes along and new discoveries are made! And here I am, firmly fixed and immovable in Christian convictions. I wonder if in my fixedness and firmness I have let valuable new information slip away. Shouldn't Christians and Christian ministers be out there on the cutting edge of learning? Are there any books on our shelves that have publishing dates beyond those years when we were in school?

Chapter VI: 251-300

"The Light of the World"

251

Jesus said, "I am the light of the world" (John 8:12). He also said to his disciples (and to us?) "You are the light of the world" (Matthew 5:14). Wait a minute. Which is right? Is Jesus the light of the world or are we? Did the scribes and translators get it wrong? Did things get mixed up in passing the scriptures down from one generation to another, and one language to another? The answer is that both passages are correct, according to scholars. They are both true. <u>Jesus</u> is the light of the world. <u>We</u> are the light of the world. Go figure.

252

I take pride in being able to walk safely down the stairs in the dark, both in my home and at my workplace. A good memory helps. Of the following I am certain: The number of steps at my home is sixteen; the number of steps at my workplace is fifteen, and I can walk down those stairs with full confidence, even in the dark. Or is it fifteen steps at home and sixteen at the workplace?

253

Reading - and understanding - a phone bill can be a headache: fees, hidden charges, this mysterious item and that unexplained item. Somebody once observed that even a brain surgeon and a rocket scientist would have trouble understanding it. Sure enough, once some television show recruited a brain surgeon and a rocket scientist. Neither could decipher the phone bill in front of them. This gives some solace to the rest of us.

254

In Lexington, Kentucky, we lived in an area up the hill from a small shopping center that contained a pharmacy, a super market, a veterinarian, a florist, and an insurance office. One day I drove down there to go to the super market and as I found my parking place I saw a woman reaching into the back of her car and obviously struggling to pull something out. I kept looking and it seemed to be getting worse for her. After I got out of my car I walked over to see if I could help. There, perched on the back seat was the prettiest Irish Setter anyone would ever see and he was stubbornly refusing to get out of the car. In spite of her best efforts, he was firmly on that back seat and humming, "I shall not be moved." So I volunteered to assist. We both reached into the back seat (the car was a two-door model which made it harder to get a good grip). She grabbed one front leg and I the other. She pulled and I pulled. Gradually, but not at all easily, we pulled the reluctant canine closer to an exit from the car. All along, the woman is saying, "He knows he's going to the vet. He does this every time." Inch by inch we pulled and pulled until the front half of his body was out, then, finally, all of him was out of the car. And then here is what happened: Immediately he ran to the door of the vet's office and sat there, wagging his tail and eager to go in. I guess he just wanted to test his owner and see if she really wanted him to go the vet.

255

I had taken a couple of vacuum cleaners to the repair shop. We waited for the verdict and when the price quoted seemed reasonable we said, "Fix them." When I went to pick them up, I remarked to the repair man that getting our vacuum cleaners back was like getting your pet dog back from the vet after having the animal treated. Then the repair man told of a dog he had once. The dog loved to go to the vet. He would jump out of the car and run to the door. Once in he would run back to one of the treatment rooms, jump up on a table - where another dog was already situated - push that dog off, and lick the vet in the face. He loved to go to the vet. Our most recent dog knew there were very few occasions to get in the car. In fact, you could bet any trip in the car was to the vet. She started shaking right after I put her in. She shook all the way to the vet. She shook on the treatment table. Her eyes were begging, "Please, please, get me out of here." It seemed nothing could settle her down. The shots were all right. The worst part was cutting her nails. I even felt the pain on those occasions. When she would get home, she would rest the remainder of the day.

256

God is somewhat of a sports fan, but hardly ever gets personally involved. One time was in 1969 when the "amazin" New York Mets won the National League championship. That was not the miracle, however. The World Series was the miracle. The Baltimore Orioles ran away with the American League championship and were heavily favored to take the Series. They won one game and the Mets won four. If anything could go wrong for the Orioles, it did. If anything could go right for the Mets, it did. Nothing worked for the Birds. Nothing failed for the Mets. In the movie "Oh God," God, played by George Burns, acknowledges taking an active part in the outcome of the 1969 World Series. Another occasion for divine intervention, on a smaller scale to be sure, might have come around 1982. Our church was in a basketball league in Burleson, Texas. There were twelve teams. Each team played the others once. Our St. Matthew Cumberland Presbyterian Church squad started out not so well, with one win and four losses (1-4). But then we took one game at a time and week after week our record improved, until, at the end of the season we were 7-4, having won six in a row. The games were played Saturday mornings, afternoons, and evenings at a local gymnasium. There was a team from the Seventh Day Adventist Church. Saturday is their Sabbath so they had to wait until dusk to play. They always played the last game of the day. We were getting closer to the end of the season. After the regular season was over, the top four teams would be in a playoff. Teams 1 and 4 would play early Saturday morning. Teams 2 and 3 would play the next game later in the morning. And then in the afternoon, the winners of those games would play for the season championship. But we had a problem. The Seventh Day Adventist team was in the chase and had a good chance to end up in the playoff as one of the top four teams. But that would mess up the schedule. They could not even play the first playoff game until after dark, and then if they won, the championship game would be on toward midnight. But somehow, someway, the Lord intervened, and that team finished fifth. We, with our 7-4 record, finished fourth, and played the first place team (and lost) on a Saturday morning. Just think of how that playoff schedule would have been totally jumbled if we had not squeaked in and captured fourth place!

257

Our daughter Kristen took her daughter (our granddaughter) Paige to work with her one day. The boss came to Kristen saying he had computer problems and could she help? Kristen walked into his office preceded by her daughter. Paige turned around and walked out of the office and as she passed Kristen she said, "Click on." When Kristen looked at the computer used by her boss that was exactly what it needed: "Click on." Paige was five years old the next month.

258

It matters not so much where a person is but in which direction that person is going. In Luke 15 the younger brother grabs his inheritance and escapes home to go out and have a good time. He is obviously well dressed, looking great, collecting a whole host of friends since he has so much money. He is set to have a blast. The way he looks, he could be on the cover of GQ. But it mattered not where he was; instead, it mattered in what direction he was going, and it was not a happy thought. Time passed, he squandered everything, lost his so-called friends, was thrown out of his plush apartment, had no money to buy a square meal, and was eating with the pigs. And then he started home. He had only the ragged clothes on his back. He looked like he had aged forty years in only a few months. He was unkempt, scraggly, friendless, penniless, hungry. He looked terrible. But he was heading in the right direction. What mattered more than where he was, was the direction he was going.

I think of this when I hear of churches growing or in decline. It does not matter so much where they are as what direction they are going. Here is a church that used to have 1,000 members. Now they are down to 150. Here is a church that struggled along with 20 or 30 members for several years and have hit their stride, gained momentum, received numerous new families, have lots of programs going, and are up to 150 members. They have the same number of members, but one is declining and the other is growing, one is disheartened, the other encouraged. A lot depends on the direction you're going.

259

The Board of Trustees of a college was in session, interviewing some individuals for the position of president of the school. Two of the three candidates had earned doctorates. One of the three had a master's degree, but not an earned doctorate. When asked about that, he said he did not get a doctorate because it was just an ego thing and he did not need the degree for his ego. I wonder if some trustees were skeptical of that reply. For one thing, in the same room at that moment, among the trustees, were at least three persons with Ph.D. degrees, one of whom was the Distinguished Professor of Mathematics at the University of Georgia. How did he feel about that answer? Was the prospective college president really being truthful? Was ego the real obstacle to an earned doctorate or were the real hindrances the foreign languages and the dissertation? Was there a lack of the determination and will needed to go the second and third mile to get the doctorate? Was he really not willing to pay the price in terms of time and energy and money and sacrifice? And I wonder who really had an ego problem.

260

This was a bumper sticker on a car in Texas:

NOT ALL WHO WANDER ARE LOST

261

This was on a bumper sticker on a pick-up truck:

PEACE TAKES LEADERSHIP
ANY FOOL CAN START A WAR

262

I once experienced the almost complete rearrangement of the scriptures, and this without scholarly assistance or council meetings. I was to preach at the installation service for a pastor in a nearby town. All went well on the way over. I had put my pulpit robe and Bible in the back seat of the car. I used them both in the service and when it was over I placed them to the side in order to enjoy the reception that followed. After the reception I took both the robe and the Bible to the car. In order properly to place the robe neatly in the back seat, I first placed the Bible on the roof of the car. Then we headed home. Several blocks and a few miles later, it dawned on me that I did not take the Bible from the roof of the car and it might just be still up there. I stopped and got out and looked, but it was gone. So we retraced our journey, going back to the church the way we came. Once on the way back, my wife saw, there on the highway, a bunch of papers in the middle of the highway and said, "I'll bet that's it," but I replied that it surely fell off the car before then and it couldn't be it, so we kept going. We re-entered the church parking lot and scoured the area but to no avail, then we started from the church and very slowly drove away, looking right and left. Then we arrived at the place on the highway where the papers had been seen previously and where I said it could not be it, but it was decided that my wife might have been right all along and so I stopped the car on the side of the road. When the traffic was clear, I ran out onto the road and, sure enough, there was my Bible, all scattered and torn apart by the wind and traffic. I cradled the pages in my arms as if it were a wounded animal, placed the scattered remnants in the back seat of the car, and drove back to our town a bit saddened. Then I did this: I drove to our church, got out, and carried the torn and disheveled scriptures into my office and placed them on my desk. They were a mess. Lamentations was now in the New Testament. Philippians was in the Old. Hebrews was missing. Jeremiah was nowhere to be found. Matthew had been drastically abbreviated. And I placed it all on my desk. The next morning, a Monday, I went into my office. I more than halfway expected my Bible to be back in place. Don't ask me why I thought that. Did I expect a miracle during the night? I was sorely disappointed to see the same mess I left the previous night. It was very difficult to give up my Bible, what with all its markings and marginal stuff and different scriptural references I had inserted in my handwriting over the years. I waited for several days before I went out and bought another Bible. Perhaps I kept hoping and praying that somehow divine intervention would take place and all would be well. It was not to be.

My mother was with us in Memphis in the early fall of the year, in 1996 or 1997 as I recall. The baseball playoffs started during that time. The Baltimore Orioles were up against the New York Yankees for the American League championship. The series was going down to the wire. The game today was crucial. I took my mother to the airport and she flew back to Kansas City, in which area she lived. The game was going right along. The Orioles had a good chance, and might have even been leading when the event I shall describe happened. Derek Jeter, the Yankee shortstop was at bat. He hit a fly ball deep to right field. The Oriole right fielder went back to the wall and camped under it, ready to catch it. As the ball descended, a boy with a baseball glove on reached down from the bleachers and caught the ball. The Oriole right fielder clearly was in the position to catch it, there, right up against the right field fence. The right field umpire signaled a home run. Yes he did. He signaled a home run although it was obvious that there had been fan interference and the batter should have been called out. The Oriole right fielder argued with the umpire. The Oriole manager ran out and argued with the umpire. Just then the phone rang. I said, "Hello." It was my mother. "I made it home." I said sharply, "Good." She said, "I enjoyed visiting with you." I replied, even more shortly, "Good." Then, as I recall, she said "Goodbye," and hung up. It was almost a decade later that I talked to her and tried to explain what was going on just as she called. The umpire's awarding of a home run to Derek Jeter still goes down in baseball history as one of the worst miscarriages of justice in sports history. But my mother got home safely.

264

This whole thing about evolution and "creationism" and/or "intelligent design" is silly. Just the labels of the latter two ideas are foolish. Regarding the last one, most of us periodically by our actions do all we can to refute the notion that there is "intelligent design" behind it all. And regarding "creationism" we should know that there is no conflict between knowing God as Creator and evolution. The two ideas are not on opposite poles and they do not contradict one another. And besides, this controversy is not new. Long before the famous "monkey trial" in Dayton, Tennessee, featuring John Scopes, an ill William Jennings Bryan, and Clarence Darrow, common sense was showing its beautiful head. Where? On the campus of Cumberland University in Lebanon, Tennessee. At that Cumberland Presbyterian college the biology professor, a faithful Christian and loyal Cumberland Presbyterian, was teaching evolution while also living by the precepts and admonishments of scripture. There was no controversy. So writes the current librarian at Cumberland University in one of the recent issues of the <u>Journal of Presbyterian History</u>. Long before the heated debates, long before the issue was politicized, long before right-wing Christians started reverting to an anti-science stance (in this and also in the global warming debate), here was a quiet, dignified, scholarly Christian gentleman showing how God as Creator and the ever-changing world go together. When was this? In the late nineteenth century.

ಸಿಂಖಿಂಖಿಂಖಿಂಖಿಂಖಿಂಖಿಂಖಿಂಖಿಂಖಿಂಖಿ

265

I'm not saying that the above-mentioned biology professor was the first to teach the absence of conflict regarding evolution and the Genesis accounts of creation, but he could well have been the first college professor to do so. But if so, it would not have been the first time Cumberland Presbyterians were the "first." The first Protestant communion service in what is now the state of Texas was held by a minister in this church, Sumner Bacon. He was also the first representative in that state for the American Bible Society. He was, by the way, ordained in a presbytery in Louisiana on the same day and in the same service as a minister named William Edward Scott, who was a pastor in the denomination for many years before moving over to the Presbyterian Church. One of his pastoral moves was to San Francisco, California, where he later founded San Francisco Theological Seminary. Its campus is now across the Bay in San Anselmo and there is a building named for Scott.

Other "firsts" for Cumberlands include: the first Protestant sermon preached in what is now the state of Arkansas; the first co-educational college in Arkansas (what became Arkansas Cumberland College and now University of the Ozarks); the first co-educational college in Pennsylvania (Waynesburg); the first woman in any Presbyterian denomination to be ordained into the gospel ministry (Louisa Woosley); the first Protestant sermon in what is now Iowa; the first (and only) Presbyterian body to write an entirely new Confession of Faith separate from the Westminster Confession of Faith used by all other Presbyterians; the first co-educational school in the nation of Colombia; the first predominantly American Presbyterian church to hold its General Assembly outside the bounds of the United States (Japan, 2008).

The ministry and mission mandate for us could be located in Mark 9:33-37 where Jesus says, "Whoever wants to be first must be last of all and servant of all." Here we are, first in so many things and hardly anybody knows it. But that's all right. We have been first in so many endeavors, and now our mission is to be last of all and servant of all, to live out the true mission of Jesus Christ as servant, not particularly caring about size or great membership or prestige or status. Church history books mention us, at best, three times: when we were organized in 1810, when we had the bitter union with the Presbyterians in 1906, and, perhaps, the fact that a remnant of the church did not go into the union and the church continues today. Sometimes the authors actually get the dates right, but not always.

266

I visited with a recent graduate of Memphis Theological Seminary. She is a hospital chaplain, and has worked in all the sections of Erlanger Hospital in Chattanooga, Tennessee. She said that just a week ago a child died three days after being born and she attempted to minister to the family. I told her that reminded me of some very bad advice I gave to a young mother years ago. She and her husband were parents of two little boys, ages about five and three. Then she gave birth to triplets who were all stillborn, two girls and a boy as I recall. There was only a small grave side service. Her husband, the funeral director, and I were the only persons present. Earlier, in the hospital room the mother had talked about whether to name the infants. I advised against it. To my mind, it would be easier to "get over" the experience if they were not named. Even talking about it now reminds me of how wrong I was. If she wanted to name those children, she should have had the right to do so. I should not have given any advice at all. Naming them could have been a comfort to her, then and in future years. It was bad pastoral advice.

267

In a suburb of Knoxville, Tennessee, we got the report that about a hundred ducks were walking around on the asphalt parking lot of a shopping center. Here is what happened, said experts on those wonderful creatures: From the sky the ducks looked down and saw what they thought was a body of water. One can imagine the surprise they experienced when they landed and there was no splash. So now they were toddling around, making duck noises, enjoying this moment of visiting with one another. As I recall, someone from Ducks Unlimited was called and soon a police net had engulfed them and they were taken to a nearby pond from whence they, sometime thereafter, flew away and continued their journey.

I was reminded of that incident when I was out in Trona, California, for some classes for the Program of Alternate Studies of the Cumberland Presbyterian Church. During the night one could hear a loud bang every so often. It turns out that what was heard was a cannon going off. Why? Flying along that desert area ducks would look down and see what they thought was a body of water. Actually, it was a chemical rising from the ground from which products like 20-Mule-Team Borax and other products were made. Trona is a company town and the trains run twenty four hours a day from that magic lake to the plant and back and forth. So the ducks would land and get mired in the muck and stickiness of the unusual lake. So the requirement of the government was to try to scare the ducks away. The boom of the cannon has seemed to do the job.

One would think that all God's creatures live and survive by instinct- birds fly south, bears hibernate. But here we see that instinct was not enough. These wonderful creations of God needed some nurture, some training, needed to attend some seminars on "How to recognize water when you see it from 2,000 feet." The conversion experience is a wonderful thing, but after that one does not live and survive (and serve) by so-called Christian instincts alone. Conversion must be followed by instruction, study, experiences of fellowship with other Christians, the give and take of vital discussion, the correction of veteran church folks, the continuing life of worship and witness in the church.

268

Mothers are wonderful people. They know so much. They do so much. They improvise. They are flexible. They make do with what they have. I was talking with a woman in her seventies who said she had polio as a child. This was evidently before physical therapy or its related sciences had been fully developed or at least were fully accessible. The polio was in her arms and legs. Her mother had her do physical activities that would challenge her arms and legs. She eventually recovered from the polio. When she went to a doctor years later regarding another ailment, that doctor said something to the effect that mothers know what to do and they do it. This woman's mother provided what today might be considered professional physical therapy and she did it out of her own love and concern as a mother. Today the woman in her seventies is, in regard to the polio, totally healthy, and thankful that her mother pushed her and helped her and challenged her.

269

My fellow preachers can appreciate this. Have you ever noticed that when you are asked to tell what your next sermon is about it sounds dull and lifeless in the telling? Even to us! Yet in the preaching of it, the sermon comes to life. In fact, if one is called upon to tell something about what we are going to say a few hours or a few minutes prior to the great moment, it may take away from the power of the sermon. This happened the night of my graduation from seminary. We were robed up, waiting with the seminary leaders and the speaker, ready to march in about twenty minutes hence. The church phone rang. It was a local reporter wanting to speak to the guest preacher. She inquired as to what the message was about. The reporter was elderly, had been the local reporter for a metropolitan newspaper for a very long time, and required repetition in a conversation, which the preacher gave. I stood near him as he repeated, more than once, what the main thoughts were. I really think that took the steam out of his message in the service, or I may feel that way because I heard him try to explain things to the reporter. Sometimes, when someone asks me about an upcoming sermon, I say this. "I can't wait to hear what I'm going to say." And I really do talk as little as possible about the sermon before I preach it.

270

We raised three daughters. They were all babies once. With our first one, we were extra careful, going by the book, Dr. Spock's book. When she dropped her pacifier, we put it in a pan of water and boiled the water for a good long time, making sure the pacifier was absolutely clean before, after cooling, putting it back in her mouth.. With our second one, we referred to Dr. Spock occasionally. When she dropped her pacifier we turned on the hot water faucet and stuck the pacifier under it for a few seconds, then, after cooling, put it back in her mouth. With our third daughter we used Dr. Spock's book as a doorstop or as something the little girls could sit on at the dinner table if they were not in their high chairs. And when the third one dropped her pacifier, we blew the dust off of it, and stuck it back in her mouth. All three grew up anyway and now live productive lives.

271

In writing and speaking one is taught to avoid unnecessary words. The most unnecessary word in the English language is "hopefully." It has no meaning. It is weak. It is impotent. It says nothing. I have asked people whether "hopefully" is an adverb or an adjective or whatever, and nobody knows. It is the most widely used, absolutely unnecessary word ever. It is better to say, "I hope." Or, "It is to be hoped." Or, "I certainly hope." Basically, the word in question really means, "I wish, and if everything goes well, good things will happen." But instead of that, people say, "Hopefully." Is there a prayer in the Book of Common Worship to help us be delivered from this word? Well, one day, hopefully, there will be.

272

I was sitting and talking with a bunch of people, many of whom were college graduates. I expressed the opinion that the split infinitive is wrong but authors and speakers ignore it and go right on splitting infinitives right and left. One person, a college graduate, asked, "What is a split infinitive?" I was on long distance with someone who happened to be an English teacher in a school in Florida. She comes from the old school and actually instructs students about the negatives of using split infinitives. She said it is difficult to continue to teach this because so many in the academic field have let it go by and view this grammatical transgression as something now to be accepted. Oh puhleeze! Give me a break! We can do better! For one thing, we can take a vow not to use adverbs. That would help. Even the Star Trek television show had it wrong, "To boldly go where no man has gone before." Take away "boldly" and you still have a strong expression. Better yet, place it somewhere else in the sentence: "To go boldly..." or, "Boldly to go..." . Steer away from adverbs and you will find yourself using fewer split infinitives, for it is the adverb that is the chief culprit, if we do not name ourselves as the culprit, which we are. But don't put all the blame on the adverb. There are other ways to split an infinitive. When Shakespeare starts saying, "To be or TO NOT be, that is the question," I'll start splitting infinitives.

273

I have had the privilege of introducing the same speaker five times over the years. In most instances, I requested the opportunity. In the 1960s I was traveling back and forth from West Tennessee (attending Seminary) to north central Arkansas (new Cumberland Presbyterian Church in Batesville). Both trips going and coming took me through Memphis. On one very late Sunday night I was crossing the bridge and began to hear a very loud noise from somewhere within my 1956 Chevrolet. When I got into Tennessee I saw a policeman and stopped and asked him to look at it, but neither he nor I could see anything with our untrained eyes. I traveled on and, still driving through Memphis, I heard it get louder and louder. Finally I found a service station that was open. Although the mechanic was not on duty (it was now about 1:30 in the morning) the one attendant easily spotted the problem: bearings. The bearings in the wheels had gone bad and any movement brought on the noise. The mechanic would be in at 7:00, more than five hours from the moment. What to do? I knew what area of the city I was in, the Highland Heights area, so, after much thought I called the pastor of the Highland Heights Cumberland Presbyterian Church, John Stammer Smith (Stammer was a family name. He was one of our great preachers. He never stammered). He gladly came over and drove me to his house, showed me a bed, and I slept well. Later in the morning, he and his wife June welcomed me to their breakfast table, after which he and I went back to the service station. By that time the repair work had been done and I could be on my way. There was one minor problem: I did not have the money to pay for the work. This fine pastor took care of it and I promised him I would send him a check to reimburse, which I did several days later. In more than one way this minister helped me get my bearings. Over the next several years, at a youth convocation, a presbytery meeting, a revival, and a couple of other events, I told this story, as I introduced him, about how he helped me get my bearings, and John Stammer Smith was here tonight to "help us get our bearings." It always went over well. And he always helped us get our bearings. In fact, throughout his ministry - in Kentucky, Texas, and Tennessee - he helped a lot of people in that regard.

274

One of the greatest and most historic military battles in history was in 1815, the Battle of New Orleans. Songs have been written about it. Probably books, too. General Andrew Jackson was the great heroic leader in that conflict. His fame spread to where he later was elected President of the United States. Only trouble was, the War of 1812 had been declared over. The Battle of New Orleans was unnecessary. I suspect church battles are fought, too, long after a truce has been declared or peace in some form has been established. Ongoing church fights just increase the tension, raise anger levels, and create groups and cliques.

275

Making changes in church takes diplomacy, tact, time, and patience. In one pastorate we had sung the "Doxology," when the offering was brought to the altar, every Sunday for five years. I, in my great wisdom, decided we might benefit from some variety. So, one Sunday there appeared in the bulletin another selection for bringing up the offering: "We Give Thee But Thine Own." The text was written by someone who was born in 1823 and died in 1897. Evidently the tune, Schumann, was from Mason and Webb's "Cantica Laudis," composed in 1850. Although it has five verses we sang only the first:

> We give Thee but Thine own,
> Whate'er the gift may be:
> All that we have is Thine alone,
> A trust, O Lord, from Thee.

I immediately had to go into conflict-management mode. One would have thought I had announced that there were four Persons in the Trinity. The hue and cry from some got louder. While others in the congregation said nothing, I am sure some of them were just silently enduring the change. I stood my ground, soft and shaky though it was. I held on for one year. During that time the persons making the loudest complaints continued. At the end of exactly one year of our singing the "new" song, the bulletin for the next Sunday contained the "Doxology" once again. Some great ideas sometimes do not pan out.

276

I was trying to lead a week-day adult Bible study group in our congregation. Along the way I asked, "If you were stranded on a desert island, what book or books of the Bible would you want to have?" One man quickly responded: "Hebrews, Ephesians, Lamentations, and Philippians!" "Why would you want Hebrews, Ephesians, Lamentations, and Philippians?" I asked. His answer: "H - E - L - P."

277

The doctrine of the Virgin Birth - Jesus was born of a virgin - has been around a very long time, and is firmly fixed in Protestant and Catholic creeds and minds. The doctrine of the Immaculate Conception is a Catholic addition of more recent vintage, proposed and announced by a pope of some centuries back. It states that the Virgin Mary herself was born of a virgin. And so, a few decades ago I was trying to lead a Sunday morning adult Sunday school class and I wanted to discuss these subjects. And so I asked, "What is the difference between the Immaculate Conception and the Virgin Birth?" To which someone quickly answered, "Nine months!"

278

I drove my car for a few days - longer than I should - with a broken speedometer. For that period of time I did not know exactly how fast I was going. My solution to the problem for that interim was to follow other drivers and keep the pace they kept. I realized how shaky that policy could be out on major highways. Let me report here and now: A state trooper does have the ability to flag down one, two, three, four cars in one fell swoop. Be sure to get your speedometer repaired quickly if it ever breaks down. I think Paul may have written something along that line in Romans 12:2, "Do not be conformed to this world." Jesus referred to the dangers of following the crowd in Matthew 6:5: "When you pray, do not be like the hypocrites..." as well as in 6:7: "When you are praying, do not heap up empty phrases as the Gentiles do..." This, too, could be added: "Unless your righteousness exceeds that of the scribes and Pharisees, you will never enter the kingdom of heaven" (Matthew 5:20).

279

You walk into a hospital and see signs with arrows pointing this way and that: Admissions, Emergency, Out-Patient Surgery, Cafeteria, Restrooms,. And this one: Surgery Waiting. We have all been there. While elsewhere in the hospital surgeons and technicians and nurses are working feverishly on the family member, we sit there waiting. You walk into a bank and you see a sign that says something like, "Wait Here for Next Teller" and in the post office, "Wait Here for Next Available Clerk." We wait for the signal light to change. We wait for the microwave to do its work. We wait for the gas tank on our car to fill up. We wait for word from distant loved ones as to whether they made it home or not. We wait for the next election. A casual look through the Bible has a lot about waiting. Psalm 25:5: (to God) "For you I wait all day long." Psalm 27:14: "Wait for the Lord." Psalm 37:34: "Wait for the Lord." Psalm 40:1: "I waited patiently for the Lord; he inclined to me and heard my cry." Isaiah 26:8: "In the path of your judgments, O Lord, we wait for you." Isaiah 30:18b: "For the Lord is a God of justice; blessed are all those who wait for him." Lamentations 3:26: "It is good that one should wait quietly for the salvation of the Lord." Waiting is probably not the American way. We should be out there working at all times. But while we are waiting God is working. In fact, a verse says that, too: "(God) works for those who wait for him" (Isaiah 64:9). The donut man in the commercial rises at 3:00 A.M. to go and prepare his product so people who walk into his store at 7:00 A.M. will have fresh, warm donuts. The modern homemaker can relax on the couch and announce. "I am cleaning my oven" as the up-to-date appliance goes through the many cycles of automatic renewal. While we wait, God is working.

280

It is hard to refrain from thinking ill of others. Especially when one boards a plane, finds one's seat, and immediately upon take off, has to cope with the seat in front that has now been pushed back as far it will go, ending up on one's chest, causing breathing problems. To be able to inhale and exhale on at least a semi-regular basis, the offended one must seriously contemplate whether or not to release one's own seat so it tilts backwards, toward, if not landing on, the chest of the innocent person immediately behind. On one occasion I asked a flight attendant to tell the person in front to pull his seat up just a little. And once, on an international flight, a trip that would take several hours, a flight attendant, perceiving my dilemma, wisely and compassionately suggested I might want to move toward the back where there were a few empty seats from which to choose, which I did. I do not think thoughtfulness, civility, and the Golden Rule stop at the door of a 747. But I'm working on my breathing just in case.

281

T-Shirts seen recently:

A young adult woman wore this message:
BROWN-EYED GODDESS

Another woman's shirt said:
I'M NOT SUFFERING FROM INSANITY
I'M RATHER ENJOYING IT, THANK YOU

282

In Jena, Louisiana, where six African-American teenage boys had been accused of beating a white young man, with at least one of the accused being tried and convicted and sent to prison, a massive protest was held in behalf of what was called "The Jena Six." Attended mostly by African-Americans, the parade was quiet, non-violent, and, in that regard, uneventful. A short time later, the white prosecutor in the case stepped to the microphone and told the press and the nation that "Jesus Christ our Lord and Savior" made the protest quiet and non-violent. While I admire his religious faith, I do not admire the slap in the face he gave to all those who were quiet and non-violent. What about their own resolve? What about their own attitudes that made the protest what it was? What about their own decisions to make it so? He gave no credit to the protestors and expressed no appreciation to them for their restraint. It was all a result of "Jesus Christ our Lord and Savior." I am sure "Jesus Christ our Lord and Savior" was involved in some way and I am certain many African-Americans know and experience him as their Lord and Savior, but it was an insult to imply that had not "Jesus Christ our Lord and Savior" been around, these good folks would have been loud and violent instead of quiet and non-violent.

283

A sign on a billboard:

I'M NOT YOUNG ENOUGH TO KNOW EVERYTHING.

284

What best defines the church? Place or people? We know that in the Old Testament, "place" was important. Genesis 28:16 has Jacob saying, "Surely the Lord is in this place-and I did not know it!" Exodus 3:5 says that the Lord told Moses, "Remove the sandals from your feet, for the place on which you are standing is holy ground." But in the New Testament, in his response to the

Transfiguration as recorded in Matthew 17:4, Peter says "Lord, it is good for us to be here; if you wish, I will make three dwellings here, one for you, one for Moses, and one for Elijah." Although Jesus has no verbal response, it was obvious that this suggestion would go nowhere. Instead of building something on that mountain, the disciples followed the Lord down to the valley where the human need was, where the people were. "Place" is important for the church - buildings, land, property. We Cumberland Presbyterians have Bethel College, Memphis Theological Seminary, the Cumberland Presbyterian Children's Home, Camp Peniel, Crystal Springs, Camp John Speer, Camp Chilhowee, Camp Lowrie, Ovoca, Camp NaCoMe, Shiloh Church, Calvary Church, Elk Creek Church, Campground Church, Mt. Pleasant Church, St. Luke Church, Hubbard Church, First Church - Lincoln, Knoxville, Columbia, McKenzie, Milan, Russellville, and on and on. The Cumberland Presbyterian Center, the C.P. Birthplace Shrine, that place under the shade tree where one felt/heard the call of God to preach, that trail one walked to contemplate God's will for one's life. On vacation we were in Annapolis, Maryland, and walked along the pier there in that town where the U.S. Naval Academy is located. On the boardwalk was a plaque, saying that on this spot, at this place, Kunta Kinte was brought to be a slave in the United States of America. Yes, place is important. We need a Place. And "People" are important, too. The church is people. We have both the Old Testament and the New Testament, both Place and People.

285

Husbands are advised that if you say the following, get ready to understand that you will say it only once in your entire marriage: The wife is in the kitchen, preparing the evening meal. You are in the family room, reading the paper, watching television, and drinking a glass of tea, all at the same time. She calls out, "Can you get that big bowl off the top shelf for me?" You reply, "Not from here."

286

Each one's call to ministry is different. Each one's moment is different. During the summer of 1958, after one year of college majoring in Business Administration, I attended several senior high camps (which welcomed college students) sponsored by different synods of the Cumberland Presbyterian Church. I also attended one junior high camp as a counselor and the C.P. National Youth Conference (now called Cumberland Presbyterian

Youth Conference). After two of these, I found myself contemplating the call. I discussed it with parents and pastor. On a Saturday afternoon between the end of one camp and the start of another, I was mowing our front yard. It was a push mower in 1958, and I was thinking. Suddenly, I would want to say, dramatically, it became clear. I could see myself doing that. I could see myself being a minister. Previously that had not been clear. Now it was. The next morning, a Sunday, I was in the choir at the McKenzie, Tennessee, First Cumberland Presbyterian Church. The invitation hymn was "Jesus Is Calling." The third verse ends, "Come, and no longer delay." That's when I went, no longer delaying. It struck some like a thunder bolt. A local dentist in the church said afterward, "Tommy, you pulled the old Statue of Liberty play on us," a reference to a trick play in football. Who knows how providential the hymn selection by the pastor was for that service. I probably would have come out of that choir with just about any hymn, but the one chosen, with the third verse ending, "Come, and no longer delay," was exactly right for the moment. To this day, I remember that occasion and every time that hymn is sung I experience the last line of the third verse as especially moving.

287

You think you know what to do at all times and in all circumstances, don't you. Well, what about this? You are away from home and you have asked the people at the front desk of the motel to give you a wake-up call at 6:15 A.M. That should give you plenty of time to get up, get ready, get packed, get to the car, and be on your way to your 8:00 meeting a few miles away. You toss and turn a little during the night, but sleep somewhat soundly otherwise. Concerned about your meeting, you wake up at 6:00, fifteen minutes before the wake-up call from the desk is scheduled. Now what do you do? Do you start the "getting ready" process? Or do you follow my example, and do nothing? You sit there on the edge of the bed and wait for the wake-up call and you are already awake! If you went ahead and took your shower would the phone ring and keep on ringing until you got out of the shower and picked up? You don't want to know. So you sit. You wait. That is time wasted, you know. You could be achieving something, solving something.. But you sit there, and the minutes go by so slowly. Finally, after what seems like an hour, the phone rings. You pick up, say "Thank you," put it back in its cradle, and move on with your life.

288

The selection of hymns for worship is a delicate task. Some pastors travel the thin line between the melody and the message. The melody (tune) makes the hymn singable (or not). The message gives the hymn substance. Both provide good reasons for the use of a hymn. Me? I come down on the side that says the hymn needs to be singable. The message is important, but if no one knows the tune, or if the singing of the melody is very difficult, very few, if any, of the congregants will end up singing. Now I know the melody is not everything. We should not sing a hymn about "Old Mother Hubbard" just because it is to the tune of "Lead On, O King Eternal" or "What A Friend We Have in Jesus." The words do matter. But what good are the words if the melody is so difficult only those trained in music can wade into it. One answer - occasionally - is when finding a hymn with an excellent message but an unfamiliar (and maybe very difficult tune) one can look to the "Metrical Index of Tunes" in the back of the hymnal to see if there is a well-known melody that would fit the rhythm and timing of the poetry in the unfamiliar hymn. We often overlook good messages because a first glance reveals an unfamiliar tune. There may be several good hymns that can be sung to the tune of "Amazing Grace" and "The Church's One Foundation" and "Faith of Our Fathers" and "Joyful, Joyful, We Adore Thee." It is possible - occasionally - to combine familiar melodies with theologically sound messages from otherwise unfamiliar hymns.

289

Familiar hymns can be sung to different tunes. For example, "It Came Upon the Midnight Clear" fits right in with the same melody as "America the Beautiful," and vice-versa. The Doxology can be sung to the tune of "Hernando's Hideaway," not that you would want to do that. "Amazing Grace" can be sung to the same melody as "The House of the Rising Sun." "Love Divine" and "All the Way My Savior Leads Me" are interchangeable, and both fit right in with "Joyful, Joyful, We Adore Thee." Recently written texts can be sung to familiar tunes with little or no adaptation. We could go on. This approach can help the worship experience, though it may drive church musicians, choirs, and song leaders to distraction.

290

Hymn selection for worship can be a mixture of old and new, comfortable and challenging. I was talking to a professor of preaching at Brite Divinity School in Fort Worth, and he gave a good definition of old and new hymns. "An old hymn is one I know, and a new hymn is one I don't know," Dr. Hunter Beckelhymer said. With that simple reasoning, we could say that it does not matter how old the hymn is. It is new if I don't know it. I like that. The oldest in existence today is one we never sing, "Shepherd of Tender Youth," written by Clement of Alexandria, c.150-220. Another old hymn, "O Sacred Head, Now Wounded," was written several hundred years later by Bernard of Clairvaux (1091-1153). To many church folks, those would be new hymns, since they have not heard or sung them.

291

There have been some famous Cumberland Presbyterians who have been known outside the circles of the denomination. The Confederate general NATHAN BEDFORD FORREST was one. The populist political leader WILLIAM JENNINGS BRYAN grew up Cumberland Presbyterian. The young teacher in the famous Scopes trial, where Bryan was involved, graduated from Illinois College, where Bryan also graduated. On the day Scopes graduated, Bryan was the commencement speaker. The father of

Scopes was an elder in a Cumberland Presbyterian Church in Paducah, Kentucky. A former governor of Kentucky, JULIAN CARROLL, was a Cumberland Presbyterian elder and denominational leader, serving on several boards of the church. The seventh congressional district in Tennessee had a Cumberland Presbyterian in the U.S. House of Representatives for several generations. FINIS GARRETT, from Dresden, had close ties to Bethel College, and may have been a Cumberland Presbyterian, I am not sure. His successor, JERE COOPER, from Dyersburg, was a member of the church, as was his successor, ROBERT "FATS" EVERETT, of Union City. Upon Mr. Everett's death, ED JONES, of Yorkville, a prominent person in the denomination, and a former Secretary of Agriculture in the State of Tennessee, represented the Seventh District in Congress for sixteen years. The string was broken, when, upon the retirement of Mr. Jones, John Tanner, a member of the Disciples of Christ, was elected. The television and film star LILI TOMLIN, is from Paducah, Kentucky, and was a part of the Margaret Hank Cumberland Presbyterian Church. Upon the death of her mother, who also was named LILI, two Cumberland Presbyterian ministers, J. David Hester and Tommy Thompson, conducted the funeral at the church in Paducah. The service was attended by many well known entertainers. Several state legislatures in the South have had members of the denomination on their rolls, and presently in the Tennessee legislature a number of Cumberlands are members: PHILLIP PINION of Troy, CHRIS CRIDER of Milan, and MARK MADDOX of Dresden being three from West Tennessee. For several years, TOM GARLAND, of the Cumberland Presbyterian Church in Greeneville, Tennessee, served in the State Senate. In Arkansas, CLYDE KINSLOW was a state representative for many years. Television correspondent JIM WOOTEN, with ABC News, was at one time an ordained Cumberland Presbyterian minister, with degrees from both Bethel College and Cumberland Presbyterian Theological Seminary (its name before moving to Memphis). His father was a minister in the church. Country music stars JIMMY DEAN and MACK DAVIS are products of the Lubbock, Texas, Cumberland Presbyterian Church. Jimmy's father was a minister in the denomination and his brother was an elder in the Lubbock church.

292

During a period of months we had to put our beloved dog, Desi, down, and then our old friend, our cat, Rico. Both had serious health problems. My wife has talked with Paige, our five-year-old granddaughter about both pets. We miss them both. One day, Paige said, "I miss Rico." Her grandmother said, "We all miss Rico.

But he is now in a better place." To which Paige replied, "But he died."

293

Do you want to hear some sad news? I once knew an unbeliever, a non-Christian, described this way: "He has every Christian virtue except faith." Now that is sad. So close, yet so far away. But here is some more sad news. I know of a few Christians about whom it could be said they have no Christian virtues except faith. Making a "decision for Christ," is essential, but "living for Christ" is also vital, but not automatic. Neither is it an instinctual thing, as if Jesus' entrance into a life will always create a complete turn around in a life - moving one from prejudice to understanding; from hatred to love; from violence to peace; from cynicism to hope in one fell swoop. God has the power to do that, and has performed such quick improvements in many lives, but in many others there is work to do. I think the writer of 2 Peter was aware of human weaknesses and the need for those who have been "saved" to work on Christian disciplines and prayer and study and relationships. The writer said this in 2 Peter 2:15ff: "Supplement your faith with goodness, and goodness with knowledge, and knowledge with self-control, and self-control with endurance, and endurance with godliness, and godliness with mutual affection, and mutual affection with love."

294

Sign outside an Assembly of God church near Little Rock:

> TWO TESTS OF CHARACTER
> WEALTH AND POVERTY

Something similar in the front yard of another church:

> BARRIERS TO SALVATION
> FOR THE RICH, PRIDE
> FOR THE POOR, BITTERNESS

295

Driving behind a big tractor-trailer, I noticed that someone had written through the dirt these two messages, the first on the left rear and pointing to the left, and the second on the right rear of the truck and pointing to the right:

EL PASO EL CRUNCHO

296

What should one make of the following two signs seen on the rear window of a car? One was on the left and the other on the right.

JESUS	AMERICA
MY	MY
LORD	COUNTRY

Perhaps PRIDE was the underlying factor, PRIDE in one's Savior and PRIDE in one's country. And pride can be good or not so good, as we know.

Maybe the message tried to convey POSSESSIVENESS: These are mine, and don't give me any trouble. Back off. This is where I stand. What are you gonna do about it?

Or it could be one of SHARING: I am honored to proclaim these truths. Please ask me about them. You too can be as happy as I am.

Perhaps, regarding America, there may have been a fierce NATIONALISM, given that the person seems to equate the two loyalties. In that case, it might be difficult to discuss this issue with the driver.

Since I did not flag down the car to ask further questions, I do not know the motivation for the rear window signs. So I do not know if the driver was militant, missionary-minded, right wing or left wing, generous, tight-fisted, liberal, redneck, against the Iraq war, for the Iraq war, or just bought the car from somebody else and had not yet had time to remove the signs.

297

I took my car for an oil change. During the time at the service station on that Saturday morning, I talked with a woman who also was having some maintenance done. One subject led to another and, in the course of the visit, she said her father was involved in the D-Day event, June 6, 1944, at Normandy. His job: pushing reluctant American soldiers off the boats and into the water toward the shore. No doubt some of them were killed within minutes. In the films of the event we see soldiers dropping on the beaches. I observed that his task must have been terrible. She said it was, and that the experience haunted him for the rest of his years.

298

Flipping through the channels I came upon a Christian-oriented program. The host and hostess were aggressively calling for donations. They were asking for $600 a year from each listener, "only" $50 per month. More than that, they were going on and on about how these donations would help the viewers. God would bless them. They would reap many rewards. Happiness would come their way, if only they would send that amount to that program. They were rather low key about how the donations would help keep their show on the air. I observed to my wife how crass and cynical all that sounded. She observed: "They might well be in some way blessed to give $600 a year, but probably not in the way they are saying. I'm not sure they need to send their money to those people." I am reminded of a Hank Williams, Jr., song:

> Preacher preachin' on TV
> In a coat and a tie and a vest
> Wants you to send your money to the Lord
> But he gives you his address.

As this is being written, Senator Grassley from Iowa has begun an investigation into the financial dealings and accountability structures, or lack of them, of some television preachers a local television news program had a segment that focused on that subject, entitled "Lifestyles of the Rich and Righteous."

299

The manager of the 2007 National League Champion Colorado Rockies baseball team, Clint Hurdle, interviewed after another victory, said, "There are two kinds of managers: those that are humble and those that are about to be." I wonder how many kinds of pastors there are.

300

A church member told this: At a Wednesday night prayer meeting, the preacher asked if there were any prayer concerns and several people came to the altar. One man said, "I need prayer for my hearing." So the pastor and the people prayed and prayed for his hearing. The pastor touched his ears and others stepped forward to do the same. There was fervent intercession. At the conclusion, the pastor asked if he was helped. The man said, "I don't know; the hearing is not until next Tuesday."

Chapter VII: 301-350

"Coming To"

301

The country singer Larry Gatlin testifies often to his Christian faith and acknowledges his drug-controlled earlier days. As he tells his story, he says, "Back in those days, when I went to sleep, I did not wake up; I came to."

302

Everybody is aware of the cycles of life: birth, life, death, birth, life death. It happened in our family in the year 2000. In late February, Mary Kathryn Coleman, Linda's mother, died in Batesville, Arkansas, after a long battle with cancer. Five months later, in late July, also in Batesville, Linda's father, Theodore Coleman, died. In early August, five days after Mr. Coleman's death, David Alexander Shanton II, our first grandchild, was born in Knoxville, Tennessee. As we moved from one event to another we were keenly aware of the realities of the cycles of life. Mourning was quickly followed by gladness. The world goes on. Life goes on. As of April 2009 Alex is a second-grader, and has been into trains, soccer, guitar, and karate. He is in the children's choir at church and in a couple of Christmas pageants over the years has been one of the three wise men in the Christmas pageant, proudly wearing a Burger King crown as he marches down the center aisle with the other two wise men.

303

A seminary student took a course in the summer with us in the Program of Alternate Studies. Work was added to meet degree requirements. In the early Fall, well before the deadline for getting homework in, Memphis Theological Seminary required a grade, so I turned in an A for the student. I informed him of the A and that I trusted that his work would be of high enough quality that he would earn the A I had already awarded him. He replied that he appreciated the grade, and would "try to live up to" my "expectations." Later we talked and I observed that this might be a great way to award grades. Record it in the registrar's office and then the ball is in the court of the student and the pressure is off the instructor! Troy said this reminded him of when he was a teenager and he went out with friends. His dad did not tell him when to be home. Instead, he asked Troy, "Now when will you be home?" Troy would say something like 10:00 or 10:30. And when the time got close, he knew to start home. He had set the goal and felt obligated to live up to the standard he himself set. By the way, the class assignments he sent in for the course were "A" quality all the way!

304

The name of the denomination to which I belong is the Cumberland Presbyterian Church. Folks have had problems with the name "Cumberland." It is too "geographical," too "local," too "limiting." Once somebody proposed "American" Presbyterian Church. That didn't go over well. Other names, such as "Evangelical" Presbyterian Church, were suggested. "Evangelical" was not acceptable, and in fact, another denomination has that name now. Geographical names abound, and, by and large, do not limit the work of the particular church. There is the Lutheran Church, Missouri Synod. I don't think this has kept that denomination from reaching out beyond its place of beginning. Of course, the Southern Baptist Church is nationwide and worldwide, the "Southern" part not being a hindrance. On the business front, we are aware that Kentucky Fried Chicken is now widely known simply as KFC. However, I do not think it is the "Kentucky" name that is the problem as much as the "Fried" part of the title. In this day when "fried" foods are anathema in some circles, it might not be wise to have "Fried" as your middle name if you are in the fast food business. And so, at least temporarily ("temporarily" now being almost 200 years) we go by "Cumberland" Presbyterian. It should do until a better name comes along!

305

A pastor was derelict in attending local high school basketball games. When confronted about this by an elder, who was a regular at the games, the pastor said, "Are you sure you want me to go and see how you and others act?" The elders said no more. And the pastor was not so sure he wanted the elders to witness his deportment either.

306

"Happiness is..." The completion of that sentence, surprisingly, is usually not some great, majestic, earth-shaking event as much as it is a small, yet important, moment that, if not happening, brings on aggravation. For example: Happiness is... tying your tie and getting it right the first time. For me, if the tie ends up too long or too short the first time, it will take, on average, five more attempts. Here is another: Happiness is...... finding the nail clippers when you need them. Here is another: Happiness is... driving into a service station when your gas gauge looks like it could not go any lower. Here is another: Happiness is... eating at a restaurant, then worrying if you have enough cash to pay plus a tip, then discovering you had a twenty-dollar bill in your billfold or purse that you had forgotten about... Happiness is... having a family that has been visiting your church for several weeks come up and tell you that they want to join this Sunday. Here is another: Happiness is... flipping through the channels and coming upon something you have heard about and really wanted to see, but had forgotten it was tonight, and you have caught it just as it is beginning. What about this: Happiness is... carrying a hot cup of coffee while opening your car door to get into the driver's seat, stumbling just a little bit, but holding on to the cup and not spilling a drop.

307

One of the first sermon ideas I ever saw was from W. E. Sangster in his book <u>The Craft of the Sermon</u>. It was about the Prodigal Son. It was a simple outline.

1. SICK OF HOME
2. HOMESICK
3. HOME

308

There are some things you do <u>not</u> want to say or hear at church. Let us say a person visits a church for the very first time, and, upon walking in, hears one of his friends ask, "What are <u>you</u> doing here?" That will not warm anybody's heart, grow churches, share the welcoming love of Jesus Christ, or encourage the first-time visitor to come back next Sunday. I must acknowledge I have heard this too many times, and, on at least two occasions it was asked of me, not as a first-time visitor to a church necessarily, but in meetings of presbyteries or at other gatherings where I was a visitor.

309

One of the goals of preaching is to make the message so simple, so easy to understand, that the listener will think two things: how easy it must be to get ready to preach, and, regarding the preaching of the sermon, "I can do that." Unfortunately, we use too many multi-syllable words, too many theological terms that need translating into plain English, and too many passages of scripture. A professor of mine at Brite Divinity School said, sort of tongue-in-cheek, that the pastor should preach one sermon a year that has lots of big words, lots of theological terms, and many complex thoughts that nobody understands so the people of the congregation can go home saying, "Our pastor is very intelligent."

On Sounding Intelligent

310

It was Christmas time in Knoxville, Tennessee. The local civic club always had a program appropriate to the season. The program chairman, himself a minister, had invited another minister to speak. Our guest was not now a pastor, but was an official in his denomination. After he was introduced, he walked to the podium, opened his notebook, and started reading. No "thank you very much." No "hello, nice to be here." He hardly looked out at the audience. And as he began to read, I came to the quick realization that he was reading word for word from an article I had read only a few days ago in The Christian Century magazine, something on how Joseph, in all the excitement over the story of the birth of Jesus, was largely ignored. At first I could not believe my ears. My faint hope was that he would, somewhere along the way, acknowledge where he got this article, and in so doing acknowledge that they were not his words. Nothing. Negative. He continued reading, and, upon finishing, sat down. The program and meeting over, we headed to the door. I came this close, this close, to saying to him while shaking his hand, "I enjoyed that. It was even better than when I read it in The Christian Century last week." But I didn't. I just shook his hand. Who did he think we were? Idiots? Did he think absolutely no one would catch what he was doing? I was insulted, and had others known what he was doing, they would have been, too. He could have made it all right by saying at the first something like this: "Ladies and gentlemen, I recently came upon an article in a religious magazine that is so good and interesting that I want to read it to you. I did not write it; somebody else did, but it is appropriate, I think, for this occasion. I think you will enjoy it." Something like that would have taken care of the matter. But he acknowledged nothing. He gave credit to nobody. This was plagiarism at its worst.

311

In the Cumberland Presbyterian denomination the local church is governed by a "session," persons in the congregation who are elected "elders." There are two ways elders can serve on the session: as lifetime members, or for three-year terms, after which they must be off the session for at least a year before they can be re-elected. In my experience as a pastor, I have served mostly new congregations where the rotation system was there at the beginning. I grew up in a church where, for most of those years, there was a permanent, lifetime session. In rotation situations, there have been persons who, once they were eligible, returned to the session with regularity, while there have been other persons who, upon rotating off, were never re-elected. I knew an elder in Lexington, Kentucky, who rotated off, and he really missed the once-a-month meetings on Thursday nights at 7:00 P.M. In fact, he said he was thinking of writing a song entitled, "The Rotation

Blues." He had a point. You are a busy, active, decision-maker for three years, and then you give up those responsibilities. The result can be loneliness, emptiness, a feeling of not being needed, and a searching for other ways to be of service in the church. The would-be songwriter was on to something.

312

The San Diego fires in October of 2007 were devastating. Almost a million people had to evacuate. Thousands of homes and businesses were destroyed. We heard on the radio an interview with a man whose house had been destroyed and here he was helping others to try to save somebody else's house. When asked why, since he lost everything he had, he was now assisting in this way, his answer was less than eloquent: "It's the right thing to do." Nothing spectacular. Nothing eloquent. He took care of the deed and cared not about any words to describe or explain the deed. Sometimes humane, community-minded service needs no words. The actions speak for themselves.

313

A nationally well known political figure wrote books on virtue and morality and they were best-sellers. He went on talk shows and news programs to highlight his views. Turns out he had a gambling problem, although when confronted by reporters, he said it was not a problem, and, therefore, not a vice. Never mind the hundreds of thousands of dollars he lost by this habit. We now know gambling is not a vice, especially if it is only a few hundred thousand dollars.

314

As a pastor I advertised in the newsletter that I would be honored to be with any of our folks at their work place for a day. I rode all night with a volunteer deputy sheriff on the back roads of a Texas county. I stood with a bank employee watching checks zip by. I walked during the night shift in a hospital behind the scenes with the head nurse. I sat in the office with the personnel director of a furniture manufacturer. I visited and rode with a woman who worked with an adoption agency. During one morning and early afternoon I was in the office of the regional director of Health and Human Services, and, it being the day food stamps were distributed, I answered the phone and informed people what time of day they could come and pick theirs up. I went with a retired executive of the city utility board and listened to him as he made the rounds explaining this and that about the total utility picture. And I sat in the receptionists' office of a middle school where the two women at the desks and phones worked together like clockwork. It was a typical day, they said afterwards: Some kids were tardy and received admission slips to get into class. A child came in who had lost her books. During recess a boy was accidentally hit on the head with a baseball bat and was taken to the doctor, later to be pronounced O.K. I was impressed with how well the women worked together. The phone would ring and, seemingly with no hand or voice signals, one would know to answer it, knowing the other was busy. They were a team. They later told me they had worked together in that office more than twenty years. All this was informative for me as I learned about the weekday responsibilities of some of our members. And maybe they enjoyed it because here was their pastor spending all or most of the work day with them.

315

Andrew Carnegie should probably be credited with the following quotation, found somewhere in a stack of my papers:

> Anyone who cannot think is a fool.
> Anyone who will not think is a bigot.
> Anyone who dares not think is a slave.

316

How long will Americans be intimidated, even governed, by fear? National leaders have discovered they can manipulate the nation's citizens by continually lifting up fear of terror and making White House and congressional decisions accordingly. I seem to recall that for more than forty years the Soviet Union had nuclear weapons pointed at the United States and we never underwent the kind of fear-mongering we are experiencing at this time in the Fall of 2007. We invaded Iraq on questionable evidence, at best, regarding weapons of mass destruction. After the invasion, the stated purposes as to why we were in Iraq changed with the seasons of the year. As I write this, Iran is now our target, and inflammatory speeches by the President, Vice-President, and others in charge are serving to ratchet up the hysteria. If there is a hidden design by some as to what the Middle East should look like in a few years and if this kind of rhetoric is part of the plan, then the sooner the November 2008 elections come, the better. Get us scared, keep us scared, and accuse anybody who differs with the plan of being unpatriotic, and you have a perfect strategy for disaster. How shall ministers of the gospel of Jesus Christ respond to all of this? Are we among those who have been intimidated? Might we learn something from the courage of the Buddhist monks in Myanmar who have put their lives on the line for democracy, even unto death?

317

What is the next step after one turns one's life over to Christ? A man in his early thirties was a reluctant church-participant at best, if at all. His wife went with the children, but he stayed home. However, it got to him. Her faithful, quiet witness plus the interest the pastor and others in the church gave, influenced his life. One day he went to see the pastor in the pastor's study and announced that he wanted to give his life to Jesus Christ. This faithful shepherd knew what to do next. He could not leave this decision hanging out there with no action to follow. He picked up the phone and gave it to the young man. "Call somebody," he said. "What?" "Call somebody. Tell them what you just did." After the shock of the strong suggestion, the young man did just that. He called his brother-in-law. They both cried tears of joy. What a good shepherd was this pastor! What loving guidance! Now this young man is studying for the ministry, and his pastor is his mentor.

318

In the Cumberland Presbyterian denomination there are no really, really large churches. A couple of them have close to 2,000 members; a few others are in the 600 to 700 stage in membership. Outside of that, not much. So when I became pastor of a church with 511 active members and 700 or so total members, I tried hard to stay humble, for, again, in our church that's a lot of people, and we were ranked 11th in size in the entire denomination!. I should not have worried about humility. Somebody else took care of that. I noticed a new family in our worship service one Sunday morning, and as we visited briefly after the service he (the husband, dad) told me the family attended a well known, very large church in the city. But, he said, they had moved to our suburb. I thanked him and his family for attending today, and he said, "We came because, well, we like the small church."

319

Some Christians take a vow of silence. Sometimes it works out all right. Sometimes not. Three men lived such a life and they were sitting on the top of a mountain meditating. The wind was blowing. It kept blowing. Finally one said, "That is a very strong wind." Three years passed. Then the second man replied, "I don't think it was all that strong." Seven years went by, then the third man stood up and said, "If there is going to be this constant bickering, I'm leaving."

320

My e-mail today consisted of many items, including an invitation to obtain a degree, or even many degrees, by mail. It looked very enticing. Part of it read: "Obtain a degree based on your present knowledge and experience." Wow! With this program I do not need to learn anything else: my present knowledge will do. I do not have to be involved in anything else: my past experiences will do. I can get a B.A., or an M.A., or even a Ph.D. from this mail-order outfit. I don't need to learn anything or do anything. I'm going to look into that soon!

Just call me doctor...

321

One of the most overlooked areas of study in churches may be on how the Bible came to be. In the instances in which any of the churches I served as pastor got involved, the time was well spent. The story of how the books were selected - which ones got in and which ones did not, the objections some people like Martin Luther had to some that did get in, the amazement one feels that a few books left out did not make it, and vice versa - is exciting. However, it is to some people a threat, because of their belief that the Bible sort of "fell" out of the sky, that no human decisions were involved, and that there should be no discussion at all about the origin and development of the Holy Scriptures. Just the other Sunday, not in a class but in a sermon supposedly based on 2 Timothy 3:14-4:5, I discussed inspiration, the Apocrypha, the period between the Testaments, the canonization of the books of the Bible, the fact that the "scriptures" referred to in 2 Timothy later comprised much of what we now know as the Old Testament, the fact that the scriptures Jesus grew up with were the Law, the Prophets, and the Writings, and that they later formed the bulk of the Old Testament. I felt and later received positive responses from some of the folks in the pews. Some had done some reading and study on these very subjects and were glad to hear them mentioned in the sermon. Our people overall are not afraid of hearing about and discussing the subject of canonization, for example. We do not give our lay people enough credit in this regard.

322

I was looking up "prophets" in Cruden's <u>Concordance</u> and found a reference to 1 Kings 18:4. But when I turned to this chapter and verse in the Bible, it said nothing about prophets. It was then I realized I had 2 Kings 18:4 and not 1 Kings 18:4. So I turned to 1 Kings 18:4, and found it, but it said nothing about prophets. Upon closer examination, I realized I had turned to 1 Kings 8:4, and not 1 Kings 18:4. So this time I flipped over to the correct passage and still saw nothing about prophets. It was then that I learned to my dismay that I had landed at 1 Kings 18:14, and not 1 Kings 18:4. So this time I turned to the right place, and it really was the right place: "When Jezebel was killing off the prophets of the Lord, Obadiah took a hundred prophets, hid them fifty to a cave, and provided them with bread and water." Any time you need help locating something in the Bible, just call on me.

323

Evidently, "buffet" means being beaten (1 Peter 2:20; 1 Corinthians 4:11; Matthew 26:67; Mark 14:65). Somewhere, at some time in a worship service, I heard a certain translation that also had 1 Corinthians 9:27 using that word: "... but I buffet (punish) my body and enslave it, so that after proclaiming to others I myself should not be disqualified." One time I heard a minister sort of tongue-in-cheek quote the 1 Corinthians 9 passage, and instead of saying, "I buffet my body," he said it this way: "I buf-FEY my body," which, in his mind, could have meant "eat hearty." So I suppose it depends on the way you pronounce it: "buffet" or "buf-FEY."

Thomas H. Campbell, my father, was Dean of the Cumberland Presbyterian Theological Seminary when it was a graduate school of theology connected with Bethel College and under the Cumberland Presbyterian Board of Education. This period was from 1945 to 1956. In 1956 the General Assembly separated the two schools (while the Seminary remained on the Bethel College campus) and since the Seminary was now a separate institution, the new Board of Trustees named him President, an office he held during the remainder of the Seminary's time on the college campus in McKenzie, Tennessee. In 1964, by action of the General Assembly, the school moved to Memphis, Tennessee, and became Memphis Theological Seminary of the Cumberland Presbyterian Church. With that move, William T. Ingram, Jr., was named President and Thomas H. Campbell became Dean. The Board of Trustees wanted a "public relations person," and they believed Dr. Campbell did not fit that description. A layman on the Board was heard to say that he thought the President of the Seminary should smoke a pipe or cigar, and Dr. Campbell did not qualify on that either. The faculty of seven consisted of three smokers (Baird, Smartt, Ingram) and four non-smokers (Todd, Irby, Gardner, Campbell). When the entire faculty traveled somewhere they went in two cars, designated above. I am told that they traveled together, in one car, at least once, with Thomas H. Campbell driving. I wonder how they managed the seating. By the time of his retirement in 1973, Dr. Campbell had seen the school take giant steps toward a more effective presence in the denomination.

Growing up in McKenzie, as one of his children, I knew of his commitment to the church and to Bethel College and the Seminary. In 1951 the Seminary moved into the north wing of a new building on the campus, with the college library occupying the south wing. The Library-Seminary Building was home to the school for thirteen years. This gave an identity to the Seminary it had not enjoyed previously.

The McKenzie Fire Department's siren carried a wailing, scary sound. It was designed to wake people up in the middle of the night and strike fear in their hearts. It would wail, and wail, and wail, and wail. One thought its sad, death-like scream would never end. Without fail, when we would be home, upon hearing that sound, my father would go to our dining room window and look eastward toward the college/seminary campus, which was just across the field and a block or two away. He would stand there while the wailing siren continued. He would watch. He would wait.

And when the sound stopped he would continue to look that direction until he was assured that nothing was amiss on the campus.

325

The day the Seminary moved into its part of the new building in the Fall of 1951 was a great moment. Almost at the same time, in Memphis, Tennessee, the newly-constructed Denominational Center was open for occupancy by boards and agencies of the church. Prior to 1951 the Seminary operated on the Bethel campus with borrowed classrooms and office space, and usually had six or eight students, and denominational offices were scattered over Tennessee. In the months following the first use of their part of the Library-Seminary Building, faculty and students experienced growth in numbers. By 1964 and the move to Memphis, there were 7 full-time professors and about 50 students. In the "lean" days, before 1951, before the spurt in enrollment, Thomas H. Campbell and the one or two or three other faculty members taught several courses each. I interviewed a minister who had served in the generation prior to the one under discussion. He said that he did not occupy a "chair" but a "sofa." as a professor. So it was with Dr. Campbell, Dr. John E. Gardner, and Dr. Bill Ingram in those days. Until the faculty was increased to its eventual seven, wide teaching responsibilities continued. By the time of the 1964 move, E. Colvin Baird, Virgil H. Todd, Joe Ben Irby, and librarian Hinkley Smartt had joined the faculty and been on board for ten or more years each, except for Smartt, who arrived in about 1957. In addition to Seminary responsibilities, some of these, prior to the separation of institutions, taught for Bethel as well. In the Seminary, teaching duties for Dean/President Campbell back then included Old Testament, New Testament, Greek, Cumberland Presbyterian History, Cumberland Presbyterian Polity, and Church History. The same kind of broad teaching duties fell on others as well.

326

The years from 1951 through 1964 - thirteen in all - were pivotal for the Seminary and the church. The school was moving toward having its own identity instead of being seen as part of Bethel College. It began to work to qualify for accreditation. Methodist students and part-time Methodist faculty joined us. Several Cumberland Presbyterian Theological Seminary graduates were easily accepted for masters and doctoral work at schools such as

Vanderbilt University, Princeton Theological Seminary, Union Theological Seminary in Virginia, and other institutions. Several General Assembly moderators, future Seminary professors and presidents and deans, future board executives, soon-to-be "foreign missionaries," those who would be new-church-development pastors, and others received their theological training within those thirteen years.

327

The seven professors and their spouses - "The Magnificent Seven" the professors would later be called - went with the school to Memphis in 1964. Most sold their homes that summer; a few kept their homes for a while longer and later sold them. All would eventually reside in Memphis. Of the seven, not a single one would resign; all would stay until retirement. Dr. Campbell's years with the school totaled twenty nine - and that was not the longest tenure! With full-time Seminary responsibilities it was difficult for any to get away and work on doctoral degrees, but as the years went by the chances were better. Some of the schools attended for masters and doctoral work by the faculty included Vanderbilt University, Princeton Theological Seminary, Union Theological Seminary in Virginia, McCormick Theological Seminary, Oberlin School of Theology, The University of Chicago, Scarritt College, George Peabody College, and Louisville Presbyterian Theological Seminary. Publishing opportunities were few, given the teaching loads, but at least three professors had books published while the school was in McKenzie.

328

In McKenzie as well as in Memphis later, wives of the Seminary professors worked outside the home. Some were school teachers, others were administrative assistants in offices at the Seminary and at Memphis State University; one was a librarian in Memphis City Schools and with Memphis State University. All the couples were active in churches in the McKenzie area before the move and continued that activity in Memphis-area churches. After retirement each professor became "emeritus." Dr. Campbell was the first to depart this life in December of 1989. Then followed Hinkley Smartt, then Colvin Baird in 1997. Bill Ingram left this world in 2001, and John E. Gardner in 2003. Joe Ben Irby succumbed in 2007. As of this writing, Virgil H. Todd, who is in his late eighties, survives. Of the wives, Vista Smartt was the first to go, then Julia Irby, then Amna Gardner. Virginia Ingram followed, and then Irene Todd in 2007. Surviving spouses are Thalia Baird and Margaret Campbell, both in their nineties as of this writing (September 2008).

In the spring of 2003 as Memphis Theological Seminary celebrated its 150th anniversary, six of the above appeared as a panel to talk about the move to Memphis in 1964. We called them "The McKenzie Six." Those on the panel were former professors Joe Ben Irby, Virgil H. Todd, and John E. Gardner, as well as three spouses: Margaret Campbell, Irene Todd, and Thalia Baird. Former MTS President J. David Hester presided. Later in the week a banquet was held and again these six were honored at a special table.

ಙಐಙಐಙಐಙಐಙಐಙಐಙಐಙಐಙಐಙಐ

329

Thomas Hardesty Campbell was born near Santa Anna, Texas, on November 16, 1907, the day Oklahoma became a state. His parents were Henry and Bell Kirkpatrick Campbell. Henry Campbell was a farmer and a school teacher. Thomas went to one-room schools and then to Santa Anna High School, graduating at age fifteen. He attended Daniel Baker College, a Presbyterian school, in nearby Brownwood, Texas, then went on to Bethel College in McKenzie, Tennessee, where he graduated in 1927. He continued on the campus and received the B.D. degree from the Cumberland Presbyterian Theological Seminary in 1929. His Seminary thesis was "In the Sunlight of God's Love," a report on the attempted union with the Presbyterian Church USA in 1906 and the steps toward recovery in the Cumberland Presbyterian Church in the years following. In 1936 he published <u>History of the Cumberland Presbyterian Church</u> in Texas, and in 1942 <u>Studies in Cumberland Presbyterian History</u>. History came into play again in 1964 when he published <u>Good News on the Frontier</u>, an updated history of the denomination. Then in 1972 there appeared <u>A People Called Cumberland Presbyterians</u>, of which he was co-author with two other writers. He received the masters degree from Southern Methodist University in the 1930s and took more graduate work at The University of Chicago during the 1950s. Bethel College conferred on him the honorary degree of Doctor of Divinity in 1949.

In my childhood and youth, a Bethel College or Seminary student would mention something about my father's writings on history as though I knew about them, which I did not. One day, in my teens, I wandered back to his study at our home in McKenzie and noticed a thesis-sized book. I took it down and its title was "In the

Sunlight of God's Love." That did not mean anything to me... yet. I began to read. With the first sentence I was enthralled. I read the complete thesis in one sitting. My education regarding Cumberland Presbyterian history had begun. He and I would have many occasions to discuss that subject in the next twenty-five or thirty years. I was present on an occasion when he was introduced to a church group as a writer of church history. When he stood to speak, he said, "I would much rather MAKE history than WRITE it." He did quite a bit of both.

330

When is confrontation advisable and when should one keep one's silence. My wife and her sister went to a movie the other night. Before it started there appeared on the screen a message asking people to turn off their cell phones. But that was not all. The manager of the theater then appeared in front of the audience and repeated the request. One would think both announcements would have done the job. No! The movie started and the woman sitting in front of my wife got out her cell phone and talked virtually throughout the entire film. Now, when does one confront another person? I inquired of my wife if she or her sister said anything to the guilty woman. No, they did not. Then she said, "I might have been shot." That fear referred probably back to a time in Birmingham when in the rush hour two women had a traffic confrontation. They had taken the same exit and were ready to turn on the main road. The woman behind was honking at the woman in front. The woman in front got out of her car and went back to talk to the other, who reached for a gun and shot her dead. Would you have said anything to the woman in the theater? In retrospect, a possible option could have been going to complain to the manager who might have been able to deal with it. In which case they both might have been shot.

331

I visited with a young woman who has sensed the call to ministry. She is married and has three young children. She has no education beyond high school. But she is not fearful or intimidated by the educational requirements nor by what the life of a minister and family would be like. Why? She grew up in a home where her father was a minister. The family moved from place to place. They had many types of experiences with many types of churches. They went through the ups and downs of ministerial and church life.

Her eyes are wide open. She is ready for the process to begin. I was impressed with her maturity and outlook. No starry-eyed illusions. No dreamy visions of personally saving the world. Instead, a gritty commitment to go and get ready to do the work God would have her to do, and thanks to a supportive husband, family, and congregation, she will find encouragement along the way.

332

The Parable of the Rich Man and Lazarus (Luke 16:19-31) is unique in several ways. First, it is the only parable of Jesus that I know of that mentions the name of a person in the parable: Lazarus. Second, it seems to be the only parable where conversations go on between persons living in Hell (the rich man) and persons in Heaven (Abraham). Inside this story we find one of the most powerful eight-word statements in the Bible. Here is the statement: "The rich man also died and was buried" (16:22b). This man had everything. He was wealthy. He had all the possessions anyone could ever want. He "was dressed in purple (royalty?) and fine linen" and "feasted sumptuously every day" (16:19). But even with all that, "the rich man died." No amount of money, no measure of possessions made him immune to going the way of all flesh, sooner or later. "The rich man died." Someone could have asked, "How much did he leave?" Answer: "He left it all."

333

A pastor's greatest nightmares number at least three: forgetting a wedding, forgetting a funeral, and forgetting a visitation appointment. I forgot an appointment to meet a young couple at the church on a particular Saturday morning (10:00 A.M. was the agreed-upon time) to discuss their upcoming nuptials and have an informal conversation about marriage and family life. Trouble is, when we agreed on that date and time I immediately laid the thought aside in my mind. I might have put it down in my appointment book, but one must consult one's appointment book occasionally in order for the book to be of assistance, which I did not do in this case. As it happened, I generally made a run up to the church on Saturday mornings anyway to check on things, make any late changes in sermon plans, read mail, and basically make sure everything was all right. Guess what! I happened to drive into the church parking lot just as this same young couple got out of their car. The time was 9:55 A.M. I looked mighty good! I gave the appearance of being efficient! I was lucky. We went in and had our visit. They never knew.

334

Sowing seed is a biblical staple. Jesus told parables about it. The idea of doing good in the world involves sowing seeds of kindness and compassion. Galatians 6:7 tells us, "You reap what you sow." One year SMU (Southern Methodist University) went to Fort Worth to take on TCU (Texas Christian University) in football on the TCU field that had natural grass. At halftime the SMU band performed. They marched in circles, stood in formation, and played some songs. A few weeks after that game, grounds keepers at TCU noticed something: The letters "S M U" appeared on the field. It seems that their band, in doing their show that day, had sowed seeds of rivalry and humor, and thus, had the last word (up to that point) in the ongoing rivalry between neighboring universities.

335

In the 1970s four Memphis teenagers left early one morning to go to Nashville and Opryland, which had opened only months before. They spent the day there, had a good time, took pictures, and then headed back to Memphis. About forty miles out of Memphis they stopped to call their parents and tell them where they were. Shortly after that, something tragic happened. Their car crashed into the concrete abutment of an underpass and all four were killed. One of them was a member of a church I served as pastor. My wife was watching TV news the next morning and heard it. Not sure if one of the last names mentioned might be a family in our church, I drove to their house. Their daughter of about twelve years of age was there. She said her parents had gone to the funeral home. I caught up with them there and went with them into the room where you viewed the different caskets and made a selection. The mother cried out in pain and almost crumpled to the floor. At the funeral for all four, I assisted. Later, for our church newsletter, the parents sent a note thanking our church for support, flowers, prayers, food, and visits. Part of the note read, to this effect: "And we all know this is God's will." I did not want to include that in the newsletter. I did not agree with it. The church secretary said, "Yes, but this is what they wrote and this is how they feel." The entire letter was published in the next newsletter. Looking back, I still do not believe the tragedy was God's will. However, I think my greatest objection to having that part of the letter published was what people might think about the pastor of that family who, some would think, might have led them to believe that. So I was thinking of my reputation at that moment, more than the needs of the family. My secretary was right.

336

At another church two decades later, another secretary was right. I had a conflict with the church session (elders) over an issue involving the use of the church van and a youth trip. There was uncertainty as to whether the person who drove was on the approved driver list. It raised quite a stir. I decided to respond to complaints and accusations. I went into my office at 6:00 one morning after this and sat down and wrote out, in longhand, a six page letter giving details of how the decision was made, why other drivers were unavailable, and what I did about it all both before and after a wedding I conducted that very weekend at the church. The letter was a defense of my actions, but it was defensive in mode, too. Yet it would have explained everything, I thought. By the time the church secretary arrived at 9:00 I had completed the letter, having written feverishly for those hours. Now I wanted her to type it and we would mail it out to all elders. Then she said these words, "Tom, let it go." I said, "O.K.," and that was that. The letter was not sent. Any such mailing would have prolonged the argument, would have heightened the conflict, and could have become a major issue in the church. As it was, I think most people simply marked it down as another major blunder by their pastor and went on with other things.

337

A church in Washington, D.C. has started what is called the "Surrender Program." Persons with warrants for their arrests can enter the church building without threat of apprehension and can sit and talk with counselors and law enforcement officials. Through this process they can find out exactly how they stand with the law and can work with officials to take care of any outstanding fines or unfinished time. As it has turned out, several have discovered that it was possible to have all charges dropped and that being "on the loose" had not been necessary after all. This makes me think that the church at large has a "Surrender Program" going on, as all of us go to the church bearing the burdens of sin and loss and grief and despair and hopelessness, and we surrender ourselves to God. No wonder we can sing in worship, "I Surrender All."

338

The issue of "gay rights" is a political football. There are candidates "for" and other candidates "against." Political-action organizations abound with this as one of the major platforms. In a moment of inspiration, it occurred to me that "human rights" is the key word, and not "gay rights." What rights should human beings have? That is the issue. But, some would say, "This is a sin," or "That is a sin," and thus human rights do not apply. Let's remember that what is a "sin" has nothing to do with what is the "law." Many of us are not in prison whose sins have not broken any laws, and more than a few are in prison whose actions were unlawful but were not sins. I recall one who was on parole/probation, and who had to go back to prison because police found a gun in the back seat of his car, a violation of his parole/probation. Was that action or moment of carelessness a sin? I think not. I do believe persons are born with homosexual or heterosexual tendencies, and others are born with a little of both, some with major tendencies one way or the other. As one person said, "When a baby is born, we know the person's sex, but we do not know the person's sexual orientation." But that aside, what rights do human beings have? At the work place? In housing? In employment? By being human, persons should automatically inherit those rights.

339

I have decided that it is better to see the movie first, then read the book. Too many times have I been disappointed in the movie after reading the book first. At least once ("The Arrangement" starring Richard Boone and others) have I walked out of the theater (very early in the film, in fact) because of sheer dismay at the way the moving picture did not come close to the book. On the contrary, I saw "The Day of the Jackal," at the movies and on the way home stopped at a drug store and bought the paperback, and had it read in two days. It was great. In fact, I could "see" the characters as I read the book. Here is some more wisdom: Do not. I repeat. Do not go to see a movie and sit beside someone who has read the book. They are likely to give you a running commentary on how what you are seeing is different from what they read, and after it is all over, if you can stand it that long, they will tell you how much better the book was. The disparity between book and film may be one reason why I have never really enjoyed movies supposedly based on the Bible. But at least I can say that "I read the book." This is one problem regarding movies like "The Last Temptation of Christ" and "The Passion of Christ." So many people objected to and protested against the first because some of it was "not biblical" but many of the same people embraced the latter even though some of it was "not biblical."

340

Our church magazine several years ago had formal and informal pictures of our General Assembly and the many people who attended. Among the candid snapshots was one of a little girl asleep on a chair in the hotel lobby with a woman sitting in a chair beside her. The woman, Barbara Hester, told the photographer that the little girl climbed into the chair, turned to her and asked, "Are you a grandmother?" When the woman said, "Yes," the little girl curled up and went to sleep.

341

I am not a fisherman. I have been fishing once, maybe twice, in my lifetime, and did not enjoy it. However, I have a deep admiration for fisher(men)(women). I drive on the highway

**Time we spend fishin'
isn't counted against us**

and see folks fishing off a bridge, or down on the bank, or in a rowboat. They seem not to be in a hurry. They seem not to be anxious about anything. They wait patiently for the fish to bite. They may or may not have read that bumper sticker on a pick up truck in Texas that said, "THE LORD DOES NOT COUNT THE HOURS SPENT FISHING AGAINST ONE'S ALLOTTED TIME." I know not their religious preferences, if any - whether they are Protestant, Catholic, Jewish, or Muslim. I know not their political affiliations, if any - whether left, right, center, or off the chart, and whether Republican, Democrat, Libertarian, or Socialist. All I can observe is that time has virtually stopped for them. Whatever they have pressing back at home or at the work place can wait. Any great social or religious issues burdening them have been put aside. I am impressed with the biblical stories about fishermen and fishing. Some of the first twelve apostles that followed Jesus were "people of the net" ("throw out your nets"), such as Simon Peter, James, John, and Andrew. After the resurrection when things were even more confused and Jesus' followers did not know what to do next, Peter said, "I'm going fishing." What a good way to clear the mind and put things in perspective. I admire all who love to fish: their patience, their patience, and their patience. When Jesus calls us to be "fishers of people" we might be wise to remember the patience it takes when we go fishing.

342

Sometimes what moves people regarding Jesus is something beyond his words. He told Nicodemus he had to be "born again." He told the rich young ruler he must sell his possessions, give the money to the poor, and follow Jesus. He challenged some to receive the kingdom as a child, and still others to "hate father and mother, wife and children" before they could be his disciples. But that was not the case with Zacchaeus in Luke 19:1-10. After seeing the despised tax collector up in the tree, Jesus summoned him and then told him he was going home with him for dinner. That's all he told him. Zacchaeus immediately informed Jesus that "half of my possessions I give to the poor; and if I have defrauded anyone of anything, I will pay back four times as much." Notice what is NOT in the story. What is not in the story is any sign at all that Jesus prompted the publican on anything. There was no sign of a lecture, or scolding, or judgmental language, or condemnation for his past ways. The appeal of Jesus in this story was his own presence. It was an affirming presence, respecting Zacchaeus, believing in Zacchaeus, and being his friend. No evangelistic talk.

No "four steps to salvation" conversation. No dialogue about being saved. I was reading the in-house history of one of our Cumberland Presbyterian congregations, and it gave the testimony of a man who was then, or was later, a state senator in Tennessee. He said he and his family visited the church and early the next week the pastor visited them. Perry Mason was on, so they all watched Perry Mason. Then the pastor went home. The next time he visited they saw Perry Mason together again. And then again. Nothing about church. Nothing about Jesus. But here was someone willing to spend time with this family and by doing so showed they were important. They all later joined that church and were leaders in the congregation for years.

343

I admire those who fish, including ministers. They find kindred spirits in the church and out, and enjoy being with friends in that endeavor. Or maybe it is playing golf, or talking baseball or football or history or science-fiction or cooking. Most pastors are people, too, and these kinds of contacts help to illustrate that fact while providing outlets and a little bit of time away from the daily responsibilities of the church. Over in North Arkansas, where the White River flows, it is said there are more fishermen per square block than in any other part of the country. Several ministers I know are avid fishermen. I sat down with one a few years ago. I knew he loved to fish. I said to him, "Neill, have you been fishing lately?" He said, "Tom, it's been a long time since I have been fishing. A very long time. At least a week." I have observed, tongue-in-cheek, that when churches in that area need a pastor they should advertise and suggest strongly that the pastor should have a boat. Furthermore, the ad should state: "Send picture of boat."

344

Here in November of 2007, our nation finds its military men and women bogged down in a quagmire called the war in Iraq. Supposedly tied to the "war on terror" directed by the George W. Bush administration, its positive possibilities look more and more dim with each passing month. The year 2007 will go down as the worst for American fatalities since the conflict began in March of 2003, not to mention the thousands of Iraqi people killed plus the disruption of the entire citizenry in that land. Four words keep coming back to haunt us: "We invaded another country." Those four words speak volumes about the soul of the nation. We invaded another country. Not for what it did, but for what we thought it was going to do. I ask: What if other countries looked at us like we looked at Iraq? And what if they took the same liberties we did and invaded us based on what they thought - based on their best intelligence estimates, as we now say - we were planning to do? Disaster has come upon us. Our leaders keep changing the explanations as to why we invaded Iraq. Nothing seems to add up. Most of the suicide bombers in the 9-11 tragedy were from Saudi Arabia. Therefore, we invaded Iraq. We thought they had nuclear weapons. Hey, the USA has nuclear weapons. What if somebody decided to invade us because of the fact that we have weapons of mass destruction, like we invaded Iraq because of a supposed fact that turned out to be false? Buddhist monks in Myanmar have risked their lives and even given their lives in protest over the military crackdown in that land. I ask, where are our churches and where are our ministers? We have been cowed. We - and others who have tried to come out against this travesty in Iraq - have been labeled as unpatriotic, or against a strong national defense, or anti-American, and thus have been largely silent. Those four words still should haunt us: We invaded another country. How tragic. And now it is obvious we have engaged in torture or at least asked other countries to do it for us, in violation not only of the Geneva Convention but also our own collective moral values. We have lost our moral compass. It is nowhere to be found. I hope we find it some day and regain our soul.

345

"Water-boarding" has been used by our government in torturing suspected terrorists. Our leaders will not admit that this is done, but will not disavow it either. I read the following about this technique, which shows we are not the first. We have chosen to be a part of a select company. Notice the long quotation below:

"The water-torture was more ingenious, and more fiendish (than another form of torture described in the book previously). The prisoner was fastened almost naked on a sort of trestle with sharp-edged rungs and kept in position with an iron band, his head lower than his feet, and his limbs bound to the side-pieces with agonizing tightness. The mouth was then forced open and a strip of linen inserted into the gullet. Through this, water was poured from a jar, obstructing the throat and nostrils and producing a state of semi-suffocation. This process was repeated time after time, as many as eight jars sometimes being applied. Meanwhile, the cords round the sufferer's limbs were continually tightened until it seemed as though every vein in his body was at bursting point.

"Richard Hasleton, an Englishman, arraigned by the Holy Tribunal of Majorca in 1588, has left a heart-rending account of his sufferings on the rack. After undergoing the water-torment, he writes, he 'could have no feeling of any limb or joint but lay in a most lamentable and pitiful manner for four or five days having a continual issue of blood and water forth of my mouth all that space, and being so feeble and weak, by reason of my torments, that I could take no sustenance.'"

My source? The book entitled The Spanish Inquisition, by Cecil Roth (pp. 95-96, W. W. Norton & Company, 1964). The United States has joined the leaders of the Spanish Inquisition as practitioners of torture. What fine company! The depths of inhumanity and degradation to which our nation has stooped bring tears of anger and shame.

346

One minister calls it a question of "coincidence or providence." The issue? Romans 8:28. The King James Version says, "All things work together for good with those who love God...." The Revised Standard Version says, however, that "In everything God works for good with those who love him..." In the first, "all things work together for good," we have Coincidence. In the second, "God works for good," we have Providence. Since this fine minister highlighted these differences in a sermon (A. Leonard Griffith, in the book What Is A Christian? Abingdon, 1962), several more translations of the Bible have come off the press. I now own a New Revised Standard Version and when I got it I could not wait to turn and see what this version would say. If the KJV says, "All things work together for good..." and if the RSV says, "God works for good..." then I wondered what the NRSV would have to offer. I turned to the New Testament, then to Romans, then to Romans 8, then to Romans 8:28. Guess what! The NRSV harks back to what the KJV says: "All things work together..." However, the notes at the bottom of the page in Romans say that other manuscripts say "God makes all things work together for good," or "In all things God works for good." Looks like this verse has been worked and re-worked by scholars and they have narrowed it down to these possibilities. Each message is quite encouraging, isn't it.

347

A church in Texas wanted to honor its pastor who was retiring. He had been there sixteen years and had been in the active ministry fifty years. I got a letter asking me (and I'm sure others got a similar letter) to write a letter telling some stories about the honoree. I wrote about this: At the Cumberland Presbyterian Theological Seminary, there on the Bethel College campus in McKenzie, Tennessee, the students between classes would go and stand outside on the front steps of the Library-Seminary Building. There they would visit, and, if the timing was right, they would watch the female college students walk to and from their classes. I would be among the group. It was also a time, especially early in the week, for students to talk about their experiences of the most recent Sunday in their churches. The one who is retiring, mentioned above, told this. "An elder last Sunday came up to me after the service and said, 'Preacher, remember, the Bible says Jesus <u>opened</u> <u>his</u> <u>mouth</u> and taught them saying...'" From that conversation Bob Covington knew he needed to speak a little louder in the pulpit. Our church members have ways of letting us know what we need to do to be better preachers and pastors.

348

My wife's parents were members of a church that relocated from one side of town to the other. We had been there thirty years earlier as pastor and pastor's wife, and now were back for the dedication service of the new building at the new location. For years I had heard my father-in-law complain about one man in the church who was always negative, always pessimistic, always finding fault, never happy about much of anything. After the service in the sanctuary and then refreshments in the family life center, some of us were walking out and I was talking with this gentleman, hesitantly, of course, and listening mostly. It was a great revelation and relief to hear him say, about the new building on the new property, "Of course, we built this for our children and their children." What a positive and hopeful statement! My impression of him changed instantly! Along with his negatives were some positives.

349

This was a message on a church sign in its front yard, two letters on the top line, statement on the second:

K J
THE WORD OF GOD

Makes one wonder if there was a "word of God" before 1611, when the King James Version was published. Not to mention whether or not the numerous translations since 1611 have a grain of truth in them.

350

Sometimes you just don't know whether to say anything or keep silent. On a Monday morning in Burleson, Texas, I drove to the town's post office to check the church's box, then drove out of the parking lot to the monthly meeting of the Burleson Ministerial Association. It was a straight shot: down Johnson Drive, past the high school, turn left at the next street, and a quick turn at the First Christian Church. Trouble was, I got into too much of a hurry and a city policeman stopped me just after I had turned left at the Christian Church. In other words, I was right in front of the church. With the blue light flashing on his car, the officer got out, walked over, asked for my driver's license and registration and gave the usual speech about slowing down. He took his time with all this. In the meantime, as I was sitting there waiting for the officer to fulfill his responsibilities, the local First Methodist pastor pulled up into the church parking lot, got out, and looked my way. Then the pastor of the First Baptist Church drove up and did the same, peering over my way, then away, then in my direction again, as though he could not believe what he was seeing. Then the Roman Catholic priest, then the Assembly of God minister, then the Episcopal priest, then the pastor of Calvary Baptist. The Lutheran pastor couldn't stand to look. He kept his eyes focused on the church building. All along the officer was talking, writing out a ticket, letting the flashing light go on and on, and taking his own sweet time about it all, if I do say so myself. When all that was over, I went into the church for the monthly meeting of the Burleson Ministerial Association. Not a word was uttered about what they saw and what I experienced. We went on with our coffee and donuts and program for the day. I think they were being nice, or trying to. But which would have been better, some discussion of this incident or the silence we evidently informally covenanted to have? Which is better, to talk about something like that, or to say nothing? Does one way bring any more comfort to the offender than the other? I have wondered about that incident of thirty years ago, and I still don't know which is the better approach. I know the entire meeting was a painful time for this vile traffic offender.

෨෬෨෬෨෬෨෬෨෬෨෬෨෬෨෬෨෬෨෬෨෬

Chapter VI: 351-400

"Killing Half a Hog"

351

I was a young adult studying for the ministry and trying to be the preacher two Sundays a month each for a couple of congregations in West Tennessee. Each would have a summer revival. I stayed in the community with the evangelist on one of those occasions, and we ate big meals for breakfast, dinner (not lunch), and supper (not dinner). Sitting at the breakfast table of our hosts, we were eating country ham. The talk wandered to killing hogs. I tried to make conversation. It did not go too well. I said, "Somebody killed half a hog and my parents bought it and our family really enjoyed eating the pork chops, pork loins, sausage, and other tasty morsels." There was silence. Then the evangelist turned to me and said, "You said somebody killed half a hog." The country ham was a shade of red, but no redder than my face.

352

Another attempt at being "country" fell flat, too. I was a college student and substituted for the pastor at a rural church somewhere in Mississippi or Alabama on a Sunday and went to a church family's home for Sunday dinner. As we were eating, I tried to ingratiate myself with the people in the home. I noticed that the butter was round, not in rectangles, like you would buy in a store, so I said something to this effect: "It sure is good to eat real butter for a change. You get tired of margarine. This is really good." Total silence. Then the clearing of a throat from the wife/mother/hostess. "We bought this at the grocery store. It's margarine." That was pretty much the end of my quest to identify with the people of the home, church, and community that day.

353

The hardest work I ever did in the church and the least satisfying service I ever tried to provide was as the director of a summer church camp. I was out of my element. I did not want the job, never asked for it, and was trying to do it only because I was attempting to serve the church in whatever capacity requested. If I worked in the camp as a counselor, or teacher, or worship leader, I knew my place and my limitations and felt fine. In case of trouble, I could always say, "Go see the director." But when I was the director, there was no place I could go. It's tough being the leader when you don't know what you are doing. You count the days and hours and minutes until it's all over. You just hope to goodness that everybody has a good time and nobody gets hurt. I count every time, EVERY time that I have been a camp director (and there were probably five or six occasions) as uncomfortable, dues-paying, get-it-done-and-go-home duties to fulfill. Every minister has one's own areas of, let us say, comfort and fulfillment. Give me prison ministry. Give me Bible study. Give me adult retreats. I'll be glad to be the director of an adult conference, or a ministers' conference, or the Program of Alternate Studies. Send me to the most out-of-the-way place to speak or run a church errand, and I'll go. But do not, in this life or the next, ask me to be the director of another church camp.

354

A license plate on the back of a car stated the obvious:

IM B4 U

355

The story on the news was that twin sisters, adopted as infants by two different families and thus separated for years, got together again at age thirty seven. Surprisingly, or not so surprisingly, their reunion was at first hesitant and then warm and joyful. Each shared her life story with the other - marriage, children, work. There was a lot of "catching up" to do and each joined right in. When things settled down they began to remember the sadness as well, the cruelty, the heartlessness of such decisions years before. It was not until they became adults that they knew there was "another" out there. One doctor even did a study of the separated twins, as though they were primarily objects of research, reminiscent of Nazi experiments. The sisters will do just fine, but they know there are many lost years, times of togetherness and shared happiness stolen from them.

356

I cannot name one thing, at this time, any more aggravating than a grocery cart that will not go straight. A "Cart Named Trouble" not only makes the super market experience go bad but also negatively impacts the whole day, if not the entire week. You push and push and guide and guide and the cart still veers to the left all the time. By the end of the shopping experience, you are exhausted. You are not worn out. You are WORN OUT, which is worse than simply being worn out. There is very little reason to think positively about any of this. Perhaps one thing is that you know, the minute you start out, that you are in for a rough time. Just hunker down and take it. Occasionally there will be a new pastoral relationship between church and minister. All signs - before the minister and family move in - point to great things happening. But from Day One the chemistry isn't there. And it won't be long before everybody will know that "This is not working." And the pastor moves on after only a few months, if not weeks. It's just like that grocery cart, wrong from the start.

357

Another church sign:

> THE GOSPEL
> OF JESUS CHRIST
> SPOKEN HERE

358

I still remember the devotional an elder in the church gave one night at the start of a church session meeting. He traced the history of the human race in about four minutes. First, in our infancy and childhood, we are Dependent. Then we grow into adolescence and we are Independent. Later we move into adulthood and realize life is about being Interdependent. It makes so much sense. This brief history is so true. The life of being Interdependent is where we eventually arrive. There's a whole lot of Christian faith and action in that big word, Interdependent.

359

A couple in their sixties attended our church one Sunday. They had moved to the area a few months prior to that Sunday. Their daughter and her family are members. After that Sunday I visited in their home and they were most gracious. During the visit I accompanied the man to his basement where he showed me his wine collection. It was extensive and he took great pride in it. Several weeks went by before they attended our church a second time. It so happened that my sermon that day was entitled "And Noah Was Drunk." When I saw the couple walk in, I thought to myself, "Oh no," for I immediately began to fear that he might think I was directing any of the upcoming sermon to him. The message was not against drinking but against being drunk. One statement I remember saying was, "Drunk isn't funny anymore." I recalled a Dudley Moore movie where the character was not funny unless he was drunk. I also recalled a time when "drunk jokes" were acceptable or at least tolerated. But now with high numbers of traffic accidents caused by inebriated drivers and with public service announcements trying to slow down the fatality rate, the text in Genesis seemed appropriate. I am sure there were

Drunk is never funny

individuals present, members of the church, who imbibed once in a while. To my knowledge there was no one present that day with a drinking problem. But I felt really bad that on the second time for this couple to attend, the preacher let loose with this sermon. They, in fact, attended a few activities within the next few weeks, but eventually joined another church in the area. I still feel bad about the whole thing. It is a disservice for a minister to direct a sermon "at" somebody. It is the height of rudeness. Occasionally, it happens that sermon and person arrive on the same day, through no conspiracy or sneaky scheme by the preacher. This, however, may not be the way the person listening to the sermon may feel about it. Besides, any time I have prepared a sermon with someone specifically in mind, that individual will not be there. There may have been thirty seven years of perfect attendance up to that point, but that individual is not there this Sunday. And that is usually all to the good. While sermons should not be so general as to have no clear focus, they also should not be directed "at" anybody.

ℬ◌ℭℬ◌ℭℬ◌ℭℬ◌ℭℬ◌ℭℬ◌ℭℬ◌ℭℬ◌ℭ

360

All of us can look back and marvel at what our mothers put up with as we were growing up. Take us three boys, for example. Consider the doorway from the dining room to the kitchen. We would measure how tall we were by standing there and marking with a pencil on the doorway. Little by little, as the years went by, the pencil marks got higher and higher. Our mother did not say a word. Even worse, the dining room was big enough where you could bounce a ball, even a regular size basketball, and run back and forth and jump and shoot the ball over the doorway. When the ball bounced on the floor it would shake the room and even the house. She would caution us every now and then about breaking things, but she never complained (as I recall). Our goal without the ball was to jump and put our hands over the top of the doorway. This would often require a running jump. For a time we could not reach the top, but then we grew taller and eventually were able to touch it and then, later, to reach over it. The story does not get any better. The dining room table - that table is in our mother's dining room in Missouri right now - was almost the size of a regular ping pong table. Somehow she let us install a net and allowed us to play ping pong there. The interesting thing was that the table had a ridge all the way around. A player keen on victory could slant a shot just right to make it go over the net but hit one of those ridges, at which time the ball flew parallel to and away from the table at an excessive speed, not allowing the other player to return it. This became a science among some family members. I seem to recall our mother's justification for putting up with all of this. It went something like this: "Well, I knew where you were." She turned 96 in October of 2008.

361

I traveled to Japan in August of 2000 on the invitation of Japan Presbytery of the Cumberland Presbyterian Church. It was the fiftieth anniversary of the re-opening of denominational missions in that nation. As we toured the area and visited our churches (twelve in all) I noticed that in many, and maybe most, of the sanctuaries the communion ware was on the table. After seeing that several times, I said to somebody that "Next Sunday must be Communion Sunday, or last Sunday was." The reply was, "No, we keep the communion ware on the table even when it is not the time in order to remind ourselves of the event." My next thought was, "What a wonderful thing!" In America we store all the trays and haul them out once a quarter or perhaps a little more often, but then we store them again. Why not display this beautiful facet of our worship and devotion all the time?

362

When I traveled to Japan in the summer of 2000, one of the Cumberland Presbyterian churches visited was in a city not far from Mt. Fuji. It is a small congregation. The pastor provides English-speaking classes for college-age young people who desire to go to school in the States. He also has numerous weddings in a hotel in the city. He has conducted so many and the requests are so numerous that he has invited other Christian ministers to take part. The weddings are Christian services and most of the couples are Buddhist. They want the Christian service because it is so beautiful. He has this agreement with every couple. "I will conduct a Christian wedding if you will give me two hours, sometime prior to the wedding, to visit with you and talk about the Christian faith." He said they always agree to that. What a tremendous witness he has had!

363

Church conflicts come and go. In my childhood days - not that there was any great conflict about it - my home church went from overhead fans in the sanctuary to central air and heating. I do not recall any fuss over this. However, I am told that in much earlier times in America there was fear that if church facilities were made to be "too" comfortable, folks would not have enough appreciation of the rigors and sacrifices of the Christian life.

Then came the debates and harsh feelings about the Revised Standard Version of the Bible, especially in saying "young woman" instead of "virgin" in Isaiah. The National Council of Churches was lambasted and tarred with various labels of anti- or un-Americanism. Today there are so many translations of the Bible we have lost count. A typical congregation will have a variety of translations out there on a given Sunday. I do not even know what the most recent translation is called.

The next conflict was over new hymnals. In the late 1980s and early 1990s many of the mainstream Protestant denominations came out with new hymnals: Lutherans, Methodists, Presbyterians, Disciples. In just about all of the new editions, some new selections had been inserted and some old favorites had been omitted. This was bad enough, but in some cases some well known songs had their words altered to coincide with the emphasis on inclusive language. This cut more deeply than any new insertions or omissions. But that, too, has passed, and in whatever ways available, church folks have adapted and moved on.

Next came "contemporary" worship. This seems to be an attempt to appeal to youth and young adults, but older adults like it, too. It does away with many of the traditions of worship, such as creeds, affirmations of faith, unison prayers and readings, confessions of sin, and other basics. Contemporary worship centers more on group singing of choruses, many recently written, led by a band or orchestra or group of musicians and vocalists. Lots of churches - large, small, and in-between - have felt the need to integrate this type into their worship life. A few try to mesh the two - contemporary and traditional - together in one service. Others have an 8:30 A.M. or 9:00 A.M. service of one, and then an 11:00 A.M. service of the other. Whether a truce has been declared or the "war" goes on, it seems that many congregations have settled in to trying to do both. Some of these churches are growing. But others, sticking with the traditional, are growing, too. Some churches are able to pull this off - have two distinct services - but a few are struggling to make the contemporary worship a meaningful event.

Whatever the style of worship, one hopes that the <u>sermon</u> would be traditional, contemporary, relevant, timely, timeless, biblical, faithful to the gospel, inspirational, heart-rending, appropriate, prophetic, pastoral, evangelistic, instructive, and much more.

ಸಿಂಜಿಸಿಂಜಿಸಿಂಜಿಸಿಂಜಿಸಿಂಜಿಸಿಂಜಿಸಿಂಜಿಸಿಂಜಿಸಿಂಜಿ

364

In a bank in Burleson, Texas, during part of the 1970s, was a display, under glass. The sign invited people to look at two one hundred-dollar bills, two fifty-dollar bills, two twenty-dollar bills, two ten-dollar bills, two five-dollar bills, and two one-dollar bills, and judge which was real and which was counterfeit, for in each category there was one of each. The two bills in each section looked exactly alike to me. And, I am sure, to others as well. One could inquire and find out which was which, but to the naked eye, they were the same. It's hard to see people and hear their claims and know if they are for real or if they are counterfeit. Sincere, well-meaning people have made decisions based on as much depth of research as they could muster, and they would later find out that the pastor they selected, the teacher they selected, the president or dean they selected, was "all hat and no cattle" as JoLean (played by Kate Capshaw) says to H.D. (played by Scott Glenn) in the movie "My Heroes Have Always Been Cowboys." Some money experts can spot a flaw in a bill immediately while the rest of us don't know what to look for or can't see it. But in regard to people, it is usually as we experience the person, and the passage of time, that we come to know whether someone is real or counterfeit.

365

A former Miss America was asked on a television talk show one time how she won so many beauty reviews that culminated in the national prize. Her answer: "Stand by somebody ugly." We need somebody to be "better than." We need to stand by somebody worse than we are so we can look good. Looking good "in comparison to" somebody else seems to be a need of ours. I know I contributed to that in my first years of living in the suburbs of a city as a young pastor. I was one year out of seminary. I would hear folks in my suburb and at church talk about "St. Augustine," and I thought they must know a lot about theology around here, since they refer to "St. Augustine" often. Turns out that is a kind of grass. Up in West Tennessee I remember weeds and dandelions and Bermuda grass and not much more. In this Fort Worth suburb, all the neighbors took care of their yards. Some of them were out there every day working on something. I just wanted to get by, and not be an embarrassment to the housing development in which we lived, so I at least kept our yard mowed. You can understand why over the years more than one family living next door to us won the coveted "Yard of the Month" award. It was easy: they were living next door to us. I think this may have been the Pharisee's logic, as well, when he went to the temple to pray. "God, I think you that I am not like... this tax collector."

366

Sign in front of a church:

> MY BOSS IS A JEWISH CARPENTER

367

The Cumberland Presbyterian Youth Conference (CPYC) has a long and honored history. It traces its beginnings back to the 1920s when the "Young People's General Assembly" (YPGA) began. My mother, age 96 in this the year of our Lord 2008, attended YPGA at Ovoca Conference Grounds near Tullahoma, Tennessee, as a youth from Oklahoma. The conference continued as YPGA until the 1960s when the name was changed to National Assembly of the Cumberland Presbyterian Youth Fellowship (NACPYF). By 1973 the name was Cumberland Presbyterian Youth Conference

(CPYC). After being at Ovoca for several years the conference was held in different places, such as Camp Cumberland in Missouri; Chickasaw State Park in Tennessee; Ferncliff Conference Grounds in Arkansas; and Bethel College in Tennessee. When Cumberland Presbyterians decided to have integrated conferences, Ovoca closed their doors to us. Bethel College was always open. At one of the events at Bethel a young African-American minister named Andrew Young was a featured speaker. Such inspiring leaders as Clark Williamson (at the start), Franklin Chesnut, Morris Pepper, Harold Davis, and Frank Ward stand out as shapers of this denomination-wide conference. Until about thirty years ago the event was for college-age youth and high school youth. But around the late 1960s or early 1970s eligibility was narrowed to young people ready for grades 10, 11, and 12, in high school, and the first year of college. In 1980 the Cumberland Presbyterian Church became involved with other Presbyterians in the Presbyterian Youth Triennium, an every-three-years event held at Purdue University in West Lafayette, Indiana. With each Triennium, the numbers of Cumberland Presbyterian youth in attendance have increased. For CP youth and adults who have attended both CPYC and Triennium at one time or another, they recognize the similarities in program and format. This can be attributed to the organizational skills and creativity of Frank Ward, now the Executive Director of the Board of Christian Education who was for over thirty years the Youth Ministry/Outdoor Ministry director for the Board. He is one of the major leaders of the Triennium where as many as 6,000 youth attend. His hard work and that of his staff of volunteers that culminates in the annual July event we call CPYC have been of great benefit to our denomination. Many leaders of the church have emerged from those wonderful experiences. When I think back to my days as a youth at YPGA and then as an adult leader at CPYC, I celebrate the patience, understanding, and vision of leaders like Clark Williamson, Franklin Chesnut, Morris Pepper, Harold Davis, and Frank Ward. Board executives have been, in succession since the 1950s, Morris Pepper, Harold Davis, Claudette Pickle (also with the Board for over thirty years, most of the time in curriculum development), and now the current leader, Frank Ward. We have been blessed!

He was in line to greet this pastor after the service. When he shook my hand he said, "I'm going into the hospital for surgery on Tuesday." I was surprised. He looked the picture of health. Turns out the situation was serious and surgery was urgent. To look at him one would have thought that all was well. But one never knows what goes on inside. Many years ago Dr. Jose Fajardo, from Colombia, South America, was preaching somewhere in the States. He told of a majestic tree in that country that had stood for centuries. One day it crumpled and came crashing down. It was then discovered that the tree was dead inside. It looked alive, but it was dead. We see one another in church, in town, at school and work. But we do not know the internal struggles, worries, anxieties, concerns, pain, or sadness that may burden others. We are wise in assuming that all people have their internal struggles and burdens everyday. All the more reason to be kind to one another.

369

Sports terminology permeates our lives. One time, Avis, the mother, stayed home from church, not feeling well. Her husband, Vaughn, and two sons Gary and Donald attended and when they got home she asked how things went and who was there. Donald, when asked about a certain couple, said, "They left at the half." Translation: They came to Sunday School but left between Sunday School and the worship service.

370

I have not read very many of Sidney Sheldon's novels, but I do know this. With each one, it is hard to lay it aside for any reason. The story moves swiftly and the end of one chapter leads on to the beginning of the next in such a way that putting the book down is not an option. Any time I talk about the Gospel of Mark I compare it to a Sidney Sheldon novel. Just look at the first chapter of Mark where in the Revised Standard Version the word "immediately" appears nine times. The same chapter in The New Revised Standard Version has "immediately" four times with phrases such as "as soon as" or "at once" replacing the word in some instances. But notice the times that both versions have the word: "And the Spirit <u>immediately</u> drove him out into the wilderness" (1:12); "And <u>immediately</u> they left their nets and followed him" (1:18); "<u>Immediately</u> he called them and... they followed him" (1:20); "<u>Immediately</u> the leprosy left him" (1:42). The remaining chapters of Mark move just as swiftly. Indeed, the full reading of the Gospel of Mark takes very little time. I once attended a chapel service here at Memphis Theological Seminary where a professional actor brought us the entire book in dramatic form in fewer than forty five minutes, perhaps within thirty. Evidently the writer of Mark was in a hurry, feeling a need to move on with the story. He only mentions that Jesus was tempted in the wilderness and does not tell what the temptations were. He does not tell anything of the Christmas story: no shepherds, no angels, no innkeeper, no wise men, no manger. You can't find any inspiration for Christmas carols in Mark! And he has a rather abrupt ending of his Gospel. So, fasten your seat belts, bring your seat backs to an upright position, turn off all cell phones, extinguish all smoking materials, and hang on. It's time to read the Gospel of Mark.

ೞಬಐಬೞಬಐಬೞಬಐಬೞಬಐಬೞಬಐಬೞಬಐಬೞಬಐಬೞಬಐಬ

371

I had a flat. It was the right rear tire. My son-in-law (husband of our youngest daughter) was available to take this tire off and put on the spare. The equipment in the trunk had never been used in the four years I had driven the car. When he arrived he took the unused spare and the jack out of the trunk. Then he did one more thing. It was shocking what he did next! He reached one more time into the trunk and came out with a most unfamiliar (to me) book.

It was the Owner's Manual. Before he lifted anything or unscrewed anything or turned anything, he took some drastic, revolutionary, scandalous action: He read the instructions. I had never ever done such a thing. Ever. As mentioned, I have driven the car for four years and have never

Have we read our owner's manual?

opened the Owner's Manual. It would have taken too much time. There would have been too much reading. I knew there would be a Part A and Part B, and instructions to raise this and turn this and fold this. Yet, my lack of experience and familiarity with the book notwithstanding, when he arrived one of his first steps was to read the instructions. He sat down on the curb and read the instructions. He not only knew where to look in the Owner's Manual; he knew what to do after he found the appropriate section. I was so grateful he was available to take care of this. I still haven't gotten over the fact that he read the instructions. Maybe my keeping a distance from written instructions goes back to when Linda and I stayed up almost all night on Christmas Eve trying to assemble different toys for three little girls. When the work was over, we always ended up with two screws and three other extra parts, making one wonder if the toys assembled would stand for very long. Maybe it's a "man" thing" - this refusal to read the instructions. We men have a reputation for not stopping and asking directions when driving and getting lost. It is a sign of weakness to admit you are lost! In regard to reading the instructions, I hope I don't ever feel that way about the Bible, whose written instructions still speak to us. Fortunately, they are not too complicated, though somewhat difficult to achieve, what with our human faults creating some problems. It is good from time to time to "read the instructions" in the Scriptures. That means taking some time, sitting down on the curb, and studiously reading what the Bible says.

372

Somewhere, long ago, I read this: The pastor was at his desk in his study during Sunday morning activities. He heard a voice: "Preacher?" But could not see anybody. Then he halfway stood and saw a little boy on the other side, whose height brought him barely even with the desk top. "Preacher?" the boy asked again. "Yes, Billy, can I help?" "Preacher, what is the littlest room in all the world?" The pastor thought and thought, and then said, "I do not know. What is the littlest room in all the world?" Billy replied, "A mushroom." The pastor went back to his work but Billy didn't leave. "Preacher?" he asked again. "Yes, Billy." "What is the biggest room in all the world?" "I really don't know," said the amused and also curious pastor. "What is the biggest room in all the world?" And Billy said, "Room for improvement."

373

The public reading of Scripture is too often overlooked as an important item of worship. Once I read where someone said that hearing some Scripture read was like "hearing the minutes of the last meeting." Ministers would do well to pay heed to this aspect of worship leadership. Some element of passion is called for, as well as personal involvement in the particular reading. I am happy to say that I have heard some very good readings of Scripture. On one occasion the one who was to be the preacher was to read the Scripture and then the liturgist (worship leader) was to return to the podium, lead the morning prayer, and announce the next hymn which immediately preceded the sermon. Communion would follow the sermon. However, the reading of the Scripture for the day was so powerful, so moving, so majestic, so expressive while flowing naturally from the lips of the one who would preach, that all of us were affected. This was truly a holy moment and I am sure some of us felt like it would be appropriate to take off our shoes, for we knew we were on holy ground. The liturgist then stood and, having also been moved, began the opening sentences for the communion service - and it was not yet time! The preacher tried to signal him; I as coordinator for the event, tried to motion to him; others did, too, until the liturgist realized something was wrong. He easily backtracked, got back on schedule and moved the service forward in an orderly manner. I remember that after the sermon, the communion, and the conclusion of the service, another minister who had been in the congregation said to the preacher, "Thank you for the sermon - both of them."

ഇരുഇരുഇരുഇരുഇരുഇരുഇരുഇരുഇരുഇരു

374

As I recall the story that I read in a civic club newsletter, it went something like this: A young man in his late twenties and just out of college moved with his wife to a small town where he would be teaching seventh grade, starting in a couple of months. He was really excited about his first teaching job, and it was to be with kids. They moved into a big two-story house on a street on the south edge of town. There was no sidewalk in front of the house so he decided to build one running from one end of the property to the other. Next door to the house, on both sides were vacant lots. So he purchased the ingredients, the wheelbarrow, the shovel, the sand, the cement mix, everything needed to make a sidewalk. He installed the long boards outlining where the sidewalk would be, prepared the mix, stirred like crazy, and poured the mix onto the ground up and down the length of the planned sidewalk. It was back-breaking work and took all day, but he finished, late in the afternoon, just about the time a softball game involving young kids was starting in the vacant lot to the left, looking toward the house. Right after he went into the house, he peered out to examine his handiwork and wait for it to harden. Just then somebody hit a ball a country mile and it landed in the soft cement. Then a couple of young players ran to get the ball and both of them managed to step into the mix as well. There were footprints and more footprints as they wrestled each other for the ball and sloshed around in the once neat-looking creation. Understandably upset, the young teacher-to-be raced out of the house and yelled at the kids. He not only yelled at them, he hurled criticisms at them, questioning the legitimacy of their origins and expressing his own preferences as to their eventual eternal destinations. In other words, he was mad. After running them off his property, he re-entered the house, still huffing and puffing. His wife, wise and insightful, said, "Honey, I thought you liked kids." Then, and only then, did a slight upturn in his expression take place when he said, "Well, I like them in the abstract, but not in the concrete."

375

The power of suggestion is always present. A young couple went to a cookout and later got very sick, almost violently ill. They were so ill that they called to see if they could bring their little girl over to stay with us while they tried to weather the stomach storm. When the young father brought their daughter over, he said, just before making a quick exit back to the car, that both he and his wife had consumed Ranch Dressing that night and it was spoiled. It was years before I could even consider having Ranch Dressing again. Every time I saw a bottle of it, I remembered how miserable and sick Mark and Elinor had become, and I wanted to keep my distance. Several years later - maybe ten or fifteen - I happened to talk with them about this and they said that it turned out that the problem was not the Ranch Dressing, for others at the cookout also ate it and they were not affected. Ranch Dressing was not the culprit. But even at that, it was months before I even tasted that delicacy again. The power of suggestion was still strong.

376

Sometimes in a conversation you want to call "Time out! Wait just a minute!" You are talking with someone. They are handling most of the conversation, giving information, stating opinions, evaluating situations. Then maybe you ask a question and the subject gets "serious." Then the other person says, "Well, I'll be honest with you," and then go on to discuss the issue. That's when you want to call a halt for just a moment, and ask, "You mean that up to now you have not been honest with me?" What does it mean when people say, "Well, I'll be honest with you." Or they say something like this: "I'll be frank with you." You mean you have not been frank up to now? Can you imagine our Lord in talking with his disciples gets to a very important point and says, "Fellows, I'll be honest with you, you cannot live by bread alone." No, his honesty shines through. There is no need to bring in this element. This phrase supposedly raises the seriousness level of a conversation, but it really calls into question the truthfulness of what has been said up to this point.

377

Nobody's perfect, and no thing is perfect. Neither is any book perfect. The classic work on preaching, <u>The Servant of the Word</u>, by H. H. Farmer (Fortress), was published in 1942, and its American version came out in 1964. One would think that proofreading that failed to catch mistakes in the first printing would have been done better for the second printing, but even at that, this great book contains at least one glaring printing error. The first sentence of the first chapter says: "If one were asked to indicate in the briefest possible way the most central and distinctive trends in contemporary Christian theology, one would be tempted to answer 'the rediscovery of the significance of peaching.'" That's right: "peaching." Not "preaching" but "peaching." And it's the first sentence in the first chapter! Now I happen to know the rest of the book discusses "preaching" and not "peaching," but one would think that somebody, in the space of twenty two years between printings, would have caught this and corrected it. I have had something to do with a couple of books and, try as we might, after hours and hours of reading and re-reading and proofreading and repeating the process, something showed up after the final printing and publishing that was so obvious one wonders how that glaring mistake was missed. Life is forever fraught with flaws - in books, pastors, churches, wives, husbands (well, some husbands), children, schools, accomplishments. We may aim for perfection but are wise in knowing it is not going to be dune and their is know weigh under hevun to make it purrfect.

378

Somewhere, in somebody's picture album, Linda and I are in a group picture with other Jehovah's Witnesses. We were, for a brief moment - but now, for much longer than that due to the picture - part of that great movement. When we lived in Knoxville, Tennessee, one of our daughters gave us certificates for two meals at Red Lobster. Instead of the restaurant nearest our neighborhood, we tried the one in west Knoxville. When we walked in we saw what looked like a hundred people, all wearing badges of some kind, and we knew we would be a long time getting served. So we jumped in the car and sped back to our familiar Red

Lobster. We were waited on promptly and our food was brought in good time. About that time a whole host of people came in, and they had the same kind of badges. They scooted some tables together and the one at the end came right up to the booth where we were seated. We were only a couple of feet away from another couple. We got to talking with some of them. I thought: These surely are friendly, nice people. They look and sound like Methodists, or maybe Baptists. And, what's more, they said they were all from Arkansas, so we had a lot to talk about. It wasn't long before they identified themselves as Jehovah's Witnesses. Their convention was being held in the Thompson-Boling Arena on the campus of the University of Tennessee. Soon someone in the group stood at the other end to take some pictures. Linda and I leaned forward for the click of the camera and we are pretty sure there are folks in Arkansas who now are asking, "Who is that cute couple at the end? Are they from your group in Conway?" "No, I thought maybe they were from Pine Bluff."

379

Jehovah's Witnesses hold their conventions in many places around the country: high school gyms, civic centers, convention centers, baseball stadiums. They are the very best in tidying up and cleaning the facilities they use, but they go beyond that to make them even neater and cleaner than before. A member of our Cumberland Presbyterian Church in Batesville, Arkansas, back in the early 1960s, was the custodian of the local high school. He reported the above after they had used the school gymnasium for a convention. Much more recently, a person who rode with them on a chartered bus that her husband drove from Mississippi to New York City for a convention in 2007 made the same observation: They left the facility in New York cleaner than when they found it. They are to be admired and respected for their diligence and conscientious actions.

380

Every person is important in church. Anyone absent is missed. Especially is this true in a small church. I recall reading about early American times - well before electricity. In some churches worshipers would bring their oil lamps and would hang them on the wall next to where they would be sitting. If they were present, their part of the church would have light. If they were absent, their part of the sanctuary would be dark. Still today, when our folks are present, they help light up the sanctuary and when they are absent, things are just not right. It is still appropriate to sing, "Brighten the corner where you are."

381

The television news this week is carrying a story about a middle school principal who has volunteered to donate a kidney in order to save the life of one of his students. All things match up. The surgery will be soon, it appears. No big thing, as far as he is concerned. It's the right thing to do. This version of "neighbor helping neighbor" moves the spirit and warms the heart. This is what people do for each other. It's a good world, and it is made better by such deeds as that of this middle school principal.

382

This was seen on the bottom of the TV screen - one of those "moving" announcements that one often misses: "In Greece a beggar is given the first slice of the Christmas loaf." That's all it said. No elaboration. No explanation. No clarification. No promise of "story at ten." But what a wonderful tradition.

383

The ballerina had finished her concert and was meeting reporters back stage. One reporter asked, "In your third presentation, what were you trying to say?" Her answer: "If I could have said it, I would not have danced it."

384

Self-reliance comes in many packages. The multi-billionaire Warren Buffet, who, incidentally, thinks the rich in America ought to be taxed much more than they are, paid the full fare for his children's college. They could go anywhere, no matter the cost, and he would pay for it. It didn't matter: Ivy League school, prestigious New England colleges, any school anywhere. But then this: Their college paid for, once they were out, they were on their own. No more help from him. And it is said Mr. Buffet brown bags it every day for lunch.

385

Our parents have been present at graduations for high school, college, graduate school. They were at every event when our sister won many honors in high school and at Bethel College. They were in Fort Worth, Texas, when I received the Doctor of Ministry degree from Brite Divinity School of Texas Christian University. They were in Washington, D.C., when Sam received the degree of Doctor of Education from George Washington University. They were in Columbia, Missouri, when Paul received his degree from the prestigious University of Missouri School of Journalism. Now I am a parent and a grandparent. I understand more now. And I appreciate their commitment to us even more than I did previously.

386

My parents were great sports fans, especially where their children were involved. We three boys had a presence on the varsity basketball team of McKenzie, Tennessee, high school for eleven consecutive years. Our sister Jo Nell, played basketball her senior year on the McKenzie High School girls team, prior to the involvement of us boys. I was fortunate as a senior to be on a team that ranked high in our district (My younger brother Paul was a freshman on the team; he would in subsequent years have some outstanding games and seasons. In his junior and senior years he would be coached, by the way, by our older brother, Sam. Sam would later move to Northern Virginia and have a great record in Virginia high school basketball. Sam in his senior year in high school - I was an eighth grader - was captain of a team that had a winning record and was one of the top teams in the district.). During the winter and spring of my senior year (1957), our father was in graduate school at The University of Chicago. He and I had talked, and he said that if we got to the finals of the district tournament he would take a train and be there for the game. Our semi-final game was on Thursday and I called him late that night to report that we had won. The finals would be on Saturday night. He took the train from Chicago to Fulton, Kentucky, on Friday, and a family member drove the forty miles from McKenzie to Fulton and was there to meet him. On Sunday afternoon, after we won the championship the previous evening, I drove him over to Fulton and he got back to Chicago by train late that night.

387

Clarence Tucker (not his real name) and his family attended the St. Matthew Cumberland Presbyterian Church in Burleson, Texas, for a few months back in its earlier years, the late 1970s. We had become acquainted before that, at the St. Luke Cumberland Presbyterian Church up the road back in the late 1960s and early 1970s. Clarence and his wife had two daughters. When we saw each other again at St. Matthew, after the passing of a few years, I learned that both daughters were married. The older, Karen, had a couple of children. The younger, Mary, had lost a little girl at birth. Clarence got sick. A heavy smoker, he contracted lung cancer. His dying was a long, painful process. The funeral service was held at the St. Matthew Church. The funeral procession moved to the cemetery where we had the brief interment ceremony. Afterwards, many people stayed at the grave site and visited. I stood back from the gathering and I heard heavy crying and wailing coming from another direction. I looked a few yards away and a woman was on her knees at a grave. She was trembling and sobbing, lost in another experience of pain and grief. The tombstone had the name of a little girl, and the dates of birth and death, one day apart. The woman was Mary.

388

George Washington was, by all accounts, a wise man. He may have been a man of few words, but what he said was usually weighty. In a book entitled The Summer of 1787 - The Men Who Invented the Constitution, there was a discussion about a standing army. When one delegate suggested that it should be limited to 3,000 men, Washington, who was presiding, said that would be well and good if we could get all our enemies to agree to attack us with no more than 3,000 men.

389

We were having some repairs done at our house and had moved sofas, chairs, tables, lamps, and cabinets around to make way. Now we were moving everything back, and a lamp just was not working. We put in a new bulb but that made no difference. The old bulb had been especially difficult to unscrew and the new bulb was no easy matter in its installation as well. And now the lamp was not working. Perhaps it had been moved one time too many. Or maybe there was a fixture loose in its inner workings. I was about to give up when my wife thought about doing one more thing, something we had not yet done: plug it in!! That done, the lamp was like its old self. It is amazing what technological knowledge will do for you. I think we would all do a little better if we were plugged in... to the right things. And if we are not functioning like we should be, we may yet be unplugged. So we plug in to God, to the Scriptures, to Christ, to Christ's concerns and compassion, to life.

390

My wife came home from shopping and among the items purchased were four little strips that she said could be installed in the bathtub so a person would not slip and fall. As of this writing, helpful as they might be, I have not installed them. In this case, "installing" them is tearing a little strip of paper away from each and pressing the remaining material onto the floor of the tub. But when I do, if I ever do, they will help me not to slip and fall. Would that there were such strips we could install on our feet so we would not slip and fall during our spiritual walk. There are many helps, but there is no complete protection. Yet we know when we fall, God is there to help us get up and keep going.

391

A fellow pastor was answering the question as to how the church was doing. "We are doing fine," he said. "However," he continued, "a couple of families have left the church because they did not like it when we started going out to the trailer park and bringing those folks and their children to church." Just when we think we Christians have a handle on what the church is all about, something happens to bring us back to the reality of our imperfections.

392

As a pastor, I had many weddings in the church where no one in the wedding party was a member of that church or even an occasional visitor. It was always with a sense of ministry that I embarked on any planning and counseling with the couple. I found there were two types of non-member and non-related couples who had their weddings in our church. There were those who wanted to use the building and there were those who wanted to <u>use</u> the building. The first honored the requests, suggestions, and regulations regarding use of the facility - cheerfully, gladly, gratefully. The second paid no attention to any restrictions and, until stopped by me and others in the church, proceeded to move pulpit and altar furniture around, willy nilly. The absolute worst happened in a little church in Arkansas where I preached on Sunday morning, driving over from Memphis. A nice Christmas tree had been placed in the sanctuary, wonderfully decorated, beautiful lights, majestic in every way. There was to be a wedding on the Saturday night prior to the Christmas program at the church on Sunday night. In this case the couple were students at a local college and were entirely unrelated to anyone in this church, had no connections, and had never attended a worship service. They just liked the way the church looked there in its rural setting set back amidst some pretty trees. Despite the instructions given and the understandings our church folks established with the couple and their party about keeping things as they were, when all of us arrived at the church on Sunday morning, the Christmas tree was out in the church yard, decorations and all, just tossed out there like so much trash. No note. No letter of apology. No request to be forgiven. No check or cash to cover church expenses. Nothing. Fortunately this is a rare occasion. Most people recognize that they are guests in a church facility and treat it accordingly. In fact, over the years of my pastorates, there have been several times when the couples involved (and their families) were not participants in the church, but they eventually did become so, due, in part, I think, to the courtesies and services extended by the church.

393

The Doctrine of the Trinity is a mystery. It deserves the capital letters it received in the first sentence. It is not specifically mentioned in the New Testament, and there are few occasions there when "Father, Son, and Holy Spirit" are in the same sentence. The Great Commission in Matthew 28:16-20 contains this, as does Paul's closing in 2 Corinthians 13:13. Christians are "Trinitarians," although that sounds like a dangerous word. This means we are not "Unitarians," although the way we emphasize one Person over the other Two sometimes would almost make us so. How best to understand this great concept has escaped us over the years. We keep trying. Most of our explanations and descriptions fall short, including the following:

Twice a week I carry out the trash. That's what the <u>husband</u> does. When I would go see my mother, no matter the time of day or night, she would have something cooked and ready to eat. For that moment I was the <u>son</u> in the story. At the wedding of a niece, none of her other uncles could be present. For that time and place, I was the <u>uncle</u>. One of our daughters got off work and rushed to a nearby town where she was going to start on a second job. She had very little time. I was afraid she would try to drive too fast. So after she had been gone for several minutes, I got in my car and followed the route I thought she would take. I looked right and left, but there were no cars in the ditch, or wrapped around trees. I kept on driving and kept on looking. Finally I arrived at the shopping mall where the grocery store was where she had begun work. Her car was there! I guess you could say I was being the <u>father</u>. On the occasion of our sister's death, we attended our funeral. I had a chance to visit with Sam and Paul. The three of us were together during the day. I was a <u>brother</u>. In recent years I have become a <u>grandfather</u>. I have been a <u>son-in-law</u> for over forty five years, and a <u>brother-in-law</u> for longer than that, what with my sister's marriage back in 1948. Just my family relationships themselves add up to these eight roles and much more besides. Yet I am one person. Is it possible to understand the Trinity, at least in part, by seeing the three Persons in the roles they fulfill? <u>Father</u>: Creator, All-Powerful, All-Wise, Omnipotent, Omniscient. <u>Son</u>: Savior, Lord, Friend, Advocate, Intermediary. <u>Spirit</u>: Ever-present, Strength, Courage, Conscience. Maybe. Maybe not. Just a thought. I realize that I may have committed the theological error of modality, but at least this helps me understand the Trinity somewhat.

394

I know very little about the German language. I have heard others say that in speaking the usual sentence, a person would say the noun at the last part of the sentence. The following story, exaggerated as it may be, is fun to ponder: Two friends went to hear a person lecture. It was to be given in German. After listening to the first fifteen minutes, one was bored and decided he had enough. He got up to go. His friend pulled him back down to his seat and pleaded, "Wait a little longer. Give him time. He hasn't gotten to the noun yet."

395

Time can be a friend or an enemy. A football coach whose team is leading but the other team is coming back strong thinks the clock is ticking too slowly. The coach whose team is behind needs just a little more time, but the clock seems to be ticking too fast for him.

A preacher can zip right through a sermon enthusiastically and simply run out of time, and all goes well. The next Sunday the same preacher can discover quickly that what was planned was not worth the saying. It is dull, uninteresting, less than urgent, and boring. Even the preacher is bored - and the sermon has been going for only four minutes! Time can be a friend or an enemy.

396

The wife wants to go shopping and the husband is watching the football game on television. She is pressing to go, but he is stalling. Then he says, and correctly: "Just two more minutes and the game will be over." So she waits. Thirty minutes later the game is finally over, what with time outs, commercial breaks, and incomplete passes that stopped the clock, "I thought you said it would be just two minutes!" His reply: "This is <u>football</u> time." Then they go to the mall. "I'll wait in the car," he says. She says, "O. K." He inquires, "How long will you be?" "About thirty minutes." He settles in with his book and the car radio. Two hours later she returns to the car. "I thought you said it would be thirty minutes." "Yes," she answered, "But that's <u>mall</u> time."

397

Back when car rentals were becoming big business, Hertz was the leader. Avis was in second place. In its advertisements and commercials, Avis made a big thing out of "We're number two!" and "We try harder." In preaching, I have tried to make a big thing out of the question: "What was Adam's second sin?" In Genesis 3 we read the account of Adam's first sin as well as his second. But what was the second sin? Just as Avis, being number two, had to "try harder," so Adam's second sin, often ignored or forgotten, has to "try harder" to be acknowledged. And what was it? What was Adam's second sin? It was the failure to acknowledge his first sin! He blamed God. He blamed Eve. But he refused to take the blame himself. It was everybody else's fault. His second sin was his unwillingness and failure to acknowledge his first sin.

398

Ed Schreiber came into our lives when he was 93 years old. He wrote a letter to a Seminary professor in Memphis who passed it on to me. Pretty soon Ed was enrolled in the Program of Alternate Studies (PAS). He lived in Nashville, Tennessee. He had degrees from New York University, George Peabody College, and other schools. In the late 1920s he was enrolled in what was then called Vanderbilt School of Religion and was told he should choose some other profession than ministry. He became a city planner and administrator, as well as an avid reader, community activist, and school administrator. He also taught school. He was on the committee that went to look at some property just east of Dickson, Tennessee, as a possible state park. He and the other committee members thought well of it. It became Montgomery Bell State Park. The Cumberland Presbyterian Church Birthplace Shrine sits within that property. Ed was an elder in the Hillsboro Presbyterian Church and later in Brookhaven Cumberland Presbyterian Church in Nashville.

In the Fall, Winter, and Spring, PAS conducts what are called Weekend Extension Schools. In the late 1990s I would drive from Memphis to Nashville on my way to one of those schools and run by Ed's house and he would join me. We traveled to South Pittsburg, Tennessee; Kelso, Tennessee; and Gadsden, Alabama, as well as other places to attend the classes. In July 1997 Ed attended our school which was held on the campus of Bethel College in McKenzie, Tennessee. We have three five-day sessions. He attended all fifteen days and did so for six consecutive years, a couple of those years even after he had graduated from PAS and been ordained. Classes and worship services were held on the third floor of one of the main building and there was no elevator. We did not want Ed to have to climb those stairs. He could come down them all right, but we were afraid about the going up. The college found a wheelchair for us and three or four times a day Ed would sit down in the chair and four able-bodied male students would turn it around and carry him up three flights of stairs. He called this his "eight-legged elevator." The Associated Press got wind of his studying for the ministry in his 90s and conducted interviews with him and me and others who knew his story. Especially was this newsworthy after he was ordained by Nashville Presbytery at the Red River Meeting House in Kentucky at the meeting of the 2000 General Assembly of the Cumberland Presbyterian Church on the anniversary of the Great Revival of 1800. Articles and pictures appeared in newspapers around the country. I received clippings in the mail from at least twenty different papers that friends and acquaintances sent.

When anybody asked him about his commitment to study for the ministry at his age, he would reply, "I want to be a credible witness for Jesus Christ." More than once he stated that one of his main goals in life was to attend the Olympics in Athens, Greece, in 2004. He didn't make it. He died less than a year before that event. He lived to be over a hundred, and only his death silenced his voice of optimism and hope, and his love for intellectual and spiritual conversation. As Director of PAS, I have had many chances to tell people they are never too old to go to school and study for the ministry. "How old are you?" I would ask a person who was complaining about being too old to do such things. "I'm 71," or, "I'm 65," or "I'm 53." Then I would tell them about Ed Schreiber.

399

"To thine own self be true." Shakespeare, or somebody, said that. One of my greatest challenges on that subject was in my youth. I handled it rather well, I think. My brothers and I were into dice baseball. Each had his players and his league. I was always an American League guy. Still am. Anyway, we had our players, our teams, our schedules. Each team played 154 games. There were eight teams in the league (this was before major league expansion of the early 1960s). We brothers were "czars" of our leagues. We traded players, named our all-star teams, pushed some into retirement and welcomed rookies. My all-time home run king was Willard Marshall who had 30 in one year. The "20 homer club" usually had fifteen or twenty players at season's end. The game had three dice. I would still be playing dice baseball if it were not for the need to support my family and try to look like a respectable citizen. I could pick up on it today and have just as much fun. The numbers were:

3 - Home Run	11 – Single
4 - Home Run	12 – Out
5 – Out	13 – Out
6 – Single	14 – Out
7 – Out	15 – Single
8 – Out	16 – Double
9 – Out	17 – Triple
10 – Out	18 - Home Run

Here is where "to thine own self be true" came into focus: What if some skinny, singles hitter in real life hit more home runs than anybody else including the big sluggers? And what if a pitcher (back then there was no designated-hitter rule) hit some home runs, too? (Pitchers were not supposed to be good hitters at all.) I always, ALWAYS, let things fall as they might. I never. I repeat, never altered anything, although the most unlikely hitters ended up as home run kings sometimes. Occasionally, a pitcher might have a no-hitter going into the seventh or eighth inning. I might hope things might work out well for him so the first no-hitter in my league could occur, but, again, I went with the roll of the dice, so to speak. I did have one no-hitter: Art Houtteman, Detroit Tigers. Perfect game. Three up, three down, nine innings. In this case, I was getting nervous as the game went on. When the ninth inning started, my hands were sweaty and I was on edge. Houtteman got one out. Then the second out. Before I rolled the dice for the possible third out I got up, walked out of my room and walked around the house, not once but twice. Then I walked carefully up the stairs back to my room and sat slowly and silently back down in my chair. I picked up the dice, shook them more than usual, and let them roll out of my left hand. It was a "seven," an out. History had been made. One day my father told me - and I had never, ever imagined that this could be - that a friend of his in high school in Santa Anna, Texas, played dice baseball. We're talking the early 1920s! My brothers and I were doing this in the 1950s. Here's one more thing. I forget whether the book was a novel or non-fiction, but someone wrote some years ago about a young man who had a dice baseball league going and he DID manipulate some outcomes along the way. Turns out he could not live with himself and he committed suicide. "To thine own self be true." In dice baseball, nobody else knows what you are doing. But YOU do.

400

To hear the commercials on the radio, you would think it was the greatest thing since sliced bread. What are they talking about? Great news! Hundreds of homes have been re-possessed and now are selling for much less than before and all you and I need to do is call this number and we can talk to an agent about buying one of these homes. In other words, somebody else's misery can be the source of my happiness. With the prime rate mortgage debacle going full blast and no solution yet in sight, these commercials continue. Maybe this bad news/good news picture has always been out there. It's raining so we can't play our baseball game. That's bad news. But the farmers need the rain and so this is good news for them. In Mark 5:1-20 a man was haunted by demons. Jesus healed him and the demons left him and entered 2,000 swine who, as one, rushed into the sea and perished. The man had good news because he was healed. But herdsmen responsible for the swine experienced bad news because they saw their livelihood drown. Is this the way economics is supposed to work? Why is it that when unemployment is higher than usual this is good news on Wall Street? Must the "have-nots" have less in order that the "haves" might have more? Must some people suffer that others might prosper?

Chapter XI: 401-450

"One Good Idea"

401

Aaron Sorkin, the creator of "The West Wing," the long-running television program about a presidential staff at the White House, now has a show on Broadway about Philo Farnsworth, the inventor of television. When interviewed, Sorkin said, "I have an idea about every nineteen years. I hope to improve on that, but I cannot guarantee it." We preachers are fortunate if we have an idea every nineteen years. We preach not to be original but to tell the gospel based on an old, old story.

402

I do not understand the concept of leaf-blowers. I grew up having to rake leaves and then put them in a can. Now there are garbage and lawn bags. Today there are leaf-blowers and the scheme seems to be that the leaves are all blown to one section and made into a big pile. But here's the rub: Somebody still has to pick them up and put them in a bag! Some day, somehow, in some fashion, the leaves must be disposed of, and that means bending down and picking them up! It seems like blowing them into a pile just uses up time that could be spent (by someone other than myself, I trust) raking and picking up.

403

I grew up in the Central Time Zone (sometimes known as "God's Time"). From early 1982 to mid-1994 our family lived in the Eastern Time Zone (Lexington, Kentucky, and then Knoxville, Tennessee). For over twelve years, at night, I would say to myself as I watched the 11:00 news, "It's really just 10:00." And I would go to bed on Central Time. But I would have to wake up on Eastern Time, like 6:00 in the morning. So, in effect, I lost one hour of sleep every night for over twelve years. Total number of hours of lost sleep: 4,380. No wonder I always look tired.

404

Happiness comes in many shapes and sizes and experiences. I want everybody to be happy. It has been my privilege to preach to churches in Colombia, Japan, and Korea. In each case a translator stood beside me and took my English words and communicated the message to the audience in their own language. It was English into Spanish, English into Japanese, and English into Korean. Now here is the "happiness" part: If the sermon was not all that good the translator could change it and make it better and I would not know the difference. Furthermore, the congregation would not know either. Therefore I was happy. The translator was very happy. And the congregation was happy, too, having heard a better sermon from the translator than from me. It's a "win-win-win" situation all around.

405

During the summer of 1989 two young men from Hong Kong were in the States. They visited various Cumberland Presbyterian congregations and conferences. They had dinner in the home of one of our church families in Knoxville and attended our worship service one Sunday morning. Then came the time to journey to West Lafayette, Indiana, for the Presbyterian Youth Triennium, a conference of 6,000 youth from three or four Presbyterian denominations. After traveling for three hours we stopped to eat in Lexington, Kentucky. It was a Jerry's Restaurant on the edge of the city. In addition to good food, the establishment had a gift shop. The two young men wanted to look for something distinctively "Kentucky." They purchased two or three little horses, good for placing on one's bookshelf or mantel. When they got back to the table the young men examined and admired what they bought. They turned the items over and on the bottom each item read "Made In Hong Kong."

406

A candidate for his party's presidential nomination went on television to give a speech that sought to ease any fears people might have about his Mormon faith. Other Mormon political leaders in our nation, past and present, have served well and honorably, and no public explanations or clarifications have ever been necessary. Yet he and his handlers thought it wise, in light of the close race, to do some explaining and try to provide clarification. He did pretty well, advocating tolerance, friendly disagreement, differences in biblical interpretation, and other aspects of faith. And he promised that, when president, he would not be influenced by officials of his church. He did all right - UNTIL he started talking about "those" people that do not believe, that have no religion, that do not attend church. At that point he drew a line between religious and non-religious people, implying, no, MORE than implying, that non-religious people are less-than-true Americans and that only religious people are qualified to hold office. In other words, he was advocating, at least through the back door and one or two of the side windows, a certain intolerance toward the non-religious. All of which flies in the face of the United States Constitution that says religion does not play any part in choosing people for public office.

407

"Wanted: More Good-for-Nothing Christians!" How does that strike you as a possible sermon title? Yes, we need more good-for-nothing Christians. I take you back to Job 1:9-11 where Satan, taunting God and trying to put God on the spot for holding up Job as a living example of faithfulness and righteousness, asks, "Does Job fear God for naught? Put forth thy hand now, and touch all that he has, and he will curse thee to thy face." Satan was harping on his thought that Job was in it for what he could get out of it. Take away what he was getting out of it, and he would lose his faith. Although Satan was a bit gruff and abrupt here, he did have a point pertinent to our day. Why are we Christians? Some have said the act of becoming a Christian is a very selfish act. It is done out of self-interest. I want to go to heaven. I do not want to go to hell. I want what Jesus can give me. I want the rewards and perks of the Christian life. Why am I a Christian? Why are you a Christian? Does Satan have a point?

408

We are, all of us, in a hurry. If we are in a meeting we are in a rush to get through. This applies to church meetings on a local and regional and denominational level as well as PTA meetings, civic club meetings, social gatherings, board meetings, and book club meetings.. We can't wait to get through. Our impatience knows no bounds. In every phase of life this need to make haste prevails. I am at the gas pump after giving a twenty-dollar bill to the cashier inside the convenience store. Everything goes well, for awhile. The dollars on the pump go from five to six to seven to eight and on up. Then the gauge gets to nineteen dollars and, right after that, slows down to a disturbing crawl. From then on, before it finally gets to twenty dollars, I have time to read <u>War and Peace</u> and half of <u>The Brothers Karamazov</u>. Worse, if I were to choose not to read anything, I could hear <u>all</u> of "El Paso" sung by Marty Robbins, a song which goes on and on and on as it tells a long and seemingly endless story. Here is something just as bad: Television commercials that go longer than thirty seconds. Those that go one minute are ads you think will never end. The micro-wave is a wonderful invention, but don't you think forty five seconds is a bit long to have to wait for something?

When we employ the above attitudes about time and immediacy and making short order of problems and situations, I think we are acknowledging our kinship to John the Baptist. He did a wonderful job as the forerunner of Jesus, but he and Jesus never were on the same page when it came to the time element. In this case, Jesus was an extreme disappointment to John, as evidenced when John was in prison and sent servants to ask Jesus (Matthew 11:2-11), "Are you he who is to come, or shall we look for another?" John after all, had promised that when the Messiah came "the axe would be at the root of the tree," and there would be "unquenchable fire (Matthew 3:7-10)." This, of course, did not happen. Jesus' ways were more patient, more deliberate, more plodding, more long-range than John's ideas of what they would be. I want the quick fix, the instant solution, the fast answer, the immediate conversion after my so-called evangelistic witness to someone.

409

The older we get the more regrets we have. I have even tried to prioritize mine, the thought being that if I could go back and change one thing, what would it be? I have a good collection of regrets, and although I know of and believe in forgiveness, I still cannot shake the sadness of those regrets, those "what-ifs." We move forward with those burdens hanging over us and we hope and pray that anyone hurt or slighted by any of our actions, or inactions, will have been able to move forward, too. One source of small comfort is that, when we have been hurt or slighted by others, we have a tendency to be able eventually to look beyond and go on.

410

Some things I cannot get over, however. They might be considered little things - by others. Our oldest daughter, Kelly Shanton, earned her Masters of Teaching degree from Carson Newman University in Jefferson City, Tennessee, a few years after earning her bachelor's at the University of Tennessee at Knoxville. The graduation service at Carson Newman was on a late Saturday morning in May, at the football stadium. At the beginning the soon-to-be graduates from the different schools and departments joined the processional, and Kelly was with her fellow Masters candidates. The music from the band went on long enough for all to reach their seats. Then on that very hot day, with the sun beating down, we heard an address by the university president followed by various other short speeches and presentations. And then the processional of graduates across the stage to receive diplomas (and in the case of Masters candidates, their hoods) began. That took awhile. By this time the sun was so hot I had slipped away from family members and walked underneath the stands to be in the shade and get a glass of lemonade. But I listened for Kelly's group to be called and when they were I walked up the ramp to see and hear everything. Soon that part was over and the service came to a close. The graduates began to march out. Down the stadium steps they came and out they went, all the while with the band playing, just as it played at the beginning of the service. My daughter's Masters group was going to be the last bunch to walk out. However, they were still standing there, awaiting their time to go, when the band stopped playing. That's right. The band stopped playing, leaving the entire Masters in Teaching class standing there at their seats in the stadium. I wanted to yell and scream and holler, "Keep on playing!" I should have, if only to register a protest. Because now, with the music stopped, our daughter and her classmates had to walk down and out of the stadium unceremoniously, unnoticed, unacclaimed, unaccompanied by appropriate music, or, for that matter, any music at all. It was a crying shame. It was an injustice. It was reprehensible. It was uncalled for. The music should have gone on. My family has tried to help me put all this in perspective, but none of their efforts have succeeded. I still remember it and I still have angry feelings. They should have kept playing! So what, if most of the crowd had left. So what, if all but one tiny portion of the graduates had departed the stadium. So what, if the band members and conductor were hot and drenched with sweat and exhausted from their much playing. There still remained this important group of Master of Arts in Teaching graduates, fresh with their degrees and hoods and with families looking on. Later I thought about writing to the university president but I never took the time. I should have. Other than that, it was a very good weekend for our family.

411

A ministerial colleague, Dudley Condron (the creator of sketches for this book), and I journeyed to Colombia, South America, in 1988 to visit our churches there, see the country, and give support to our Cumberland Presbyterian missionaries. He carried with him a new video camera the Board of Missions, his employer, had recently purchased. He preached at a few churches and I did, too, with translators standing by our sides. I remember that on a Sunday night at the San Lucas Church in Palmira, the sanctuary was full. As the service proceeded, at every window there were children on the outside looking in. They were standing there. They listened to the music. They saw the people. They saw the worship service. If anyone ever fit the description of "seekers," they did. They were quiet, evidently trying to absorb it all. I still remember, nineteen years later, the children peering in. What a wonderful opportunity for that church and pastor with those inquiring eyes, hearts, and minds.

412

While in Colombia we were riding with Boyce Wallace and were stopped by a group of army officers patrolling that section of the country. Boyce was calm. He said to hide the camera under a blanket in the back seat of the car. We stayed in the car and could hear him explaining who we were and what we were doing. I heard "pastore." That means shepherd as well as minister. I wondered if perhaps the officers asked, if we were shepherds, where were the sheep? We were soon on our way again, no harm done.

413

We want to "do well" in our lives. That is, we desire to be "successful" in our many endeavors. And if this, perchance, means making a pretty good living, with health care and a dental plan, so be it. That means we are <u>really</u> "doing well." But alongside "doing well," we also want to "do good." That is, we desire to be responsible citizens, compassionate neighbors, trusted friends in our relationships, forgiving of others, gentle friends to animals, honest in business dealings, ethical in all matters, with hands and feet of helpfulness for the less fortunate. Probably - and this is just a guess, from an economic standpoint - we worry more about our "doing well" than our "doing good." Jesus went about "doing good." In the eyes of his peers, he likely was not seen as doing all that "well." An obscure poem summarizes the case in our day, many think. It says that "Jesus went about doing good, while most of us are content with just going about."

414

I was not in my high school plays, as a junior or a senior. Nor did I try out for drama early in college. However, in my third year, sort of on a whim, I showed up when they announced that "Abe Lincoln in Illinois" was going to be the spring play, and it would be outside with the historic Log Cabin on the Bethel College campus as the backdrop. I not only showed up, I got a part. I would be Joshua Speed, a close friend of Lincoln's in Springfield, Illinois. I was told to grow a beard and learn to smoke a pipe as these would be two of my "props." The play was well publicized, weeks before the three consecutive evenings when it would be presented. With the publicity and my frazzly excuse for a beard, people began to assume I was going to play the part of Abe. I began to feel like John the Baptist: "After me comes he who is mightier than I, the thong of whose sandals I am not worthy to stoop down and untie." "I'm not the one; he is," "he" being a fellow student with much more dramatic experience than I. He could not grow a beard because he was to play Abe in his younger days, before the beard, and then grow a beard (in this case, a fake) before going off to the White House. So I was increasingly "not the light, but I came to bear witness to the light." When I would say "I am not the one," I think some people assumed I had wanted to play Abe. To the best of my recollection, as they used to say in the Senate hearings, I do not recall desiring that role. But I think I did learn just a little of how John must have felt, always trying to brush off any tendency to assume I (with the beard) was going to be Abe in the play. The three evenings went off well, although on the last night, it clouded up and thundered a little, and the director had us skip a couple of scenes in order to get to the final part of the story. The next day I was glad to get that poor excuse for a beard off my face. And I put the pipe down for good, although I sort of liked the aroma of pipe tobacco.

415

Another church sign (this one in the front yard of Highland Heights United Methodist Church in Memphis, Tennessee)

PEACE STARTS
NOT AT A MIDEAST TABLE
BUT AT A MIDEAST STABLE

416

It is very seldom I get to keep very many of the promises I make, but I can tell you of one time when I was successful in doing so. I was in the seventh grade. It was early Fall of 1951. The baseball season was drawing to a close and the Brooklyn Dodgers and New York Giants were locked in a best-two-out-of-three championship playoff. The Giants won the first game and the Dodgers the second. Now they were in the contest that would decide the National League pennant. At school some of us would gather in an empty classroom to listen to the radio and hear some of the play-by-play. Then we would rush back to class. I had been listening to the Giants-Dodgers game and then had gone to Mrs. Esch's class. Soon there came a knock on the classroom door. Mrs. Esch walked all the way from her desk past all of us students to the door. As she opened the door, Jimmy Young, a junior in high school, blurted out these words: "Tell Tommy Campbell that Bobby Thomson just hit a home run and the Giants have won the pennant!" Mrs. Esch slammed the door, walked quickly back up to the front, looked sharply at me and said, "Don't ever let that happen again!" I have kept that promise. Bobby Thomson has never hit a pennant-winning home run again. The Giants and Dodgers have never again gone to a best-of-three playoff, Ralph Branca has never again been the pitcher in a Giants-Dodgers playoff game, and Jimmy Young has never again knocked on the classroom door, at least for that purpose. Do I keep my promises, or what?

417

A biography of the actor Jimmy Stewart by Marc Eliot (<u>Jimmy Stewart: A Biography</u>, Harmony Books, 2006) tells that he was a native of Indiana, Pennsylvania. He and his family were members of the local Presbyterian church. When he entered show business he drifted away from church life. When Stewart married, his wife brought young twin sons into the family. In Hollywood the family attended the Bel Air Presbyterian Church. Mrs. Stewart taught a Sunday school class, and Jimmy and the boys were regular participants in the church. Both boys went away to Viet Nam. One of them was killed in action. On a day in the middle of the week the funeral was held in the church. By the time of the start of the service, the keys to the organ had not been found and no one on the staff knew where to look. The service proceeded without instrumental music. The family naturally was upset by this. Soon they started attending Hollywood Presbyterian Church. However, they never got over the pain and anger of the former church's failure to provide normal ministries in their loss (p. 268).

418

You will have friends that say they take the Bible literally. "Oh?" you will ask. "Yes, I take the Bible literally. Every word." "Well," you might inquire, "When Jesus said 'I am the door' in John 10:9 are you saying he had hinges and a door handle and he was a certain size piece of wood?" "No, of course not," might be the reply. "That really means..." "Wait a minute," you might reply, "You just said you take the Bible literally, and now you are saying that a certain passage 'really means' something else? You are not at this moment taking the Bible literally." Any time somebody says "It really means this or that" it is an acknowledgment, expressed or not expressed, that they don't take the Bible literally, at least that part, regardless of their persistence in saying they do.

419

Our English language seems easy to us (although we butcher it sometimes with split infinitives and abused gerunds and misplaced apostrophes and prepositions that come at the end of sentences). We may forget how difficult it is for those trying to learn it as a second language. We had a family from Iran in our church in Lexington, Kentucky. At a church dinner on a Sunday night after the Kentucky Wildcats had racked up another basketball victory on Saturday night, I was sitting by the patriarch of the Iranian family and talking about the game. My words went something like this: "They had us with our backs up against the wall, but we kept our nose to the grindstone and before it was over we ran their socks off." I wonder how much of that, if any, made any sense to this gentleman still struggling to learn the English language. We preachers can be more diligent in trying to make sure that people - both those native to English, and those that are not - can understand what we are saying.

420

We forget sometimes how descriptive we are in our conversations. We use all manner of figures of speech to try to tell our story, get our message across, and help others understand what we are talking about. One can imagine how difficult this makes it for those seeking to make English their second language. Examples follow:

- you heard it straight from the horse's mouth
- pretty as a picture
- big as a house
- slippery as an eel
- nutty as a fruitcake
- crooked as a snake
- slow as Christmas
- slow as molasses
- thin as a rail
- eats like a bird
- dead as a doornail
- sick as a dog
- white as a sheet
- nervous as a long-tailed cat in a room full of rocking chairs
- memory like an elephant
- eats like a pig
- wise as an owl
- quick as a cat
- he saw the handwriting on the wall
- quick as a wink
- poor as Job's turkey
- bored to death
- happy as a lark
- happy as a clam
- he bit off more than he could chew
- getting a leg up
- loose as a goose
- crazy as a loon
- pure as the wind-driven snow
- rich as Rockefeller
- pretty as a peach
- cute as a button
- pleased as punch
- smooth as silk
- fresh as a daisy
- naked as a jaybird
- right as rain
- hard as nails

hit the nail on the head

421

Here are some more figures of speech no doubt confusing to someone new to the English language:

Everything but the kitchen sink
back against the wall
nose to the grindstone
ear to the ground
piece of cake
guilty as sin
hungry as a horse
fast as a deer
blind as a bat
strong as an ox
weak as a kitten
quiet as a mouse
cold as ice
living high on the hog
flat as a pancake
red as a beet
soft as a baby's bottom
sharp as a tack
straight as an arrow
the patience of Job
the wisdom of Solomon
rained cats and dogs
angry as an old wet hen
proud as a peacock
fit as a fiddle
slick as a whistle
he told him how the cow ate the cabbage
hot as a firecracker
cool as a cucumber
sly as a fox
high as a kite
learning the ropes
cried like a baby
cute as a bug
tight as a drum
graceful as a gazelle
helpless as a baby
a pig in a poke

a razor-sharp mind
put your money where your mouth is
he came unglued
she went into orbit
eye like an eagle
he has lost all his marbles
his elevator doesn't go to the top floor
the boss cleaned his plow
he is not working with a full deck
he should not try to jump the gun

422

The Bible contains many such word usages, at least as the scriptures appear in English. This includes sayings of Jesus but also words by others as well. Here are some from the Old Testament book of Hosea and from two of the Gospels.

I am the door (John 10:7)
I am the vine (John 15:5)
You are the branches (John 15:5)
I am the bread of life (John 6:35)
I am the light of the world   (John 8:12)
You are the light of the world (Matthew 5:14)
You are the salt of the earth (Matthew 5:13)
He saw the Spirit of God descending like a dove
    (Matthew 3:16)
I am like a moth to Ephraim (Hosea 5:12)
And like a dry rot to the house of Judah (Hosea 5:12)
I will be like a lion to Ephraim (Hosea 5:14)
And like a young lion to the house of Judah (Hosea 5:14)
They are like a heated oven (Hosea 7:4)
Ephraim is like a cake not turned (Hosea 7:8)
Ephraim is like a dove, silly and without sense (Hosea 7:11)

423

Sign outside a business establishment:

RELAX
GOD IS IN CHARGE

424

This place of business must have had more than one location, but the sign could have been confusing to some passers-by:

SECOND TO NONE # 2

425

An elder (a lay leader in the church) was elected Moderator of the General Assembly in 2000 in Bowling Green, Kentucky. He spoke of former pastors, all of whom had a positive influence in his life, he reported. I was one of them. He mentioned one who had helped him in evangelism, another with an emphasis on small groups, another influenced him in something else. Along the way he mentioned my name and said "race relations." I was shocked. I recalled talking about the subject and having disagreements with him on the subject. I do not recall that anything I said was convincing or weighty. I guess you never know when what you say touches somebody else. I was moved by his words of appreciation.

426

Occasionally you see two apparently contrasting passages in the scriptures and wonder, first, if the transcribers and scholars and translators got it right, and second, how to reconcile the two. Such is the case with Luke 9:50 and Luke 11:23. In the former, Jesus says, "Whoever is not against you is for you." In the latter, he says, "Whoever is not with me is against me." Laying aside the differing references to "you" and "me" we do here have two contrasting thoughts. I have tried to preach on these as they stood alongside one another, but always to no avail and with a total absence of gospel truth that mattered. Then one day, still wrestling with the two, I began to see that possibly the following was a good way to look at them: The first - "Whoever is not against you is for you" - is how we should look at others. We should give people the benefit of the doubt. We should honor and respect the religious and non-religious. Many non-religious people are worthy and honest and responsible and would do not harm to the church. They are not against us. And, when we meet strangers, why should we have the right to assume they are not Christians and start "witnessing" to them in their faces? They are not against, so they are for us. The latter passage - "Whoever is not with me is against me - is how we should look upon ourselves. We should be much harder on ourselves than on others. With Christ, there is no neutral ground for us. We are either for or against. And if we are not for him, then we are against him. We should be harsh on ourselves and respectful and tolerant of others. I wonder if that is something close to the solution of how to stand those two passages side by side.

427

This old and wise quote came from somewhere:

> "When all is said and done,
> there will be more said than done."

428

There was a time when the Chief Executive Officer of a company received maybe 45 or 50 times the amount of the average worker in the same company. Now that figure has grown to enormous heights, something like 500 times the amount of the average worker. And it doesn't matter how well or poorly the company does. Sometimes the CEO is fired by the board of directors but still walks away with millions in severance pay and bonuses, as though the company were making great progress instead of being run into the ground by this same CEO. Therefore, it is unusual to hear about one CEO who broke away from the pattern. Several years ago this executive decided to give Christmas bonuses to all staff and workers above and beyond the usual ham or gift certificate. In fact, he provided each of them unusually high bonuses plus shares in the company. When he was criticized by fellow CEOs his answer was, "What am I going to do with all my money, eat more food?"

429

I read about a man who owned a steak house. The place burned and while repairs were being made and the establishment was closed, he continued to pay his employees their regular wages. His reasoning was, first, he did not want to lose them to other restaurants. Second, it was his way of thanking them for staying with him through the bad times as well as the good.

430

At first glance, the words "epitaph" and "epithet" resemble one another, and they might appear to have similar meanings. Not so. "Epitaph" is when, at your funeral, they say nice things about you. "Epithet" would be those words we say in anger and rage toward another person while we are living. The more "epithets" we utter in our lifetimes, the more imaginative and creative those who give our "epitaph" will have to be upon the occasion of our funeral.

431

The television sitcom "Mad About You" was a long-running success. It starred Paul Reiser and Helen Hunt. Along the way she became pregnant. About that time his uncle became seriously ill and was in the hospital facing death, so the report said. The uncle, played by Mel Brooks in a cameo role, had one request: When he died, would they name their baby after him? It was a biblical name, he said. They quickly agreed. Then they realized everybody knew him by his nickname and nobody had ever called him by his real name, and they did not know what it was. They rushed to the hospital to check on the uncle and he was out of the bed, singing and dancing and having a great time. They were relieved he was doing better. They were really relieved he was better when they found out what his real name was, the name they had promised to name their child if the uncle died, the biblical name. What did they promise to name their little baby? "Deuteronomy."

432

In the 1960s during the intense civil rights struggles, voting rights for African Americans kept the nation's attention. Folks from other parts of the country came to the South to help in the project. One white lady from Detroit, Viola Liuzzo (sp?), drove blacks from the church to the court house to register, and then back to the church. Somebody drove beside her car and fatally shot her. I heard church people say, "Well, she just shouldn't have been there. She should have stayed home with her family in Detroit." When Chaney, Goodman, and Schwerner, three college-age civil rights workers, were murdered in Mississippi, church folks said, "Well, they just shouldn't have been meddling in things that were not their business. They should have stayed up north and gone to school and worked." I was riding along with a fellow member of my civic club in Burleson, Texas. Six nuns had recently been raped and murdered in Central America. "Well," he said, "They just shouldn't have been there. They had no business being there." Truth is, the nuns had gotten off a plane in a Central American city to go to their place of work. Some men met them and told them they were there to take them to their destination. The men drove them to an isolated spot, made them get out of the van, raped them, then shot them. "Blame the victim" has been going on a long time. "Well, she asked for it." Or, "They asked for it." Let us remember who the perpetrators were and blame them. Nothing any of the above did warranted death. In fact, they were all doing good. And that was a threat to many.

433

Did you hear about the man who kept receiving mail addressed to "Occupant"? Included in the pile of junk mail was a request for donations to a certain cause. He wrote a generous check and signed it "Occupant."

434

There are two different kinds of "tired." One can get tired _of_ one's job, and one can get tired _in_ one's job. The first can be negative and disillusioning. The second is to be expected and calls for periodic rest and time away. But the second, if not recognized and honored, can lead to the first. Perhaps this was what Paul was referring to when he said in Galatians 6:9, "Let us not grow weary in well-doing." If we allow ourselves to "grow weary _in_ well-doing," and no rest is on the horizon, we may become weary _of_ well-doing. And, lo, it is called burn-out.

435

I need to confess something. Can we talk? As a young child, one of my life's ambitions was to be in the fourth grade. I knew some people who were in the fourth grade and they were taller and seemed to know what they were doing. I thought that if I could make it to the fourth grade, the rest would be smooth sailing. I am happy to announce that my dreams were fulfilled and I was not disappointed. It was a great experience. I would recommend it to anybody. Those were three of the best years of my life.

436

While I have your attention, I must tell you that I have actually had two ambitions in life. The other, besides making it to the fourth grade, was directing a band in some of John Phillip Sousa's marches. By the time I was in my mid-fifties that had not yet occurred, so, on a church talent night I arranged to get some tapes of Sousa marches. I put chairs all in a row on the stage in the fellowship hall. A musician on the church staff who worked at a music store provided a majestic hat that only band directors would wear. When my time came on the program I announced that we were happy to have the Philadelphia Philharmonic Orchestra, the University of Tennessee marching band, the Powell High School marching band, and the all-star band from other high schools in East Tennessee. I had someone go to the door to let them in and as he held the door open, my imaginary musical guests entered the room. In fact, there were so many of them I had to get more chairs put on the stage. When "they" were all ready, I tapped the lectern for quiet, lifted my arms, and let her fly. The technician operating the tape machine (the same musician on staff who loaned me the hat) flipped it on and the great march "The Thunderer" came on. I "directed" my guest band with great flair and dignity. When that march was over, on came "The King Cotton March," truly one of the great musical selections of all time. I pointed over here and the bass drum boomed loudly. I pointed over there and the clarinets came on strong. I pointed over the other way and the trumpets sounded gloriously. It was a great experience. I enjoyed my moment of directing a couple of Sousa marches.

437

A minister had an old and much-used copy of the New Testament that he treasured. It contained his markings and marginal notes. But it was falling apart, so he went to get it bound with a hard cover. When the bindery had finished the minister noticed, with a smile, that on the front was the full title - "The New Testament" - and on the side, the abbreviation: <u>TNT</u>. So he took his old and trusted friend, the New Testament, to his car, and drove back to his church, hoping beyond hope, and praying fervently, that some day his preaching would, in some way, make way for the explosive and dynamic gospel contained therein.

438

The Program of Alternate Studies (PAS) of the Cumberland Presbyterian Church is a part of the tradition of the denomination whereby alternate routes to ministerial education are provided for those who cannot go to seminary. Seminary life is Plan A. PAS life is Plan B. A young high school math teacher bought an interest in a mattress factory. Why? So he would have something to "fall back on." PAS fills the bill on that score. And you heard about the man who could not decide whether or not to buy a certain mattress in a furniture store. A recent cartoon in the newspaper told of it.

Because of his indecision, he decided to "sleep on it." They found him the next morning and called security.

439

There is some question as to who the first PAS student was. Our records go back to 1984 when the program officially started, but I think the first student might have been Amos, the prophet of Old Testament times. He had many of the characteristics of a PAS student. Until the Lord called him he was working two jobs: "I am a herdsman, and a dresser of sycamore trees." But then "the Lord took me from following the flock, and the Lord said to me, 'Go, prophesy to my people Israel'" (Amos 7:14-15). Notice that Amos accepted God's call, but he kept his other job as a "dresser of sycamore trees." It seems he could not at that time break away and attend the official school of the prophets.

440

A PAS education is not enough. A Seminary education is not enough. A Ph.D. is not enough. The main purpose of education is to create a hunger to learn more. The truly educated are not satisfied with what they know or what they have learned. I know of persons who, after their formal education would have been expected to be over, after retirement from their careers, after Social Security and retirement checks had been coming in for many months and years, have gone back to school - to art school, to auto mechanics school. They have taken music classes, learned to play an (or another) instrument, studied astronomy, traveled to places not previously seen, studied psychology, learned the fine art of cooking, delved into computers with great depth. In other words, they never stopped learning.

441

Two church signs:

>   HOME IMPROVEMENT
>   TAKE YOUR FAMILY TO CHURCH
>
>   GOD LOVES YOU
>   JUST THE WAY YOU ARE

442

Advertisement on a theater screen (along with other ads) prior to the showing of the previews and the main feature:

>YOUR SPIRITUAL OASIS
>JOE'S LIQUORS AND WINES
>Midtown Memphis

443

A television program featured Gatlinburg, Tennessee, a tourist town. Some people had lived there and moved away and, upon returning, commented on how the town had changed. It just wasn't the same anymore. A city councilman was interviewed. He said, "If you want to see how things have changed over the years, just look in the mirror." Then he added, "When you're green, you're growing; when you're ripe, you rot."

444

The book <u>Legacy of Ashes: The History of the CIA</u>, by Tim Weiner (Doubleday, 2007) tells of a special agent who "had buried weapons all over Europe, but when the crisis came, no one could find them." (p.129) We Christians have much stored up for our use in the battles and struggles of life, if only we can remember where to go to find them.

445

In the same book on the history of the CIA, the author reports that the CIA in its early days "had a great reputation and a terrible record" (p. 55).

446

"The First Nowell" or "Noel" - written by "Traditional" - is a popular Christmas hymn. Only trouble is, it switches stories without warning and, in fact, gets it wrong. The first verse says:

>The first Noel the angel did say
>Was to certain poor shepherds in fields as they lay;
>In fields where they lay keeping their sheep,
>On a cold winter's night that was so deep.

So far, so good. But the second stanza has these words:

> They looked up and saw a star
> Shining in the east, beyond them far;
> And to the earth it gave great light,
> And so it continued both day and night.

The third stanza adds to the confusion:

> And by the light of that same star,
> Three wise men came from country far;
> To seek for a king was their intent,
> And to follow the star wherever it went.

The writer of the hymn has brought together the Luke story and the Matthew story of Christmas, and combined them into one song, which has both the shepherds and the wise men following the star. I have searched and searched in Luke and find no mention of a star. There is no evidence to show that the shepherds followed "the same star" or that they followed a star at all. Having puritanical, consciously self-righteous tendencies anyway, I find this discrepancy a delight about which to nit-pick.

447

Football can be a lesson in life. I know all about football. I played one year back in the eighth grade. We used the old single-wing offense, mainly because the high school team did and many on our team would be playing at that level the next year. Here is what I learned in that one experience: Every offensive play that is diagramed by the coach and learned by the team is designed to score a touchdown. If all of the players block their respective targets, the one carrying the ball should score every time. However, this occurs, on average, only about 5% of the time or less. Why? If the diagram shows how it should be, why does it not occur every time? Probably because the opposing players do not cooperate. They elude the attempted blocks, they push the would-be blockers away, they run faster than they are supposed to, they go left instead of right, they reach out and tackle the ball carrier. The audacity of all that! How dare they! Well, if about 5% or fewer plays result in touchdowns, would it not be accurate to say that most football teams are failures on offense? Yes, every time we see a ball carrier tackled, the play is a failure. Except that this is the way it is in life for us all. Very little goes as planned. Our dreams and ambitions are thwarted. Every aspiration is subject to change. The times do not cooperate. The weather does not cooperate. Other people do not cooperate. Our abilities and inabilities do not cooperate. Yes, football is a lesson in life. It teaches that we go on, charge ahead, move forward, keeping our eyes on the goal. Recently a quarterback threw a pass to his star receiver. The receiver uncharacteristically dropped the ball. It was a sure touchdown had he held on to it. The team came out of the huddle for the next play and the quarterback threw the very same pass to the very same receiver. This time he caught it and raced into the end zone for a touchdown. Failure was followed by success.

448

Exodus 1:22 reports, "Pharaoh commanded all his people, 'Every son that is born to the Hebrews you shall cast into the Nile, but you shall let every daughter live.'" Matthew 2:16 says, "Then Herod... sent and killed all the children in Bethlehem and in all that region who were two years old or under according to the time which he had ascertained from the wise men." Power is always nervous, scared, looking over one's shoulder, non-trusting of others, suspicious. No wonder these two kings had the children killed. One of the children might grow up and be instrumental in ousting the one on the throne. Power can deal with other Power, such as armed might, military strength, and boasting and bluster similar to its own. But Power has trouble with the common people who stand up to it. Power does not know how to deal with ideas, courage, challenges from the ordinary folks. In China a young man stood in the pathway of an armed tank. The tank turned away. Brute force may remove people from the scene but their ideas live on. This is what those kings were afraid of. This is what Power today is fearful of. The Church does not belong with Power. It belongs out there with the common people. The Church that cozies up to Power feels proud but loses its soul. The Church that thinks it can control a government or a political party has already lost its way. We belong with the outcasts, the riffraff, the forgotten, the people with no lobbyists in Washington, the uninsured, the homeless, the hopeless, the helpless, the weak in body and wealth.

449

In the early 1960s I sat in a pew in the chapel of the Cumberland Presbyterian Theological Seminary in McKenzie, Tennessee, and heard the local Methodist pastor, J. K. Stuart, deliver the following quote, which was the theme of his sermon: "The church that marries the spirit of the times is a widow in the next generation." Some statements you hear stay with you over time. That one did with me.

450

Out in Burleson, Texas, in the 1970s a young couple joined the church: Orvis and Noelle Schechter. Of course, and you would expect this, when I introduced them to the congregation I mentioned that she was the "first Noelle" to join St. Matthew Church. I have found that, so far, she is the "only Noelle" to have joined that church.

Chapter X: 451-500

"God With Us"

451

Sometimes we feel that God is <u>against</u> us. At other times we may feel that God has <u>forgotten</u> us. Still on other occasions we feel that God is <u>for</u> us. But Matthew 1:23 reports that the name of the forthcoming Messiah would be "Emmanuel (which means, God with us)." God <u>with</u> us. The last is best of all. We are relieved that God is not against us and that God has not forgotten us. We are much happier knowing that God is for us, rooting for us, if from a distance. But most of all and best of all, we are elated to know that God is with us, by our side, supporting us, holding us up, guiding us, through thick and thin, through plenty and want, through the good times and the hard times. God is with us. A person more observant than I in biblical matters has pointed out that the Gospel of Matthew begins with "God with us" and ends the same way: "Lo, I am with you always" (28:20).

452

We never know and cannot anticipate when a song might "grab" us. We sing our hymns and love them - the tunes, the words, the messages. Often we rush right by some powerful lines, however, that when looked at closely bring strength and comfort. Such is the third verse of "It Came Upon the Midnight Clear," one of the great Christmas hymns. Edmund H. Sears penned the words:

> And ye, beneath life's crushing load,
> Whose forms are bending low,
> Who toil along the climbing way
> With painful steps and slow,
> Look now! For glad and golden hours
> Come swiftly on the wing;
> O rest beside the weary road,
> And hear the angels sing.

453

I don't think taunting is appropriate at any time, and that includes in football after a touchdown or a successful tackle or fantastic interception. When a player does that after a touchdown, it doesn't seem to matter to the offender that his team is penalized fifteen yards for the kickoff. At least he got to show off. There is something called sportsmanship that should still be in the picture and it often is not. Don't the players know that their actions merely raise the ire of the other team and make them more determined to come back even harder? Run the ball, score the touchdown, put the ball down, receive congratulations from teammates, and head toward the sidelines as the extra-point team comes in. It's that simple.

454

While we are on the subject of football and the antics of players after a job well done, what about the defensive tackle who gets by the blocker and sacks the quarterback for a twelve-yard loss? That being accomplished, now he has to charge forward a few steps, look up into the crowd, and beat his chest like he is King Kong or Tarzan or Godzilla. He has to say, in effect, "Look what I have done. Isn't that great!" Hey, that is what he is in there for, to get the quarterback. That's his job. Why brag about it? Why create such an uproar? Why make the other team any angrier than they already are, what with the twelve-yard loss and everything? I know there is no room for humility in football, but, again, sportsmanship is not so old fashioned that the defensive tackle cannot turn around, go back to his place in the defensive line, and await the next play. It just makes good sense.

Now we see kids in peewee football and junior high and high school football doing the same, trying to emulate their college and professional heroes. Jesus performed miracles and told folks not to tell anybody. He said, "When you give alms, sound no trumpet before you" (Matthew 6:2). Perhaps still another scripture could apply as well: "Pride goes before destruction, and a haughty spirit before a fall" (Proverbs 16:18). The early part of Isaiah 2:11 could easily say it also: "The haughty eyes of people shall be brought low, and the pride of everyone shall be humbled."

455

Presidential candidates were having a televised debate. The subject of religion emerged. The moderator, a network news anchor, asked the group if they took the Bible literally. "If you do, raise your hand." What is wrong with this picture? First of all, any answer given would offend many in one's party. Second, one could ask what is meant by "literally." Third, the presumptive nature of the question was repugnant. Fourth, a better question, since a president takes an oath to uphold it, would be, "Do you take the Constitution literally?" I didn't stick around to hear the answers or see the show of hands. It was that bad. But an excellent response by one, or some, or all of the candidates would be, "That is none of your business!" And an adjective of some descriptive nature before the word "business" would have been in order. What is it with religion and politics? It's the Constitution that matters.

456

For some reason I hardly ever see the television program "My Name is Earl." I wish I could catch it more often than I do. I love the concept. It is great. The main character, haunted by the harm he has done someone many years ago (and he has a long list), sets out to remedy the situation and otherwise make compensation for the pain he has caused. Every week there is a new episode and a new project to make things right. However, nothing ever seems to go as planned and his efforts usually end up as unmitigated disasters. The heart is in the right place, so to speak, but the resulting actions end up twisted and flawed. All of us have regrets and may have even thought of trying to go back and make things right. A biography of Andrew Jackson says he was planning on joining the Presbyterian Church. His pastor said things would not be right until Jackson forgave all his enemies. I told that story in a sermon one time and at the door afterwards a church member said that Jackson would have trouble with the forgiveness project because most of his enemies were dead by that time. Most of us live with regrets that bother, even haunt us. We can only hope that, if we cannot go back and make things right, the offended persons have long ago forgiven us. We hope we have been inclined toward that when we have been the ones hurt or offended.

457

I started watching a show called "The Weakest Link" when it first showed up on the television screen. The idea of this quiz show is that with every round someone is voted off, presumably the "weakest link." But the person is not just voted off. There is a brief period when the moderator seems to go out of her way to belittle and ridicule the unsuccessful contestant, who then slinks away in utter shame. It's sort of a "survival of the fittest" mentality. I don't watch this program anymore, for it reminds me of what the church should <u>not</u> be, and I hope what the church is <u>not</u>. The church invites the "weakest link" into the fellowship. We are all weak. We need one another. The spirit by which the different contestants on the show are discarded resembles, in a dark way, the Nazi efforts to weed out the supposedly weak in their society. I keep going back in my mind to Isaiah 42 where the prophet speaks of God's servant, with whom we can compare to Christ very easily: "He will not cry or lift up his voice, or make it heard in the street; a bruised reed he will not break, and a dimly burning wick he will not quench; he will faithfully bring forth justice" (42:2-3).

458

The entire "Survival" series on television seems to have the same kind of theme. The fittest survive, the weak do not, whether it is on a lonely island, in the deepest heart of a jungle, or in the hottest desert. There are winners and there are losers, and the losers have no place in the world of "survivors." Here again, there is no resemblance to the church, what it is or what it ought to be. In the church we are there for each other. All of us are strong in some things, weak in others. When one suffers, all suffer. When one rejoices, all rejoice. For sure, the church includes many "survivors" - survivors of the death of loved ones, survivors of divorce, survivors of financial downturns, survivors of health problems, survivors of shattered dreams. But it also embraces those who are now involved in some of those struggles and who may not "survive." Still the church is there for them. We toss nobody from the ship.

459

Sign in front of a condo:

STOP
LOOK
LEASE

460

A sermon is better off without including a lot of statistics. Citing a host of figures tends to weigh heavily on a message and slow it down to a crawl. Statistics are usually spoken to convince and persuade. One does not want to be inaccurate but the preacher does not want to burden the listeners with so much stuff. I am convinced that 60% of the preachers of the land agree with this at least 75% of the time. I am 51% certain of these statistics and am persuaded that 90% of the time we would be better off without

80% of the numbers we are apt to quote, though I am guessing three out of five preachers do this at least half of the time.

461

The founders of the Cumberland Presbyterian Church - Finis Ewing, Samuel King, and Samuel McAdow - in forming Cumberland Presbytery, took many things into consideration back in 1810 as they made that fateful decision. But they may have overlooked one item: the date. February 4 seemed at the time to be a really good day. Back then it was, and throughout the denomination, we have celebrated what we call "Denomination Day" in special worship services, dinners, dramas, and sermons on the Sunday closest to February 4. Cumberland Presbyterians cherish their great history and are conscientious in passing the story on from one generation to another. February 4 is an especially important day in the church year. But in the recent past, that date has also been special for another reason: the Super Bowl. Now we ought not to fault Ewing, King, and McAdow for this. They did not know. They had no inkling. Football had not even been invented in 1810. The Green Bay Packers were only a distant dream. But recently the conflict in dates has been a problem. It may have kept some people at home when they might have otherwise attended a special Denomination Day service. I know, I know. There should be no contest (if you'll pardon the pun), but sometimes immediate concerns take precedence over eternal matters. We can say, Blessed are those who get out and go on to the church services on that Sunday evening, knowing they might miss the first half. They will receive their reward in heaven.

462

This is an old, old story, original teller unknown. In a Sunday School class the children were asked where Jesus was born. "Pittsburgh," said one child. "No," said the teacher. The same child came back, "Philadelphia." Again, "No, that is not correct." The teacher continued, "Jesus was born in Bethlehem." To which the same child said, "I knew it was somewhere in Pennsylvania."

463

When I was in Japan in August of 2000, my last night there arrived. My hosts said we could go see sumo wrestlers or a big-league baseball game. I chose baseball. Just before the game, as the music swelled, the giant scoreboard in left field showed a huge sun rising. An announcement was made, and although I could not understand it since it was in Japanese, I suspected something. Sure enough it was an announcement that the national anthem was going to be played and would everyone rise. My hosts, two Cumberland Presbyterian ministers, cried out, in English, "No, no, no!" And they did not rise. Neither did about one-third of the crowd. I sat with my hosts and did not stand either. It was explained to me later that the national anthem depicts the emperor as a god and that there is a movement afoot to militarize the nation again and urge more reverence for the emperor. Christian churches in the nation, including Japan Presbytery of the Cumberland Presbyterian Church, are negative about all this as they recall what happened in World War II when emperor worship was forced on the churches there as well as in Korea, a nation that the Japanese occupied. It dawned on me that not all countries revere the flag or the government or its rulers the same way as others.

464

The college basketball coach was telling a reporter about his star point guard. "I was at this high school game actually to see another player, but this other young man caught my eye and now he is our leader on the floor." It is reported that a major league baseball scout went out to watch a game on the campus of Columbia University in order to look at a highly touted outfielder. While there he noticed another team member who hit the ball hard every time and fielded really well at first base. His name was Lou Gehrig, who became a Hall of Fame star at first base for the New York Yankees and a teammate of Babe Ruth. Sometimes we find what we are not looking for. We keep our eyes open to what God has in store and often receive gifts for life that we never requested or expected.

465

In Nashville I drove down a highway and saw to my right the world headquarters of a denomination. Outside were flagpoles and the national flags of every nation where that denomination had missionaries and churches. I thought, "What a wonderful idea." But then I remembered a debate at the General Assembly of the Cumberland Presbyterian Church held in Jackson, Tennessee, in 1992. Some well-meaning commissioner (delegate) introduced a resolution to display the American flag, along with the Christian flag, at all subsequent gatherings of the General Assembly. This seemed like a pretty good idea to some until the Assembly was reminded that we are an international church and many nations, not only America, are represented in our annual meetings. This was followed by the pretty good suggestion that at every General Assembly we fly the flags of all the nations where we have missionaries and/or churches. You should have heard the protests by our international commissioners. In many of the countries where there is a Cumberland Presbyterian presence there is corruption, tyranny, oppression, and an absence of freedom of speech, not to mention the persecution of churches in some instances. There was no way we would display those flags. The national flag, for some, meant fear and not freedom. All attempts at flag displays failed. We all thanked God for the decisions made by the Assembly not to go with the flags.

466

I am not a stranger to band instruments, having tried the trumpet (coronet), french horn, and baritone. There was never an oboe in the high school band while I was there, and I am not that acquainted with its story. However, I have heard a couple of things about the oboe, whether they be fact or legend or something in between. First, the oboe is very hard to play. It takes a lot of energy and wind from the instrumentalist. The second characteristic is that the oboe cannot be tuned, which means that all other instruments must be tuned in harmony with the oboe. It is not flexible. It is as if the oboe refuses to work with other instruments, is uncooperative in meeting them halfway, and insists that everything must be as it demands. Well, when I came upon this, I found an occasion to say these very things about the oboe in a sermon and somehow made reference to people in churches who seem to take this same attitude. The service was not over but a few minutes when a man in the church rushed up to me and asked, "Were you talking about me when you mentioned the oboe?" I was caught off guard and, being earnest about peace in the church, said, "No." But he was really the person I had in mind. Call it bad manners by the preacher. Call it lack of ministerial ethics. Or call it hitting the nail on the head. I did not mean to be that direct, but, on the other hand, if the shoe fits. I realize that the best preaching is often indirect, coming through the back door or side window instead of the front door, but this time I must have just barged right in. Oh for a parable from Jesus on oboes, but a complete search of the New Testament reveals nothing on the subject.

467

A few years ago a church leadership magazine had a cartoon - funny at the time - depicting a futuristic church that had surrendered to the spirit of the times. The phone had rung, and an automated voice was saying, "Thank you for calling Calvary Church. To reach the senior pastor, press 1. To reach the associate pastor, press 2. To talk with the director of Christian education, press 3. To talk with the church secretary, press 4. For counseling services, press 5. To discuss service opportunities, press 6." Back then this scenario was unthinkable. Today this is no longer an imaginary occurrence.

468

Have you ever called up a company or a church or a business and asked for a certain person that you know works there, only to hear these words: "Mr. Smith is no longer with us"? And that's all they tell you. You are left with many questions. Is Mr. Smith dead? Is he sick? Did Mr. Smith take another job? Did Mr. Smith get fired, or, these days, down-sized? Did he leave amid scandal or was it an amicable separation? Did he take another job just down the hall with another department of the same company or does he now live halfway around the world? Is he out on the streets with a sign "Will Work for Food" or did he "move up" to Assistant Chief Executive Officer of the firm? We'll never know. We know only this: "Mr. Smith is no longer with us." The phone rings. Thomas answers. "Is Judas there?" "Judas is no longer with us." Another time: "Is John the Baptist there?" "John the Baptist is no longer with us."

469

The actor Matt Damon has appeared in three closely-related movies. Their titles are "The Bourne Conspiracy," "The Bourne Ultimatum," and "The Bourne Identity," but not necessarily in that order. Just like the "Rocky" movies that now number in the double digits, it seems, there could be more "Bourne" films. Here is a suggested title if our hero has one of his capers in America: "Bourne in the USA." If he has a torrid romance but she leaves him, we can have a movie entitled, "Bourne to Lose." And when our main character gets religion? That's easy. Here it is: "Bourne Again."

470

Another church sign:

> DO THE MATH
> COUNT YOUR BLESSINGS

471

I appreciate subtleties and the niceties and delicacies of <u>soft</u> speech, such as the tender message seen at a Chili's Restaurant near Dallas:

> CHILI'S PARKING ONLY
> ALL OTHER CARS WILL BE
> CRUSHED AND MELTED

472

I have been reading a lot about Abraham Lincoln lately. In the Civil War he became exasperated and frustrated with Union generals who would not fight. They would prepare and prepare, and then report that they were not quite ready and, besides, they needed more supplies, mules, horses, cannons, rifles, men, or something else. They kept putting off marching into battle. Lincoln's famous complaint to one general still echoes. He said to one of them, "Sir, if you are not going to use your army, may I borrow it?" It was not until General U.S. Grant came to the highest military leadership role that the Union forces began to make significant progress. It appears that some folks are always getting ready, always preparing, always needing just a little bit more before they can do what they were called on to do. I recall that some well known author had a story about a man who was constructing a boat, but, just as he was about to finish it, he decided it needed a different design, so he tore it down and started again. And, sure enough, as he got to the finish line and it was almost ready to launch, he concluded that it should be revamped, and he broke it down and started again. He never put a boat out to sea.

473

Another church sign:

> DO YOUR BEST
> GOD WILL DO THE REST

474

Our denominational executives in 2006-2007 were asked by a special task force to assess their own work. There were also opinions expressed in a questionnaire distributed to a handful of other, at-large, people in the church. There were mine fields galore in this exercise. The whole thing was unfair, uncalled for, and loaded with pitfalls and pot holes of the worst kind. I saw the results of the 1 to 10, poor to excellent, project. . Some executives rated themselves a "4" and others gave themselves an "8." Another put down a "10" and another a "5." What the at-large folks gave was different most of the time. The executives who gave themselves rather high marks sometimes had lower ratings by the few that were interviewed in the church. And those who gave themselves low marks sometimes had higher scores from the church. It was a no-win situation. If you rated yourself lower than the public sees you, you have no self-esteem, you are too humble, you do not know your capabilities, you think less of yourself than you ought to think, you are <u>out of touch</u> with the church. But if you gave yourself high marks but the average from the church was lower, then you are ego-centered, you think too highly of yourself, you are <u>out of touch</u> with the church. And in both cases, you are not worthy to hold an executive position in the church. See you later. Furthermore, some of the at-large persons interviewed knew nothing about the work these good folks were supposed to be doing, or if they knew that, they did not have day-to-day knowledge of the intricacies of the work. Yet they gave them a grade, based on what, I do not know. Self-assessments that are not private are an idea whose time has not come. And

by the way, the General Assembly instructed our boards years ago to do a biennial evaluation of their executive directors, and they have been abiding by that requirement. Who better than board members to evaluate these good people? Did the evaluations of the respective boards count for naught in the recent study? Were the boards consulted?

475

It is very difficult to assess one's own life. It is better when others do it. Anything done by ourselves concerning ourselves could easily appear to be ego-centered or, the opposite, falsely humble. Once I took a hospital chaplaincy class under the auspices of Texas Christian University in Fort Worth, Texas. At the end of the semester the chaplain, our instructor, called each of us in, one at a time. When I sat down in his office, he asked me what kind of grade I should get. I told him what kind of grade I hoped to get, but there was no way I could tell him what I deserved; that was his responsibility. But he kept on insisting that I suggest a grade. The same thing applied here as I described above. I don't even remember what the grade turned out to be. I know I was not qualified to make any suggestions. Self-assessments, at least for others to see, are fraught with danger and can serve no good end.

476

One more thing about personal assessments. Isaiah 49:4 begins in despair but ends in hope: "I have labored in vain, I have spent my strength for nothing and vanity; <u>Yet surely my cause is with the Lord, and my reward with my God.</u>" Do we need a New Testament corollary? How about 1 Corinthians 15:58, the last words of Paul's classic chapter on Resurrection: "Therefore, my beloved, be steadfast, immovable, always excelling in the work of the Lord, because you know that <u>in the Lord your labor is not in vain.</u>" Now those are good assessments!

477

The reader of the paper for the group I was in, George Estes, highlighted two great men, Dietrich Bonhoeffer and Martin Luther King, Jr. They both could have lived more comfortable lives than they chose. Bonhoeffer, born and raised in Germany, watched Nazi rule take hold and protested at every opportunity. To escape imprisonment or worse, he fled to the United States having been urged to do so by friends. However, his heart was with his country, and he returned, later to be imprisoned and found guilty of helping in the plot to assassinate Hitler. Some of his writings while incarcerated were published as <u>Letters and Papers from Prison</u>, a classic work for Christians. He formed an underground seminary and wrote <u>Life Together</u>, another classic. Just days before the Allies stormed and liberated the prisons, Bonhoeffer was executed. He was 39.

Martin Luther King, Jr. was a Baptist minister who was urged by friends to get involved in the Montgomery bus crisis. He became the leader of the civil rights movement. He was an inmate in the Birmingham jail and wrote a "Letter from the Birmingham Jail." He was an advocate of non-violence and an admirer of Gandhi. He went to Memphis to lead the march in the garbage workers' strike and was assassinated. He was 39.

Both could have been more laid back, more obscure, more comfortable in their lives. They believed, however, that one must do what is best for one's people, even if it leads to sacrifice and death. In their activities, both were vilified by others, even sometimes by their own people. Both died premature deaths, but the quality of their lives and the depth of their commitment to righteousness and justice motivated them to take risks.

It was a good paper about these two witnesses and martyrs.

478

One of our Memphis Theological Seminary professors was the guest minister at a United Methodist Church in Memphis whose former days had more splendor than the present. People have moved to the suburbs and joined larger, growing congregations, leaving the city churches with a nucleus of the faithful and growing numbers of opportunities for community involvement. The attendance Sunday was in the sixties, the professor said. Then we talked about the hardships and challenges of churches that stay instead of relocating. The professor, Lee Ramsey, said that in the Book of Acts Jesus said to stay in the city: "While staying with them, he ordered them not to leave Jerusalem, but to wait there for the promise of the Father" (Acts 1:4).Later the mandate to be "my witnesses in Jerusalem, and in all Judea and Samaria, and to the ends of the earth" (Acts1:8b) was given. We are grateful for those churches and their pastors who choose to stay in the city to do vital ministry.

479

Life is good, and tragic. Martha Roark grew up in McKenzie, Tennessee, graduating from the local high school. She married young and became Martha Roark Stoker, had a son named Johnny, and divorced. She started to Bethel College and, as a single mother, held down a job while going to school. I was a student at Bethel, just out of high school, and I remember her, for she was an "older" student (at least thirty years old!!). Martha worked hard, against all odds, and graduated. I didn't hear about her for several years, but then learned she was a professor in a college in West Virginia (maybe West Virginia University) and had married someone who was also a professor there. But the way I learned about her was not good. The article was in the local paper, The McKenzie Banner. The details were sketchy, but they went something like this. Someone (was Martha at home?) playfully reached for a rifle or shotgun on the shelf. The gun was empty. The person playfully pointed the empty gun at Martha and playfully pulled the trigger of the gun that was not loaded. The blast from the unloaded gun killed her instantly. Here was one who had worked hard, overcome personal adversity, and reached great heights as a college professor, only to have her life end in such a tragic, foolish, crazy way. I learned nothing else, whether anyone was arrested, tried, convicted, or whether it was ruled an accident. This was sometime back in the 1970s. I still feel great sorrow over that.

480

Another church sign, this one in Missouri:

>KING JAMES
>BIBLE BAPTIST CHURCH

481

Should the above have been arranged this way?

>KING JAMES BIBLE
>BAPTIST CHURCH

482

An interesting quote from a book on worship has stayed with me through the years. Paul W. Hoon wrote The Integrity of Worship:

Ecumenical Studies in Liturgical Theology, Abingdon, 1971. Keep in mind the era in which this was written, because it is not necessarily inclusive language. On page 23 we read: "A seminarian once suggested the kind of attitude appropriate to our task (of looking at worship) in comparing a man's decision to enter the ministry to his decision to marry. 'To marry,' he said, 'is to choose the woman one would most like to be unhappy with, and to enter the ministry is to choose the vocation one would most like to be a sinner in.'" I will leave that with no comment, except to say, again, the quote has not escaped my memory these many decades.

"Is this the person with whom you have chosen to be unhappy?"

483

Sometimes words and phrases directed to or spoken about somebody, and intended to be derisive or critical, end up being considered complimentary. This happened a few years ago. A professor at Memphis Theological Seminary was attending a conference in Washington, D.C., with teachers from other theological schools. Someone asked the MTS representative where he taught, and he said, "Memphis Theological Seminary." To which the person responded, "That's that 'blue-collar' seminary, isn't it?" To which the MTS professor proudly answered, "Yes." We are in midtown Memphis, not in the suburbs. Students and faculty are involved in many inner city ministries. Students here mix seminary classes with their work. They go to work, break away to go to class, then return to work. About 40% are African-American. Approximately 40% of the students are female. The curriculum of the MTS points one toward the pastorate, mostly. There are over thirty denominations represented in the student body of over 300.

Of the fourteen faculty members, eight denominations are represented. Yes, we are that "blue-collar" seminary and working hard at being a better one.

484

I heard the other day that one way for the church to make inroads into the youth culture of today is to pay more attention to video games for that is where kids are to be found during many hours of the day. So we need to meet them where they are. It didn't help and I don't think anybody laughed when I suggested that one way to start would be this game: "Dungeons and Dragons and Deuteronomy." At least it would be a start.

485

Exit polls on election day are an abomination. According to the media, they make possible the prediction of the outcome when less than 2% of the ballots have been counted. Oh, I pray for the pundits to be wrong again and again! How many people are going to stay up and watch the election returns on into the evening if the networks have named "the winner" at 7:10 P.M., ten minutes after the polls have closed? Viewer enjoyment comes when at 8:30 P.M. they declare a different candidate "the winner" and then at 11:15 P.M. they go back to the one they named first, only to have to change one more time at 2:30 A.M. when the final tally finds the winner to be not the one proclaimed at that premature hour the previous evening. There is a way to beat this system. Folks can lie when asked how they voted. Or they can refuse to reveal how they voted, which is their inherent right. If necessary, they can say something to this effect: "None of your business." I love it when all the polls get it wrong... so long as my candidate wins.

486

A few decades ago, on "The Tonight Show With Johnny Carson" a brief film was shown of some birds flying but having trouble landing. I think they are called "gooney birds," and do not know whether that has anything to do with their inability to make safe landings. Anyway, the short movie showed them flying in the sky - nothing prettier, no birds more graceful. But then it showed them descending and hitting the ground in a most unbird-like fashion. They all hit the ground hard with their feet and then stumbled, rolled over, tumbled, and/or crashed. Such grace in flying, such awkwardness in landing. Somehow that reminds me of starting a task, working on it really well, making great progress, but unable to close it out, not able to finish the work.

Beware being a gooney bird

487

However, in contrast to the gooney bird discussed above, there are other types of birds that cannot fly at all. They have wings. They barely get off the ground only to return, never able to soar. The gooney bird can't land; these birds can't fly. Both have their weaknesses. Some folks, like the birds that cannot fly, seem to have all the ingredients of soaring through life, but they cannot get started and when they finally do, they don't go far.

488

Outside sign at First Cumberland Presbyterian Church, Owensboro, Kentucky:

OUR SUNDAYS
ARE BETTER THAN
BASKIN-ROBBINS

"Our Sundays are better than Baskin Robbins'?"

489

At one pastorate there was an annual work day at the church, and members were invited to do various tasks in and around the building. There would be cleaning, fixing, painting, and yard work, including taking care of the flowers and shrubs. We would have some mulch brought in the day before and folks would spread that in the flower beds and among the shrubs. Every year, and I mean every year, in the next newsletter I would list the names of those who worked and would thank them. And I would always end by saying, "Thank you very mulch." That was just one thing the folks put up with for nine years.

490

Sign at a used car lot in Nashville, Tennessee:

> WE HAVE MORE RIDES
> THAN OPRYLAND

491

Phone number on a sign outside a barbecue restaurant in Chattanooga, Tennessee:

> 499-0INK

492

This was on the sign of the First Cumberland Presbyterian Church in Columbia, Tennessee:

> IF AT FIRST YOU DO SUCCEED
> TRY SOMETHING HARDER

493

Pardon me while I put forth a theory. I start with the game of baseball. Many of the best and most successful managers in the game were not great players. Two come to mind immediately: Ralph Houk with the New York Yankees and Walter Alston with the Los Angeles Dodgers. You won't find either of them in the Hall of Fame as players or in any of the record books insofar as their playing careers are concerned. They and others were mediocre and sometimes had only brief major league careers. There have been exceptions, of course, but it could be safe to say that some of the best managers were not on the list of great players. What is this suggesting? Perhaps that the one who was a mediocre, at best, performer on the field has a greater understanding of how hard it is to excel as a player and would likely have more patience. The average, or worse, player who later becomes a manager would seem to possess empathy with struggling catchers, pitchers, infielders, outfielders, and, from the plate, hitters. If some or all of that came easy, then it would be harder to understand the difficulties of striving to improve and be a winner.

This elaborate, and too lengthy, analogy brings home the notion that ministers and other spiritual leaders for whom the Christian life is sometimes a struggle may be more effective than those for whom prayer and study and righteousness seem to come so naturally. The one who preaches on prayer and makes it sound so easy and always with happy results may be out of touch with real people. The preacher who speaks of facing temptation and brings a message of triumph and victory may not be honest with his or her inner self. Acknowledging the difficulties of prayer and of resisting temptation, to mention two constant issues, may be more honest and also more helpful to the listening audience.

494

At the gathering of the McKenzie, Tennessee, High School Class of 1957 on the occasion of the 50th anniversary of our graduation, we reminisced. Stories of the past over the years have gotten more and more colorful in our meetings over time. We mourned the loss of classmates by death in the past few years. One who is deceased is Dr. Stanley Patterson. He was a brain surgeon in Memphis, Tennessee. In high school he played football and was one of the co-captains in his senior year. Stanley also was not bereft of mischief. So when we gathered as a class in his absence, and when stories of past misdeeds were being told, it was tempting to blame everything on Stanley, since he wasn't there. In fact, it got to be expected. The blowing up of part of the chemistry classroom was Stanley's fault. The stuffing of the bell in the balcony of the old gym so that when the class bell rang it would have a certain muffled sound was Stanley's doing. The tricks played on our English teacher, Miss Polly Rucker, were instigated by Stanley.

I think we have a tendency in Christian circles to do to Adam what the Class of 1957 in good fun did to Stanley Patterson: blame everything on him. Have I sinned lately? Blame it on Adam. Is humanity seemingly on a downward spiral due to greed, lust, sloth, avarice, and other signs of decadence? It's Adam's fault. Even the short poem says it: "With Adam's fall, we sinned all." Where does blaming Adam give way to taking responsibility for our own deeds and words that alienate us from God? Right now, all I have to say is, "Thank you very much, Adam!" The good news in that expression of gratitude is it's not my fault. The bad news is Adam set the pattern and we have all followed in his footsteps to the detriment and degradation of the human race. Yes, "Thank you very much, Adam! Thanks for nuthin!'"

495

It doesn't hurt to generate a little publicity for your church, a little spin, a slight tweak so the surrounding community might sit up and take notice. Back in 1978 the people of St. Matthew Cumberland Presbyterian Church in Burleson, Texas, were ready to construct another building. They had a small sanctuary, restrooms, classrooms, pastor's study, a very small fellowship hall, and an even smaller kitchen. The addition would give the church twice the current space in the form of a much larger fellowship hall. A groundbreaking service was set for a Sunday immediately after morning worship. The local newspaper was invited to send a photographer. There were four sets of twins in the church - in the Wilbanks, Murray, Martin, and Hewgley families. These eight children and youth would be the first to turn the dirt. In the Burleson Star a few days later the picture showed the four sets of twins shoveling the dirt. The caption said it all: "ST. MATTHEW SEES DOUBLE." A few lines under the picture told the complete story and gave the names of the twins at the groundbreaking.

496

Tornadoes ripped through the South in February of 2008, bringing almost total devastation to Union University in Jackson, Tennessee. Several students were trapped for hours under the rubble of crumbled dormitories. All lived through the ordeal. One student spoke to his mother and said, "I've lost everything." She replied, "I've got you. I haven't lost anything."

"We didn't lose anything"

497

A sermon title by a fellow minister preparing to preach about Adam's fall and how it affects us:

I'VE FALLEN AND I CAN GET UP

ఏ౧ఇఏ౧ఇఏ౧ఇఏ౧ఇఏ౧ఇఏ౧ఇఏ౧ఇఏ౧ఇఏ౧ఇఏ౧ఇ

498

The turning points in life are often easily noted but often more subtle. It is helpful to look at the life of Joseph in the Old Testament. We are not certain whether he was a spoiled child or not, but his brothers evidently thought he was. It bothered them the most that he got a lot of mileage out of being spoiled and pampered and favored by his father. They may have loved their brother but they did not like him. Like it was said of John Adams in the play and movie "1776" Joseph was "obnoxious and disliked." So when the older brothers had a chance to "take care" of Joseph they came "that close" to finishing him off. Cooler heads prevailed, however, and they "only" sold him into slavery. But before they sold him into slavery he spent some time in a dry cistern. His brothers put him there sort of for safe keeping. As it turned out, that time down deep in that cistern was a "turning point" in the life of Joseph. Look closely and you will see that this was a B.C. and A.D. moment: Before the Cistern and After the Deep. Before the cistern he had all the aggravating traits anyone would find annoying. He was self-centered, self-righteous, haughty, condescending, arrogant, and audaciously sure of himself. But after the deep we see none of that. Though taken into slavery and literally in prison for awhile, Joseph rose in favor with authorities and was soon a government official, perhaps the equivalent of Secretary of Agriculture, or something like that. He was gracious, sensitive, helpful, generous, and a host of other good things. It looks like the "turning point" was that cistern. Lots of people can point to a "turning point" in their lives. They, like Joseph, can say, "This is where and when my life changed." The Bible contains several other examples, one of the most obvious being Paul's experience on the Damascus Road (Acts 9). Zacchaeus certainly had his turning point, when Jesus invited him down from the tree (Luke 19). The disciples had theirs, when Jesus called them to come and follow him. The Prodigal Son had his turning point, when he "came to himself (Luke 15)." People in our day can testify of similar turning points in their lives: when their first child was born, when their teenager got into trouble, when cancer struck, when the call to ministry occurred, when they were confronted with the invitation and demands of the gospel, and many others.

Our "cisterns" might not have been literal cisterns, but we know what it means and how it feels to come up out of one phase of our lives and move on to another.

499

There is another part of the story linked to the one in #494. The Apostle Paul reminds us that, just as Adam brought it all down on us, so to speak, and we have him to "thank" for all this misery, so has Jesus Christ lifted it from us in his death on the cross. We read in Romans 5:15b and following: "For if the many died through the one man's trespass, much more surely have the grace of God and the free gift in the grace of one man, Jesus, abounded for the many... If, because of the one man's trespass, death exercised dominion through that one, much more surely will those who receive the abundance of grace and the free gift of righteousness exercise dominion in life through the one man, Jesus Christ." There you have it. We can say, "Thank you very much, Jesus!"

Thanks for everything, Jesus

500

I wonder if the phrase "mountain-top experience" stems from the story of the Transfiguration as recorded in Matthew 17:1-13, Mark 9:2-8, and Luke 9:28-36. Jesus went up into the mountain with three of his disciples and there he was transfigured and the disciples saw him standing and talking with Moses and Elijah. When it was all over, Peter wanted to build something permanent and even possibly stay on the mountain. However, Jesus mentioned the need to return to the valley where the people were so they could minister to the hurts and sorrows and illnesses of humanity. Young people sometimes have trouble coming down from the mountain of church camps and convocations. Adults sometimes struggle with coming down from the mountain of a weekend retreat or lay evangelism conference. These problems may be compared to when astronauts experience "re-entry" into the earth's atmosphere. Despite all of these problems, I am confident we will continue to describe great spiritual events as "mountain-top experiences."

Chapter XI: 501-550

"Decadent Love-Oriented Christians!!!"

501

Let us hear no more of that "love your enemy" nonsense!

Adolf Hitler had us Christians pegged in the 1930s. He really did. He was giving consideration to going into Spain to help non-communist efforts there while also establishing a Nazi foothold. He "hated the Spanish Catholic Church," so writes Stanley G. Payne in his book <u>Franco and Hitler: Spain, Germany, and World War II</u> (Yale University Press, 2008). Payne tells us, "Hitler considered Islam, with its simple theology and ethos of holy war, the best of the major religions. He believed that the highest culture ever seen in Spain was that of the Muslims, since it was so refreshingly non-Christian, and later lamented that the Muslim expansion had been checked in France. Hitler conjectured that if the Germans had been converted to Islam, rather than to DECADENT LOVE-ORIENTED CHRISTIANITY (capital letters added by T. Campbell), they might already have conquered the world in the Middle Ages (p. 20)."

So there you have it. To Hitler, our "decadent love-oriented Christianity" did not fit his plans for world domination. While unfortunately some professing Christians in Germany got caught up in the frenzy of the Nazi movement, and they lost their spiritual bearings, the good news is, that hysterical and sinister period of history ended with Hitler's plans and practices in ruins. What a wonderful compliment from one who represented all that is evil in the world. He did not mean it as a compliment. We pray, we earnestly pray, that we Christians are always a part of this "decadent love-oriented" pilgrimage.

502

In a church that I served as pastor there was a member who was an artist. He sold a few of his paintings along the way. He knew art, too. He was telling me that Cezan' - and excuse the spelling if it is incorrect - had a habit of leaving some phase of his work unfinished. This appealed to me in regard to sermon work as well. If we wrap our sermons up in nice neatly tied ribbons leaving nothing for the listener to process or mull over, we preachers may do a disservice. If, like Cezan' we leave some phase of the sermon "unfinished," the listener might be challenged to think through some ideas and ponder some thoughts offered by the preacher: a little more to chew on, a little more to think about, some work still to do by the listener. That's a good goal of preaching. These thoughts were confirmed when I read something from the well-known and highly respected homiletics professor and preacher Thomas Long, who, in what publication I do not recall, remarked on some of the very same thoughts about the very same artist. Now all that is something for us preachers to think about, mull over, and ponder.

503

We saw the movie "School of Rock" starring Jack Black the other night. It is full of fun and it is crazy with great rock music. But the best part of the story is that the character played by Jack Black, posing as a qualified teacher when in truth he has just been fired from a rock group, comes on as one of the best teachers around. He encourages every student every step along the way. He never tells his students they are not capable. On the contrary, he enforces the belief that every person has worth and can achieve. At every turn, when faced with potential negative attitudes or actions, the pretend-teacher affirms and encourages and, in the end, celebrates with the kids. He keeps telling them, "You can do it." And they did.

504

I am surprised that more churches have not given themselves the name "St. Barnabas." St. Barnabas United Methodist Church. St. Barnabas Lutheran Church. St. Barnabas Episcopal Church. St. Barnabas Cumberland Presbyterian Church. St. Barnabas Presbyterian Church (USA). St. Barnabas United Church of Christ. Barnabas was one of the true heroes of the New Testament. He exemplified the spirit of Christ in his words and deeds. He was called "Son of Encouragement." He could have been one of the "encouragers" in the movie "School of Rock" mentioned above.

505

Being a guest preacher has its ups and downs. You don't know the people. You don't know their situation. You don't know what the pastor has been preaching lately that you might hook up on. You do your best under the circumstances. On two occasions I was to be the preacher and a text was assigned. The first was when I was a pastor in Lexington, Kentucky, in the early 1980s and Presbyterian churches (including Lansdowne Cumberland Presbyterian) were sponsoring noonday Lenten services. I was asked to preach on a certain day and the text was to be Matthew 26:6-13, which included these words of Jesus in verse 11: "You always have the poor with you." I accepted the assignment and hoped it blended in with the other sermons at the noonday services. The second occasion was in February of 2003 in San Francisco, California, at the First Chinese Cumberland Presbyterian Church in the English service (later in the morning would be services in Mandarin and then Cantonese). I was out there to conduct some classes for the Program of Alternate Studies and had been invited to preach that Sunday morning at First Chinese. The pastor was out of town. He had been doing a series from the Beatitudes and I was informed that I would continue in that series. Moreover, my Beatitude was "Blessed are the peacemakers, for they will be called the children of God" (Matthew 5:8). This happened to be on the same weekend when a nationwide protest against the imminent invasion of Iraq by the United States was being held. In all other places across the country the protests were held on Saturday, but that was the day of the celebration of the Chinese New Year, so in San Francisco the protest was set back one day, to Sunday afternoon. Now I'm about to preach on "Blessed are the peacemakers" and the lay leader in worship gives the morning prayer which includes something to this effect: "Bless those who will be protesting today." And then I stand up to expound on "Blessed are the peacemakers." What a moment! In the early afternoon from our hotel room we saw the huge crowd in the streets of San Francisco and we heard speakers, including the actor Danny Glover. Here were real peacemakers, trying to make a difference. I only preached about it. Neither approach changed any minds in the U.S. administration, and we know how the rest of the sad story goes. But I did appreciate the assigned scriptures on the two occasions mentioned above.

506

I have a word of advice for those who preach without notes. It is this: Never say in your sermon, "There are four things I would like to say about this." Trust me. You'll be lucky to remember three of them. It might be best this way: "There are several things I would like to say about this," or "I wonder what comes to mind about this matter," and then start listing the ideas accordingly. That way you haven't made any promises you can't keep. Many of the writers and teachers in speaking of preaching without notes say this aspect is one of the dangers of that approach. But they also say that it is a small price to pay for the luxury of looking at your congregation more often and communicating better. In fact, preaching without notes usually means not having any lengthy quotations, if any at all. It means no long poetry, if any at all. It means no lengthy statistics, if any at all. But that is still a small price to pay for the value and satisfaction of speaking to your congregation face to face every Sunday.

507

There was a street in Memphis, Tennessee, named Shotwell. Then the federal government put the Veterans' Hospital on this street, making its name increasingly inappropriate and demoralizing. So the city fathers gave it another name: Getwell. This is revealed in a recent video in the "Memphis Memoirs" series for public television.

Strange names occur without planning. I heard there was a town in Tennessee named Only. I have not visited there. It is not on the map so far as I can see. It used to be just off Interstate 40 between Jackson and Nashville. I think there was, or is, a state prison there. If there is a town by that name, one would assume that there are churches, perhaps named the Only Baptist Church and the Only United Methodist Church and the Only Church of Christ.

In some state in the south I heard there was a town or village named Halfway. Now how would it be if there were a Halfway Baptist Church or Halfway United Methodist Church or Halfway Church of Christ or Halfway Cumberland Presbyterian Church?

I honestly and truly saw, somewhere in Arkansas, this sign in front of a dental office jointly owned by two professionals in the tooth department: SHARPE & PAYNE, DENTISTS.

And of course, given the emphasis on global warming by Al Gore, I heard of one dentist telling how unpleasant a toothache can be and using modern terminology in a newspaper ad: AN INCONVENIENT TOOTH.

508

This is a ministerial confession to lay people. We preachers need just one or two more days in the week to get our sermons ready for Sunday. Seven days between each Sunday morning worship service is not enough time. Give us eight, maybe nine days (and nights) between preaching moments and we can come up with some whiz-bang, earth-shaking, mind-boggling masterpieces. But seven days? No way. Many preachers can testify that some of their best material for sermons comes on Mondays following the Sunday service, when it's too late.

But here is another part of the confession. We preachers know that a complete, finished sermon is not the goal. We may be tweaking it, fiddling with it, even changing it in our minds even as the hymn or anthem is being sung immediately prior to sermon time, but we never ever get it just the way we want it. There is always something else we feel we need to do to enhance the sermon's quality or power or focus.

And so we go on week after week preaching incomplete sermons, not quite finishing them before it is time to preach them, and after we preach an incomplete, not quite finished sermon, we are compelled to start thinking about the next sermon seven days hence. Here is the good news. God takes what we bring and uses it for good. A veteran preacher, wise and helpful, said, "When a sermon is preached, somebody is helped."

509

It seems every culture, race, tradition, and family has its stories. I once heard a wonderful rendition of how the races came about, especially the different colors. As the story goes, God, in forming human beings, put them in the oven to get just a little texture and refinement. When God brought them out of the oven, those people were white and God said, "I did not leave them in long enough." So another group went into the oven, and this time God waited somewhat longer before removing them. The people this time came out black, and God said, "Oh my, I left them in too long." A third bunch was placed in the oven and this time when they were pulled out they were brown, and God said, "Perfect. I finally left some folks in for just the right amount of time." This, of course, would be a story told by a culture where the people are brown.

510

An Old Testament object of envy for preachers is young Samuel.

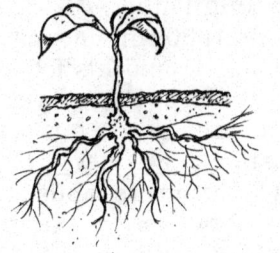
Some seed fell on good ground

Here is what is said of him in 1 Samuel 3:19: "As Samuel grew up, the Lord was with him and let none of his words fall to the ground." Those who walk to the pulpit every Sunday sometimes feel as though ALL their words "fall to the ground." Did anybody hear what I said? Was anybody listening? Was there anything said that was worth hearing?

Stand that scripture up alongside Matthew 13 where we have the Sower and the Seed. In this parable, EVERYTHING fell to the ground as the sower planted the seed. Some seed fell on "the path." Some fell on "rocky ground." Other seed fell "among thorns." But others fell on "good soil."

Maybe, just maybe, even though we may think all of our words fall to the ground, some words may fall on welcoming ears, open hearts and minds. In other words, good soil. I believe that is true more than we think.

♪11

Sign seen on a passing truck:

>   JESUS IS LORD
> NOT A SWEAR WORD

512

To show that a name does not necessarily convey what something is all about, I read the other day about Father Charles E. Coughlin, the Roman Catholic priest of the 1930s in America who called for an American version of fascism. He and his followers hated Jews, Communists and labor unions. His movement published a directory of non-Jewish merchants in portions of New York City, so says the <u>Dictionary of Christianity in America</u> (Inter-Varsity Christian Fellowship, 1990) and its members "abused and physically attacked Jews in the streets". Now here is the irony. Coughlin published a monthly paper entitled "Social Justice." Yes, that is right. The name of the publication was "Social Justice." Sometimes a name belies what it is really all about.

513

Sign outside a middle school in Columbia, Tennessee:

WHAT DID YOU READ TODAY ?

514

One of the greatest hymns ever written is "How Firm a Foundation." The tune we usually sing it to, "Foundation," brings its own power and adds to the total experience. The other tune, "Portuguese" (the same as "O Come, All Ye Faithful") does not capture the essence of the hymn nearly as well. When I was helping to plan my father's funeral service, I suggested "How Firm a Foundation." After the service one of my father's colleagues said that the same hymn was sung at his wife's funeral and he was able to experience its power once again on this occasion. All the verses are wonderful. I especially appreciate verse 2:

> In every condition, in sickness, in health,
> In poverty's vale, or abounding in wealth;
> At home and abroad, on the land, on the sea,
> As your days may demand, shall your strength ever be.

Again, every verse is powerful, including what is usually the last verse:

> The soul that on Jesus hath leaned for repose,
> I will not, I will not desert to its foes;
> That soul, though all hell should endeavor to shake,
> I'll never, no, never, no, never forsake!

515

There are those who want, and pray for, the United States to become a "Christian nation." Some maintain it started out that way. I'm not so sure it started out that way. Go ask Benjamin Franklin or John Adams or Thomas Jefferson or George Washington about that. Some, or all, of these might refer to "God" or a "Higher Power" and say we all should worship such a One, but hardly ever do these or other founders of our country center in on Jesus. Reference to "God" can be very general and take in a lot, but a focus on "Jesus" narrows the view and shines the spotlight on one belief, one approach, one way of life. I am bothered by the cry for us to be a "Christian nation," and fear that those who plead for that and work for that might get what they want. In fact, I do not believe they would really want what would follow. Would there be a Department of Christian Values with its Secretary in the President's Cabinet? Would there also be room for a Department of Jewish Values? And Buddhist Values? And Muslim Values? Or would we leave other Americans out if we were to become a "Christian" nation? It seems the more we try to make our country a "Christian" nation the more intolerant we are, the more hate-filled we are, the more divisive we become. Go figure.

516

The new pastor came in like a house afire. Evangelistic zeal, looking for souls to save, powerful and bombastic sermons mostly about sin. This Sunday sin, next Sunday sin, last Sunday sin. Finally, after a few years, he resigned, and one lady, trying to give a compliment, said on his last day: "Pastor, we didn't know what sin was until you came here."

I didn't know what sin was until you became my pastor

517

Sign outside a church:

THOSE WHO BURY THEIR TALENTS
MAKE A GRAVE MISTAKE

518

I suppose those committees who compile hymnals must keep the songs to a limited number of verses, though the author may have more than four or five. I know this is true about Washington Gladden's "O Master, Let Me Walk With Thee." One of the seldom seen verses in "How Firm a Foundation" is this one, written especially for us older folks:

> E'en down to old age, all My people shall prove
> My sovereign, eternal, unchangeable love;
> And when hoary hairs shall their temples adorn,
> Like lambs they shall still in My bosom be borne.

519

Sign outside First Cumberland Presbyterian Church of Columbia, Tennessee, upon the death of a former pastor and beloved friend to many in the area:

> THANK YOU REV. WAYNE PARKS
> FOR YOUR FAITHFUL SERVICE

520

I heard a song on a "Gospel Network" radio program. It was "We Want America Back." I listened closely and I think I heard the vocalist singing that America was founded on the Bible and we have departed from the Bible and we need to get back to the Bible as a country. I hope I live by the Bible and I hope I teach and preach it faithfully, but the Bible is not the basis for our nation and never has been. The Declaration of Independence is our song of freedom. The Constitution is our foundation of government. We would not want a President or a Congress or a Supreme Court to support or in any way push for a government and a national life based on the Bible. First, laying aside the Declaration of Independence and the Constitution (for argument purposes only), who would decide what part or parts of the Bible we would live by? Would those who broke the law be stoned? Would Sabbath laws be enforced? From what would our laws derive? And how tolerant would we be or not be to those who decided not to live "by the Bible?" Furthermore, not everybody sees the value of the Bible as much as we do, and, indeed, may not be believers at all.

Additionally, what would classify one to be a believer? If the answer to that is "believing in Jesus" what about Jews and Muslims, and Hindus and atheists? Would they not have a place in our national life? And who would be the arbiter on what the Bible says about such subjects as women and the poor? With all due respect, I am afraid that many who argue for a nation built on the Bible are unknowingly pushing for a Theocracy. As one person said, "If you want to live under a Theocracy, move to Iran." We Americans are a "people of the book," and the book is the Constitution.

On being a people of the Book

Children and their bedtime prayers are wonderful to hear. Take the following, for example.

A little girl wanted to be a high school cheerleader. She was already practicing when she prayed, "God bless Ma, God bless Pa, God bless me, Rah, Rah, Rah."

And the little boy who had a pet prayed: "God bless Mommy and Daddy, God bless me and my brothers and sisters. God bless my dog, Butch, who stinketh to high heaven."

"And God bless Fido"

522

In a Fort Worth suburb some folks started a new church, with the support and supervision of the Presbytery. The name was St. Luke Cumberland Presbyterian. I got there in 1965, one year after the "Fellowship" had been started. In February of 1966 we were officially organized and 35 people were charter members. Growth was steady in the next few years. One aid was the weekly mailing by the Welcome Wagon. We received lists of new families moving into the communities in the area for zip codes 76134 and 76133. Our new church was in the heart of the 76134 region and we were the only church in the neighborhood. I would go and visit families almost as they moved in, and on a couple of occasions, got there before they did and returned a few days later. In addition to the Welcome Wagon information our church received, the church folks themselves would let me know about new families. Someone in the church told me about this young family that had moved in two doors down from them and pretty much right around the corner from the church. So it was that on a warm, lazy, sunny afternoon I went to the home of the young family - father, mother, two little boys, my informants said. When I got to the house I noticed toys outside - tricycles, balls, bats, other items. And, since it was around 2:00 in the afternoon and thinking the boys might be having their afternoon naps I decided not to ring the doorbell, but instead to knock softly on the front door. The young mom came to the door and whispered, "Yes, may I help you." And I was glad I knocked instead of ringing the bell, for that might have awakened the boys. Her whisper told me that. So I whispered back, "I am the pastor of the new church right around the corner and I wanted to welcome you to the community and invite you and your family to Sunday school and worship." I was rather proud that I was able to adjust to the circumstances by whispering. Evangelism and outreach must accommodate the situation at hand, I always have said. So my whisper seemed to go all right. Until she said, "I have laryngitis; you can talk out loud."

523

Here are the final words of a movie called "Mississippi Burning" - an important film about the civil rights movement. The abused wife of a convicted law enforcement officer tied to the murders of three civil rights workers, says to the FBI agent who had worked the case, and to whom she had given testimony that helped to break the case: "If you are ever in Des Moines, don't send me a card." You'll have to see the movie to get the full story on this.

524

You heard about the fellow who won the lottery and then experienced both good news and bad news. The good news was he won a million dollars. The bad news was that he will receive one dollar a year for a million years.

525

Is there anything longer or more tedious than a two-minute commercial on television? We are accustomed to fifteen-second or, at most, thirty-second messages. When I see the Nutri-Systems commercial coming up, I switch channels. They go on and on and on about Nutri-Systems, how much weight they have lost, how much better they feel and look. It is the longest two minutes in recorded history. This reminds me that we preachers should have sermons that move instead of just standing there. If a boring two-minute commercial is so bad, just think of what a boring twenty-five minute sermon sounds like. It had better be good.

526

David Ramsey was a great organist and a great person. A Cumberland Presbyterian throughout his life, he was frequently the accompanist for meetings of the General Assembly. He was a teacher in the music department at Rhodes College in Memphis and was at different times organist and music director for leading churches in the city. He perhaps was best known in the Memphis area, however, as the organist out at Auto Zone Park, and before that, Tim McCarver Stadium, for all home baseball games of the local professional team. He died in early 2008. A sign outside a local jewelry store said it well:

DAVID RAMSEY MADE MEMPHIS A BETTER PLACE

527

I keep coming upon, or being confronted by, analogies about the church. The other day I walked into a Pizza Hut. I like the Pizza Hut. Their Pizza Hut Supreme Sandwiches are the best. However, this time nobody noticed me. I walked to the area where you are supposed to stand so they will notice you and seat you. Nobody came. I walked over to the cash register where one would think somebody would be there, but, again, nobody. Oh, all the workers were busy. The cooks were cooking. The servers were serving. The clean-up crews were cleaning up the different tables. But nobody noticed the newcomer (me) walking in and standing there. The workers were busy going about their duties but appeared to be ignoring anybody new. They were taking care of what they had. I have seen churches that were very busy on Sunday mornings. Everybody was doing necessary things. But nobody noticed the newcomer entering the building. In truth, the newcomer, the visitor, should be our top priority. We are serving not only our own, but others. It is those "others" that the church needs to be focused on. By the way, after being unnoticed for several minutes and continuing to give the workers the benefit of the doubt (surely somebody will come up here), I walked out of the place. They lost a customer.

528

We have all heard the advice: "If you can't say something good about somebody, then don't say anything at all." Alice Roosevelt Longworth, daughter of Theodore Roosevelt, was a well known Washington, D.C. personality. She had a sharp tongue and a love for gossip and scandal. She turned the phrase around this way: "If you can't say something good about somebody, then come and sit down beside me."

529

Where did I hear this a long time ago? It's about marriage and it goes something like this:

ANYBODY WHO MARRIES FOR MONEY EARNS IT

530

Something else on marriage. A couple splits up. Somebody heard one of the couple saying, "We expected too much." The reply was, "No, you did not expect enough."

531

Chapter 37 of the Book of Ezekiel has the story of the "valley of dry bones." God instructs Ezekiel to "Prophesy to these bones and say to them: O dry bones, hear the word of the Lord (37:4)." Ezekiel writes in verse 7, "So I prophesied as I had been commanded; and as I prophesied, suddenly there was a noise, a rattling, and the bones came together..." Sometimes God has the prophet to speak AFTER the event happens. Sometimes God has us to speak DURING THE EVENT. In this case, God told the prophet to speak TO MAKE IT HAPPEN. This shows the power of words. A basketball team plays the first half in a lethargic way but comes out for the second half and turns up the energy and speed and pressure and wins going away. What happened? In the locker room the coach spoke them into high gear. Did the coach instill encouragement, or criticism, or fear, or judgment, or challenge, or all of the above? Whatever it was, the words did it. Churchill spoke England to victory in World War II. Martin Luther King, Jr., spoke and non-violence triumphed over violence. Franklin D. Roosevelt in his "fireside chats" challenged America not to live in fear but in faith and determination during the Depression years. I think along the way somebody has been an Ezekiel for us, speaking us out of despair or grief or anger and into new life. And, though we may not be aware of it, we have probably been an Ezekiel for others as our words have lifted them out of their distress into new adventures. The dry bones of death and destruction rallied to come alive again in the time of Ezekiel. God is still using the power of the spoken word to instill new life.

532

Sometimes a person just can't get it right. Often it is not right because the person does not open the two eyes given by God to use every day. I was a good speller as a child, and still am. In fact, I sometimes pride myself in being a good speller. I won the

McKenzie elementary spelling bee as s sixth grader and went on to win the Carroll County Spelling Bee, which sent me to the Mid-South Spelling Bee in Memphis. We will not go into how brief my appearance on the stage in Memphis was. In the seventh grade I won the McKenzie contest again but in the Carroll County event thought too much, had too many second thoughts, got crossed up in my mind, and misspelled "thieves." However, as an eighth grader, I bounced back, taking the McKenzie event again as well as the Carroll County contest, and again going to Memphis, but true to form, bowing out early - very, very early. And so, I have a pretty good record.

Why, then, can I not spell Ezekiel? The above item (# 531) has that name sprinkled throughout. I had it spelled "Ezekial," and could not understand why the red line kept showing up under the name on the computer screen. I did catch the mistake, finally. As a matter of fact, when I have listed this prophet as one of the scripture readings in the Sunday bulletin, it has always been "Ezekial." In a course on the prophets, which I sometimes teach in weekend schools for the Program of Alternate Studies, it has always been "Ezekial." To remedy this, there was really one thing I needed to do: look in the Bible closely, very closely, and then look again, and I could have noticed clearly that the book bearing this prophet's name is spelled "E-Z-E-K-I-E-L."

ಖಬಲಾಖಬಲಾಖಬಲಾಖಬಲಾಖಬಲಾಖಬಲಾಖಬಲಾಖಬಲಾಖಬಲಾ

533

A pastor does not have just one career, but many, covering several stops along the way with different churches. Every church situation is another career. So I have had a ministerial career with several Cumberland Presbyterian congregations: in Batesville, Arkansas, with the Faith Church (1961-65); Campground Church, Strawberry, Arkansas (1963-65); Hopewell Church, Cord, Arkansas (1963-65); in Fort Worth, Texas, with the St. Luke Church (1965-72); in Memphis, Tennessee, with the Whitehaven Church, (1972-75); in Burleson, Texas, with the St. Matthew Church (1975-82); in Lexington, Kentucky, with the Lansdowne Church, (1982-85); in Knoxville, Tennessee, with the Beaver Creek Church (1985-94); and, since assuming the office of Director of the Program of Alternate Studies at Memphis Theological Seminary, preaching on Sundays for the Searcy, Gum Springs, and Pleasant Grove churches, in Searcy, Arkansas (1995-97); and then, preaching on Sundays for the Lebanon PCUSA Church, in Toccopola, Mississippi; and Monroe PCUSA Church, in Algoma, Mississippi (1997- to the present).

Why so many "careers" by one pastor? Because a minister cannot expect to take programs and ideas and even sermons and expect to use them again in the next place with no changes or improvements. Situations are different. Cultures are different. People are different. Besides, one should expect to change and grow and mature as a minister and what a pastor did a few years back should have been replaced or certainly refined into something better in the present. One of our pastors, Dr. Morris Pepper, when I mentioned that he had had sixty years of ministerial experience, with a smile modestly said that it was one year's experience sixty times. But those who heard him say that knew better, for in his eighties and early nineties, years after he had retired as a pastor, he was still eager to learn and grow and adjust to different situations

So my many "careers" have culminated in the present position of Director of the Program of Alternate Studies. I try to help present and would-be pastors to be equipped to cope with the changes and adjustments sure to come in the pastorate, church after church after church.

534

Eighteen of the first twenty-one years of my pastoral work were spent in new-church development congregations. I had the privilege of being the organizing pastor for three congregations (Faith, St. Luke, St. Matthew - see #533 for the years). During my last few months in Fort Worth I was honored to be asked to preach for a new group in Burleson, just five miles down the highway, a group that eventually named itself "St. Matthew Cumberland Presbyterian Fellowship." I would return in a few years to be their fulltime pastor. And while at the Whitehaven Church in Memphis, I had the honor of preaching for the new Germantown Fellowship for three months in an early Sunday morning service as that group was getting started, just before I moved to Burleson, Texas, to the St. Matthew Fellowship. I had been in Memphis for three years. Those in the Germantown Fellowship included some members of the Whitehaven Church who had moved into the Germantown area of Memphis. These things I learned: Being a part of a new church is exciting, scary, hopeful, scary (again), and demanding. While the other adjectives might be self-explanatory, what is it with the "scary" part? A new church is fragile, having just started a few months or a year or two ago. Every person is crucial. Every offering is vital. Every crisis is a danger to the very existence of the new church.

The exciting part is fun to talk about. New people, many from different parts of the country, come in. There is no "tradition" - at least of that church - to have to follow. We can do new things. New members usually join knowing of the challenges ahead: property, construction of a building, maintaining a certain level of offerings, the crucial importance of each family and individual, the financial commitments needed from everyone. Until I went to the Beaver Creek Church in Knoxville, Tennessee (organized 1833), all the other churches served (except for the two rural congregations in Arkansas while also serving the new Faith Church) were less than twenty years old. I have had the privilege, with George Estes of the Board of Missions, of co-teaching a class in new church development at Memphis Theological Seminary, in five different semesters in recent years. And here is another gem of truth: Every church that ever existed, no matter how old, was once a new church.

535

I saw this scene in a short television clip. I think it was part of a movie that never got released. Art Carney is sitting in the doctor's office. The doctor tells him, "I have bad news. You have one month to live." Art, playing whatever character in the film was assigned to him, is in shock. He is speechless. He sits there in silence. He is visibly shaken. Finally, after a minute or two, he speaks, "Well at least I have thirty days." The doctor replies, "Well I have some more bad news." "What's that?" The doctor answers, "This is February."

536

This sign was outside a Church of Christ in Arkansas:

>HELP STOP TRUTH DECAY
>BRUSH UP ON YOUR BIBLE

537

I drive into the state of Mississippi every Sunday morning to preach at two small churches. Mississippi has several towns, cities, and counties with long names, probably given by native Americans, who lived in that area for years. Towns like Kosciusko and Pascagoula.. Counties like Issaquena and Ittawamba. Other towns like Itta Bena and Noxapater and other counties like Noxubee and Oktibbeha. One day a man in a car with an out-of-state license stopped and went into an eating establishment in a Mississippi town with a very long name. When he went to pay he asked the cashier, "How do you pronounce this place?" She gave this answer, slowly, looking him in the eye: "DAAAIIRRRYYY QUEEEEEEEN."

538

I am a bit bothered when pastors and others who lead worship "fade away." What in the world am I talking about? The "fade away" moment comes at the Responsive Reading, or during the Lord's Prayer, or the reciting of the Apostles' Creed or some other affirmation of faith, or in the praying of the Prayer of Confession - any segment of worship where someone is leading the people in that particular aspect of worship. What is the "fade away" I so negatively mention? This occurs when the worship leader or pastor gets the people started with a relatively strong voice, then, instead of continuing to lead, "fades" into the background, is no longer heard from, as though that person had joined the Foreign Legion, and the remainder of the recitation or prayer drags along with no audible leadership. Here's my "solution" to the "fade away" leader: Stay strong with your voice. Stay at least one one-thousandth of a second ahead of everybody else. Keep the unison moment going. Don't run and hide. Stay in the forefront and encourage the people, by your good leadership, to go boldly forward with their voices. When you accomplish that, you may wish to step back and be only one-half of one thousandth of a second ahead!

539

This sign outside a church in Missouri seems to indicate that egg hunts are not all that one of our church seasons is about:

> EASTER IS WORTH MORE
> THAN DYEING FOR

540

I went to a service where the Presbytery ordained a minister and then installed that person as the pastor of the church where we were gathered. They let me preach. I had looked in the scriptures for some good examples of pastors, but with very little success. That is, until I came upon the Book of Job. Nestled within its second chapter is an account of not one, not two, but three excellent examples of a good pastor... almost. After so many bad things had happened to Job, three "friends" heard about it and came to him from three different directions. When they saw him at a distance they wept. Then they came closer and, for seven days and seven nights, sat with him in complete silence. Though not officially pastors, these three men were filling the role exceptionally well. For seven days and seven nights. Silence. No talking. Total and complete silence. They were being great pastors. They were shining examples of that role. But then the visit started going downhill fast. Why? They started talking. Before long they and Job were arguing back and forth, hurling accusations, debating the finer and coarser points of sin and repentance and punishment and all the related matters. One by one, the friends accused Job of deserving his suffering, asserting that one suffered to the extent of one's sin. If one had sinned only a little, one would suffer only a little, and since Job was suffering a great deal, his sin must have been horrific. They urged him to repent, to turn to God, to admit his wrongdoing, to quit blaming God, to "fess up" to his sins. Job argued back, claiming that he was not that bad a sinner and stubbornly refuting their crude attempts to help him make sense of it all.

If you and I could confront these three so-called friends, we would probably say that they should have remained silent. They would cry out, "But Job started it!" And they would be correct. But their mistake was in responding to Job's laments. They should have just listened and not argued. They should have let Job go on and on and on about his grief and suffering and loss and pain. Let him vent. The moments when one is suffering intensely are not occasions for reasoning and deciphering the innards of suffering and arriving at logical conclusions, and that is the mistake the friends made. Moments of grief deserve their space and time. When sufferers cry out, "Why?" that is not the call for us to start our explanations... as though we had the answer.

§41

A man in the congregation pleaded guilty to a crime and was taken off to jail. Many members of the church were there for the sentencing, and it was a very sad time. My wife and I drove to the family's home, following the man's wife. We walked into the house together and suddenly the wife crumpled to the floor, her body draped over the stairs that were just inside the front door. She wept openly, almost screaming. My wife stepped over to her as if to console her and help her stop crying. But she instead stepped back, realizing that the wife needed to unleash all the pain and loss and grief that was inside her soul. In a while, she had become quiet, her open sobs now giving way to soft whimpers and soon there was silence. But she needed that time. No words were needed. And she needed the time and space for unrestrained grief.

542

I got a call from Faye, a member of the church. Marie's son had died after returning home from the dentist. An innocent visit and tooth extraction resulted in an almost sudden death of the young man, whose home was in western Kentucky. We were in East Tennessee and now his mother was home in total grief. I got over there as quickly as I could. When I walked into the house there in the family room was the grieving woman, lying on the floor, sobbing, lamenting, loudly venting her recent loss. Faye, the woman who had called me, was sitting on the floor beside her, rubbing Marie's arms and shoulders, saying not a word. I sat down on the couch across the small room from them. The grieving mother continued in her lament. Faye continued sitting beside her, rubbing her arms and shoulders, saying nothing. This went on for an hour or more. I marveled at the silent ministry Faye was performing. No words like, "Don't cry." No attempts to slow down or stop the audible feelings being expressed. No words at all. I was proud of Faye. I saw her Christian witness there in as strong a way as I have ever seen it in anyone. I sat there another hour, then part of another. I did nothing and said nothing. When it was time to talk, Marie let it be known. And even then Faye used her wisdom and Christian maturity to walk gently into the arena of conversation. I had only a slight ministry of presence. Faye was Marie's pastor that day. And I was proud of her.

543

I have conducted over a hundred and fifty weddings and had about that many counseling sessions with potential brides and grooms. Thus it was that Kenny and Natalie (not their real names) got married. We had met (more than once) to talk about marriage and then to get into the specifics about the ceremony. She was bringing two young children into the marriage. This was his first. After the wedding they seemed all right for a time. But then there was strife. It seemed to be constant. The two children were somewhat of a discipline problem. The wife spoke sarcastically of the husband. His parents were very concerned. Before too long Kenny and Natalie separated. Then it dawned on me. In all our visits and counseling and planning, I failed to ask this question of him, "Do you love her?" and this question of her, "Do you love him?" And I now recall that I never heard "I love you" from either of them toward the other. What was this marriage about?

ಬಿಜಿಬಿಜಿಬಿಜಿಬಿಜಿಬಿಜಿಬಿಜಿಬಿಜಿಬಿಜಿ

544

Still another church sign touting the favorite translation of so many:

GET THE NEW LOOK
WITH THE OLD BOOK
KJV

ಬಿಜಿಬಿಜಿಬಿಜಿಬಿಜಿಬಿಜಿಬಿಜಿಬಿಜಿಬಿಜಿ

545

A professor of mine at Brite Divinity School, Dr. Charles Kemp, in a class on family counseling, said that the following questions are good ones to ask of any prospective bride about the groom-to-be or to the groom about the bride-to-be: Do you like her/him? Do you love her/him? Do you trust her/him? He said that if a person cannot answer YES to at least two of the three questions, the marriage is already in deep trouble before the ceremony is held and the vows are said.

ಬಿಜಿಬಿಜಿಬಿಜಿಬಿಜಿಬಿಜಿಬಿಜಿಬಿಜಿಬಿಜಿ

546

In 1980, in anticipation of my receiving the Doctor of Ministry degree from Brite Divinity School at Texas Christian University, the St. Matthew Cumberland Presbyterian Church asked me to order a new pulpit robe and the church would pay for it. That robe carried me through twenty-six years of ministry before dying on me in 2006. This happened first: I was preaching along in one of the two small Presbyterian churches in northern Mississippi where I go every Sunday. I was being expressive, I guess you could say, waving my arms and being very active in the pulpit. After the service, almost everybody in that little congregation said they saw something fly out of my robe as I was preaching. Turns out it was the right shoulder pad. I never saw it happen. A few weeks later the robe began to be contrary, in that the zipper would not stay zipped. I could tug on the robe just a little and it would come undone. I recall a trip to California to preach an ordination sermon. I was sitting in one of the chairs ready to be the next on the program. I looked down and the robe was completely undone. I came home and put it away and announced to my congregations that it had gone the way of all robes and I had sent it on to robe heaven, and that I would get me another robe someday. A few weeks later came Christmas and both churches, in addition to the nice bonus they give me every year at that time, presented to me a total of $780 to go and buy another pulpit gown. I was overcome and so grateful. It took about six weeks after I went to Cokesbury Book Store in Memphis to get measured and order one, and then it arrived. I wear it every Sunday at those churches in Toccopola and Algoma, Mississippi. But I am on guard for any flying shoulder pads!

547

Our five-year-old (almost six) granddaughter went with her mother to get her shots prior to registering for kindergarten. In one visit to the doctor she received five injections. They stopped by the house later and she showed us her five colorful, sparkling band aids on her arms. Her mother then, and her daddy later, talked about how brave Paige was in getting those five shots. She didn't cry, much, and she made it through all right. A few days later Paige was talking to her grandmother and said softly, "I wasn't brave," and a tear rolled down her cheek. Oh, but she was. Talk to the people we call "brave" and they will not see themselves that way. Being brave doesn't mean you are not scared. It means, more often, that you are scared but you go ahead and do what needs to be done anyway.

The true meaning of courage"

548

I saw a western movie forty five years ago. I forget the title. One of the male characters was named "Regret." How would you like to carry that name around all your life? One of our church founders was Finis Ewing. "Finis" is Latin, I think, for final, the last one, no more. He and his wife, I seem to remember reading, had ten children. The eighth one they named "Finis," but it was not to be. Two more children came along. Johnny Cash sang a sad song, "A

Boy Named Sue," in which he lamented the name his parents gave him. People are awarded nicknames along the way: "Shorty," "Red," "Tex," "Pete," "Stretch," "Freight Train," "Shipwreck," "Speedy." One fellow was asked his name and he said, "Tex." To the question, "Where are you from?" he replied: "Louisiana." "Well, then, why do they call you 'Tex?'" His answer: "Because I don't want to be called 'Louise.'" Names - and nicknames - do matter. Simon Peter got a nickname from Jesus, the modern-day equivalent of "Rocky." James and John were "Sons of Thunder." My name is Thomas. My father's name was Thomas, but we had different middle names. In childhood and youth it was Tommy, and longtime friends and family members still call me by that name. Later it was Tom. Now I am becoming Thomas again in my own mind out there in the public. But it is still Tommy or Tom among acquaintances. As someone once said, "I don't care what they call me, just so they call me to dinner."

549

Highway signs are interesting. Sometimes it depends on how the words on the signs are placed. For instance, this one:

SLOW
MEN WORKING
25 MPH

But what if the words were arranged as follows:

SLOW MEN
WORKING 25 MPH

I guess if we wanted them to work slower the sign would read "15 MPH."

550

I attended a worship service in a small United Methodist Church in Arkansas and noticed the attendance board. "Last Sunday" they had 37 in the worship service and an offering in the amount of $850. "Today" they had 36 in worship and an offering totaling $320. I thought: I want to meet that person that did not come back "Today"!

Chapter XII: 551-600

"Don't Forget the Resurrection"

551

I did it! I did it! The very thing I had criticized others for doing, I did myself! It was an 11:00 Easter service. Our pianist was out of town. The other 21 worshipers and I were singing the closing hymn, "Crown Him With Many Crowns!" I was "leading" the singing. We sang verse one and then verse two. I noticed the time and the fact that we were struggling a little bit through the hymn. So after verse two I announced quickly, "Verse four!" We were not past the first line of verse four before I realized my terrible mistake. You have already figured it out, I am sure. The verse we omitted, verse three, reads this way:

> Crown Him the Lord of life! Who triumphed o'er the grave;
> Who rose victorious through the strife For those He came to save;
> His glories now we sing, Who died and rose on high;
> Who died eternal life to bring, And lives that death may die.

And it was Easter Sunday! Every verse counts. The poets and song writers would not have written certain words if they felt them unimportant. The Broadman Hymnal, which we were using in our 11:00 service, contains four verses of the above-mentioned hymn. The United Methodist Hymnal (used in the Sunrise Service early that morning) contains six verses of the same hymn. We sang all six in that service.

552

The Graduation Service for the Program of Alternate Studies occurs on the first day of the July school held at Bethel College. Those set to receive PAS certificates return, after having concluded their work, to participate in the pomp and ceremony of the program and we congratulate them, their families, and their churches. Since I seem to want to follow set patterns, the first hymn for at least the past half dozen years, if not more, has been "To God Be the Glory." The closing hymn has been, for at least that many years, and probably more, "Footsteps of Jesus." We used it in every year up to 2008. The latter hymn has seven verses. We sing them all. Each year I announce that we will sing them all, sort of half apologizing for not omitting any of the seven verses. But I say, each time, that there may be a verse, or a line, or a word that, if omitted, would fail to touch someone it needs to touch and who needs to be touched by it. Just look at the following verses of "Footsteps of Jesus" and tell me which, if any, you would leave out if you were to arrange the program that celebrates the ongoing work of those who are ministers in the church:

> Sweetly, Lord, have we heard Thee calling, Come, follow me!
> And we see where Thy footprints falling Lead us to Thee.
>
> Though they lead o'er the cold, dark mountains, Seeking His sheep;
> Or along by Siloam's fountains, Helping the weak.
>
> If they lead through the temple holy, Preaching the Word;
> Or in homes of the poor and lowly, Serving the Lord.
>
> Though, dear Lord, in Thy pathway keeping, We follow Thee;
> Through the gloom of that place of weeping, Gethsemane!
>
> If Thy way and its sorrows bearing, We go again,
> Up the slope of the hillside, bearing Our cross of pain.
>
> By and by, through the shining portals, Turning our feet,
> We shall walk, with the glad immortals, Heav'n's golden street.
>
> Then at last when on high He sees us, Our journey done,
> We will rest where the steps of Jesus End at His throne.
>
> Refrain:
> Footprints of Jesus, That make the pathway glow;
> We will follow the steps of Jesus Where'er they go.

In 2008 we finally changed our closing hymn. It is "Forward Through the Ages," sung to the same tune as "Onward, Christian Soldiers." Great message. Easy to sing. I was presiding. I called for the benediction and completely forgot the hymn. However, the PAS pianist started playing it before we got too far into the recessional and we stopped and sang the hymn. Then we marched out.

553

A colleague here at Memphis Theological Seminary was on the phone with her mother, who is retired. Her mother had to cut the conversation short: she had things to do and places to go. Retirement has not slowed her down. In a church where I was pastor, an 80-year-old woman and her husband visited our church one Sunday. It took a good four or five weeks to work out a time I could visit with them. They were both so busy. The woman, in fact, wrote me a letter in which she gave her daily schedule for a given week. It included bowling, bingo, quilting, visiting the public library, her sorority meeting, and a half dozen other commitments. As I recall, there was an opening between the hours of three and four in the afternoon on Thursday, if I hurried and confirmed. Another colleague at the Seminary retired and first looked forward to his own retreat and office in the home of his sister, where there was a large library, plenty of peace and quiet, and much time for uninterrupted contemplation, prayer, and meditation. He lasted one week. That would not do, he decided. He needed to be more active, to be with people, to stay in touch with the rush of society and the push of events. He accepted an interim pastorate (that lasted at least three years). He stayed in touch with the Seminary. He was alive again. As I contemplate retirement, someday, I have no idea what I will do. Perhaps the examples given here will remind me that I may be busier than I am now and might wish for the comfort, security, and pace of a steady job so I can get some rest.

554

People are making political hay out of the preaching of a pastor in the Midwest whose communicants in the church he has been serving include a presidential candidate. Someone seemed to recall some inflammatory words the preacher said around the time of the invasion of Iraq. Whereas many were saying, "God bless America," this pastor said in his sermon "God damn America." This is usually where most people stopped. They did not read or hear the rest of the sentence. "God damn America," and the rest is this or similar to this, "for presuming to see herself as a god, as superior, as above the law." This will probably hurt the chances of the candidate, who has been criticized for not getting up and walking out, or casting his church membership elsewhere, or publicly rebuking the pastor then instead of six years later during the campaign. It has been pointed out that many of the statements of the late Dr. Martin Luther King, Jr., were inflammatory, too, as he called America a "criminal nation" for its injustices, oppression of the poor, and civil wrongs. The pastor, Reverend Jeremiah Wright, weeks later attempted to bring his words into context and clarify his thoughts while emphasizing the uniqueness of the black church. However, some of this seemed to backfire on him and he became the issue, thus causing his parishioner, Barack Obama, to have to renounce Pastor Wright's statements.

But let's see this in a broader context. The leader of the free world, the President of the United States, invades another country which leads to violence and bloodshed amounting to over 4,000 American military personnel killed and thousands more wounded, not to mention the hundreds of thousands of Iraqis killed or displaced; condones torture of enemy prisoners; vetoes a bill passed by Congress that would instruct the CIA to abide by the Geneva Conventions and thus not torture; lowers taxes for the rich while laying more burdens on the middle class and the poor; authorizes phone surveillance of American citizens; and then closes his speeches with "God Bless America." Now which is more obscene. You tell me. We all should instead say, "God Forgive America," or "God Cleanse America," or "God Save America," or "God Restore America." I read a letter to the editor in a magazine from the pastor of First United Methodist Church in Indianapolis, Indiana. He wrote that he has been pastor of that church for fifteen years and a faithful member and regular attender is U. S. Senator Richard Lugar. The pastor said he would hate for Senator Lugar to be held responsible for anything he ever said.

555

I heard about a newspaper ad seeking a housekeeper. The job description was not unusual: "hard-working, honest, punctual, clean." Then it added: "A cheerful Christian, if possible." A tall order. On the one hand, the good news of Jesus Christ brings cheer to the believing heart. But on the other, the conscientious Christian will not pretend all is well with the world and ignore its problems in which we are all involved. Furthermore, I am sure the owner of the house would not want anyone who just pretended to be cheerful, only in order to get the job. But at the same time, grumpy and sour and pessimistic Christians do not normally spread goodwill to neighbors. The writer of the ad must have known all this, for the ad reads: "A cheerful Christian, if possible." It does not say, "A cheerful Christian." It adds "if possible." Yes, I think the compiler of the ad knew the ins and outs of such a requirement.

556

You are walking along in the mall. A young man is going about the same speed and is talking to you. Or so you believe. A closer listen to the conversation quickly erases that assumption. He seems to be carrying on a personal conversation with himself. It is rather animated. Should we track down Security and alert them to this crazy man? Then he goes in front of you and you see what is really his problem: He has an ugly cancerous growth in his right ear. It looks very serious. It is only as he moves along that it occurs to you that he is talking on his cell phone to someone else and that the horrible growth in his right ear is the phone itself. I have lost count of how many conversations I thought I was involved in only to learn that the person is on the phone to someone else. The person may be looking at me, and may be walking toward me. It doesn't matter. When you see such a scenario do not assume anything, and especially do not assume you are about to engage in conversation with someone.

557

Luke is the only one of the four Gospels to tell of the "Road to Emmaus" experience. His 24th chapter relates how two men on Easter afternoon were walking the seven-mile stretch from Jerusalem to Emmaus and a stranger caught up with them and joined in on their conversation. He helped explain the events that were rumored to have happened that morning - empty tomb, resurrection, women at the tomb - And also informed them regarding the scriptures, all the way back to Moses. When the three arrived in Emmaus the two persuaded the stranger to stop and come in and eat with them. During the meal their guest seemed to take over the meal and made it very special with his words and presence. By that time the two men realized who he was and then the stranger was gone. It was night by that time, bedtime for many. But the two men felt compelled to go back to Jerusalem, not waiting until morning, to tell the disciples of their experience and to proclaim that Jesus had truly risen from the dead. And so they walked - or did they run - back to Jerusalem, seven miles again! The Road to Emmaus is only part of the story. The Road FROM Emmaus is an important part, too, the going, the telling, the witnessing.

558

A church sign on display during Lent:

> 3 NAILS + 1 CROSS
> 4 GIVEN

559

Another church sign:

> DEAR GOD PLEASE MAKE ME AS GOOD
> AS MY DOG THINKS I AM

ಸಿ)ಲ3ಸಿ)ಲ3ಸಿ)ಲ3ಸಿ)ಲ3ಸಿ)ಲ3ಸಿ)ಲ3ಸಿ)ಲ3ಸಿ)ಲ3ಸಿ)ಲ3ಸಿ)ಲ3

560

By the time this article and the book containing it see the light of day by getting published and tossed out into the world, a new American president and administration will be in charge. Perhaps the justifications sent forth by the administration now in power (late 2008) for the war in Iraq will have been replaced by truth and change and withdrawal from that strife-torn nation, a nation we helped to destroy. One of the most cynical lines from the present crowd in Washington is that to withdraw now would mean that the 4,000 Americans that have been killed over there "would have died in vain." Now let me get this straight: The more of our own that die in Iraq the less likely they all "would have died in vain." Well, the numbers will undoubtedly increase. We will reach 5,000 before too long, then 6,000, then 7,000. Let me offer this opposite viewpoint: They ALL died in vain. That is the tragic part of the story. They ALL died in vain. The whole thing - the invasion, the bombing, the killing, the destruction, the abolishing of the Iraq army, the displacement of hundreds of thousands of Iraqis - was unnecessary and unwise. They ALL died in vain. This will not be said by any public official or office holder. Nobody wants to hear it. It is too painful. We as a nation must have our crusades and this was one that was contrived and concocted out of half-truths and wishful thinking. Patriotism was promoted and anybody who opposed the invasion was considered unpatriotic. News organizations surrendered their integrity to go along with the hysteria of the moment. Bill O'Reilly on one of his radio shows before the invasion said, "If you oppose this war, we know who you are and we are coming to get you!" Discounting a lot of his rhetoric as so much hot air, he was reflecting the administration's spin and promoting the "patriotic" and "unpatriotic" divide that prevailed in early 2003 and beyond. They ALL died in vain, and those who will die in the future in Iraq - and there will be many more - will also have died in vain. Sad, but true. Nothing is better than it was. A former government official who was one of the enthusiastic promoters of invading Iraq was interviewed the other day and said, while the war is longer and costlier than planned, at least the U.S. achieved its goal of ousting Saddam Hussein from his rule. Except that was not the stated reason for going in. It was that Hussein was suspected of harboring and increasing his supply of "weapons of mass destruction" and invasion and war were the only ways of handling that. As usual, here was another one of the war-promoters who had changed his rationale five years after the invasion and occupation began.

561

The idea that the longer the Iraq war goes on, the less likely our people "would have died in vain" reminds me of some of my preaching. I can get into a sermon and quickly realize I have not said much of anything worthwhile and I have not said it that well. Then I think that if I keep talking, perhaps I can say something good. But instead, it gets worse and worse and worse. Going longer just makes it worse. Admit failure, have your closing prayer, sing the closing hymn, and pronounce the benediction. It's over.

562

We have all heard stories about the sacrifices our great-grandparents and grandparents and parents made to go to school - how many miles they walked in the cold and hot weather, how chores at home sometimes made it difficult to stay in school, how they had no money and one pair of shoes, and so forth. I am afraid I will not have any such stories to pass on to my children and grandchildren. I walked one block to elementary school and two blocks to junior high and high school. Going to college and seminary was a little bit more challenging - three blocks. So I drove. That was too far to walk. I have kept to that strict physical regimen throughout my adult life.

563

We go to Buffalo, Missouri (on U.S. Highway 65, 30 miles north of Springfield), every so often these days because my mother lives there, and my younger brother, Paul and his wife Rebecca, do too. He is editor of the weekly newspaper in Buffalo. On a recent visit Linda went to a local antique store and came away singing the praises of a dining table and its four leaves and six chairs. There was no way to get them home so she laid the thought aside, for awhile. But the desire never left and the longing was pronounced. I returned to the area a few weeks later on my way to a meeting of Missouri Presbytery. Before departing Buffalo to go on up to the meeting I dropped by the antique store and bought the dining room set, still not knowing how we were going to get it down to Memphis. The folks at the store said they could have it delivered to my mother's garage only a half mile away and that they would have it delivered Sunday afternoon. Not five minutes after I drove into town on Sunday, the pickup truck drove in, too, and we found that some of the items - four chairs and the four leaves - could fit into my car. That left the table without the leaves, and two remaining chairs, sitting in my mother's garage. Two weeks later a tornado, or at least a violent storm, swept through Buffalo and blew away the antique store. The little town had been hit hard by an ice storm a little over a year earlier, and now this. Other buildings in addition to the antique store were hit pretty hard this time. Buffalo recovered from the ice storm; it will bounce back from this tragedy as well. And the table and chairs are safe. A few weeks later two members of the family went to Buffalo in a vehicle large enough to hold the remaining items and brought them to Memphis.

564

In the midst of so much "God Bless America" rhetoric, this bumper sticker on a car in our condo area is like a breath of fresh air:

> GOD BLESS ALL PEOPLE
> (NO EXCEPTIONS)

565

We have heard, read, and seen a lot about the nation of Libya and its dictator, Colonel Ghadafi. I have a question: If he is so all-fired powerful, how come he is still just a colonel? One would think he could promote himself to general or something.

566

In the summer session of The Program of Alternate Studies one year I "taught" Cumberland Presbyterian Polity (government). It so happens that there was going to be a Sunday afternoon ordination and installation service at a nearby church. I thought it was a brilliant idea to have the members of the class attend and see first-hand how the government of the church works. A man was to be ordained as a minister and installed as the pastor. I was the guest preacher and, not being a member of West Tennessee Presbytery (I am a member of Missouri Presbytery) within whose bounds the church was located, I was not an official member of the presbyterial commission that conducted the service. I thought my main and only responsibility was to preach the sermon and did not notice until the service was well along that in the installation phase I was to "declare" that the minister had been installed as the pastor of the Trezevant Cumberland Presbyterian Church. I went ahead when the time came and "declared" that the minister was officially and duly installed. When I sat down I then realized that I, a member of Missouri Presbytery, had just done an official act that someone from West Tennessee Presbytery would have rightly taken care of. In other words, I violated the Constitution, so to speak. Furthermore, those ministers and elders from West Tennessee Presbytery who were on the commission and sitting with me on the platform were now exhibiting nervous and anxious looks as they realized what had taken place. Worse, the members of my Polity class were present. Back in the classroom on the Bethel College campus, we had a lot to talk - and laugh - about on the subject of Polity.

567

Church growth experts tell us the congregation should be a "visitor-friendly" church. That is, any first-time attender should be able to experience some degree of comfort upon entering the building and meeting the people. At least two things might hinder that. First, rightly or wrongly, a visitor usually believes that everyone knows everyone else and therefore as a visitor one sees a tight circle into which it will be difficult to enter and feels like an outsider. Second, church bulletins and announcements spoken in worship raise barriers when people are identified on a first-name basis. The bulletin might say, "The women's monthly meeting will be Tuesday at 10:30 A.M. at Freda's house. Bring a covered-dish." Well, who in the world is Freda? What is her last name? Where does she live? What is her phone number? How do I, if I am a woman, know whether I am invited or not? Will somebody show me the way? In addition to the bulletin, public announcements from the pulpit may make a visitor feel out of the loop: "We congratulate Howard and Marsha on the birth of their son John, who came into this world last Tuesday at 11:14 A.M.. And congratulations, too, to the proud grandparents Ron and Judy, and Jim and Janice." Who, pray tell, are Howard and Marsha, and Ron and Judy, and Jim and Janice? I don't know them. I am sure everybody else knows them, but I have never heard of them. Could

I at least have their last names please? It's things like these that may tend to alienate or scare off newcomers to the church.

568

I was chatting with one of our Cumberland Presbyterian ministers the other day. He told how he and his family became a part of this denomination before he entered the ministry. He and his wife came out of other denominations. His secular work took him to East Tennessee and on one Sunday they and their children, after visiting one or two other churches previously, decided to visit an area Cumberland Presbyterian Church. A greeter met them at the door and showed them around. He introduced them to several church folks along the way. Then instead of telling them about a Sunday school class they might enjoy visiting, and instead of just showing them where it was, or, better yet, taking them to the class and leaving them there, he walked with them to the class, introduced them to all the members and sat down with them for the entire Sunday school hour. What a wonderful thing to do! Needless to say, they joined that church and it was out of that congregation that this first-time visitor to one of our churches surrendered to the ministry and went on to college and seminary. Now he is a faithful and talented pastor in the denomination. A lot of gratitude can go to that greeter on that Sunday morning years ago.

569

Telling jokes in the pulpit is, to my mind, out of bounds. Telling stories that have humor in them or using words and sentences that convey humor is totally acceptable in many cases. I try to tell beginning preachers, "Never tell jokes. Tell stories." Never call it a joke. If you call it a joke, and the people do not laugh, most likely the rest of the sermon will be a joke. There is absolutely no need to feel that you need to start out a speech or sermon with a "joke." Unrelated and irrelevant attempts at humor just to get on the good side of an audience or to break the ice or to show them how good a sense of humor you have are an abomination. But humor well-placed, timely, appropriate, in good taste, and offered with some ease is often appropriate. Humor at the expense of someone else is off limits and usually reflects not on the object or subject of the humor but on the speaker, and may turn the audience against the speaker all too quickly. It is true that humor is conveyed by some preachers more easily than others. One must be oneself in the pulpit, but one can enjoy the time in the pulpit as well. The reverse is true, of course: Untimely attempts at humor, such as when discussing grave issues during serious times can send a congregation's respect for a pastor plummeting. Appreciating the seriousness of the moment is crucial for a faithful pastor. Being lighthearted in grave moments may indicate that the pastor doesn't "get it."

570

I went to Japan in the year 2000 at the invitation of Japan Presbytery to help in the celebration of fifty years since Cumberland Presbyterian work was renewed in that country. Japan Presbytery held a big three-day celebration in a hotel. Before and after that convention I visited our churches and saw some of the country. I am herewith announcing that all pictures of Mt. Fuji are inaccurate if the postcard was produced before 2000. Why? Because I reached out and grabbed a fist-sized chunk of that great wonder of nature and brought it back to the United States. Yes, they need to go and take another picture of Mt. Fuji. What you see now is not the true picture; I reduced it with my fistful of Fuji.

571

Editorial errors can be glaring and even humorous. The library staff of Memphis Theological Seminary had a stack of books to discard. They could be purchased for 50 cents for hardback, and 25 cents for paperback books. I bought a paperback book entitled The Protestant Churches of America, by John J. Hardon (Newman Press, 1964). I looked for references to the Cumberland Presbyterian Church. What caught my eye was an example of what was probably someone's handwriting that got printed incorrectly. On page 200, the book mentions

"1810, when the Cumberland Presbytery seceded to form a separate denomination (not quite accurate; there was no secession), known as the Cumberland Presbyterian Church. Its grievance was the Calvinist doctrine of predestination, which was rejected as 'fantastic.'"

I have never heard any Cumberland Presbyterian describe "the Calvinist doctrine of predestination" as "fantastic." I have heard many describe it, however, as "fatalistic," and I suspect that is what the author meant for the book to say.

572

More errors in printing come to mind. Several years ago some letters to the editor of "The Cumberland Presbyterian," the church's denominational magazine, carried on a discussion of whether pastors should display their degrees on the walls of their offices. Back and forth went the arguments, pro and con. The mistake of all mistakes occurred when one minister wrote to say, regarding diplomas or degrees, that he had "none" on his wall. Sadly, the magazine had him saying "nine." The correction that followed in a subsequent issue of the magazine notwithstanding, that minister's academic achievements, if only for a brief time, were quite impressive.

573

It was in mid-December and shoppers were crowding the malls. Parents were taking their little children to see Santa, sit on his lap, and have their picture taken with the gentle old man from the North Pole. It happens that a little girl and her mother were walking along in the mall and up ahead they saw Santa coming their way. "Look, Mommy, Santa Claus!" And when they got closer, the little girl cried out, "There is Santa! Hi, Santa!" To which Santa growled grumpily and in a noticeably unfriendly way: "I'm not on until eleven." As a minister I have had problems knowing how to take a day off. I would more likely take time off in a given day. It is not that I work that hard; it is that, not being good at planning ahead, I have not found it easy to get away from the church and its work. And even if "off" for a day, do I not continue as the pastor of the church? Do I let emergencies interrupt that day off? And on my day off when I see someone at the supermarket am I not still their minister? Being of the "old school" I have not been able to shut the door to the responsibilities of the pastorate even when "off" the job temporarily. And besides, you don't turn off your concern and then turn it on again. It is always there. Do you share my confusion on this?

574

H. H. Farmer's book on preaching, mentioned much earlier in this book because it talked about "peaching" instead of "preaching," is a very good treatise on the subject. On page 44 he writes, "A sermon... should have something of the quality of a knock on the door. A knock... is a call for attention in the first instance; but it is also more than that, it is a call for an answer." Why is it that some people, such as Dr. Farmer, can say in a few words things that are so powerful yet so simple, what it takes the rest of us paragraph after paragraph to say in our sometimes futile ways?

575

The New York Times is a prominent and influential newspaper, but it can be "used" just like any other entity. In the run-up to the Iraq war, as the Bush administration was looking for a rationale to invade, the following tactic was used: Someone in the White House would "leak" something to the New York Times. The Times would print it. Then someone else in the administration would go on "Meet the Press" and say, "The New York Times is reporting that such and such, and so and so," and with a straight face no less.

576

Let me get this straight. According to many in the United States, giving financial help to banks, lenders, Wall Street firms, airlines, big oil companies, tobacco companies, and other corporate giants, is good business, and good for America.

However, providing financial help for the middle class and the poor - such as with universal health care - is Socialism.

Now, did I get it right? Please correct me if I'm wrong.

577

More than sixty years ago I heard Franklin Chesnut, director of a church camp, tell this story: There was a family of skunks. The mom and dad had two sons, In and Out. Only trouble was, they had trouble controlling them and keeping them in the same place. When In was in, Out was out, and when Out was in, In was out. It was all they could do to struggle and have In in and Out in at the same time. Sure enough, one time supper was ready and the mom saw that Out was in but In was out. So she said to Out, "Out, please go out and see if you can bring In in." So Out went out searching for In, hoping to bring In in. It wasn't too long before Out came in bringing In with him. His mother was impressed. "Out, how was it that you found In so quickly." "It was easy," said Out, "Instinct."

578

As a very young boy, I was told not to eat grapes from the grapevine in the backyard. One had a tendency to eat too many and get sick. But I did. I went outside and ate some grapes, and when I went back into the house my mother asked me if I had been eating grapes. I said, "No, I have been eating onions, but they smell like grapes."

579

In the heat of emotion I have never been able to say things just right. I get too excited and say things wrong. I was very young and my teenage sister had been left in charge. Our mother had told her, "Do not let Tommy go outside." But I headed for the door. Jo Nell said, "Tommy, do not go outside." I responded with anger and emotion, "Don't tell me what to do; I'm not your mother!"

580

My little cousin was at home with her grandparents in charge while her mother worked. They said, "Don't go outside." Next thing you know, she is coming back in. "Did you go outside?" "Yes, I had to sneeze," she explained.

581

The following may not matter to most people - or even to God - but I'm bothered by the incorrect use of the word "previous." That word is an adjective, not an adverb. The word "prior" is an adverb, but not the word "previous." Yet writers and speakers will often say something like this: "He came to the building thirty minutes previous to the start of the program." No, it should be, "He came to the building thirty minutes PRIOR to the start of the program." I'm sorry, but that is the way it is supposed to be. Now I know the two words can be interchanged along the way: "I have a prior commitment." "I have a previous commitment." Both sound all right, and are probably grammatically correct. And in both cases they are adjectives. But in most other situations "prior" is an adverb. Pardon my puritanical ways regarding grammar. And are you now thoroughly confused? Then I've done my job.

582

I was reading a biography of Daniel Boone. The book is entitled <u>Boone</u> (Algonquin, 2007) The author, Robert Morgan, on page 141 is talking about Lord Dunmore, the British leader who was trying desperately to help his nation hold on to the colonies in the 1700s. He tried everything else and nothing worked, so he introduced fear. Then the author writes: "A classic way of increasing and maintaining one's power is to make people afraid." Gee, I am certainly relieved that no modern leaders have resorted to that.

583

Another church sign:

NOW OPEN FROM EASTER TO CHRISTMAS

584

I was preaching in the morning worship service. My wife was in the choir. Our three girls - ages 7, 5, and 3, were scattered among the church folks in the sanctuary. The sermon may have been about family life; I do not recall. Or it may have been on how nobody is perfect. But somewhere along in the sermon our youngest somehow got loose from whoever had her beside them and went to the second pew from the front. There she lay down and then put her feet over the back of that pew. Just as I said something like, "Nobody is perfect," Linda stepped out of the choir and went over to sit with Kristen and slowly and quietly helped her to sit up in the pew and face forward. After the service one man said, "You planned that, didn't you." The answer was "No, I did not. It just happened." And that was the truth. However, if we retain something like 10% of what we hear and something like 50% of what we see, then the object lesson for that Sunday was most helpful!

585

The Vice-President of the United States in the Bush administration was on a Sunday morning talk show. The moderator said: "Two-thirds of the American people think we should not be in Iraq." The Vice-President's response: "So?" "Does it bother you that they feel that way?" "No." If two-thirds of the shareholders of a company were against a policy or action, and the CEO or his chief advisor went ahead anyway, does anyone think the CEO or the advisor would be around much longer? If a pastor and session knew that two-thirds of the congregation felt one way but pastor and session felt another, how many ticks of the clock would there be before some confrontation occurred? And what can a pastor and session do if they lose the trust of the people of the congregation?

586

It was 1950. I was eleven years old. We three brothers and our mother had been to Chicago for a few weeks where our father was in graduate school for the summer session at the University of Chicago. We traveled there by train. On the way back to Tennessee we were to change trains in Guthrie, Kentucky. Our train was late so we missed connections. The next one to McKenzie, Tennessee, would be something like seven or eight hours. So we waited, and waited, and waited. Guthrie, Kentucky, according to 2005 calculations, had a population of 1,452. One can imagine that it was no larger in 1950. That town is about five miles from the Tennessee line and not far from Clarksville, Tennessee, on the road to Russellville, Kentucky. But Guthrie was where we were to change trains. There was nothing to do. It was a hot summer day. There was no place to get something to eat. I complained. I undoubtedly cried. I suppose my brothers were quite uncomfortable and restless, too. But the worst was yet to happen. When our train finally arrived we boarded and I could see out the window and I noticed that our trunk - that held all our clothes - was not on the wagon that stood beside the train. I told my mother. I cried and otherwise expressed great concern about our luggage, all contained in that big trunk. Mother reassured me that everything would be all right. When we arrived in McKenzie, there was no trunk. I was right. It never got put on the train. I sure hoped somebody knew where it was. One thing for sure, it certainly was not at the train station in McKenzie, Tennessee. I think it was about a week before our stuff arrived. Mother never lost faith that it would arrive soon. I never believed it would. Faith won out over doubt. Ever since then when I board a plane and I see workers loading the baggage, I look for mine. Most of the time I don't see it and I try very hard to have the faith my mother had back there in Guthrie, Kentucky. Most of the time my luggage does arrive and comes down the chute with a rush just as I am beginning to think it did not get put on the plane. Just a few months ago I flew from Little Rock to Dallas-Fort Worth to El Paso. I had one bag and a suit bag containing my pulpit robe and best Sunday suit. It was the first time the robe had every traveled by air. I was very concerned. I wasn't on the ground ten minutes and as I stood at the baggage claim area with my host I was wondering out loud whether I could go somewhere and buy a suit and whose robe I could borrow. And the baggage had not even started coming out of the chute yet! My stuff was included in the chute-dumping so all was well. But that is where I am. Little or no faith. Much doubt. I need to listen to my mother more often.

587

Luggage can really be a problem. Especially if yours does not arrive. I was on the last leg in a return flight to Memphis after being in Korea for ten days. I had been up more than thirty hours. I boarded a Northwest flight in Minnesota for the final journey home. I sat beside a minister who was going to Memphis to attend the meeting of the General Assembly of the Presbyterian Church in America. He had come all the way from Vancouver. During the flight he asked if I might help him make sure everything went well after landing: getting his luggage, finding a taxi, making sure of the hotel. Later we stood by the baggage-claim area. Eventually my two bags shot out of the chute. We continued to wait for his one piece of luggage. It was light green. There were several items that resembled his just a little bit, but none fit the bill. We waited and waited, thinking there might be another batch to be brought out. I was hot. I was dirty. I was tired. But I had promised and I surely did not want the fine minister from Vancouver to lose his way or feel all alone in Memphis. So we waited a while longer. The only consolation was that, early on, Memphis Grizzlies general manager Jerry West was standing there as well, but when he got his luggage, he moved on. We kept standing there. Finally my friend walked over to the office where owners of lost luggage stood in line to report their misfortune. He came back in a few minutes. They had tracked it down. It never left Vancouver. I gave him some American money, flagged down a cab, told the driver the name of the hotel, and he was on his way. A few days later he called to say his luggage arrived the next day and he appreciated my help. After leaving the airport I arrived at my house and family members were waiting. I said hello, then went and took a shower. I thought I should burn those clothes that I had been wearing for more than a day and a half. My wife probably had to run them through the washing machine twice. Luggage can get lost. Be concerned. Be very concerned. It could happen again.

588

Team nicknames are sometimes appropriate, sometimes out of place. The Minneapolis Lakers were well named as one of the National Basketball Association teams, for Minnesota has a thousand lakes, they say. But then the team moved to Los Angeles and they became the Los Angeles Lakers. The Vancouver Grizzlies club was moved to Memphis where they became the Memphis Grizzlies. I am sure there are plenty of grizzlies up around Vancouver. The only ones in Memphis are in the Memphis zoo. A pro basketball team in New Orleans was called the New Orleans Jazz. But when the team moved to Utah, they became the Utah Jazz. I don't even know if they allow jazz in that state. It has been fifty years since the Brooklyn Dodgers moved to Los Angeles and remained the Dodgers, but it never has seemed quite right. The Dodgers belong back in Flatbush. The same is true of the New York Giants who became the San Francisco Giants. Somehow the nickname just does not resonate. What if the Colorado Rockies moved to Florida? The Houston Oilers moved to Nashville and had the decency to change their name to the Tennessee Titans. The St. Louis Browns baseball team moved to Baltimore and became the Orioles, a natural change since the local team fifty years earlier had the name and the AAA minor league club did, too.

589

One of the vital aspects of church polity/government is property. The Cumberland Presbyterian Church, like other denominations, is connectional. The local church does not own the property; the Presbytery does. There are three main occasions when property becomes an issue and we forget what our Constitution says about property. One time is when a church closes. A family four generations back may have donated the property and the deed says that if it ever ceases to be a church the property reverts back to the family, now scattered to the four corners of the earth. No, the Presbytery owns the property. A second way that property becomes an issue is when a pastor and people seek to leave the denomination and decide they want to stay on the property and use the very same facilities they were using before they decided to leave. They may be going into another denomination or may be planning to be a non-denominational church. Either way it doesn't matter: The Presbytery owns the property. If they leave the denomination they must leave the premises. A third way is when a denomination votes to unite with another denomination and a portion of the members want to stay and perpetuate the denomination to which they belong and in which they have been nurtured. This was a litigious issue after 1906 when the Cumberland Presbyterian Church officially, but by a narrow margin, voted to be absorbed into the Presbyterian Church USA. A large minority chose to stay and keep the Cumberland Presbyterian Church not only afloat but going about its mission. Different state supreme courts in most cases sided with the Presbyterian Church USA as did the United States Supreme Court. The "faithful" Cumberlands had to start over. There was very little left. But they knew that there was more to "church" than property, and they continued with the mission they believed God had given them.

590

When the Cumberland Presbyterian Theological Seminary was on the same campus as Bethel College in McKenzie, Tennessee, the annual Cumberland Presbyterian Ministers' Conference would be held there every January. In 1960 one of the speakers was Dr. Ralph Sockman, well-known and long-time pastor of Christ Methodist Church in New York City. He was a popular preacher on the Protestant Hour radio series. He was about to retire, having been the senior pastor of that church for more than forty years. It was the only congregation he served after seminary. He preached and lectured several times during that week. There was a question-and-answer time one afternoon over in the Seminary chapel. One minister asked Dr. Sockman how he prepared for his Sunday evening sermon. He said he chose his scripture texts for both Sunday morning and Sunday evening early in the week. Then he spent the study hours the rest of the week working on his Sunday morning sermon. On Sunday afternoon he would start in earnest with his evening message. He said that, having chosen the text on Monday, he would often have it on his mind during the week even though he may not have done any focused work on it, so that when he sat down after lunch on Sunday he would not be starting empty-handed.

591

Many preachers will occasionally have a sermon series over a period of several Sundays. This is a help to the congregation (sometimes) but a special help to the preacher. As Ernest Campbell reminds us, we can do all of our reading on the one theme over time. Positives of a sermon series are that one can use an extended period of time to cover a general subject or theme in some depth. Negatives are that one can go too long. I always made it a practice of going one or two Sundays longer than I should have. After six or seven Sundays, sometimes even I was bored.

592

Some sermon series are very good and helpful. Others may go too long. I think in many of my series I went one or two Sundays longer than I should. Even I was bored by that time. But there are some good, sound series possibilities that many pastors have employed, such as the Apostles' Creed, the Lord's Prayer, the Beatitudes, the Ten Commandments, the Fruit of the Spirit, the Temptations of Jesus, the Miracles of Jesus, and the Parables of Jesus (at least some of them; all in one series might be too much). The plan would be to preach on one aspect of each of the themes. For example, one sermon from the Lord's Prayer would be: "Hallowed be thy name." The next sermon could be "Thy kingdom come, thy will be done." From six to ten sermons could be presented out of the Lord's Prayer. There are nine Beatitudes, ten Commandments, nine items in the Fruit of the Spirit.

593

A preacher may get "carried away" and have a series of sermons that may stretch the limits of reason regarding the scriptures. Mark 2:1-12 tells of the healing of the paralytic. The house where Jesus was teaching was crowded. The doors were shut and the windows were blocked. No one else could get in. Outside there was a paralyzed man who was being carried on a stretcher by four friends. They took him up on the roof, made a hole in the roof and let him down so he could be with Jesus. Well, who were these four men? They represented Faith, Hope, Love, and a fourth thing, maybe Determination or Persistence or some other virtue. Or, consider Acts 27:39-44, the shipwreck where Paul was involved. He and others floated in on "the broken pieces of the ship." What were those "broken pieces of the ship?" Faith, Hope, Love, Determination, Persistence, Patience, Kindness, Self-Control, and a host of others. The worst of all might be "taken" from John 21:4-14, the story of the risen Christ on the beach with Peter and other disciples fishing. They are not catching any fish so Jesus suggests they "cast the net to the right side of the boat, and you will find some." Verse 11 reports, "So Simon Peter went aboard and hauled the net ashore, full of large fish, a hundred fifty-three of them; and though there were so many, the net was not torn." What were those one hundred fifty-three fish? Why, they were Faith, Hope,

Love, Determination, Persistence, Patience, Kindness, Self-Control, Happiness, Peace, Generosity, Joy, Goodness, Gentleness, Studiousness, and on and on. The Lord may forgive us for such chicanery. Maybe. We hope, too, our people will forgive us.

594

I walked into a supermarket many years ago. In addition to food supplies they (for some reason) had some records on sale, 33 1/3 records, which reveals how far back this story goes. Anyway, I was walking toward the back, pushing my grocery cart, and noticing those records on display as I got closer to them. There was an album, perhaps by Porter Wagoner, and the title of the album was (and this was the way the words were arranged:

BACK IN THE GOOD OLE DAYS
(When Times Were Bad)

When we think realistically and soberly about the past we can acknowledge there is some truth to the album title. We remember "the good ole days." We sometimes long for "the good ole days." But when we take the time to ponder about those days, we remember that they were not all rosy or peace and quiet or promising or just or encouraging.

I heard someone a few years ago talk about the movies of the 1940s and 1950s and how good and family-oriented and clean and non-profane they were. I like to watch them to this day. Some of the plots are rather simplistic and the acting and camera work not so advanced. But one of the main reasons NOT to long for those "glory days" of film was the place (if any) of African Americans in those films. We are thankful for the advancements made in the past few decades in this regard.

595

Here is another church sign:

GOT JESUS ?

596

If one is troubled one can go to counseling. If one is grieving there are welcoming groups to help in that area. Should doubt be a problem when one desires faith, there are people to go to.

Sometimes solitude is the best medicine. Sometimes being with other people provides the best therapy.

But sometimes you just want to kick back, turn your radio loud, and sing along as loudly and as unselfconsciously as you can with whatever song is being played. Especially if it is this one by Tanya Tucker, the chorus of which goes:

> When I die, I may not go to heaven.
> I don't know if they let cowboys in.
> If they don't, just let me go to Texas.
> Texas is as close as I've been.

The second time the chorus comes around you can hear a crowd gathering and a few folks joining in:

> When I die, I may not go to heaven.
> I don't know if they let cowboys in.
> If they don't, just let me go to Texas.
> Texas is as close as I've been.

The third time when the chorus rolls around things are much louder. There is a lot of whooping and hollering in the background and lots more people are singing, and it's a whole lot more rambunctious:

> WHEN I DIE, I MAY NOT GO TO HEAVEN
> I DON'T KNOW IF THEY LET COWBOYS IN.
> IF THEY DON'T, JUST LET ME GO TO TEXAS.
> TEXAS IS AS CLOSE AS I'VE BEEN.

I won't begin to try to describe how things are by the time they get to the fourth chorus. The noise is high volume. It sounds like everybody in the place is laughing or talking or singing. And you are driving in your car across the Mississippi River bridge going out of Memphis toward Arkansas with the volume turned up high and cutting loose with your loudest, most unselfconscious vocal efforts. That is pretty good therapy. In fact, real good.

My colleague who is also one of my mentors, Dr. Robert M. Shelton, has written about "testimonial preaching." He said, as I recall, that occurs when the one in the pulpit tells one's own personal story and it comprises most if not all of the sermon. As I recall his comments on this, this is a very limited way of preaching. Why? Because after the telling, which would probably take the length of one sermon, there is no more to report, unless one repeats oneself over and over in future messages. Therefore, after the "testimonial preaching" it is then appropriate to go to the scriptures for future sermons.

598

Our friend and colleague Dr. Paul Dekar retired from teaching at Memphis Theological Seminary recently to return to his home country of Canada where his and Nancy's grandchildren live. A minister in the Canadian Baptist Church, Paul exemplifies the Christian faith in all its dimensions. He teaches, preaches, and lives the basic Christian tenets of peace, love, fellowship, honor, non-violence, justice, and service. He has said that one thing that attracted him to Memphis was the Civil Rights emphasis in a city where Dr. Martin Luther King, Jr., was assassinated. In his thirteen years at MTS, Paul Dekar was an advocate for human rights at home and abroad, traveled extensively (especially to Australia) on his sabbaticals, and belonged to and wrote about the Baptist Peace Fellowship of North America, as well as the Fellowship of Reconciliation, out of which the BPFNA emerged. While at MTS he became closely associated with the Board of Missions of the Cumberland Presbyterian Church, and was, in fact, present in the Cumberland Presbyterian Church in South Korea on the Sunday that new church was organized. He has been to Japan and has visited in CP churches there. He has led "immersion experiences" with students to Choctaw Presbytery in Oklahoma, and to other Native American locations in the United States, not to mention similar excursions to Trinidad and other countries. By the end of his tenure at MTS I quit asking him what countries he had been to, and started asking him what countries he had NOT been to, since there are fewer of those! We will miss Paul Dekar. He has been an integral part of MTS and a close friend of the Cumberland Presbyterian Church.

599

Occasionally I will talk with a minister who claims not to follow the church year. We in the Cumberland Presbyterian Church (along with other mainstream denominations) find ourselves in the happy place of being somewhere between the liturgical brethren and sisters on one side and the free-church brethren and sisters on the other side. We can go in both directions at different times and often do so. Many of our pastors and churches do follow the church year: Advent, Christmas, Epiphany, Ash Wednesday, Lent, Holy Week, Palm Sunday, Easter, Ascension Sunday, Trinity

Sunday, Pentecost, and sometimes several other named seasons or days. So, occasionally I'll hear someone saying, "We don't follow the church year." I want to ask, but hardly ever do so: "Do you observe Christmas?" I am sure the answer would be "yes." "Then, you are following some of the church year." "So you observe Easter?" "Yes, of course," the imaginary answer might come forth, "of course we observe Easter." "Well, then, you are observing some of the church year." Without acknowledging to themselves or others, some pastors and churches do observe the church year, at least in part, which is what many of our churches are doing, observing the church year, at least in part. Some churches and pastors take in some or all of the church year; others participate in only a little.

600

The following messages were all on the back of one pickup truck (and there were other messages):

> GOD LOVES YOU
> WHETHER YOU LIKE IT OR NOT
>
> IF GUNS CAUSE CRIME
> MATCHES CAUSE ARSON
>
> WHEN THE FINAL TRUMPET SOUNDS...
> I'M OUTTA HERE

Chapter 601-650

"The Rich Man Also Died"

601

Occasionally you read something shocking, absolutely shocking, in the Bible. I came upon that as I read the Parable of the Rich Man and Lazarus, Luke 16:19-31, the other day. It had been there all along, of course, but the power of the statement spoke very loudly this time. The parable tells us that the rich man, of course, lived and ate well "every day" but he also ignored the poor man at his gate who was afflicted with physical pain and hunger. The story goes on: "The poor man died and was carried away by the angels to be with Abraham." Then we read the shocking words. Get ready. Can you hear this? Here are those shocking words: "The rich man also died and was buried." There you have it. "The rich man also died." Death, the great equalizer. Death, the non-discriminatory force. Death, the inevitable fact that eventually knocks on the door of every life. No matter how wealthy he was, no matter how well he ate, no matter what his social standing was, no matter whether he was consulted on great projects for the city and served on boards and councils (I doubt if he even cared about any of that!!), "the rich man also died." It happens to everyone eventually. His riches did not keep death away. His fine food did not keep death away. "The rich man also died." What a shocking, sobering thought. I am still riveted by that statement.

602

Sign outside Highland Heights United Methodist Church in Memphis, Tennessee:

COME JOIN OUR PROPHET-SHARING PLAN

603

I took typing as a junior in high school. One of the first things learned was to identify the "home keys." Thereafter, the teacher, to start the class, would call out, "Hands on home keys." It was always important to start off right. A good start is very important. If I do not begin with "hands on home keys" when typing, it is a mess. Let us assume the final sentence for this: paragraph is, "It is important to begin well." If I move my hands just one key to the right and get the "home keys" thing wrong, the above sentence reads like this: "Oy od o,[ptysmy yp nrhom er;;/" In every important venture, we need to have a good beginning.

604

When the apostles met together on Sunday night after the resurrection and Thomas was not there (John 20:19-23), it was a sad thing for Thomas. The others had to tell him what they had experienced in seeing the risen Lord. Later he saw for himself but the sad thing was he missed the first meeting. All of us have regrets in missing, by plan or circumstance, what turned out to be important events, such as a reunion, an important church event, or a speech. Now, was the absence of Thomas a blunder of some kind? Did he misunderstand the announcement passed around among the apostles? "I thought you said MONDAY night!" Or did Thomas just choose not to show up?

605

Isn't it aggravating when you get a form letter from some agency and they write like they know you? Something like, "Dear Thomas Campbell: Because of your excellent credit rating, we are offering you this credit card, so forth and so on and so forth and so on." Well, it is obvious they do not know me. They got a bunch of things incorrect in only a few words. The writer of the letter knows me about as well as my fellow minister did who complimented me on my "piety" earlier in this book.

606

Have you ever been somewhere and then wished you were somewhere else? In Fort Worth and in Memphis years ago I would attend the golf tournament when the professionals came to town. The spectator at a golf tournament needs to decide whether to follow one player around all the time or to stay put at one hole and watch the approach shots and putts of all the players or to jump around from one hole to another without any plan at all. A discouraging experience at a golf tournament is to be at, say, the ninth hole, and you hear a tremendous roar from the crowd coming from the thirteenth hole. And you weren't there. You were here. Now, do you rush over to the thirteenth hole. It's too late, you know. Or do you resign yourself to having missed a great sports thrill (perhaps somebody sank a forty-five foot putt) and stay where you are? It is a guessing game. The most memorable experience I had in following one player was in Fort Worth, toward the end of his playing days, when I trailed along with Fort Worth native Ben Hogan and the other golfer playing with him as well as a hundred or so fans. I tried to ignore the loud cheers coming from elsewhere and set my face in the direction Hogan was going. It was a good decision. After following Mr. Hogan for awhile, I wandered and did the "no plan at all" routine.

607

Eighteen of my first twenty-two years as an ordained minister were spent as a New Church Development pastor. The new churches, all Cumberland Presbyterian, were Faith in Batesville, Arkansas (1961-65); St. Luke in Fort Worth, Texas (1965-72); and St. Matthew in Burleson, Texas (1975-82), respectively. Whitehaven Cumberland Presbyterian Church (1972-75) was in between the Fort Worth and Burleson experiences. And the Lansdowne Church in Lexington, Kentucky (1982-85) was a church redevelopment venture, the church having started in 1967 but having sort of an official re-start in the early 1980s. I enjoyed the challenge of the new church situation and derived a great deal of satisfaction and accomplishment out of even small progress in those churches. My only truly "established" church was the Beaver Creek Church in Knoxville, Tennessee (established 1833). The new-church fever still comes on every now and then, though at seventy years of age (in 2009) the energy is not there. With George Estes from the Board of Missions I have had the opportunity in Memphis Theological Seminary to lead classes in that subject five or six different semesters. Occasionally, I will hear of a new church start and imagine myself "doing it" again. I'm told that some ministers have a "knack" for that sort of thing and some do not, just as some enjoy prison ministry or evangelism or counseling or inner city work.

608

Can't find the words to pray, except for much-used words and phrases of the past? Feeling dry as a bone as if there were a famine in the land of prayer and you know not what to do or where to turn, except to pray, "God, be merciful to me a sinner"? That prayer is certainly the place to start, but if you want to go further, why not reach for a church hymnal and discover again, or anew, how many hymns are prayers. The old Broadman Hymnal of the Southern Baptist Church contains many of the great traditional selections that have enriched our lives. For example, No. 4, "Come, Thou Almighty King" is a prayer, and just the first verse can help us lift our hearts and voices in prayer:

> Come, Thou Almighty King,
> Help us Thy name to sing,
> Help us to praise:
> Father, all glorious,
> O'er all victorious,
> Come and reign over us,
> Ancient of Days.

Some hymns are about God. Some hymns are directed to God. Those that are directed to God are prayers. Here is another, No. 13:

> Savior, like a shepherd lead us,
> Much we need Thy tender care;
> In Thy pleasant pastures feed us,
> For our use Thy folds prepare:
> Blessed Jesus, Blessed Jesus,
> Thou has bought us, Thine we are;
> Blessed Jesus, Blessed Jesus,
> Thou has bought us, Thine we are.

No. 19 in the Broadman Hymnal is "Love Divine" and this is the first verse, a prayer:

> Love divine, all loves excelling,
> Joy of heaven to earth come down!
> Fix in us Thy humble dwelling;
> All Thy faithful mercies crown.
> Jesus, Thou art all compassion,
> Pure, unbounded love Thou art;
> Visit us with Thy salvation,
> Enter every trembling heart.

No. 56 is "I Am Thine, O Lord" and a couple of verses will suffice to indicate the power of this hymn as a prayer. We all know the refrain, "Draw me nearer, blessed Lord, to the cross where Thou hast died." Here are two of the verses:

> I am Thine, O Lord,
> I have heard Thy voice,
> And it told Thy love to me;
> But I long to rise in the arms of faith,
> And be closer drawn to Thee.
> Consecrate me now
> To Thy service, Lord,

By the power of grace divine;
Let my soul look up
With a steadfast hope,
And my will be lost in Thine.

These are just samples. There is a rich prayer life within the different hymnals that we use in all of our churches. Yes, it is somebody else's prayer, somebody else's poetry. So? We sing these hymns. Why not "pray" them, too?

609

In the Cumberland Presbyterian system, the presbytery is central. Every church in a particular region is a member of the same presbytery. Usually this body meets about twice a year. It elects a moderator to preside over the meeting whose membership consists of all ordained ministers who belong to the Presbytery as well as elected delegates (elders) from the sessions of the different churches. The key to a successful meeting is the moderator. In the many interviews ministerial students have conducted with those who have served in that role, almost without exception the first requirement is to know parliamentary procedure. A weak moderator can hamper a meeting. A strong, well-informed moderator can facilitate the meeting. One area where even good ones may go wrong is in calling for the vote. A motion is made. The moderator should wait for a second to the motion. The moderator should not ask for a second. Once the motion has been seconded, the one presiding then repeats the motion and asks for discussion. Once discussion has ended, the presiding officer says, "Those in favor of the motion, say Aye." And here is where some go wrong. They then say, "Those opposed, like sign." Or, "Those opposed…" and offer no specific guidance on what to say. It should be this way: "Those opposed, say No." Something clear. Something easy. Something directly opposite to the favorable vote. All of us are working on this. Anyone serving as moderator of a presbytery will want to adopt this easy, clear approach to voting.

610

I almost messed up at a meeting of presbytery, and it was in the interest of history, at least that's my story and I'm sticking to it. The year was 1983. All presbyteries were being called on regarding whether to adopt the new proposed Confession of Faith for Cumberland Presbyterians. Presentations in Cumberland Presbytery (in Kentucky; I was pastor of our church in Lexington) had been made and we were ready to vote. The moderator asked for those in favor and there was a fairly strong outpouring of voices in favor. Then he asked for those who were opposed and the voices were very weak. Perhaps they were weak because the moderator may not have given those opposed a clear word to say. Anyway, the moderator declared the motion passed. No one objected. But I, in my so-called interest in history, stood and suggested that, since some history was being made here and we and all the other presbyteries were voting, it would be good to have a standing vote so it could be recorded for posterity. No one disagreed so we had a standing vote. It was a one-vote victory for the new Confession of Faith. Something like 12-11 or 17-16. I remember it was just one vote. Evidently in the first vote the positive voices were stronger than they were really were, and the negative voices were weaker than they really were. We could have had a real problem. The moderator had already declared - after the voice vote - that "the ayes have it." What would we have done if in the standing vote the result would have been the opposite? I can't go there. Thank goodness, and thank God, the vote stayed in the affirmative, though the second vote was much too close for comfort. Remind me to keep my big mouth shut next time.

611

In a small town in West Tennessee four churches sit atop a little rising hill in view of the main highway. One of the them is the Cumberland Presbyterian Church. These churches and their people have been neighbors for years. Each parking lot literally joins another. Newspaper articles have been written and pictures shown of the four churches in that town. I attended an ordination and installation service for the new pastor of the Cumberland Presbyterian Church early one Sunday afternoon. Many of us attending were from out of town. We did not know where one parking lot ended and the other started. After the service and the reception, with punch and cookies and cake and nuts, I left to return to my regular duties. As I approached my car, a man was emptying some trash in the nearby dumpster. I didn't know him. He didn't know me. As I got closer to the car, he called out, "Are they through in there yet?" I said, thinking this conversation was on a courteous and friendly note, "They are just finished in there, I think." Then he called out again, "Tell those people they need to move their cars!" I did not try to frame a reply, for by that time I had opened the door to my car. But I did reflect on the occasion as I drove away. I asked myself the question: "How many times in all these years have the people from this small Cumberland Presbyterian Church ever had such a good attendance that the cars overflowed into the adjoining parking lot?" And, "How many of those other three churches would be having services or activities at that time of day on a Sunday afternoon?" The answer to the first question was probably, None. The answer to the second question was also probably, None. That made me ask myself, What was all the fuss about? We weren't bothering anybody. We weren't encroaching on somebody else's space to the detriment of any other church. In fact, the place where others and I had parked was right next to the side of the Cumberland Presbyterian Church and the entire parking lot for that other church had exactly one car on it and the whole space was the size of half a football field. A stranger would naturally assume the space adjoining the Cumberland church was that church's parking lot. But it wasn't. But who would have known? Needless to say, the joy and inspiration of the worship service and fellowship afterwards were a bit soured by this man's apparent belligerent attitude. I should have said what the comedian/actor Steve Martin said in one of his movies: "Well, excuuuuuuuse me!"

611 "Wellllexxxxcusssmmmmeeeeeee"

612

Sign in the front yard of the Atwood (TN) Church of Christ:

DON'T POINT A FINGER
LEND A HAND

613

I heard this one years ago and have told it often: A woman was at the city park and there were eight children running around yelling and screaming and laughing. An onlooker approaches and asks: "Pardon me, lady, are all these your children, or is this a picnic?" The reply: "They are all my children and, believe me, it's no picnic."

614

I recently saw a light-hearted movie produced sometime in the 1980s. It starred Susan St. James and it was entitled "I Take These Men." She was unhappy in her own marriage and began to fantasize about being married to someone else. What would it be like to divorce her husband and marry this man in their circle of friends, or this one, or this one? She projects into the future and finds that, while these guys all looked to be desirable and dependable and downright good husband material from a distance, none are worth the effort. Each has his own peculiarities, bad habits, hang-ups, and flaws. She decides, in the end, that the husband she has is really the best way to go. She and he decide to make the marriage work and to make it work better than it ever has before.

615

Our older brother Sam returned to the West Tennessee area from his home in Virginia in 2007 for a reunion of his Medina High School girls' basketball team that won the district tournament fifty years earlier. One year later, in 2008 he came back to attend the Gibson County Athletic Hall of Fame gathering to witness the induction of Brenda Morris, a star player on that 1956-57 team. At lunch that day, prior to the program that night, Sam told us that Brenda started the year as a forward. Back in the 1950s the forwards were on one end of the court and they did the scoring. The guards were on the other end and they defended the forwards from the other team. The forwards never had to defend and the guards never got to shoot. Normally, the forwards got most of the glory because they made the points and their names were in the newspapers. Sam said that, four or five games into the season the team was mediocre at best. Brenda went to him and volunteered to move from forward to guard. He said that turned the team around and they went on to win their district tournament and win the first game in the regional tournament before finally losing, ending their season with a record of 20-12. This spoke volumes about Brenda. She was more concerned about the team than personal recognition. Her talents, though, could not be overlooked. Thus the Hall of Fame award.

616

Robert Morgan in his recent book, <u>Boone: A Biography</u> (Algonquin, 2007) devotes some space (p. 372) to a discussion of "boating in the west." There were "bull boats" made of "bull" buffalo hides.

There were canoes. And there were flatboats. Morgan says the flatboat was propelled by the current. Then he wrote: "A flatboat could travel only downstream, and when its destination was reached the wood was sold for building or firewood." It could "travel only downstream." We Christians might pay heed to this analogy. If all we can do is float downstream, never going against the trend, never arguing against the status quo, never challenging tradition, we are like the flatboats of the late eighteenth century. Daniel Boone himself, though raised among Quakers, never opposed slavery, for example. He never owned more than two or three slaves at a time, but he did not protest. All of us are like the flatboats in many areas of life, I am sure, but there are occasions and issues when we cannot relax and be swept on downstream without resistance. If in my later years a grandchild (or great-grandchild) should inquire about my activities in the years that I have lived (from 1939) I would say immediately that I had the joy and pain of living in a time when the civil rights movement in the U.S. was at its strongest and would say gladly that social customs regarding segregation and all its aspects have changed drastically in these times. The changes occurred because hundreds of American citizens, black and white, fought against the downstream, easy, "acceptable" way. But I will be embarrassed if a grandchild (or great-grandchild) asks about my involvement or lack of involvement in those matters during that time.

617

Sign outside St. Stephen's United Methodist Church, Memphis, Tennessee:

> LOOKING FOR A SIGN FROM GOD ?
> THIS IS IT

618

Sign on a billboard advertising a Parks and Recreation event:

> Remember when PLAY wasn't a button?

619

In his biography of Daniel Boone (Algonquin Books of Chapel Hill, 2007) author Robert Morgan wrote that someone once asked Boone in his later years if he was ever lost while hunting and fighting and living in the wilderness. He said he was never lost but he was once "bewildered for three days."

620

Sign outside a Baptist church in Memphis:

> IF YOU DON'T FEEL CLOSE TO GOD
> WHO MOVED?

621

Our five-year-old granddaughter has been saying the blessing at family meals:

> God is great, God is good.
> Let us thank him for our food.
> Amen.

But recently she amended her prayer, like this:

> God is great, Jesus is good.
> Let us thank him for our food.
> Amen.

Before anyone could ask, she explained, "We ought not to leave Jesus out."

622

Micah 6:6-8 ends with these triumphant and eloquent words:

"He has told you, O mortal, what is good; and what does the Lord require of you but to do justice, and to love kindness, and to walk humbly with your God?"

From many accounts, the ways in which people of the times tried to please God were with "burnt offerings" (6:6) or "thousands of rams with ten thousands of rivers of oil" (6:7) or, worse, with the sacrifice of their "firstborn" (6:7). Notice how violent all of these are. Killing. Fire. More killing. Bigger fires. Murdering one's own child. And in the name of God. Violence. Killing. Was that how they felt they should please God?

Micah said, "Not now. Not this time. Not anymore." It was this: Do justice, love kindness, walk humbly with God. Non-violence. Quiet goodness. Fairness.

Notice, too, that the first two requirements have to do with other people, not with God, at least not directly with God. This "jealous God," this "angry God" this "righteous God" that people were trying to please and appease was in fact not any of those. In fact, two of the three requirements had to do with people's relationships with other people. The third called on them to "walk humbly with God."

Some world leaders still think violence is the key. You don't like the way another country is doing things. Nuke them. Bomb them. You don't like what you think they MIGHT do to our country some day? Go after them now, before they blow us up.

Yet Micah's interpretation of God's demands was a pattern of non-violence. We have hardly learned anything on this. It took a non-Christian, Gandhi, to exemplify what Jesus himself had taught and exemplified. A former president of the United States visited with Hamas, an enemy of Israel. He was roundly criticized for his "Don Quixote" visit and sit-down with Hamas leaders. But I ask, "Was anybody killed while they talked? Did his nation or the other group bomb each other while they were visiting? Does it hurt to talk? While this was going on, one prominent presidential candidate said, "If I am elected president, I will be Hamas's worst nightmare." Is he going to bomb these people? Will he call for an invasion? Is that the answer? Is that the way to please God? To be a nation that bombs and kills and destroys and lays waste the nations?

623

The more I dwell on matters, the more I am persuaded that the most destructive negative image and most enduring blot on this country to come out of the most recent years of the American government will be the legacy of torture that we have created. The worst foreign policy blunder, the Iraq war, will certainly be up there. The firing of U.S. attorneys for strictly political reasons will be high on the list. The fiasco following Hurricane Katrina will be up there as well. So will the program of invasive listening. But the most lasting blight on the American image will be the torture of "enemy combatants" and the excuses we have used to inflict the torture, including saying it isn't torture. This evil mark will stay with us for decades to come, I am afraid, and will, of course, put our military personnel in harm's way if and when they are captured by the enemy, whoever that might be. We will have no argument. We will have no high moral ground to stand on. We cannot make the humanitarian plea. And we cannot self-righteously point to ourselves as examples of how to live by the code of justice and decency. No, this will go on and on, this scar on our national conscience, this ugly chapter in our history. And now, after revealing documents have to come to light, the administration that EXPRESSED surprise in April 2004, when pictures of dehumanizing actions by our people against those of the other side were made public, really just FEIGNED surprise. They knew all along. Shame on them. Shame on us.

624

Four people stood up to offer special music at church. They sang the first verse of the hymn in unison. Then, starting with the second verse, they sang the song in parts. They were harmonizing. They were in harmony with each other. There was no harmony during the first verse because they were lifting up the hymn in unison; they were all singing the melody. The harmony took place when they were singing different parts, but the same song. Harmony in the church may not mean everybody is doing or thinking the same thing. It may mean that everybody is singing the same song, but in different parts.

625

The Summer Extension School of the Program of Alternate Studies, held every July at Bethel College in McKenzie, Tennessee, is a fifteen-day school that breaks down into three five-day sessions, or Blocks. Many students attend one Block only, and have to get back home because of work or other responsibilities. A few are able to attend two Blocks. And perhaps one fourth to one third of them attend all three Blocks, fifteen consecutive days from 6:45 in the morning until 9:00 at night, non-stop. One year, toward the end of the fifteen-day marathon of classes, worship, meals, fellowship, and late-night hymn-singing, I was talking with my friend and colleague, Alfonso Marquez, himself a PAS graduate. He said, "Going all fifteen days at PAS is like eating a Jalapeno pepper. You enjoy it, but you suffer." No more apt description has ever been given.

626

I have been a pastor and I have talked with many pastors over the years. Among the problems in a given congregation, "control issues" top the list. Most pastors I know believe that the church can make progress, do the Lord's will, nurture children, grow in membership, and develop new leadership if the "control issues" can be dealt with and put to rest. Whether it is the desire for power, or a psychological hunger that compels people to assert themselves in controlling ways, or even a desire to wreak havoc in the church out of meanness or evil or jealousy or a need for revenge for some harm done to them in the past, the people who feel they must exercise power and control top the list of pastoral concerns. Pastors and congregations can handle just about anything else, but this one is a difficult item.

627

Some events return over and over in our minds. At least a decade back, a man with a wife and three little children bought a new SUV, and it was to be the wife's to drive around while he would drive the other, older car to work. On the very first day after they bought it, the family went for a drive, with the wife/mother at the wheel. On the highway from their home in eastern Arkansas toward Memphis, she swerved to avoid an animal in the road. This caused her to veer off the road into a ditch that had water in it from recent rains. Her husband said, "You get out now and I will get the babies." She forced the left front door open and exited the sinking vehicle. In seconds the car was submerged in the water. There was silence from the car. Her husband and the children drowned as he was attempting to free them and bring them out. It happened so suddenly. A happy, excited family was virtually wiped out in one split second. A young mother lost her husband and three children. I still think about that. What a tragedy. What great sadness. What a great loss.

628

This happens to many pastors, I am certain. I ring the doorbell of one of the families of our church. A little girl comes to the door. "Is your mother home?" "Mommy, its God."

629

On another occasion as a pastor I called a young family on the phone. Their little girl answered and I asked for her mother. She called out, "Mother it's the Creature."

630

I have always admired Micaiah, one of those Old Testament prophets that did not get a book named after him but accomplished great things. In 1 Kings 22 we find four hundred prophets called together by the king who asked them if he should go to war. They were "yes" men and easily said, "Yes, go up." But the king still was uneasy for he knew there was one prophet out there with integrity and his name was Micaiah, who was not at the meeting. He did not believe going to war was the right thing to do. He was encouraged by other prophets to "go along" and when asked by the king, did that very thing, though he was lying through his teeth and the king knew it. This response was unsettling to the king and the king came back at him saying, in effect, "Tell me what you really think." When he shared with the king his inner convictions on the matter the monarch got so mad he had Micaiah thrown into prison. It was hard being a government-paid prophet. When the fellow in charge is surrounded by people who want only to please him, the chances are slim that anybody will step up with views contrary to the big guy's. I am not wrong in supposing that tradition has continued to this day. Unfortunately, loyalty trumps integrity almost every time.

631

This was on the front license plate of a car:

> Buckle Up For
> JESUS
> (Proverbs 3:6)

632

One of the Sundays in the Church Year is Ascension Sunday. Ascension Day comes forty days after Easter and the Sunday following that day is Ascension Sunday. Ten days after Ascension Day (fifty days after Easter) is Pentecost Sunday. I suspect not all churches observe the Ascension in their Church Year. It is often overlooked. I try to preach about it every now and then, usually not knowing much to talk about and often adding little or nothing to the conversation. But the last time around I did come up with one thought: Ascension is supposed to be the shortest holiday in the Church Year. How do I know? It's in Acts, Chapter 1, Verse 11: "Men of Galilee, why do you stand looking up toward heaven?" In other words, don't celebrate too long. It's time to get on back to doing the Lord's work. Observe the Ascension. Preach about it.

Sing about it. Pray about it. Then move on. I guess this is verified in that we do not list the Sundays following as "First Sunday After the Ascension," "Second Sunday After the Ascension," "Third Sunday After the Ascension," and so forth. No, it's time to put that behind us, quit looking up toward heaven, set your eyes back on this earth where the work is, where the pain is, where the grief is, where the mission is.

633

Winning isn't everything. A college women's softball game - in fact an important playoff game - was on the line. Sara Tucholsky of Western Oregon University hit the ball over the centerfield fence with two runners on base to win the game and the championship against Central Washington University. However, as she rounded first base she missed the bag, and, in turning to go back and touch it, twisted her knee and she could not get up. It was determined that a pinch runner could only stay at first and the home run would have been ruled a single. If her own teammates tried to help her she would be called out. Finally members of the opposing team asked if there were a rule against their carrying Sara around the bases. No one could find a ruling against that. So the first baseman and shortstop carried Sara around the bases. She touched each base, including home plate, with her good foot. The Central Washington team members contributed to their own loss by this act of good will and sportsmanship. This is one of the great sports stories of the century.

When winning is not the most important thing

634

This was a bumper sticker on the back of another car:

>REGIME CHANGE
>STARTS AT HOME

635

I have never gone to the racetrack. I have never bet on a horse. I would like to go to the racetrack sometime. I always watch the Kentucky Derby and the Preakness and the Belmont Stakes each year and hope there is a Triple Crown winner this time. I lived in Lexington, Kentucky, and had dozens of opportunities to go to the races in Lexington and Louisville in those almost-five years of living in the area, but did not. So, I have yet to go to the window to place a bet and to say something like this: "Twenty dollars on Number Five." That is, I would be betting $20 on horse number 5. But I think I come close to that experience every time I use cash to purchase gas for the car and walk in to pay. I say this: "Twenty dollars on Number Five." That is, Pump No. 5. Just the other day I did just that. "Twenty dollars on Number Three." A couple of days prior to that it was, "Twenty dollars on Number Nine." I am doing that more often these days. By the way, my horse has never won.

636

In the Cumberland Presbyterian Church, the Presbytery is the heart of its church government. The congregation elects elders who comprise the "session." The Presbytery consists of all ordained ministers and elected elders from the different sessions of congregations in a given region. Since Cumberland Presbytery was organized on February 4, 1810, thus laying the foundation for what became a formidable denomination in the United States and the rest of the world, the Presbytery has been, to use my words in some classes on polity, "where it's at." It is the Presbytery that authorizes the start of new churches. It is the Presbytery that approves the calling and installing of pastors for the different churches. It is the Presbytery that nurtures and ordains persons to ministry in the church. From the very first, what seems to be the main function of the Presbytery has been this last matter: nurturing and ordaining ministers. In fact, you look through the Minutes of early meetings of Cumberland Presbytery and its succeeding presbyteries and find that almost the entire proceedings were given over to its responsibilities in regard to ministers. Today the same holds true. No one but the Presbytery ordains ministers. No one but the Presbytery receives ordained ministers from other denominations and makes requirements of them. It has ever been so. Long let it continue.

637

I went to Jim McKee's funeral. This veteran of World War II, husband, father, grandfather, educator, former quarterback on the Bethel College football team, former chair of the trustees of Bethel College, former president of Bethel College, and church leader, was characterized by his pastor, William Warren, as a person who quietly and faithfully did "the right thing." William compared Jim's life to that of Joseph, the husband of Mary, the mother of Jesus. Joseph never called attention to himself, seemed always to go about his life in an unassuming yet focused way, and always did the "right thing." William gave several examples in Jim's life of such moments. During the service I was reminded of the only time I ever saw Jim McKee on television. It was the local evening news. He had been stopped by the police on the streets of Germantown, a suburb of Memphis. Why? They were promoting good driving, and he had been stopped to receive the commendation of the Germantown Police Department for his safe driving. He was doing the "right thing." Jim was somewhat embarrassed by all this attention, as I recall.

638

I was involved in a conversation about forgetting names. Most of us told how we had struggled with recalling names. I think pastors are especially conscious of this. One fellow said, "I had trouble remembering names until I took that Sam Carnegie course."

639

I remember, with fondness mostly, Vacation Bible School from my childhood. For many years, it lasted two weeks. You went from 9:00 to noon every morning for five days each week, with the closing program on the night of the last day. That evening, things the kids made would be on display and different classes would present a skit or a musical number or some other item for the program. Later many churches reduced their VBS activities to just one week, with a five-day school. Now it is not unusual to see churches with a three-day or even one-day VBS. The down-side for me as a child was that the "vacation" part of the name was not quite true. It almost never failed that the church I attended would have its VBS the very next week after the public schools let out for the summer. There was no time in between. I am tired of school, and now, without any respite, we go to school again? No way! I remember complaining, even whining, but to no avail.

640

Another church sign, this one in the front yard of St. Stephens United Methodist Church in Memphis:

> HEAVENLY FORECAST
> "REIGNS" FOREVER

641

I have had moments of reflection about my senior year at McKenzie High School, and especially the basketball season. We went 23-8, won the district tournament, and ended the season with a loss in the first game of the regional tournament. I tallied up the scoring. We averaged 62 points a game. Our opponents averaged 52 points a game. Billy Webb and I were the seniors and co-captains on the team. Seniors Barry Baker and Herb Blumenthal were the team managers. Coach C. D. Parrish was in his fourth year at the helm. The previous year we were 16-7 and the year before that 20-7, so we had a reputation to uphold. Willie Chandler was what we might today call our "point guard," though we had never heard of that term in 1956-57. Willie made very few of what we called then "floor mistakes," what we now call "turnovers." I remember how he handled the ball so well. Bobby Gwaltney and Marvin Townsend rounded out the starting five. Bobby had the physique of a football player and was one of our best rebounders. Marvin had the best shooting touch of the whole bunch, though he often had to be told to shoot more. As mentioned, Billy and I were seniors and, more often than not, one of us would end up being the high scorer for most of our games. Willie and Bobby were juniors. Marvin was a sophomore. Among the reserves was my little brother Paul, a freshman, who would make a mark for himself and his team in his junior and senior years as one of the greats of McKenzie High basketball fame. Naturally, when Billy and I talk - he lives in Kentucky, I in Tennessee - the conversation inevitably gets around to that senior year, and how we could have been 28-3 instead of 23-8. And, of course, the last time we played, we lost, in the regional tournament. It is a sobering thought that most basketball teams lose the last game they play. Such are the memories after more than fifty years.

642

It is often forgotten, if ever known by many in the first place, that the first theological seminary west of the Mississippi River was founded by two Cumberland Presbyterians, Finis Ewing and Robert D. Morrow at New Lebanon, Missouri, in 1821. "Morrow taught the scientific courses; Ewing taught theology." This from a history of Presbyterianism in Missouri entitled <u>Presbyterianism Spreads Westward</u>, by Kenneth R. Locke and J. Joseph Trower (Locke Printing, 1997). They write, "During long summer vacations, Ewing and Morrow along with their students went on preaching tours in the territory and holding camp meetings. Young would-be preachers rode beside their mentors reciting their lessons as they went from place to place. Thus in this early theological institution, theory was combined with practice." These days in seminaries they call those kinds of trips "immersion experiences." A wonderful way to learn, according to the testimony of many.

643

A strange event happened during the previous basketball season, the 1955-56 year when we went 16-7. For one thing, the brackets for the district tournament were all askew. Our team had lost only two games all year among district teams, and both losses were to Paris Grove High School. Yet when the pairings were announced we were in the same bracket with the Blue Devils of Grove High School. We were in the same bracket, not at the semi-final level where you might expect, but at the quarter-final level, very early in the tournament. So there we were, set to play our main detractors, a team that had beaten us decisively twice in the season. The game was in their gymnasium, where the tournament was being held. We did not do well, and at the half they were twenty points ahead and looking unbeatable. We went to the dressing room for the halftime talk and what was hoped to be a renewed energy and effort. But while we were down there the lights went out. The coach told the manager, Don Richardson, to "go and get those lights back on." Don came back pretty soon and said, "Coach, the lights are out in the entire city of Paris. Somebody hit a light pole." And so it was that the second half of the game had to be postponed to the next afternoon. We got dressed in the dark and filed out of the gym slowly. We learned later that the city police, with flashlights, helped families, friends, and fans get out of the gym in the same way, slowly, carefully. On the way home we were discouraged. It didn't look good for tomorrow. A few were undecided as to whether we ought to go back and play the second half at all. I have been reminded many times that I thought we ought to go back. "We can beat those guys," I am reported to have said. To this day, teammates of that year say, "Campbell convinced us to go back. Blame it on Campbell." We went back the next day. Now the Grove players had been rested from the first half and were set to come out fresh, again. They blasted us in the second half, too. We might have lost to them eventually in the finals or semi-finals of the tournament anyway. But to have to play them - again the only team to beat us all year in the district - that early in the tournament was a terrible injustice. We still talk about that when we get together in McKenzie and rehash that year. It was especially unjust and unfair for our two main seniors, Jackie Hall and Gene Hale, who were our leaders on the team that year. They, and we, deserved better.

644

I have told this story so many times it is imperative that it be in this book. I don't know where I read it or heard it, but it has been passed on to many people. It seems a young man was in his first pastorate. The sermon on his first Sunday was a stem-winder. The sermon on his second Sunday was almost as good. However, on the third Sunday the message faltered somewhat, and on the fourth it was worse than before. The fifth, sixth, and seventh Sundays got progressively worse. Finally, the church board asked him when he prepared his sermons. He said, proudly, "I am so busy in the week being a pastor to the people that I don't work on my sermon until Sunday morning when I walk from the manse/parsonage (across the driveway) to the church." The church leaders immediately passed a motion to sell that house and buy another one for the minister and family ten miles away.

645

This sign in an examination room at an animal clinic:

> HEAVEN IS WHERE ALL THE DOGS
> YOU EVER LOVED
> ARE THERE TO GREET YOU

646

The Boy Scout executive and I were visiting in the fellowship hall prior to the regular Monday night meeting of our local troop. He was there to help with some special projects. I don't know how we got off on this subject, but he said, "Humans breathe in oxygen and breathe out carbon dioxide, and plants breathe in carbon dioxide and breathe out oxygen." Then he said, "Somewhere out there, there is a plant that is glad you are alive."

647

Isn't it funny how different words and phrases are used these days as substitutes for others? These days, you are not "fired" from your job, and not even "laid off" any more. Instead, you have been "downsized." The U.S. military has a weapon - perhaps a rocket or a bomb or an otherwise very large weapon - called the "peacekeeper." It used to be called a "rocket," or a "bomb" or a "very large weapon." One of my favorites has to do with cars. It's not "used cars" any more. And it's not even "pre-owned cars." I like what has taken their place: "pre-loved cars."

648

In 2008 Pentecost was on the same Sunday as Mother's Day. Our "time for children" leader talked to the kids (and to the adults indirectly) about Mother's Day. I emphasized Pentecost. In my introductory announcements, I mentioned the question of how to bring those two special days together. And then I thought of it: Pentecost is the Mother of all special days in the church year!

649

In June of 2008 the General Assembly of the Cumberland Presbyterian Church met in Tokyo, Japan. Years ago a Church Growth motto emerged: "Cumberland Presbyterians Can." And they can, including having their annual international meeting in another country besides the United States, for the first time in history. Most likely this is the first time an American-based Presbyterian denomination has met in another country. This is just like Cumberland Presbyterians! This small denomination - approximately 50,000 active members and around 750 churches - is tiny by all measures. Yet the church just keeps doing what to observers would be the impossible. It is what some call the "bumble-bee factor." From all scientific accounts that I have heard fourth- and fifth-hand, the bumble-bee cannot fly. Its body is so big and its wings are so small that there is no way it can get off the ground or, doing that, stay in the air. But nobody ever told the bumble-bee that! With one college (McKenzie, Tennessee), one seminary (Memphis, Tennessee), and one children's home (Denton, Texas), and each enjoying great growth and success, the church continues to witness and serve. With churches in Japan, Colombia, Hong Kong, Brazil, Mongolia, Laos, and a half-dozen other countries, the church continues to do mission. With an outstanding denominational Christian education ministry, including an annual youth conference that has capacity enrollment every July, the church continues to nurture and teach. With new opportunities opening up often for new church development, the church continues to start new congregations. We could go on. Cumberland Presbyterians Can!

650

Sign in the front yard of First Presbyterian Church of Antlers, Oklahoma:

GOD ANSWERS PRAYER
YES   NO   WAIT

Chapter 651-700

"Be Careful What You Ask For, Preacher"

651

We preachers need to be careful what we say when we challenge our people to committed discipleship. They might take us at our word and do it. Randy Jacob of Choctaw Presbytery told of a member of a church where the pastor preached the necessity of total commitment to the church. A meeting of presbytery was held a few weeks later that went from Thursday through Saturday. The man missed work on Thursday and Friday to attend. When he returned to his job on Monday he was fired. He went to his pastor and said, "I did what you told us to do. I gave my all to the church. Now I need help getting another job." The pastor told him that next time use better judgment on when to miss work. The man replied, "But you didn't say that. You said to give our all; you challenged us to total commitment!"

On taking the preacher too literally!

652

Another, similar, incident happened in Kentucky. A pastor went on and on about the sins of tobacco use. He condemned those who smoked it, those who grew it, those who sold it. All in all, he tore into the total industry. A church member took the pastor at his word and went and cut down all his tobacco crop. Then he visited his pastor and said, "I did what you preached. My tobacco crop was my living. It fed my family and put a roof on our heads. Now I need your help in finding new work." This time, if I heard correctly, the church helped him in his distress. Sometimes we preachers get all up tight about some things and fail to deliver a message that takes into account the life situations of people and where they really live and what they really do.

653

Was this a dream come true or a nightmare? I am preaching along and I call for total commitment to Christ and his church. I may even use some of the apostles as examples, as they left their boats and followed Jesus. I invite people, even urge them, to "give of their best to the Master." After the service, fifteen people wait around to talk. They want to do what I called for. Do I have any work for them to do? What a dream come true! But my answer is, "Not really. Everything in the church is covered at this time." What a nightmare! I need to be careful what I ask for in the name of the Lord.

654

I had a book-burning incident one time and loved every minute of it. My seventh-grade health class workbook was of terrible paper quality and when writing in it with my pencil I experienced a terrible, almost disgusting feeling. In fact, I dreaded to have to write in it, filling in the blanks, answering questions, because of what the whole experience did to me. It was worse than fingernails on a chalkboard. On the last day of school, I took that book home and went out to our back yard. Within a certain fenced-in area - where my older brother used to keep some chickens as a 4-H project and where we sometimes burned trash - I tore that book with my bare hands, page by page, and then placed everything in a pile. With great pleasure I struck a match to the cursed book. I relished the moment. It was all over. The torture was now behind me. I could live again.

655

Sometimes what a preacher promises does not get done. In doing a bulletin early in the week, I list a sermon title and usually come close to having that as the theme. Recently the text was Acts 3:1-10 where Peter and John come upon someone in need and begging alms. They say, "Silver and gold have I none, but what I have, give I unto thee. In the name of Jesus Christ, walk!" I listed the sermon title as "Give What You Can," because these two disciples did not have any money so they gave what they had, which was words of healing. But during the week something happened in my studies and the sermon actually came around to saying that what the disciples gave was greater than what they would have given had they had some money. The man lame from birth was not asking for enough. He requested alms, and had the disciples provided it his future days would have been exactly what they had been in the past, each day lying at the door of the temple begging. Instead, their words of healing brought him to his feet and he jumped for joy and praised God. So the sermon was not at all about "Give What You Can." Instead, it was about how God provides for us much more than we ask.

656

This happens frequently. A little boy goes to sleep on the couch in the family room. Later, at bed time, the father picks up the child and upstairs they go. In the morning the child wakes up in his own bed. He went to sleep downstairs. He woke up in his own bed upstairs. I have heard this wonderful story used as an illustration of heaven. We die. Then we wake up in another place. While we slept our Father carried us to our comfortable place.

657

"This… is CNN." Those used to be the signature words proclaiming the presence of that great television news organization. I guess CNN is short for Cable News Network. The voice belonged to actor James Earl Jones. Someone asked him one time how he got the invitation from CNN, and what instructions they gave. He said, "They told me, 'Just sound like the voice of God.'" No doubt, he came closer than anybody else ever has. And he did so with his own voice, no pretense, no hype, no "acting." When we preachers mount our pulpits, if we ever presume to be the "voice of God" we should do so in our own voices, and not in some new tones or fake accent or some holy verbal attitude that belies who we really are. My mother, unable to read because of eye problems, has been listening to books by audio for a few years. She also listens to the Bible being read. The reader? James Earl Jones.

658

The folk singer and philosopher Utah Phillips died recently. One of his quotes was this:

"Before you call someone a hero, make sure they're dead, so they don't blow it."

659

Church fights are to be expected. How to deal with them is always a question. The other day, I was visiting with someone who was telling about a historic downtown church in a major city. During construction, members were at odds over the shape of the bell tower. They solved it this way. They built two. The bell tower on one side of the church is square. The bell tower on the other side is round. What a wonderful compromise!

660

Sign outside a wine and liquor store in a Middle Tennessee town:

CONGRADULATIONS
2008 GRADUATES

661

"Do you want a box?" That is a question a server might ask at a restaurant after it is obvious I am not going to eat any more of my meal and it is also obvious that more than half of the meal has not been touched. "No, thank you," is my reply. It has mystified me how people can ask for a box to take the remains of a meal home that they just ate part of and are filled to the brim and can't stand to look at the food anymore and probably will not want to eat any of the leftovers for several days if at all. I see a lot of people exiting eating establishments carrying their boxes. So, one day, I was eating out with our daughter, Kim, and I brought all this up. Why? Why? Why? Her answer, short and to the point, set me straight and made me understand. She said: "Dad, you don't cook."

662

"Remember the Sabbath day, to keep it holy." We grew up with that admonition in our house. Back then it meant, basically, not doing those things you really enjoyed, like playing any sports or listening to them on the radio or watching them on television (black and white in the 1950s). My parents later mellowed and softened their approach to this major unhappiness on our part, but one thing our mother never wavered on, and it didn't have as much to do with "keeping the Sabbath" as it did "getting ready for the Sabbath." We took <u>The Nashville Tennessean</u> newspaper on Sundays. If given half a chance we boys would open up the paper and read all we could until told to get ready for Sunday school and church. Then, we would go reluctantly and risk being late. So our mother would make it a point to get the newspaper before we did and hide it. That's right. She would hide the paper. No amount of begging or whining or bargaining would do. The Sunday paper would be unavailable until we got home from church. This went on for years. We would search and search but would never find it. We finally gave up and surrendered to the policy that had been adopted. I think Mother would hide it one place one Sunday and another place the next. She is now 96. Recently I asked her about this and where she hid the paper. She was reluctant to tell, even more than half a century later. Finally, she told: behind the piano, under the couch, behind the couch, under a pillow, and a dozen other places, and never the same location two Sundays in a row.

663

At the funeral of our brother-in-law, J. S. Reynolds, who had married our sister Jo Nell in 1948, the three Campbell brothers gave personal testimonies and told stories about J. S. One brother told of how when we would go and see their family, J. S. would sometimes bring out the playing cards, especially when our parents were elsewhere. We were taught the ways of the world by an uncle (see above item) and a brother-in-law. Isn't this the way it is supposed to happen? One of the brothers testified that one time when he was about nine or ten, he was riding with J. S. out on a U.S. highway near their Missouri home. Out of the blue J.S. asked, "Would you like to drive?" The brother, whichever one it was, was surprised and did not know what to say. Before he knew it, he was in the driver's lap with both hands on the wheel (and with J.S. not holding on to the wheel). It was not a "crash" course in life, because the car did not crash. But it was a quick learning experience.

664

Possessing and enjoying what were called "playing cards" were strongly discouraged in our house as we grew up. I'm talking of those with aces, kings, queens, jacks, and the rest. It didn't matter the game; you didn't play with those cards. Rook was O.K. Old Maid was a nice game. And, in a gesture of compromise, our mother let us play with those otherwise despicable cards so long as we played games like Crazy Eight or other harmless endeavors, but definitely not Gin Rummy and, of course, never Poker. Then an uncle came to live with us while he went to college. The pace picked up. Clay taught us three boys a lot. Our love for sports intensified when he was with us, for he was so competitive, whether it was in the backyard playing basketball, or inside playing electric football or dice baseball. The goal was to win. He taught us three songs which I still remember and can sing to this day. And he also helped us to bring out the playing cards and enjoy them. We knew our mother did not approve. Once we were upstairs engaged in a card game while at the same moment the record player in the room was playing, at high volume, "I Just Got Lucky." We heard Mother coming up the stairs, fast. We were not swift enough to conceal everything. She came in, and, just as Jesus overturned the tables of the money-changers, did the same in our case, if not literally, at least figuratively. Then she turned around and went downstairs and sat down at the piano and played a hymn. This was not unusual. Anytime she was disturbed or angry or concerned lest her children might be drifting away from the faith, she would sit down and play a hymn. Usually it was the same one: "Will Jesus Find Us Watching?" We could hear it, easily, from upstairs.

665

By the time I was a sophomore in high school I had not yet driven a car. Our uncle Clay had a car. We brothers were over on the college campus one evening and our uncle said to me, "Would you like to drive?" Before I could answer, he had me in the driver's seat, hands on the wheel. All I remember about the relatively short drive home is that I failed to stop at a stop sign, ran over at least one curb, and, when it came time to stop completely, braked so quickly that all in the car were jerked forward for a moment. By the time I got around to the task of officially learning to drive, our father did not have to endure that first attempt; it had already been made. Now I was a little more at ease.

666

Psalm 46 is an interesting scripture. Especially 46:6a, which reads: "The nations are in an uproar, the kingdoms totter." Recently we heard in the news that in Napal the parliament voted to abolish the monarchy. In the country where monarchical rule had been in effect for two hundred years, the people's representatives were now saying it was over. In fact - and this had to be a terrible blow to the ego, self-importance, and regal splendor of the reigning king - parliament was giving him fifteen days to vacate the castle! Fifteen days! After two hundred years, the deadline was fifteen days! To quote Donald Trump, "You're fired!" "The nations are in an uproar, the kingdoms totter."

667

Psalm 46 also reminds us that terrible weather has been around a long time. In the past months, all over the world, there have been tornadoes, hurricanes, cyclones, tsunamis, earthquakes, and other natural disasters. The writer of Psalm 46 must have been keenly aware of those kinds of tragedies when he wrote," God is our refuge and strength, a very present help in trouble. Therefore we will not fear, though the earth should change, though the mountains shake in the heart of the sea; though its waters roar and foam, though the mountains tremble with its tumult" (46:1-3). The disasters he described may have been called by other names in those days, and, indeed, some people may have bestowed on them a more divine meaning and purpose than we might today. But there seems no doubt that the sea and the mountains were elements to be concerned about. It is easy to tell someone else not to be afraid, especially when we are a safe distance away. This writer seems to have been right there in the midst of the danger. His faith was put to the test. Still he did not fear.

668

"I'll pray for you." That is a good thing people say to each other. However, on a few occasions I have been wary and even resentful of that news because I felt that the other person would really be praying that God change me, or at least change my way of thinking. I knew they were not going to pray that they themselves might reach a better understanding of the issues, or of me or my opinions. They were going to pray that God achieve what they could not: Change me. I doubt if this is the highest form of prayer.

669

I was in my study at the church early one afternoon and got a phone call. On the other end was a young man, probably in his thirties. He and his wife and one child were occasional visitors to our church and lived only two or three blocks away. I had visited them once or twice over the weeks and months. But now the phone call came: "Can you come over to the house?" That's all he said. I did not hesitate. I dropped whatever I was doing and rushed to the car and drove quickly to that address. My pastoral instincts were clicking, my pastoral heart was pumping, the pastoral-care segment of my ministry was at the ready. What was it he wanted to talk about? Was there a family or marriage problem? Was there a spiritual problem? Did he want to talk about giving his heart to the Lord

On being careful what you ask

and, maybe, church membership? Did he have questions about the church, its doctrines, its practices, its government? Yes, it was going to be church government. If not that, maybe something about the three adult Sunday school classes we had going and which one he and his wife should start attending. Or perhaps it was a question or two about the class their daughter would be a part of. I drove into his driveway and almost jumped out of the car. I felt something was urgent and I wanted to be there with him. I knew his wife was at work and his little girl was in school. I rang the doorbell. He came to the door. "Let's go back to the kitchen," he said. We went back to the kitchen and he invited me to sit at the counter across from him. Then he opened his mouth and talked to me saying, "Could I interest you in some life insurance?" I hid my disappointment. I pretended to listen to him give his sales talk. I feigned interest. My face did not change expression from the moment I walked into the house. While I appeared to be enthralled by his pitch, I was churning inside. What a fool I am, I thought. I should have known. He got me to his house on false pretenses and now I am trapped. Can I be polite through all this? I was too polite. I was so polite that, when all was said and done, I signed on the dotted line for a life insurance policy. I had been "had." His tactics worked. I don't remember whether they ever attended that church again.

ೞಚಃೞಚಃೞಚಃೞಚಃೞಚಃೞಚಃೞಚಃೞಚಃೞಚಃೞಚಃ

670

The late Supreme Court Justice Hugo Black kept in good physical shape. He loved to play tennis. He said one time, "When I was forty my doctor advised me that a man in his forties shouldn't play tennis. I heeded his advice carefully and could hardly wait until I reached fifty to start again." (As quoted in A History of the Supreme Court, by Bernard Schwartz, Oxford University Press,

1993, quotation taken from The Dictionary of Biographical Quotations)

ഔങ്കാരകാരകാരകാരകാരകാരകാരകാരകാരകാര

671

It was June, 1958. I was nineteen years old, with one year of college under my belt. The General Assembly of the Cumberland Presbyterian Church was having its annual meeting in the East Lake Cumberland Presbyterian Church in Birmingham, Alabama. For years, "fraternal delegates" from the black Cumberland Presbyterian denomination would be in attendance at our meeting, and we would send "fraternal delegates" to theirs. But in 1958 tensions were high. Birmingham had already had some racial strife. When our General Assembly convened, the daily newspapers in the city did not talk much about the issues. Instead, they highlighted the fact that African American ministers would be in attendance, although in the 1950s the terminology was different. The White Citizens Council was strong in the Deep South and in Birmingham, and their voices were heard through the newspaper articles, warning of trouble. By mid-week, fearing trouble, all but one of the four guest ministers had gone home, leaving one, the Reverend S. A. Nelson of Muskogee, Oklahoma, a longtime friend of the church. When asked why he did not leave, he jokingly said that he looked more like an Indian than a black man and they might overlook him. The week went quietly, all things considered. Then everyone left for their homes across the country.

In 1982, in Owensboro, Kentucky, the General Assembly was meeting. Announcements were being made about the 1983 gathering, to be held in Birmingham. I received permission to speak, having recently written about some of this. I contrasted 1958 with the way 1983 would certainly be. When I sat down, the Reverend James Talley of Hopkinsville, Kentucky, rose to speak. He had been pastor of the East Lake Church in 1958. He told us something no one else knew. During the Assembly that week, he and Jamie Moore, the chief of police in Birmingham and a member of that church, agreed that officers in suits and ties would sit in the Assembly as though they were delegates. They would be on the alert for White Citizens Council disturbances. No such events occurred. We never knew, until 1982, how much danger was possible or how much the law enforcement folks of Birmingham were protecting us. Somehow "Bull" Connor, the police commissioner, was not around and evidently had nothing to do with the protection provided. I was there. I remember the talk in the halls about the newspaper articles. I remember Carl Ramsey of the Board of Missions trying to persuade the black ministers to stay, but knowing that they feared for their lives and understanding why they left.

672

Sign outside a Church of Christ building in Alabama:

A S A P
ALWAYS SAY A PRAYER

This was posted outside at another Church of Christ in Alabama:

HOPE IS REALLY
THE BEST MEDICINE

A Baptist Church in Alabama had this sign:

WHAT YOU BEHOLD
IS WHAT YOU BECOME

673

My father was pastor of small congregations in Texas and Louisiana in the 1930s and 1940s. In one congregation, he and my mother sang quite a few "specials" together and each one sang several solos, too. Why? They said there was a woman who loved to sing but was not very good. No, she was horrible, but she thought she was good. Other church members quietly expressed disgruntlement and concern to the Campbells at the thought of her letting loose with still another song in the Sunday morning worship service. The reason Daddy and Mother sang more often than they really wanted to was that, each Sunday morning, as they walked into the church, the woman met them and asked, in these words, every Sunday: "Are you going to sing today or do you want me to?" They would say, "We have something ready," or one would reply, "I think I'm going to sing today. Thank you, though." Occasionally, they would let her proceed with her musical efforts but those times were much more seldom than the lady desired.

674

A PAS (Program of Alternate Studies) student is Director of Christian Education in the Cumberland Presbyterian Church in Cleveland, Tennessee. Jennifer Newell sent me some information I had requested about her upcoming sermon at our Summer

Extension School. Then she wrote the following and, at my request, gave me permission to use it:

"Sorry this is late... I am up to my neck in VBS planning and a playground installation. As my husband loves to point out when I feel overwhelmed by VBS, 'Jesus never held VBS.' Maybe, though, that is ALL that Jesus did---they were outside most of the time, had snacks, lots of object lessons, and parables...!"

675

Country music and Gospel music tell many stories and, occasionally, tell us something, if only be chance, about the church. The group called Alabama has a song with this great line: "If you're gonna play in Texas, you gotta have a fiddle in the band." We know it takes people of varying talents to make up the church, and if some parts are missing, it is not the church it needs to be. "You gotta have a fiddle in the band."

The great quartet, The Oak Ridge Boys, in my mind the best gospel quartet in the land in the 1970s, went "country" late in that decade. One of their hits in the late 70s and early 80s was a song that seemed to defy labeling. It has this refrain: "Nobody wants to play second guitar behind Jesus; everybody wants to be the lead singer in the band." The church has plenty of supportive roles and some of the most valuable members are in the background, away from applause and publicity. They don't mind playing "second guitar behind Jesus" and have no desire to be the "lead singer in the band."

676

Another church sign:

> GOD GRADES ON THE CROSS
> NOT ON THE CURVE

677

I was meeting a new student at a church in Middle Tennessee. The student was coming into the Cumberland Presbyterian Church from another denomination. We were waiting for the local pastor to come and unlock the door to the church he had so graciously permitted us to use for some PAS classes. Right after he drove up on his motorcycle and the two of them met each other, the host pastor cut to the chase. To this new Cumberland Presbyterian who was coming to us from another denomination, he said, "If you can be a minister in this church and not have the attitude that we are the only ones, and if you can work cooperatively with churches and ministers of other denominations and other fellowships, you will do well." I thought, "Wow!" I thought some more, "Craig said it so well, so straight, so clearly." Then another thought: "That is who we are as Cumberland Presbyterians."

678

I thought I would try to tackle an obscure Old Testament passage of scripture several weeks ago. The text was Numbers 21:1-9. As Moses was leading the people through the wilderness many complained. This made the Lord angry and "the Lord sent fiery serpents among the people and they bit the people, so that many Israelites died." The survivors came to Moses to acknowledge their sin of speaking against the Lord and asked Moses to pray to the Lord to remove the serpents. Moses did pray to the Lord and God said: "Make a fiery serpent and set it on a pole; and everyone who is bitten shall look at it and live." So Moses followed the instructions and made a serpent of bronze and put it upon a pole, and anybody who was bitten by a serpent could look at the pole and live. It did not occur to me until a church member mentioned after the sermon that physicians and pharmacists use the pole and the serpent as emblems of healing today. Another church member, a pharmacist, said that pharmacists have one serpent around the pole and physicians have two. Those symbols are used to this day. We can thank Numbers 21:1-9 for that.

679

I have some shocking news. It is too startling to mention, but I will go ahead with it. Here it is: Most of us spend from one-fourth to one-third of each day doing absolutely nothing. That is scandalous. Surely we can do something to correct that. Furthermore, during that one-fourth to one-third time that we are doing absolutely nothing, we are stretched out parallel to the floor as though some magician had performed an act of levitation. What a waste! Just think what we could be doing with those non-productive hours. But, no, we choose to do nothing. By the way, this is called sleeping.

680

In 1969 the General Assembly of the Cumberland Presbyterian Church met on the campus of Trinity University in San Antonio, Texas. Two other Presbyterian assemblies had been held, or were going to be held there: The United Presbyterian Church in the USA (North) and the Presbyterian Church US (South). The occasion for these gatherings at that site was the 100th anniversary of Trinity University, which Cumberland Presbyterians founded in Tehuacana, Texas. At the CP Assembly one morning there was a breakfast sponsored by Bethel College and Memphis Theological Seminary. The speaker was Dr. R. Douglas Brackenridge, professor of history at the university, who had just written a book on the history of the denomination in Texas. Now he was with us and telling something of his observations about the Cumberland Presbyterian Church. Four decades later I still remember his presentation and its three major themes. He told us that the denomination had three main characteristics in the 19th and early 20th centuries. We were Evangelistic in Purpose. We were Ecumenical in Posture. And, lastly, we were Elastic in Procedure. This last one drew loud applause and much laughter. We knew what he was talking about. All three help to tell who we are as a denomination.

681

On more than one occasion, when I have had the privilege of speaking to groups about the history of the Cumberland Presbyterian Church and its mission and ministry, I have started with Dr. Brackenridge's (see # 680 above) three main points, giving credit and citing when they were spoken. But I have had fun in adding to those major themes, using the same "E in P" model. The emphasis was on what I hoped and prayed the characteristics of the church could be, as well as what the church is now. I don't have those notes any more and I forget what I added, but it was something like this: Excellent in Preaching. Ethical in Practice. Effusive in Praise. Energetic in Planning. Endless in Possibilities. Easygoing in Pageantry. Experienced in Pandemonium (oops!!). Educational in Publications. Eccentric in Particularities (ouch!!). Earnest in Perseverance. Elaborate in Playfulness. Euphonious in Presentations. Exceeding in Passion. Errant in Perfection. Economical in Property. You get the idea.

682

A few years ago a minister in the Cumberland Presbyterian Church wrote to me about the Program of Alternate Studies. The letter was very critical of one or two of our instructors, without naming names. In fact, he called one of them a "soteriologist." As Director of PAS I thought, "If he accuses somebody of being a soteriologist, this is serious. That teacher has got to go!" Then I said to myself, "Before I take such drastic action I will go to a theological dictionary and find out what soteriology is." I was shocked, SHOCKED, at what I found in the reference book. Here it is. Get ready. No wonder this letter writer was alarmed. <u>The Westminster Dictionary of Theological Terms</u> (Donald McKim, Westminster John Knox Press, 1996, page 265), reveals the following scandalous information: "Soteriology: The doctrine of salvation." And there is more; it gets worse: "Soteriological: Pertaining to the doctrine of salvation." There you have it. One of our instructors - the one accused of being a "soteriologist" - was teaching PAS students about SALVATION. I must acknowledge that this is still going on. Please don't tell anybody about this. I have been derelict in my duty, for that instructor is still with us.

683

Educational institutions get saddled with labels like "liberal" and "conservative." People do, too. We forget how those two names are relative. It depends on where you are standing. If I am standing beside several people who are around five feet tall, I, at six feet one, seem tall. But if I find myself beside three or four NBA players, all at 6' 10" or more, I am short. So someone's "liberal" may be someone else's "conservative." And vice-versa. But I doubt if all "liberals" think alike and I doubt if all "conservatives" think alike. The trouble is that both get carried to extremes, so that a liberal can say to another liberal: "You are not as liberal as I am; therefore I am authentic, and you are not." And a conservative can say to another, "You are not as conservative as I am; therefore I am authentic, and you are not." What is forgotten is that many people - and we shall use the same labels out of convenience - are liberal on some things and conservative on others, and some are conservative on some things and liberal on others. For example, I know people who are staunch biblical literalists (they say) and strong right-wing Christians. They are conservative politically but their social habits are liberal: social drinking, slack Sabbath observance, dressed to the nines, the latest in cars, dancing fools. And I know political liberals who are uptight about just about everything; they are rigid observers of religious rituals and squeaky-clean in their personal behavior. Today conservatives, if they want to nail people really bad, call them "liberals." It's almost a dirty word now. But, of course, it's those dirty rotten liberals who gave us Social Security, Medicare, the Minimum Wage, the Forty-Hour Work Week, Aid to Dependent Children, and the Voting Rights Bill, all features of our society we take for granted. I saw a portion of a panel discussion on C-Span one time. The theme question was: Is the Republican Party the voice of conservatives today? Are they one and the same? The same question could be put to the other side: Is the Democratic Party the voice of liberals today? Are they one and the same? The answers to those four questions should be, No, No, No, No. But I am afraid that is not the case.

684

Charles Turner was a Cumberland Presbyterian pastor in West Tennessee in the 1950s when I was attending church camps. He would be the vesper (evening worship) leader from time to time. During the years when I was ten, eleven, and twelve, I was giving no thought to becoming a preacher, but I did notice a certain pattern to his preaching. I thought he was maybe not putting enough effort into his messages because he was simply following, verse by verse, what the scripture of the day was saying. He was easy to listen to. His messages were so simple and easy to understand. I had heard some very good preachers by that time. Charles Turner was not an orator, not a polished pulpiteer at all. He spoke to the kids gathered for worship in conversational tones and, as I observed, put the scripture out there and followed it almost step by step with each message. After these many years at attempting to be faithful to the scriptures and trying to preach the good news, I have come to the conclusion that Charles Turner was on to something. Some teachers of preaching rightly say, "Present the scripture, then get out of the way and let it speak." He did just that. The more I think about it, the more respect and appreciation I have for what I saw and heard as a youngster going to Junior Camp and Junior High Camp and hearing the pastor of the Morning Sun Cumberland Presbyterian Church, Cordova, Tennessee.

685

My wife and I took a trip on Amtrak from Memphis to Chicago. In the hotel where we stayed we met several staff members. We found that three, all African-Americans, were originally from Coldwater, Mississippi. They did not know that about each other. One staff member had a daughter who had recently graduated from high school and was headed to the University of Iowa, if flood waters receded in time. We joked with them about having a "Coldwater, Mississippi, Reunion" in Chicago some day. Later I reflected on the fact that African-Americans migrated from the South to the North by the thousands throughout the twentieth century. This was partly because of better opportunities for employment. But another reason was that the practice of lynching was so much a presence in the South that blacks everywhere knew that nobody was ever free from that threat. Supposedly, the rationale for lynchings, said white people, was to protect the purity of white women, who, supposedly had been sexually insulted, abused and/or killed. Usually black men were the targets of accusations. However, this so-called altruistic motive belied the real reasons for such horror and depravity, for many lynchings were committed when African-Americans got too "uppity," when they did well in business, when they seemed to be making progress in life, when they were elected to leadership positions in towns and villages. Lynchings were a way to warn them not to take this too far. These atrocities had nothing to do with protecting white women, but everything to do with power and the fear of losing power. For decades Southern senators and congressmen resisted calls for laws on the subject while the threats, intimidation, and murder went unabated. The madness continued through the century in most southern states and other states as well. The need to take the law into their own hands thrilled and excited the mobs. No one person would have had the courage to try this alone, but otherwise sensible and rational people would lose all reason when in large groups and mob rule would take effect. In most cases, no one would be convicted of any of the lynchings, because no one in the different communities where they occurred would speak up in court. Police reports would specify that the despicable deeds were done "at the hands of persons unknown." But of course they were known, but no one would stand up and testify. I thought about all that after meeting and visiting with African-American staff members at the Congress Plaza Hotel in Chicago.

686

While in college I preached at two little churches fifty miles away, one on the first and third Sundays, the other on the second and fourth Sundays. On one of those Sunday morning trips, I was driving along and a buzzard sitting on a fence on the right side of the road decided to fly across the road at a leisurely pace. Trouble was, he traveled at windshield level and he flapped his wings directly into the car. Half of him landed on the highway; the other half was on the windshield and in the floorboard. It was a terrible scene. When I finally got back and went to the local insurance office I told my story. Then the agent filled out a form and I could see that he marked "Act of God." There were several categories he could have checked. He checked "Act of God." I have wondered about that ever since. Is that something we do when we cannot otherwise name the cause of some disaster or accident? Or is it an insurance term normally employed to explain the unexplainable? We blame God for a lot of things. We give God credit for a lot of things, too. Just when is something an "Act of God"?

687

I was in one dramatic production in my college years. It was "Abe Lincoln in Illinois," a three-night production on the Bethel College campus. I learned a lot about stage productions and have come to appreciate what goes on to make an event like that happen. As the director was having auditions and was casting people for the different parts, and as some people got large roles and others got small ones, the director remarked: "There are no small parts, just small actors." That told me that what you do with what you are given is what matters. You can seek excellence in even the small role you might have. I have noticed this in different movies, where well known movie stars who would normally be the top names in films would have so-called supporting roles and would, therefore, be listed far below the main actors in the credits. To me, this is a sign of a great actor, for the person is one who is so secure and so confident that the ego is not the issue; the story is.

And I sometimes think that is when actors have the most fun, in those small roles. Robert DeNiro in "Jackie Brown" and Tom Cruise in "Magnolia" come to mind. In those movies neither had top billing and both were far down the list of credits.

688

Fear can play a great part in our lives if we let it. We can conjure up almost any rumor or scare tactic and spook ourselves and others. In the 1980s there emerged some sinister warnings about what some musical numbers on phonograph players sounded like if played backwards. When I was pastor of our Cumberland Presbyterian Church in Lexington, Kentucky, a young mother mentioned to me that a neighbor girl had told her child that if you played a certain record backward it talked about the devil and Satan and other such evils, and now the child was very upset. The mother then calmly asked, "And do you have any friends that have record players that play songs backward?" The child said, "No." That took care of that. A person can create a scare and give others the heebie-jeebies with just about anything. For instance, did you know that if you rearranged the letters that spell Santa they would spell Satan? Now run with that.

689

Sign in front of a church in Memphis:

> MONEY
> GREAT SERVANT
> TERRIBLE MASTER

690

Another sign at a Memphis church:

> FREE TRIP TO HEAVEN !
> DETAILS INSIDE !

691

Timing is everything. The University of Tennessee football program is such that fans can expect a winning season every year, which will include a major bowl game and a high ranking in the national polls. In the late 1980s two enterprising journalists decided they would fill a void in UT football by starting a magazine-type of publication that would be completely about the Volunteers and their ongoing season. Ordinarily this would have been an instant hit. The men were talented in their field. They knew the game of football. The moment was right, one would think. But fate would deal them a deathly blow. In an unusual turn of events the UT football team lost their first six games. This unprecedented and totally unpredictable occurrence doomed the infant publication. It fizzled after only a few weeks. One never knows. I hope nobody tried that during the 2008 season.

692

A well known excuse students use for not bringing their homework to the teacher is, "My dog ate my homework." When nothing else would work, a person could always use that as the reason for not turning in an assignment. But this actually happened in a Cumberland Presbyterian Polity class I taught at Memphis Theological Seminary a few years ago. Eric came forward to report that event, and then produced pictures of the evidence. There was the homework, what was left of it, all torn to shreds by his dog, and the reason the rest of it was not there was that the dog had eaten it! Since that time I have had greater respect for that excuse, I mean, reason, for not turning in one's assignments. It was truly a great moment in that class. It made the semester even more memorable.

Stranger than fiction

693

Sign outside a Church of Christ in Atwood, Tennessee:

A SERMON THAT PRICKS THE HEART
HAS MANY GOOD POINTS

694

In the baseball season of 2008 the Tampa Bay Rays are tearing up the American League. They have the best won-lost record in baseball two-thirds of the way through the season. Earlier fans voted for their favorites for the All-Star game between the American League and the National League and guess what! Not a single player from the Tampa Bay team was voted on the team. One or two were later placed on the reserve roster by the American League manager, but nobody from the Tampa Bay team was named to the American League starting lineup. I think that speaks well for the team. There is no one "star." They all work together. They are a team. It doesn't matter who gets the credit. They are out to win the pennant. And, guess what: They did win the pennant.

695

A phrase I grew up hearing was this: "Reverend So-and-So will be filling the pulpit next Sunday." "Filling the pulpit." That's been another way of saying somebody will be the guest preacher at that church next Sunday. "Fill the pulpit." That can carry negative messages as well as positive. I know I have "filled the pulpit" many times in the past. I have "filled" it with empty words, hard-to-understand ideas, and highfalutin' gobbledegook. I have "filled" it with tired phrases, much-used theological terms that need CPR, and half-baked moralisms that scold and condemn and judge from the safe "coward's castle" of the pulpit. I have filled it with predictable structures, oft-repeated stories, and truths barely connected to a text, if at all. Yes, I have "filled" the pulpit. I hope I have not filled it with hatred, prejudice, or smug "me-and-Jesus" platitudes, and I wish I had not filled it with all the above-mentioned palaver. Nowadays, when I hear that someone has "filled" the pulpit, I wonder, "What did they fill it with?" And who is going to go in and clean it out after that guest preacher leaves?"

696

Sign in the front yard of Highland Heights United Methodist Church in Memphis, Tennessee:

> THERE IS NO HEAVIER LOAD
> THAN A CHIP ON THE SHOULDER

697

Bumper sticker on the back of a Tennessee car:

> MAKE TEA
> NOT WAR

698

It had been more than fifty years since I rode on a train when Linda and I decided to take Amtrak from Memphis to Chicago. An overnight trip on a Monday brought us into the Windy City mid-morning on Tuesday. Then late Thursday we caught Amtrak back to Memphis, arriving around 8:00 A.M. on Friday. While in Chicago we saw the White Sox play, visited the Navy Pier, saw a modern version of Shakespeare's "Comedy of Errors," took a Chicago River tour and then a Lake Michigan tour, and walked to the original Marshall Fields store and enjoyed its old splendor. While on the train going and coming, we heard the train whistle several times, usually to warn car and truck and bus traffic that might be wanting to cross that the train was coming. I once heard at a civic club meeting how long it takes to stop a train. It takes a very long time. That's most likely why the trains send out their sounds, to warn folks up ahead. Since our trip, we have heard of two or three occasions when an Amtrak train collided with a car or truck trying to cross the railroad track when the driver either did not hear or ignored the train whistle. Now as I sit in my Memphis office I hear the occasional train whistle. I appreciate that sound even more now, having traveled the rails once again. Trains do remind us of times past. An old bluegrass song goes, at least in part: "The conductor doesn't wave from the train anymore, the way he did back in 1954." Yet as airline fares rise and additional fees pile up on air travelers, going by train may become more and more appealing. The leg room is great!

699

In Chicago, along the sidewalk entrance to the famed Navy Pier right there at Lake Michigan, there is a statue of the entertainer Bob Newhart as he was seen in his television show in which he played a psychologist. The external shots of the show - and maybe some of the internal ones - were filmed in downtown Chicago and the people of that city proudly claim him as one of their own. I took a lot of pictures on our trip to that great city. Beside the statue of Newhart in his famous pose in the easy chair within his office sat a couch, in bronze just as the other fixture was. I asked Linda to sit down there and pretend to be talking with her counselor, Bob Newhart. After taking some pictures of her, I exchanged places with her and she took some pictures of my intense conversation with the psychologist. The pictures turned out well. We both looked very concerned. And, I'm happy to report, Newhart was a good listener.

700

Let me get this straight. Somebody step in and correct me if I'm wrong. The United States has nuclear weapons, but we don't want anybody else to have them. Therefore, we put pressure on countries like Iran and North Korea to cease production and show proof that they have done so. Yet we have nuclear weapons. Did it ever occur to anybody that one reason other nations might be developing these instruments of mass destruction is that they are afraid the United States, well known to have nuclear weapons, might use those things against their nation? What moral right does the U.S. have to dictate to other nations what they should or should not do, when we are doing the very thing we are accusing others of doing? Oh, I forgot. We are on the moral high road. We are the moral leaders of the world. Our weapons are for positive use only. Let me think. The only nuclear weapons used in combat were employed by the U.S. in 1945 against Japan: Hiroshima and Nagasaki. Not to mention that early in this century we invaded another country, Iraq, on the false assumption that they had weapons of mass destruction and (at this date in September of 2008) almost 4,500 American military personnel have been killed, not to mention countless Iraqi civilians. And, oh yeah, American war profiteers galore are in Iraq cleaning up financially while others die for their ill-gotten gains. The Truman Commission in late World War II took stern measures against U.S. war profiteers, those making tons of money off the backs of war-torn countries and war-weary soldiers. Nothing like that, absolutely nothing, is in place now to corral modern profiteers.

Chapter 701-750

"Words of Assurance"

701

This age-old bit of advice has carried me through many a hard time: "Cheer up; things could be worse." Sure enough, I cheered up, and things got worse.

702

On not needing a good excuse to give flowers

More than four decades ago I attended a PTA meeting at an elementary school in suburban Fort Worth. I may have had the invocation or was scheduled to have the benediction, I don't remember. A Methodist minister was the guest speaker. I still remember two stories he told. Since it has been at least forty years since I heard them, I can honestly say that I have been faithful to tell these stories on the average of once a year somewhere and in different settings. Just before a husband left the house to go to work his wife said, "Honey, I bet you don't know what special day this is." He said, "Of course, I do," but he had no clue. On his way to work and while at the office he racked his brain: anniversary? birthday? What might it be? To be safe, the man ordered flowers and they were delivered to his wife at the house. When he got home, she expressed her thanks. "I have never received flowers on Groundhog Day," she said.

703

The second story, still remembered, told by the Methodist minister at the elementary school PTA meeting in a Fort Worth suburb was about a nervous bride just moments before going in on the arm of her father. The director, seeing her panic and trying to calm the bride, said, "There are three things to remember. When you start to go in you will see the AISLE. Then you will walk a little further and see the ALTAR. As you go farther you will see HIM. Remember, say this over and over again: 'AISLE, ALTAR, HIM. AISLE, ALTAR HIM, I'LL ALTER HIM," Lots of luck on that.

704

The late Bernie Mac was a comedian and an actor. He grew up on the south side of Chicago and worked long years to be a success. One of the movies he starred in was "Mr. 3000," about a star baseball player who retired after getting his 3,000th hit, thereby making sure he got into the record books. However, the story goes, some time later the major league office reviewed the video or otherwise looked again at one of his "hits" and determined that the fielder made an error and it was not a hit, and that, thus the official scorer got it wrong. This meant he was back to 2,999 hits. He decided to become an active player again in order to retrieve his 3000th hit. On the last day of the season, still at 2,999, Bernie Mac is at bat. He has a choice. He can make a sacrifice hit, moving a base runner along, and thus not reach his goal, or he can forget about the team and think only of himself and try to get that elusive hit. He decides to be a team player and the movie ends with his so-called failure to get into the record books, but he doesn't care. He has sacrificed for the team. A good ending to a good movie.

705

Sign outside a Lutheran church in Tampa, Florida:

> FAMILY REUNION
> EVERY SUNDAY
> YOU'RE INVITED

706

In his earlier years of leadership in Great Britain, Winston Churchill experienced a mixture of success and failure, and in military matters, victory and defeat, but more defeat than victory. Other leaders did not trust him, being afraid he would too eagerly engage in another war at the slightest provocation or opportunity. So writes Arthur Herman in his book <u>Gandhi and Churchill: The Epic Rivalry That Destroyed an Empire and Forged Our Age</u> (Bantam, 2008). In November of 1918, after World War I was over, Churchill was appointed to the War Council as secretary of war. "He complained that there was not much point to the post if the war was over. Andrew Bonar Law answered for all of (Churchill's colleagues). 'If we thought there was going to be a war,' he said pointedly, 'we wouldn't appoint you War Secretary (p. 249)'".

That's similar to my being appointed lifeguard at the community swimming pool for the winter months, when the pool is closed and the water has been drained.

707

My apologies to the hundreds of people who have heard this, some of them more than once.

Invariably, somebody I greet in a given day will ask, "How are things going?" I usually reply, "So far, so good." Often - too often, I am afraid - I cannot resist prolonging the conversation by telling the following story. A man fell from the 37th floor of a hotel. As he passed the 24th floor somebody saw him and asked, "How are things going?" and he replied, "So far, so good."

708

Christians are rightly called "People of the Book," the "Book" being the Bible. In the United States, we are, all of us - Christian, Jew, Muslim, Buddhist, Hindu - also "People of the Book," the "Book" being the Constitution of the United States. It amazes me - and frightens me - when people get those two books confused, when Christians say the "Book" of the country should be the Bible. In fact, many say, "If only everybody in this country lived by the Bible, all would be well," forgetting that millions of people do not call the Bible their Book, not even in religious terms. What makes us one nation is not the Bible, but the Constitution. We live by the Constitution, and those of us who are Christians and who adhere to the Bible, or try to, should be keenly aware of the fact that the Bible is not the nation's common Book. The Constitution is. We are not a theocracy. We are a democracy.

709

There are THREE dreaded words a husband/father will READ and there are FOUR dreaded words he will HEAR. Regarding the first, see # 208 above where "Some Assembly Required" is mentioned, usually seen on the boxes of Christmas toys that need long hours of tedious work to make them ready for Christmas morning. And what are the four words most dreaded? They are spoken by the wife and they are these: "We Have to Talk." Put the newspaper down. Turn away from the television. Look toward the other person. Appear to be interested. All activities come to a screeching halt. And, usually, it's something the husband/father did or did not do, or something equally as serious that he needs to be doing or not doing. There is some guilt involved. Not always. But most of the time. If Eve had thought of that with Adam, perhaps a lot of trouble for them, and us, could have been avoided.

710

A pickup truck in Tennessee had this bumper sticker:

> SUPPORT YOUR
> LOCAL UNIVERSE

711

Maybe it's because I was an English major. Maybe I was an English major because of my propensities in the direction of purity of grammar. Whatever the cause, in my work as director of a program that helps to prepare persons for ministry, I mark up papers with bad grammar, punctuation, and spelling. Occasionally - but probably not often enough - I tell would-be preachers, "Somewhere out there in your congregation there will be an English teacher who will endure your bad grammar for a short while, then will confront you on it." I was relating this to a fellow minister and he added this: "If the English teacher does not approach the preacher about the bad grammar used, the teacher will stay silent and just cringe every Sunday and approach each service with dread and foreboding and the preacher will soon lose that person as a listener." The second sounds as ominous as, if not more ominous than, the first.

712

After church one day a man in the congregation got some tomatoes out of his car to transfer to our car (church members know we love tomatoes), and as he did so his cell phone rang. I heard his end of the conversation: "Hello." (Then the other party spoke)... "We just got out of church services." (Then the other party spoke again)... "He told us to do right." I laughed and enjoyed that in my mind for a very long time. The sermon was on three of the twenty-three recommendations or commandments or guidelines or suggestions Paul gives in Romans 12:9-21. The three, because they seemed to go together were: "Rejoice in hope, be patient in suffering, persevere in prayer" (12:12). I hope at least one of those three items from Paul's writing helped us all to "do right."

713

Those studying for the ministry come from varied careers. One of our students in the Program of Alternate Studies, Tom Spence, from Burns Flat, Oklahoma, had a career in the Marines. When he came to our Summer Extension School at Bethel College in McKenzie, Tennessee, in July of 2008, he placed this sign on his door, a sign he says all Marines know of and often post. You gotta love it! Tom's loyalties run deep.

MARINES WELCOME ANYTIME
RELATIVES BY APPOINTMENT ONLY

714

"Blame the victim" is the temptation we succumb to at times. Hurricanes come to New Orleans and the Gulf Coast and Florida and the rains flood houses all the way to the roof and the winds blow away houses and cars and uproot trees. "Well, they shouldn't have been living in that area in the first place," may be our words of wisdom concerning the people affected. Tornadoes ravage towns and villages in Kansas and Oklahoma and Texas, and we echo the same words, repeating the theme that it is the fault of the victims. We heard this regarding the Tsunami in Indonesia and the riots in Los Angeles and Detroit. Earthquakes kill hundreds in China or India and we blame the victims. Volcanoes erupt and, well, "They shouldn't have been living so close to that thing." People move to the suburbs supposedly to "get away from the crime" of the cities and the crime follows them. Really, is there actually a "safe place" anywhere? There is an old, old story that I remember reading in a book by a minister - I do not remember name or title - and he told of a man who lived amid the ravages of World War II somewhere in Europe. He had the means and the wherewithal to move, so he decided to find an island nobody ever heard of and move out there, safe and secure and away from all danger forevermore. The little island he moved to was a tiny, obscure thing called Guadalcanal, wrote the minister.

715

My mother is the oldest of seven children in the Estes family. The seven siblings have had successful careers in varied fields. Their childhood was anything but easy. Their father, Samuel Russell Estes and their mother, Grace Barefoot Estes, raised those kids on practically nothing. He was a Cumberland Presbyterian minister who had to work at other jobs to make a living. When they moved from one church to another it would likely be because he felt God calling him, but part of it might have been that the current pastorate did not pay him anything at all and he could not survive. More than once a member of the family had to go to the church treasurer's house to ask for his salary. When the family moved they would pile on the bed of the wagon or truck and ride to the next little town where their new church was. "The Grapes of Wrath" could have been patterned after some of their struggles, except they stayed in Oklahoma and did not go to California. "Brother Sam" - as he was called - had a pastor's heart and "Gracie" did, too. We grandchildren called her "Nanny." This couple were examples of how Cumberland Presbyterian ministerial couples made it through such times as the Depression out there in Oklahoma where, as one of our ministers described it, they had "dust, debt, and depression."

716

As mentioned in #715 above, the Estes children, having scraped their way through their early years in hard times out in Oklahoma, succeeded in life. Margaret, my mother, who attended ten or eleven schools in her elementary and high school years, graduated from Rocky, Oklahoma, High School in 1930. That was her only year in Rocky. The family lived in four different houses in that year. She would attend college and then have to drop out because of lack of money. Then she would start again in a few years. But she made it and became a high school English teacher and later a special education teacher. Malnor, the next oldest, also finished college a little later than she would have preferred and became an English teacher in Borger, Texas. Sam, Jr., the oldest boy, became a Cumberland Presbyterian pastor and served churches in Mansfield, Missouri; Denton, Texas; Owensboro, Kentucky; and Lubbock, Texas. Loyce, the next oldest boy, also became a Cumberland Presbyterian pastor and was in churches in Longview, Lubbock, Austin, Fort Worth, and Jefferson, all in Texas, and in Marlow, Oklahoma, and Hampton, Arkansas. David, the fifth child was in the marines in World War II and became a radio and television announcer in Springfield, Missouri, and later the Kansas City area. He wrote some country songs, one of which was Porter Wagoner's first single, "Headin' for a Weddin'." In Porter's autobiography, "Satisfied Mind," Uncle Dake is mentioned as helping Porter record his first songs in the studios of KWTO in Springfield. Olive, the third daughter, was an in-demand court reporter in Fort Worth, Texas, with most of her career in family court. Clay, the youngest of the seven, had a career in education, mostly in the state of Virginia, coaching basketball and serving as a high school counselor. All seven attended Bethel College in McKenzie, Tennessee, and the other six lived with Thomas and Margaret Campbell and family at one time or another while attending Bethel. As of this writing in September of 2008, Margaret is 96. Malnor is 92; Sam is 89; Loyce is 88; David is in his mid-80s; Olive is 80; and Clay is 78 or 79. This group has gotten together at David's farm in southern Missouri every year for more than two decades, usually around the Labor Day weekend. Age and bad health are getting to some of them but as of early September 2008 they were gathering again.

717

I went to a baseball game at the local Memphis park a few years ago. The Memphis Chicks were in town. Just before the start of the game, another minister, a good friend, came ambling up and, since the stadium was not nearly filled to capacity, we sat down together, ignoring where our tickets said we ought to sit. Mike and I stood for the national anthem, and, as we were sitting down, but not all the way down yet, he turned to me - again while we were not yet settled in our seats - and asked, "What do you think is the future of the mainline church?" I gulped and then laughed. He and I had never talked about the future of the mainline church. Furthermore, I was set to look at the scoreboard to check the starting lineups, not consider anything related to the church. Not at this time. Not here. Not this way. I was taken aback and do not remember whether we actually discussed anything concerning the future of the mainline church. I seem to remember that during the course of the game we did "talk church" but I thought it amusing and even hilarious that this question came right off the bat, to borrow a baseball word. But, thank goodness, my ministerial friend has always been ready to talk church at a baseball game, or baseball at a church event. It doesn't matter. And it's always a delight.

718

One of our students at the 2008 Summer Extension School, Phillip Anders of Arkansas, sang a Ray Stevens-type song in one of our worship services and again, by request, at our morning devotional time a few days later. The name of the song was "You're In My Pew," about a poor guy visiting a church for the first time. He sat in one of the pews and got the strangest looks from the church people. In a short time a woman came, stood over him, and said, "You're in my pew." He quickly and quietly moved. After worship there was a time of visiting in the fellowship hall. Refreshments were served. He wandered into the church kitchen but was caught short by a strong voice saying, "Get out of my kitchen!" At our school it was suggested that the attitudes expressed in the song would NOT contribute to church growth. And that would be an understatement.

719

You may be wondering how Pakistan got its name. No? Well, it is still an interesting story. After World War II, when Hindus and Muslims in India were still having trouble getting along, it was decided to create a new state, run by Muslims, leaving India to be run by Hindus, to make a long story short. But what about the name for the new country? Years before the separation became official, in 1933, a Muslim student at Cambridge came up with the name. It was P for Punjab, A for the New West Frontier Province or Afghania, K for Kashmir, S for Sind, and TAN for Baluchistan. Taken together they formed the word Pakistan, which meant in Urdu "Land of the Pure." Pakistan is the largest Islamic nation in the world (p. 409, <u>Gandhi and Churchill</u>, by Arthur Herman).

720

The comedian Groucho Marx said he once entered a Groucho Marx look-alike contest and finished third. One of the really good Charles Bronson movies depicted him not as the rock-em, sock-em vigilante hero he usually portrayed, but as a good guy in the west who becomes the target of some bad guys. They shoot and kill someone they think is he, but it is really someone who was pretending to be he. He is celebrated, lionized, deified, and placed on a national pedestal. Thereafter the real guy appears (Charles Bronson) but no one will believe he is really who he is. They have made him almost a god and therefore he can't really be alive. He is an impersonator and a not-very-good one at that. Bronson becomes totally frustrated. This lighthearted movie has fun with the he-man who cannot convince anybody that he is really the national hero they have honored. This leads me to wonder how we would react of Jesus showed up in the flesh. Because of preconceived notions of what he should look like, he might not fit our requirements. Furthermore, what he would say and do might not, either. What is our performance record when we meet the real thing?

Will the real Groucho Marx stand up?

721

In a worship service the reading of the Scriptures should be done well. The reader or readers should speak loud enough to be heard and clearly enough to be understood. These efforts will enrich the service and draw people closer to the Bible. This phase of worship should not be a "dead" moment. However, the preacher in delivering the sermon is wise to assume that nobody was listening or reading along in their own Bibles during the lesson or lessons. Whatever the text for the sermon, the one in the pulpit should, I think, bring the passage out again for full view, even to the point of reading it again in the context of the sermon. If the chosen text is to be emphasized in the sermon, which, of course, it should, it behooves the preacher to make sure the people know what it says.

722

Personalized car license plates run the gamut of messages. One that I saw recently indicated that a personal lifelong quest had been fulfilled:

FNLYHPY

723

I know we preachers would like for every one of our sermons to be a whiz-bang, stem-winding, earth-shaking, Spirit-filled, heart-warming message for the ages. However, the reality is that our wishes will never come true. Recently I read what, for me, is something that not only brings great consolation on that subject, but also makes good common sense. It is in the book entitled Power in the Pulpit: How America's Most Effective Black Preachers Prepare Their Sermons, edited by Cleophus J. LaRue (Westminster John Knox, 2002). I cannot find the page or remember which of the many writers contributed the helpful thought. It is this: "We may not hit a home run with every sermon, but we can get on base." In baseball terminology, that is good news for the preacher. Just get on base. Make an inroad. Open the door. Plant a seed. Make a connection. Bring forth something to build on. Get on base. Try not to strike out.

724

It is good to plan ahead - but it is also advisable to take care of immediate matters as well. Forty years ago I was driving on a Fort Worth street. A railroad track lay ahead and just beyond it sat a white car, possibly a Ford, looking as if it planned to move out in traffic at any time. I thought: "I will watch that car very closely and if it decides to get out on the street I will be ready." In that short moment, I felt pretty proud of myself, thinking ahead like that. I was thinking those good thoughts as I crossed the track, looked to my right, and saw a train barreling down on me, no more than fifty feet away. I reflexively accelerated and got across the track easily. It was only after it was all over that I had time to think how close I came to being hit. I should have handled the immediate task and not look so far ahead. I learned later that two women in the church I served at the time were coming the other way and saw the whole thing and, not knowing it was their pastor doing that foolish thing, asked one another, "What is that driver doing?" or some such like.

725

Not since childhood have I been in a congregation that sang the great hymn "Safely Through Another Week." As a pastor and worship leader, I have selected that classic message and melody more often lately. I don't know what kept me away all these years. Perhaps my pastor's instincts are finally kicking in and the hymn is now more meaningful. The names of John Newton (of "Amazing Grace" fame), who wrote the text, and Lowell Mason ("When I Survey the Wondrous Cross" and dozens of other great hymns of the church), who wrote the music, stand atop the page beside this title. Perhaps as one gets along in years this hymn takes on more power and importance.

> Safely through another week
> God has brought us on our way;
> Let us now a blessing seek,
> Waiting in his courts today:
> Day of all the week the best,
> Emblem of eternal rest:
> Day of all the week the best,
> Emblem of eternal rest.
>
> While we pray for pardoning grace,
> Through the dear Redeemer's name,
> Show Thy reconciled face,
> Take away our sin and shame;
> From our worldly cares set free,
> May we rest this day in Thee:
> From our worldly cares set free,
> May we rest this day in Thee.
>
> May Thy Gospel's joyful sound
> Conquer sinners, comfort saints;
> May the fruits of grace abound,
> Bring relief for all complaints:
> Thus may all our Sabbaths prove,
> Till we join the Church above:
> Thus may all our Sabbaths prove,
> Till we join the Church above.

726

You are sitting in a church during a worship service. All is solemn and reverent. Then you hear a click, then, after a few seconds, another click. Then another. You recognize the sound. Someone is engaged in the trimming of fingernails. It gets on your nerves. You begin to wonder if and when it will ever end. You estimate how many clips per fingernail and multiply by five for each hand. You pick up on the count: 7, 8, 9. You think of the hero in a B western movie counting the shots from the bad guy's six-shooter. However, unlike our hero who jumps the villain when he knows the villain is out of bullets, you cannot jump the church villain. The pain must be allowed to go on... and on... and on. You do not even want to think about where the droppings are landing: on the floor? In somebody's purse? On the pew? Go away, bad thought! Go away! Finally, the misery ends. You did not turn around to see who the culprit was. You wanted to. And you don't turn around now. Yes, you do. You do, sort of. You sort of stretch and yawn and twist and turn your body and just happen to glance around. You know you should have done it while the terrible event was going on. You'll never know who it was. You have suspicions, but no certainty. You will carry this terrible experience with you the rest of your life.

727

With money markets, mutual funds, hedge funds, bailouts, mergers, home-buying messes, and fluctuating interest rates, this bumper sticker on the left side of the back of a pick-up truck belonging to a farm family in Missouri brought a smile:

THE ONLY STOCK I BUY
HAS FOUR LEGS

728

The same pick-up truck, on the right side in the back, had this message, possibly the thinking of many farmers:

GOLF COURSES:
A TERRIBLE WASTE OF GOOD PASTURE LAND

729

This sign outside a church in Missouri carries an important message:

THIS CHURCH IS PRAYER-CONDITIONED

730

Just about every year in the Summer Extension School conducted on the campus of Bethel College by the Program of Alternate Studies of the Cumberland Presbyterian Church, we have eight or ten Spanish-speaking students, who attend classes in their own language. In morning devotionals, translations are from English to Spanish, or from Spanish to English, depending on who is leading. The same is true in worship where sermons are also translated. We learned from each other and tried to speak each other's language, at least with a few words. Toward the end of the week in our 2008 school, I knew we English speakers had gone too far and had corrupted our Hispanic colleagues when a Spanish-speaking student walked up to me, shook my hand, and said, "Howyadoin?"

731

A religion magazine published in October 2008 says a reporter asked one of the principal national political candidates about the Pledge of Allegiance. The answer: "If it was good enough for our Founding Fathers it's good enough for me." Of course, reports the magazine, the Pledge was written "not by the founding fathers but in 1892 by Francis Bellamy, a Christian socialist and Baptist minister, with the intent of pledging support for poor and excluded Americans." Furthermore, the phrase "under God" wasn't added until 1954. (The Christian Century, Vol. 125, No. 20, p. 8)

732

Sometimes I hear a song incorrectly. It has been this way since childhood. We all know of the little boy who wanted to sing about the "cross-eyed bear" at church. You know, "Gladly the Cross I'd Bear." I grew up hearing what I thought was "The Church Is One Foundation." That meant I did not know exactly how the next line fit in: "Is Jesus Christ her Lord." I have always wished the church was "one foundation." A country song that Crystal Gale sang was "Don't It Make My Brown Eyes Blue," but it sure sounded like "Donuts Make My Brown Eyes Blue." A long time ago, in the late forties or early fifties, there was a popular song, "Don't cry Joe; let her go, let her go, let her go," but the words came out for me as "Don't cry Joe; let it snow, let it snow, let it snow." A children's song was "Brighten the Corner Where You Are,' but my ears heard, "Right in the Corner Where You Are." And, of course, the kid who prayed, "Dear Andy," thus confusing his parents, explained it was from a church song: "Andy walks with me, Andy talks with me." And I always thought the Christmas/Epiphany carol had the wise men as citizens from "Orientar" and they lived a long, long way off: "We three kings of Orientar, Bearing gifts we traveled so far..." And a perfect song to sing after a huge church dinner was "We Can Sing, Full Though We Be" although its correct title is "Weak and Sinful Though We Be."

733

Occasionally we hear of a great professional athlete who while in high school could not make the varsity team, or who never was on the starting team in college. Furthermore, we hear that such greats as Albert Einstein and Winston Churchill had learning problems as children. I finally am reading a book from my shelf entitled <u>As I Remember</u> (Harper, 1953), an autobiography by Edgar J. Goodspeed, the great biblical scholar who has a Bible translation named after him and wrote many books on biblical subjects. At what was later called the old University of Chicago he and other teens were taking college preparatory classes. One of the subjects was Greek. On the first test, some made in the nineties, others in the eighties and seventies. The lowest grade with a number was in the thirties. Goodspeed and one other student made so low the teacher did not place a number beside their name. This one who would later be a renowned, widely known and respected expert in the Bible and its languages, failed the first Greek test he ever took (p. 48)! A college here in West Tennessee advertises on the radio and includes this theme: "The potential of a student is not necessarily judged by one's past performance." Thank goodness, and thank God on behalf of all of us!

734

On making rash decisions

When I was ten years old I was hit by a car. In the summer of 1949 we were visiting grandparents in Muskogee, Oklahoma, and our parents had let my older brother Sam and me go with a couple of neighbor boys to downtown Muskogee to see a minor league baseball game. We caught a city bus and then walked a few blocks to the ball park. After the game we were on our way back to the bus stop. I was sort of running and skipping along and, being in a hurry, decided to run across the street ahead of the others. A car hit me. I do not know how fast it was going. I turned a flip and landed either on my feet or side and, miraculously, was not hurt. But I was crying. The driver, fully innocent in all of this, was right there with me, apologizing and asking me how I felt. Not a bone was broken although I think I had a sore wrist for a few weeks. When everything was seen to be all right, we walked the few remaining steps to the bus stop and boarded the bus for the ride back to the neighborhood where the grandparents lived. On the way home nobody said anything about the accident. I woke my parents up and told them what happened and said I was all right. After that, nothing else was mentioned. I guess everybody was just so relieved and felt that there was nothing else to say. I was fortunate. I tried to get ahead of the rest of the group. I should have stayed with them and crossed when they did. It was not the last rash decision I ever made.

735

Sign outside a church in Memphis:

> SOMEDAY IS NOT
> A DAY IN THE WEEK

736

My closest brush with death, however, came fifty nine years later, in early June of 2008. It was a Saturday morning. Our 1997 Chrysler Cirrus, with over 150,000 miles on it, was overdue for an oil change since the last one was about 4,000 miles ago. I decided I would go to a service station that provided such things. I got in the car and started out. After about three blocks, the car speeded up without my help. I put my foot on the brake to slow it down and it speeded up even more. Next I pushed as hard on the brake as possible but the car accelerated further. By now I was going somewhere between 50 and 60 miles an hour on a Memphis city street in an out-of-control car. I saw a major intersection ahead and, with the speed increasing I approached. My traffic light was red, having just changed, and, fortunately traffic on the street to my left had not started up and I turned right at full speed, looking for a way out. A large church was now to my left. The first parking lot was not possible, nor the second. The third might be. No traffic was coming toward me so I made a quick left turn into the church parking lot. I barely missed a school bus parked in the lot as well as a small bus for boy scouts. Still going full speed I saw in front me a light pole or two and some trees. It was time (really overdue) for me to do something drastic. At the last possible moment I put the gear into PARK and the car skidded to a stop, its motor racing wildly and loudly. I turned it off. Now I thought everything might be all right and I started the car again, still in PARK. The motor revved up so loud it was scary. I turned it off. I knew I had probably ruined the transmission with my shoving it into PARK at sixty miles an hour but there was no choice. I called my wife and then our middle daughter, Kim, who came to get me. We went home and Kim and Linda went to the computer to find possible cars to buy. I drove back over to the scene in my car with Linda also going. I called a wrecker who took the car to the dealer where we would be shopping for another automobile. He turned the ignition on, and again it revved up in a frightening way and he quickly turned it off. At that location, we bought another car and sold our old one. Looking back, several terrible things could have happened but nothing did. Fortunately I hit no one, hurt no one including myself, and damaged no property. I was very relieved. As you read this, you have my permission to insert God into the story at any time. Perhaps God was in the part where our little granddaughter was not in the car; just a day earlier she and her grandmother traveled a short distance for a brief shopping trip. Perhaps God was in the part where I did not go to the Cumberland Presbyterian General Assembly in Japan, starting that very day. Had I made that trip, perhaps someone else in the family would have driven it that day and faced the same trials. Perhaps God was in the part where I got to the intersection and I turned right unimpeded. Perhaps God was in the part where I was able to turn left onto the third parking lot of the large church. Perhaps God was in the part where I avoided the school bus as well as the small bus for boy scouts. Perhaps God was in the part where I put the car in PARK just before a collision with a light post and a tree. And, oh yes, as I turned right at the signal light, to my immediate right was a man on a bicycle, waiting for the light to change. I turned in front of him while he was still standing there. Perhaps God helped him to decide not to go forward at that very moment. So, take your pick. Any and all of those are eligible. I do thank God for whatever part God had to play in that potentially horrible incident that turned out not to be.

737

Use your own judgment in discerning any meaning - if any - of the message on the back of somebody's shirt:

>HELL IS FULL
>SO I'M BACK

738

Sign on the back of a pickup truck, owned by a confident sportsman:

>FISH TREMBLE
>AT THE SOUND OF MY NAME

739

Different church groups have names that they revere. The Presbyterians have John Calvin. The Baptists honor the name of Roger Williams. The Quakers revere the name of George Fox. Cumberland Presbyterians honor the name of Finis Ewing. Lutherans gladly do so with Martin Luther. John Wesley is at the top of the list for Methodists. And the Christian Church (Disciples of Christ) and the Church of Christ remember with gladness the names of Thomas Campbell and Alexander Campbell.

Well, my name is Thomas Campbell. And my father's name was Thomas Campbell. In the late 1940s and early 1950s Thomas H. Campbell (my father) attended graduate school at the University of Chicago Divinity School. Housing was a problem and they finally found room for him in the Disciples House, though he was a Cumberland Presbyterian. He was treated well. When I did graduate work at Brite Divinity School of Texas Christian University in Fort Worth (a Disciples-sponsored institution), I was in a class once where on the first day each student was to introduce oneself. I happened to be at the back of the room and they started at the front. I was, in fact, the last student with a self-introduction. I was prepared. "My name is Thomas Campbell." Everybody laughed. Really loud. I built on that. "I am actually a used-car salesman, but I thought the class needed somebody famous!"

When I was a pastor in Lexington, Kentucky, my father and I, both history buffs, went out to Cane Ridge Meeting House near Paris, Kentucky. Cane Ridge is the birthplace of the Disciples movement, the site of great revivals and religious awakenings which were a part of the Great Revival of 1800 and afterwards. We toured the area and the tour guide had us sign the Guest Book. My father signed in as "Thomas Campbell." I signed my name "Thomas Campbell." The guide looked at what we wrote and I think I heard him mutter, "We get a lot of that."

740

Sign outside a pet grooming establishment:

        FUR PET'S SAKE
        DOG GROOMING

741

An obsessive poet who loved to do puns got sick and had to be hospitalized. Try as they might, the staff could not keep him in the bed. Every time he got an inspiration for a poem he would get out of bed, go over to a desk, and write it down. His wife could not control him either. One time the phone rang in the room and she answered. Someone on the other end wanted to know how her husband was doing. "Not too well," she replied, "He has gone from bed to verse."

ഈ‌ൽഈ‌ൽഈ‌ൽഈ‌ൽഈ‌ൽഈ‌ൽഈ‌ൽഈ‌ൽഈ‌ൽഈ‌ൽ

742

Dogs are not human, so far as we know. Yet they have a way about them that often ministers to folks. Six examples follow. First, in nursing homes, where some older people go and have to give up practically everything to do so, including their pets, we ministers and other church folks have tried to bring cheer and hope. Sometimes we do a pretty good job, sometimes not. Some nursing homes, one day a week, have "pet day" and some of God's creatures come and visit. Of most comfort are dogs, who give love and accept love unconditionally. I am positive some spiritual renewal takes place when dogs are around.

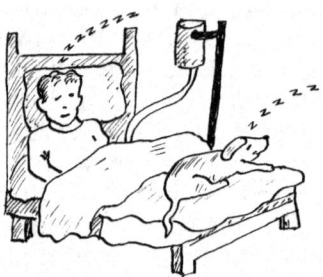

On the healing presence of dogs

Second, it has been found that patients awaiting surgery are helped immensely by a visit from a friendly canine. We have seen on the television news that organizations provide these gifts from God on a daily basis. The dogs traipse up and down the hospital hallways and drop in on people, especially those facing operations. They put their paws up on the beds and are loved and petted by the patients, with smiles all around. What a ministry!

Third, both in men's and women's prisons, life takes on new meaning for inmates who are given a dog to care for and feed and train over a period of time. The very best kinds of therapy take place in the hearts and minds of the inmates as they experience self-worth, and take care of one of God's lovely creatures. The dogs are trained by the inmates to go out and be someone else's pet or helpmate and the prisoners have to give them up. This is understood from the first. But it does not erase the sadness and heartbreak they experience when they see their best friends leave to make a home with someone else. However, very soon another dog is theirs to care for and train and they are involved again with another one of God's great gifts that will help the residents find life more worth living.

Fourth, dogs have innate qualities that enable them to detect problems. They, like other animals, knew something was wrong well before the Tsunami hit Indonesia and surrounding areas, and fled the territory. Our most recent canine pet, Desi, knew a storm was coming well before the weather man on TV did. She would start shaking almost uncontrollably. We would try to comfort her and lessen her shaking, but to little avail. It is said dogs can detect cancer, oncoming epileptic seizures, and diabetic emergencies in people.

Fifth, dogs are wonderful companions and can bring out the best in us. In a book entitled <u>A Friend Like Henry; The Remarkable True Story of an Autistic Boy and the Dog That Unlocked His World</u>, by Nuala Gardner (Sourcebooks, Inc. 2008), we see another way in which dogs can bring healing and peace to people's lives. A couple's little boy was autistic and communication between parents and child was difficult. Henry came along. He became the son's best friend and drew him out, thereby helping him in every way such as socially. The parents learned to communicate with the boy through the dog and he talked with them through Henry as well. Today, both the parents and their grown son credit that warm relationship with Henry for helping them through the hard times.

Sixth, a book entitled <u>Izzy and Lenore</u>, by Jon Katz (Villard Books, New York, 2008), contains a wonderful story of an author who decided to receive training for ministering to Alzheimer's patients as well as in hospice situations. He took along Izzy, a beautiful dog. Izzy took the classes, too. When Jon Katz would visit a home and they would stand beside the bedside of a patient, at a given moment, with no signal, Izzy would jump up on the bed and cuddle close to the patient. At that moment the patient would respond with a pat or a light hug and would almost literally "come alive." After about fifteen minutes, again, with no signal needed, Izzy would jump off the bed. The next visit would be the same. There is no question that our canine friends have innate qualities that have served humankind well and endeared them to us in the warmest ways.

743

Words of wisdom on another church sign:

AN APOLOGY IS THE BEST WAY
TO HAVE THE LAST WORD

744

While living in Burleson, Texas, in the 1970s and taking graduate work at Brite Divinity School at Texas Christian University, I first heard the name of Fred Craddock. Two facts were emphasized: He is the best preacher in the Disciples of Christ church, and he is short, no more than five feet five inches tall. Thereafter I began to read his books and occasionally had opportunity to hear his sermons on tape. In 1985 we were fortunate enough to have him on the Bethel College campus as the preacher for that year's Cumberland Presbyterian Ministers' Conference. I was on the planning committee and then a pastor in Lexington, Kentucky. As I drove onto the campus in McKenzie, Tennessee, that first morning, I found myself following another car. I recognized Dr. Craddock as he got out of his car and I decided to wait until we got inside the auditorium where the services would be held before trying to meet him. I followed at a distance as he walked in and went right down the middle aisle toward the pulpit. There he walked around it, stood at it, grasping it with both hands. By that time I had arrived at the pulpit and heard his first words, "I'll need a box." Indeed, without the box, his face could barely be seen over the pulpit. We got a box. The good news is that the other major speaker, Dr. William Ramsay, then a faculty member at Bethel College, was no more than an inch taller than Dr. Craddock. They both needed the box, which meant we could keep it there for the entire conference and they could see their audience and the audience could see them.

745

Pulpits come in all sizes, heights, and even shapes. Some are built like corrals, others are as small as little lecterns. Some hold a lot of material that can be easily concealed from the audience. Others hide nothing and hold very little, and sometimes that which they hold can easily slide off onto the floor. Some pulpits in churches that have television programs are almost nowhere to be seen, and some that are visible are see-through kinds of pulpits. Don't all church people know you need a pulpit with a couple of shelves below for storing old bulletins, old sermon notes, old Sunday School literature, and a few hand-held fans from local funeral homes? I am told that some pulpits are adjustable and can be lowered or raised. I have never stood at one, however. At six feet one, I have experienced both the highs and lows of pulpit life. Some have been so low that I had to hold whatever materials - Bible, notes, manuscript - in my hands in order to read them. Some are so high that even at my height they seemed too elevated. Once I stood at a pulpit for about four nights in some special services where - and I exaggerate only a little - I had to stand on tiptoe to preach. That is not a bad way to preach. You finish quicker. You say only the essential words and omit any unnecessary ones. There is an added urgency as your legs get tired pretty soon. Yes, the kind of pulpit in front of you can affect the delivery of the sermon.

746

Some statements you never forget. Dr. Robert Middleton, then pastor of First Baptist Church (American Baptist) in Birmingham, Michigan, was the preacher for the Cumberland Presbyterian Ministers' Conference at Bethel College in the early 1980s. In one sermon he used two phrases that had clear meanings and challenges. On the one hand, he said "there is the nerve of failure." On the other, "there is the failure of nerve." The first is risky, challenging, exciting, fraught with possibilities and disappointments. But at least the person is willing to try. The second is not risky at all. It has us not trying at all, not risking anything, not going out on any limb, not attempting the impossible, and maybe not even attempting the possible. I like "the nerve of failure." I do not like, and hope I have few if any moments of, "the failure of nerve." This reminds me of the Parable of the Talents in Matthew 25:14-30. The five-talent man and the two-talent man exercised the "nerve of failure." They could have lost it all. The one-talent man had the "failure of nerve." He was afraid to risk any of it.

747

One of our PAS (Program of Alternate Studies) students has a sister who lives with her husband and family in the Washington, D.C. area. Both husband and wife have high-powered jobs in Washington. One works in the Pentagon. The wife's position is as high and well-paying as the husband's. Both are in decision-making roles in their work. Yet, when the weekend rolls around they go to a church in Alexandria, Virginia, where the wife is not allowed to accept any leadership roles. She cannot teach other adults. She cannot serve as a lay speaker. She cannot serve on the

Board of Deacons. She cannot even think of becoming an ordained minister. Her denomination has said in its faith statement the woman's place is "to serve as (her husband's) helper in managing the household and nurturing the next generation." However, as The Christian Century reports in its October 21, 2008, issue, page 9, some leaders in that denomination are concerned, what with evangelical Sarah Palin running for vice-president and thousands of members of this particular denomination enthusiastically supporting her. The church leaders may want to revise their position on women in public life. The Palin issue is only one of many where the service of women in society is recognized while their voices are stilled in their churches, and the contradiction is embarrassingly visible.

748

Many great preachers have been featured at the annual Cumberland Presbyterian Ministers' Conference. If one were to look only at the late 1970s and then into the 1980s one would see the names of William Willimon, David Buttrick, Fred Craddock, Robert Middleton, Oswald Hoffman, John Killinger, William Carl, Ernest Campbell, Eugene Lowry, and Thomas Long, and that is not the complete list. In the 1990s and on into the 21st century the committee that plans the event has continued to bring outstanding preachers to the conference. All the above spoke on the campus of Bethel College in January of certain years. In the past few years the conference has moved to Nashville, Tennessee; and also to Fort Worth, Texas; with stops at Bethel in between. Russellville, Arkansas, is also on the schedule.

What's more, along with those outstanding preachers there was also another person featured, and that was the lecturer. Usually, each one had three presentations each. There were three worship services with a sermon in each, and there were three sessions with the lecturer. In the recent past, on a couple of occasions, one person did both. Our denomination has been blessed with nationally known speakers who, we found out, are just down-to-earth people, easy to visit with. It has always been good to gather at such conferences and to be refreshed by the wisdom, inspiration, and leadership of such outstanding people.

749

At this writing (late October 2008) a national election is drawing near. Millions of people will probably vote for a person who is an African-American. Some whites may have to grit their teeth to do so, for it may be the first time they have ever voted in this way in any election. One sobering thought could be this: How many years, how many generations (during those times they were allowed to vote) have African-Americans had to grit their teeth and vote for a white person? Isn't it about time for a turn-about-is-fair-play moment? The same could be said about the other ticket and the possibility of a woman as vice-president. Whoever wins, history will be made in a big way.

750

By the way, even before the general election, the primaries and the general election were history making events. Why? Because, down to the "final four" we had someone from Hawaii and someone from Alaska, our two newest states. That's one for the books, too.

Chapter 751-800

"Carroll County, Tennessee"

751

I grew up in Carroll County, Tennessee, which is situated in the northwest part of the state, only about forty miles from the Kentucky line. One of its many bright spots is Bethel College in McKenzie, in the county since the school's founding in 1842. Natives of the county have gone on to be well known in their areas of work. DIXIE CARTER of "Designing Women" fame on television, is a native of the county and maintains a home in McLemoresville, where she grew up. GENE HICKERSON, who died in October of 2008 after a long bout with Alzheimer's, though born in Gibson County, grew up in Trezevant in Carroll County. He was an All American lineman on the Ole Miss football team and went on to be an NFL all star for the Cleveland Browns. He ran interference for Jim Brown and other great Browns running backs. Hickerson was recently inducted into the National Football League Hall of Fame. PATRICK WILLIS, a graduate of Central High School in Bruceton, also in Carroll County, completed a great career as a linebacker for the Ole Miss Rebels and is now playing for the San Francisco Forty Niners. WILLIAM ALEXANDER, the son of a doctor in McKenzie, grew up there and went away to school. He became an educator and is credited by most as being the "inventor" of the Middle School concept. His brother, JIM ALEXANDER, was a political leader in Tennessee and served as State Treasurer in the Frank Clement administration. TOM WINSETT grew up in McKenzie and later went on to play outfield for the Brooklyn Dodgers. DALE KELLEY grew up in Huntingdon and graduated from Bethel College. He has been mayor of Huntingdon for several terms. He was a member of the House of Representatives in the Tennessee legislature for a few years and served in the cabinet of Tennessee Governor Don Sundquist. In the world outside of the county he is best known for his work as an NCAA basketball official, having refereed on the highest level, including the Final Four. He has been the supervisor of officials in several basketball conferences. BOBBY BROOKS played football for McKenzie High School and then starred as a running back for Memphis State College (as the University of Memphis was known then). RAYMOND OWEN, a graduate of McKenzie High School, class of 1951, grew up as a member of First Methodist Church in McKenzie, served in the military in Germany and South Korea, entered the ministry, attended Oklahoma City University as well as Perkins School of Theology at Southern Methodist University in Dallas, Texas, and also Scarritt College in Nashville, Tennessee. He served as pastor of churches in the state of Oklahoma and represented his denomination in many national and world organizations. After eight pastorates in that state, he was elected as a Bishop in 1992 and served in that great office in the Southwest Texas Conference and the Rio Grande Conference. GORDON BROWNING, a native of Huntingdon, fought in World War I, was elected to Congress, and then was elected and served several terms as Governor of the State of Tennessee. RAY MORRIS grew up in McKenzie, attended Bethel College, then graduated from Tennessee Tech in Cookeville. Within a few years he started his own business, Venture Construction Company in Atlanta, Georgia. Ray has done well, has seen his company grow nationwide, and has been a strong supporter of the two colleges that he attended and that touched his life. There have been others who came out of Carroll County to have an influence in the world at large. These are a few of the well known Carroll County natives of the past. Also on the list, of course, is EVERY MEMBER of the class of 1957 of McKenzie High School.

752

As a guest preacher in revival services I have looked out upon a congregation I have never met before and had these thoughts over the duration of the week. On the first night, I see "faces." On the second night, after getting to know the people a little better, I see "faces with names." By the third and fourth night, I look out and see "personalities." On about the fifth night I look out and see "characters." With each passing evening I get to know the people better. And I sometimes envy the pastor for being honored to serve with and minister to such great folks.

753

There was a big front-page article in the paper about the Tampa Bay Rays baseball team. During the off-season the team changed its nickname. It used to be Tampa Bay Devil Rays. This year it became the Tampa Bay Rays. They got the Devil out of there. The newspaper article told of some Christians who said the team was helped when they took the Devil part of the nickname out. The evidence cannot be disputed. In 2007 they finished last in their division, with the worst won-lost record. In 2008 they finished first in their division, beat the White Sox in the division playoffs, and then the Red Sox in the league championship series. Quite a difference! I don't know how much the alteration of the team nickname had to do with it, perhaps some. It also helped that their pitching staff got better. Their starters did well and their bullpen was outstanding. In the movie "Crimes and Misdemeanors" a man looks back to his past in a Jewish household. And remembers that a rabbi prayed that a particular boxer would win his next fight. After the prayer one of the women sitting around the dinner table said, "It won't hurt if he has a good punch." The Tampa Bay Rays in 2008 had some pretty good "punch" on offense and really good work in the field and on the mound.

754

Do you want to know the most frightening time for a pastor? It is when a guest minister comes in to preach a revival. No matter how heralded, no matter how trusted, no matter how good friends the two ministers might be, it is still a scary time. Each night during the three, four, five or six night series of services, the pastor leads the worship service and then, about halfway through, turns the program over to the visiting preacher for the message of the evening, and also, turns the people over to the visitor as well. And then, for twenty or twenty-five or thirty or thirty-five minutes, or more, the pastor has no say-so, no voice, no leverage, no power, no influence. In truth, this pastor is turning the people over to this visitor, this stranger, this interloper, this intruder, this so-called guest. And for that period of time each evening, the pastor is helpless as the visitor preaches on and on and on, for better or for worse. This good pastor, who week in and week out, has nurtured the congregation, buried the dead, married the young, confirmed the children, celebrated with the youth, counseled the grieving and disturbed, and listened to heartache and sadness and joy and victory and defeat - this pastor, who has truly been "pastor" to the flock, turns the flock over to this visiting shepherd. What a dangerous moment each evening! What a scary time! Theology and doctrine and faithfulness to the scripture and good manners and good grammar and attention to congregational needs may be thrown to the wind. I have been both a pastor and a visiting preacher in these situations. I am coming to the belief that the pastor is the one to be thinking of. Once the guest preacher and wife literally "took over" wherever we were that week and it got so bad I left town on the pretense that I had to see somebody in a hospital in a nearby city. The guest preacher can preach and then skip the country. The pastor is left to clean up after the hurricane that just swept through. The people the next Sunday settle in again to listen to the sermons of their local minister and resume the routines of "church" that were broken during the special week. Sometimes, unfortunately, there is much from which to recover and it may take months to get back to "normal" for the congregation and pastor. It truly can be a dangerous time. Fortunately the several pastorates I have had have included mostly very good and very thoughtful and considerate visiting evangelists. They were good church people who taught me a lot and shared common concerns. But just occasionally there was the other kind. As for me, I fear I may have been one of those visiting preachers that folks had to clean up after upon my leaving. While I may not have been equal to a hurricane, I may have appeared as a slight wind, mostly "hot air" that took some getting over. I do know that in my most recent "revival" meetings as a guest preacher, I have been more thoughtful of what the local pastor is going through. I have adopted this personal policy as a guest preacher, interloper, intruder, disturber of church routine, in a revival in somebody else's church: DO NO HARM.

755

Sign outside a church in McKenzie, Tennessee:

> WHAT CAN THIS SIGN SAY
> TO GET YOU IN CHURCH SUNDAY?

756

The following does NOT contain a typographical error:

In the movie "Melinda and Melinda" one of the characters is asked, "What do you want?" She answers, "I want to want to live."

A powerful statement indeed... I not only "want to live." I "want to want to live."

757

Pastor Appreciation Day (or is it Month??) has been around for a few years. When I was a resident, fulltime pastor, in the 1960s, 1970s, 1980s, and early 1990s, that special day was not in vogue. No church was doing it that I knew of. Somebody dreamed up this idea and it caught on. Now, sometime in the fall of the year, churches are encouraged to observe Pastor Appreciation Day (or Month). Thinking back, I am afraid I would have been on shaky ground as a pastor on some occasions, and would probably have wondered if there would be any positive effort on the part of the session and congregation. I'm sort of glad I was out of that phase of my ministry by the time that caught on. I don't know how it would have gone. I read of one church's raising money from within the congregation to send pastor and wife to the Holy Land. My fear would be that for us it might be a pair of one-way tickets. Even without the special day, the good folks in our congregations have demonstrated their appreciation of their pastors in many good ways. Sometimes, over the years, I have felt under-appreciated as a pastor. At other times, I have felt that there was sincere and genuine gratitude for work done and that gratitude was evidenced in many good ways, and maybe too much. Occasionally, I have felt that there was greater appreciation than deserved. Since I have taken on the work of Director of the Program of Alternate Studies at Memphis Theological Seminary, Linda and I have traveled on Sundays to, and have been blessed to have spent two years with, three small Cumberland Presbyterian churches in the Searcy, Arkansas, area from 1995 to 1997, and then almost twelve years (since October of 1997 and still going) with two small Presbyterian Church (USA) (total combined membership:25) congregations in northern Mississippi (in the beautifully named small towns of Toccopola and Algoma). The three churches in Arkansas, and now the two in Mississippi, have shown love and appreciation to us and we are grateful.

758

We went to vote early today, one week before the 2008 presidential election. There was a long line, as there has been every day, according to reports. I timed our stay there. From the moment we got in line outside the Berclair Church of Christ in Memphis, until we voted, it was one hour and ten minutes. Not bad, really. I did get tired of standing all that time. During one especially tiring stretch, I did a little thinking out loud, and said, "I am really tired, but every time I think I am too tired to keep standing here, I think of Valley Forge." The person behind me smiled and agreed. We occasionally just need to put things into perspective.

759

One of the many joys in preaching has been to have a series, a Sunday-by-Sunday string of messages (from three to about six or eight or more) tied to one theme, or text, or subject. The Ten Commandments became a series, as did The Beatitudes. The Fruit of the Spirit in Galatians brought on this approach as did the parables in Luke. Various passages in Genesis were involved in a series as well. One time I had a series where the titles of all the sermons started with "Coping With..." "Coping With Loss," "Coping With Grief," "Coping With Loneliness," "Coping With Happiness," "Coping With Doubt." I had a sermon ready to deliver entitled "Coping With Indecision," but never could decide when to preach it.

760

This sign outside of Highland Heights United Methodist Church in Memphis, Tennessee, should be heeded by all political candidates:

MUD THROWN
IS GROUND LOST

761

The young boy got it wrong, but got it right, when he called the Book of Revelation the Book of Revolutions.

762

For many people, the book in the Bible immediately after John is called The Book of Acts. For others, it bears the title The Acts of the Apostles. For the Choctaw Indians in southeastern Oklahoma, I am told, it is, simply, The Apostles.

763

Modern technology gets more and more "modern" with each passing day. As of this writing, we are in the computer age. Only God knows what age we will be in months or years from now as new ways of communicating are discovered and individuals become even better equipped to communicate with one another. It wasn't that long ago when, in moving from one church to another and into a new pastorate, my greatest thrill was to walk in and see in the pastor's study an electric typewriter. Previously, I had sat down to manual typewriters. I thought, "This is as good as it gets." Right around that time, after we had used hard-to-use erasers to try to wipe out a mistake on the typewriter, there arrived "white-out," a liquid in a little bottle that, when applied to the mistake on the typewritten page, could make the problem disappear. But this was not all: Later there came typewriters that, when a mistake was made, could back up, and, in typing over the blunder, make way for the correct letter. Wow! I was "up town" there in Lexington, Kentucky: an electric typewriter, some "white-out," and, later a machine that does its own erasing. But there still remained the messy stencils that were used and then placed on the dreaded mimeograph machine. Somehow, some way, the copying got done, and we had bulletins for Sunday and a newsletter to mail out to church members. All that is history, including the cursed "address-o-graph" that was at one church I moved to. The previous pastor had tried his best to get rid of it, lowering the advertised price considerably over several months, but still no takers. We moved it from one storage closet to another in the church and kept advertising, always with a still lower price tag. Finally, I think we just threw the thing away. But then along came the computer, and, one by one, church offices and pastors' studies had them. How things have changed in only a few short years. In the 1960s you typed a term paper or thesis for college or seminary, and, to make three copies, you had three sheets of typing paper with two sheets of carbon paper between them. Always the third copy was very dim. Now we have copying machines. It doesn't get any better than this. Or will something else come along?

764

A ministerial colleague saw this bumper sticker:

> WORK IS FOR THOSE WHO
> DON'T KNOW HOW TO FISH

765

The book entitled <u>Capitol Men: The Epic Story of Reconstruction Through the Lives of the First Black Congressmen</u>, by Phillip Dray (Houghton Mifflin, 2008), has a little section telling about white plantation owners who lost their property in the Civil War. On page 49 the author tells of one "Henry Stewart, a 'hard master' who promoted the rebellion (secession and the Civil War) in every possible way except to take up arms himself." Where have we seen and heard of that before, of national leaders who "promoted (war) in every possible way except to take up arms (themselves)?"

766

Robert Reich, a former secretary of labor, has written that in 2006 (the last year for which we have data) "The richest 1 percent of Americans took home 23 percent of total national income." Back in 1980, he reports," The richest 1 percent took home 8 percent of total income." He concludes, "The last time (prior to 2006) the top 1 percent took home more than 20 percent of total income was in 1928, just before the Great Crash." (The American Prospect, November 2008, p. 52)

767

It is the morning of November 5, 2008, the first day of Barack Obama's tenure as president-elect of the United States of America. The outpouring of positive reaction over the world and in this country is heartwarming. His election is truly historic, something that will be noted in all future books on American history. It ranks alongside other historic moments, such as the U.S. Supreme Court's 1954 school desegregation decision and the day baseball great Jackie Robinson played his first game for the Brooklyn Dodgers and the "color line" was broken in the major leagues. These three events - along with others - will always be known as defining moments in American history.

768

The young man and young woman were dating and were progressing toward a possible wedding. Since marriage was a possibility, the young woman thought she ought to be straight with her future fiancé and husband. So one day as they were discussing all of this, she said, "I need to let you know something about me before we go any farther. I'm a vegetarian." Without hesitation, he said, "That's all right; we'll go to your church one Sunday and mine the next."

769

A recent newspaper article reported that in Somalia a 13-year-old girl was stoned to death by authorities. Why? She had been raped by three men and had reported it to community leaders. In their understanding of the laws of the land, it was the girl - not her attackers - that had brought shame to the community. Therefore, she should be the one to die. They took her out to a public place and stoned her until she was dead. I am sure the town leaders were doing exactly as their ancient scriptures instructed. They took their inherited teachings literally.

770

Jephthah is one of the "heroes of the faith" mentioned in Hebrews 11, the "faith chapter." "And what more should I say? For time would fail me to tell of Gideon, Barak, Samson, Jephthah, of David and Samuel and the prophets…" (Hebrews 11:32).Jephthah had been called to lead an army into battle, but, uncertain of his own abilities and those of his men he prayed to God for victory and made the promise that if he came out victorious he (Jephthah) would sacrifice the first person he saw when he returned to his village. All this is found in Chapter 11 of Judges. He won the battle and upon his return the first person he saw was his daughter. Though he lamented this terrible turn of events, Jephthah felt obliged to go ahead and keep his promise to God. He would offer his daughter up to God as a "burnt offering" (Judges 11:31). And he kept his promise. Before a person was burned in the sacrifice the victim was taken to a public place and stoned to death. Then the burning took place. Do you figure Jephthah witnessed this happening to his daughter, his only child? Do you think he may have even participated in the ritual?

So far as we know, the above story is the only reason Jephthah is mentioned in Hebrews 11 as one of the "heroes of the faith." A sad reason indeed. Several years ago, I heard of a minister, in speaking on the Judges passage, say that "there are some promises we ought not to keep." Well said. We ought to be careful what we promise. Then we need to be careful about keeping the promise, lest it have been a rash, unreasonable, eventually cruel promise.

771

Often in intense conversations and times of conflict and confrontation I cannot think of anything to say. It may be a day or a week or a month or more before something comes to me that I should have said at the time. In the Presbyterian system, the Presbytery has authority over individual churches insofar as their calling of a pastor. The church (its elders) calls the pastor and the Presbytery approves and then installs the pastor. But when the church has someone preaching for them who is not a minister in the denomination, the Presbytery wants to encourage the people of the church and show concern just as it does for the other churches in the area. So it was that I was a part of a committee making a routine visit with a church session (elders) and their preacher, who was a minister of another denomination. He had been preaching for them for several months and no one was sure if there would ever come a time when this minister would leave and they would get a Cumberland Presbyterian minister. I - innocently, I might say - inquired of the minister what his plans were and how much longer he thought he might stay at this church. To this day, I believe it was a rather soft, non-threatening question. He exploded. He barked loudly that the matter was none of my business or the committee's either. He would leave when he felt ready. The question, in his mind, was out of order and intrusive. I felt scolded and rather intimidated, and said nothing in the rest of the meeting. Moreover, I felt so bad, that from then on in casual meetings elsewhere with any of their elders or with this minister I went out of my way to be nice, to be overly thoughtful and considerate, and in other ways express by my actions my deep apologies for being so rude. I kid you not: Twenty years later, and this was all of a sudden, it dawned on me. "Hold on here," I thought. "Hey, I am a member of a committee assigned to work with churches without an ordained Cumberland Presbyterian pastor and I have a perfect right, no, an obligation, to inquire as to your plans, sir. I am carrying out my duty as a presbyter. I am trying to fulfill my responsibilities as a minister in the Presbytery on an assignment to visit with this church and this preacher. And, sir, I still want an answer to my question!" But, sad to say, those thoughts did not occur to me at the time. It took two decades for the full impact of that visit to penetrate my brain and heart. I think I would like to go back to that time and finish the conversation on a little stronger note than I actually did.

772

I couldn't find a hymn about Barabbas in any hymnal, so I wrote one. It can be sung to the tune of "In Christ There Is No East or West," or to the tune of "Amazing Grace." Back in the 1970s and 1980s this was used in a couple of worship services, sung to the first tune, when this biblical character was discussed. Feel free to use it as you feel led.

HYMN OF BARABBAS

1. "A stranger died," Barabbas cried,
   "Between two men like me.
   He suffered loss, he bore my cross,
   And set this prisoner free."

2. "What can I say? What can I pay,
   For all he did for me?
   He knew me not, yet cast his lot,
   And set this prisoner free."

3. "Time cannot dim my debt to him,
   Its meaning now I see.
   Instead of strife he gave me life
   And set this prisoner free."

4. "Jesus, our Lord, we trust your word,
   We laud your victory.
   For from that time your cross sublime
   Has set the prisoner free."

5. "And now impart to every heart
   Our special ministry:
   With joy proclaim your saving name
   That sets all prisoners free."

773

Occasionally I am asked about a certain minister who is a candidate to be pastor in a certain church. What do I know of that person? Would I recommend this one to this church? How about pulpit skills? Does the minister visit? My record is spotty, at best. To begin with, sometimes I do not know the person and cannot say one way or the other. Sometimes I do know the person and can easily recommend the church's continuing to be interested. On more than one occasion, I have absolutely, without a doubt, flat-out said "you don't want that person." Half the time churches back away; half the time they go ahead anyway, and, surprise of surprises, half of those times the pastor-church relationship is good and half the time the pastor-church relationship is not so good, as feared. Sometimes a person has had bad experiences in several previous pastorates and there seems to be no indication that pastoral characteristics, or lack of them, have changed. To sum up, we don't know. It's like marriages. She is going to marry him? Why? And then they have fifty years of wedded bliss. The same is with pastors and churches. We never know. Where there appears to be excellent "chemistry" and a "can't miss" situation, one should not be surprised if pastor and church part ways before six months. And where there are questions all over the place, and hundreds of doubts, and a lot of foreboding, be ready to celebrate with pastor and church the fifteenth year of their relationship. So, if you need advice, or help on calling a pastor, just come to me. I predicted "M A S H" would not make it as a television series. In my own mind, I doubted if a young man still in seminary could go to a small, suburban church in Texas and make anything of it. That was about twenty years ago. Right now he is still pastor of that "small" church and it has almost 2,000 members. Yeah, just call me; I'll set you straight.

774

Message outside a church in northern Alabama:

> BELIEVE AND RECEIVE
> DOUBT AND DO WITHOUT

775

The presidential election of 2000 saw one major candidate receive 500,000 more votes than the other major candidate, but lose in electoral votes. For several weeks, there were questions and concerns and disputes over the vote count in one state. In the end, the United States Supreme Court declared the candidate that happened to have the lower count in popular votes nation-wide as the winner of that particular state, which put him "over the top" and awarded him the presidency. During and after the legal arguments over the vote in that particular state, some commentators - radio talk show guys especially - were hollering at the other side, "Move on! Our guy won! Get over it! You're a bunch of losers and cry-babies!" Finally, it was suggested by several commentators -not the radio talk show guys, though - that since the vote was so close, the new president would have to govern "from the center." That did not happen. Following both the 2000 and the 2004 elections, both very close, that president ignored the "center" and governed from the far right.

In 2008 the other side won. The candidate of the winning side had a plurality of 3,000,000 or more votes and had an overwhelming victory in the electoral college. Some commentators - especially including the radio talk show guys - are saying, "It is not a mandate! It is not a landslide! He will have to govern 'from the center!'" Hey! Is there a double standard here? The group that should have governed "from the center" and did not has been discredited and practically disregarded as the transition from one administration to another begins. Many of them are the ones crying that "It was close!" No. It was not close. The new president may choose to govern "from the center" but he has the support and the votes to take the progressive route if he chooses to do so and sees that it is in the best interest of the country. American politics seems to run in cycles. The pendulum seems to swing back and forth over time. Now the cycle has continued and the pendulum has swung. It's the other side's time. Get over it. Step back and let the process continue. Monitor how they do. Criticize when necessary. But do not say the 2008 vote was "close." It was not.

776

Someone I know vacationed in Hawaii. On one afternoon he went swimming in the ocean but drifted a little too far so that he could not see the shore. He became confused as to which direction to swim to get back to the beach. Was it the curvature of the earth that made this a difficult moment? Whatever, it was a terrifying experience. Fortunately, he chose the right direction and was back on shore after seeing it and swimming vigorously back to safety. On a much less serious note, but still serious, preachers would be advised as they deliver their messages not to wander too far from the text and the main message. Too often a preacher will drift away from the subject and, in doing so, get so far away that a loss of direction takes effect.

777

It is good and understandable that church folks take pride in their buildings, keep the facilities clean, and have ongoing maintenance where needed. The other day I heard, though, one of the best mission statements made anywhere. A church had moved into their new structure: shiny tile floors in the lobby and restrooms, brightly painted walls, excellent lighting, everything easily accessible to all, brand new carpets. The statement, made by the pastor but shared by the entire membership was this: "The sooner we wear out the carpet, the better." Isn't that a great attitude! The church is for people, and the more people the better - all during the week. Boy scouts, girl scouts, community groups. Bible study groups, youth activities, committee meetings, session meetings, breakfasts, lunches, dinners, collections of groceries for the needy. With all that, the carpet may wear out. What a testimony to the church in mission!

778

Jesus turned the water into wine. The Burns Flat, Oklahoma, Cumberland Presbyterian Church turned a grocery store into a church. When the town's only grocery store went out of business (there had been three or four owners/managers but no lasting success) the folks at the local Cumberland Presbyterian were looking to expand. Their present property and facilities were limited for growth. The church, with encouragement and counsel from the Board of Missions of the denomination, bought it, made plans for renovating creating a church facility within the building, and provided most of the labor. Along the way the church sold its other building to the local Assembly of God congregation, which has grown a lot since the move. So has the Burns Flat Cumberland Presbyterian Church. This is more than a "storefront" church. It's a whole store!

779

Small sign on the desk in a motel room:

> TALK IS CHEAP
> REALLY, REALLY CHEAP
> (Free phone service)

780

Message in a church front yard somewhere in Tennessee:

> GOD DOES NOT CALL QUALIFIED PEOPLE
> GOD QUALIFIES THE CALLED

781

Burns Flat is in the western part of Oklahoma. About twenty miles away is another little town named Rocky. It was in Rocky that the Estes family lived for about a year in 1929-30, enough time for their oldest child, Margaret, to be a senior in the high school and graduate with her class. She had attended almost a dozen schools in her lifetime as her father, Samuel Russell Estes, Sr., found jobs in different localities. Among those in the senior class were people who became lifelong friends. I rode with one of my hosts over to Rocky to see the town: the abandoned service stations, one of which undoubtedly Billy Sparks (later known in Cumberland Presbyterian circles as Army Chaplain and General Assembly Moderator John W. Sparks) worked as teenager and young adult before going off to college. There was the site - now a vacant lot - where the Cumberland Presbyterian Church was located. The old school building was replaced in 1941 by another building built by the WPA. As we rode around the little town I pictured Margaret Estes as a teenager enjoying senior class activities in the school and community. Margaret Estes became Mrs. Thomas H. Campbell in June of 1935. Three sons, born in 1936, 1939 (me), and 1943, added to the family which also included a daughter, Jo Nell, by my father's first wife who had died in 1933. Seeing Rocky, Oklahoma, and knowing a little of what the Estes family (with seven children) went through in those hard Depression years makes me think of John Steinbeck's <u>Grapes of Wrath</u> and the hard-scrabble times those Oklahoma folks went through.

782

Driving in western Arkansas, on an interstate, at night, in heavy rain, can be risky and nerve-wracking. Unless you are behind a nice big tractor-trailer whose lights you follow. I followed it pretty much all the way across half of the state on into Oklahoma and felt safe and secure and very positive about my trip under extreme weather conditions. It is good when somebody else runs interference for us, when another person stands up for us, when others pave the way so we can have a smooth journey in the hard times. We benefit from our predecessors, from those Christians who have gone before us, from those who paid the price so we who followed could have easier times. One would not want to take this analogy too far. I came this close to following the truck into the weigh station but decided I had received enough assistance after getting into Oklahoma and could make it the rest of the way, especially since the weather had cleared.

783

"Bait and Switch" is a common term employed - if not spoken - by some stores and, maybe, churches. Back in 1964, less than a year after we got married, we saw an ad in the Memphis paper about a nice bedroom set for a very acceptable price. When we walked into the furniture store, however, we found that the items we had in mind were way, way back in the rear of the store. In fact, you had to walk around other furniture, almost climb other items, fight through a couple of cobwebs (I may be exaggerating here) to find - there in the semi-darkness - the things we saw in the ad. In fact, while we were in the store, the folks really tried to sell us other items that were much more expensive. We did buy one thing. We bought a coffee table for nine dollars. Forty five years later we still have that coffee table. I get concerned sometimes when churches send out huge advertisements and lavish invitations, but when people arrive what they see and experience may be anything but what was advertised. Perhaps churches need to be concerned about "Bait and Switch" too.

784

Coleman Thomas Shanton, our little three-year-old grandson, had to go to the hospital for something and when the time came to go home he still had his little hospital bracelet on. When the family got home, he wanted to keep it on. He wore that thing around for days. Sometimes we need to let people know where we've been, what we've been through, how tough life is. He was just conveying a much-needed message.

785

I had just sat down in a restaurant and a woman in her mid-thirties (I would guess) sat down several tables away. From the start, she seemed to be looking for someone in particular. I knew this was the case when she waved the server away, indicating she would wait for a few minutes as she was expecting someone. Minutes passed, and she kept glancing toward the front door, but to no avail. Finally she ordered her meal, and while awaiting her order she continued to look toward the door. She ate slowly, again often looking up and around, obviously looking for someone. She finished her meal and still the chair across from her was empty.

On the pain of being "stood up"

After receiving her ticket, she continued to sit for a few minutes, even after paying. Then she stood, looked around the restaurant as though thinking the other person might be somewhere in the establishment, and walked to the door, always keeping a watchful eye out for the other person. Through the window I saw her when she got to her car. Before she got in, she stood there, looking around, still hoping, still waiting, still obviously thinking the other person might arrive.

After getting in the car, she sat there for several minutes before starting it. Still no one appeared. Then she drove away. Who was it that did not appear? Was this a new acquaintance, perhaps someone she met on the internet? Or was it a male friend from years gone by and with a chance to renew the acquaintance? Was this planned as a clandestine meeting that might perhaps lead to romance? It was obvious there had been an agreement: O-Charley's, noon on Thursday. But the other person did not show up. I felt a sadness in this. The woman was obviously anticipating a meeting that never happened, at least not then and there. One can only guess. Did they finally get together? Did they make connections? Did they get their signals crossed and go to different restaurants by mistake, one not knowing the other was at the other place? These missed connections can happen. They sometimes work out; sometimes they don't. Nevertheless, I felt a sadness for the woman. I hope things turned out well for her.

786

Occasionally I am asked to preach in chapel services at Memphis Theological Seminary. The biggest laugh I ever got was not intended as humor, but I am happy any time there is that response, even when it is not anticipated. The response came after I spoke the first sentence of the sermon. The sentence was, "I have discovered the key to understanding Paul." After the laughter, it dawned on me that the entire scholarly world has attempted to understand Paul all these many centuries, largely to no avail, and the hilarity of anyone's suggesting a solution in the first words of a sermon must go down as justified. I went ahead, meekly and humbly, to suggest looking for the word "therefore" and the words that follow will be Paul's message on the subject discussed. That may be at least one approach to understanding Paul. For instance, in 1 Corinthians 15, a chapter on the resurrection, there are 58 verses. It is in the last verse that we find Paul's "therefore." He writes, "Therefore, my beloved, be steadfast, immovable, always abounding in the work of the Lord, knowing that in the Lord your labor is not in vain." In this scenario, the first 57 verses are prelude, introduction, preparation for hearing the main message that waits until the very last to appear. This approach has helped me. Therefore I will continue to use this as one of the tools for understanding Paul.

787

Many preachers experience some satisfaction in preaching sermons in a series: three or more messages over a period of Sundays linked by a common theme, text, chapter, or book in the

Bible, or based on various lists, such as the Ten Commandments, The Beatitudes, The Fruit of the Spirit, The Gifts of the Spirit, or other such emphases. I could not help but notice that in that great hymn, "Tell Me the Story of Jesus," by Fanny J. Crosby, we find a wonderful summary of the life, death, and resurrection of Jesus Christ, and, therefore, some possibilities for series preaching.

Notice these items listed in order as they appear in the hymn: **His birth**: Tell how the angels in chorus, Sang as they welcomed His birth, "Glory to God in the highest! Peace and good tidings to earth."

His temptations: Fasting alone in the desert, Tell of the days that are past, How for our sins he was tempted, Yet was triumphant at last.

His rejection: Tell of the years of His labor, Tell of the sorrow He bore; He was despised and afflicted, Homeless, rejected and poor.

His crucifixion: Tell of the cross where they nailed Him, Writhing in anguish and pain,

His burial: Tell of the grave where they laid him.

His resurrection: Tell how He liveth again.

His wonderful story: Tell me the story of Jesus, Write on my heart every word; Tell me the story most precious, Sweetest that ever was heard.

788

I know, I know: The King James Version (KJV) of the Bible is not the one and only true translation of the Bible. And I know that other, more "modern" translations convey more accurately the message and meaning of the Hebrew and Greek. And I know that the KJV is not a translation of the "original manuscripts" but a revision of existing translations of its time. And I fully acknowledge that the KJV is one of the hardest versions of the Bible to read and study because, for one thing, every verse is a paragraph, leading one to experience difficulty in discerning the full message of a paragraph or a chapter or a book. Years ago around the start of my ministry I laid the KJV aside for the Revised Standard Version, and since about 1993, have read, studied, and used the New Revised Standard Version. Many other folks embrace the New International Version, or the New King James Version, or The Message, or The Living Bible, or Today's English Version, or some other translation or paraphrase of the scriptures It is a mystery to me why so many ministers and groups of Christians stubbornly believe that the KJV is THE Word of God, no other translation being blessed by God, I suppose. It behooves me to ask them, at least rhetorically, "How did Christians make it before 1611 without a Bible?" And, furthermore, what about those millions of believers who have found the way to salvation through one of a half dozen other translations? Is their conversion invalid?

That said, I find the KJV the most beautiful book ever written. One of the pastorates I moved to had pew Bibles and they were the translation called Good News for Modern Man (Today's English Version). In my previous pastorate we had the Revised Standard Version in the pews and often engaged in unison readings of the scriptures. I was going to try this at my new place and first turned to the 23rd Psalm. No thanks! That version may have been more accurate, it may have been more clear, it may have been more this or that, but the familiar and comfortable music and rhythm and flow of the 23rd Psalm were nowhere to be seen! The same was true of most of the other psalms and most of the other familiar scripture passages such as The Lord's Prayer. We turned to the back of our hymnal for responsive readings where familiar versions of familiar texts were found in, as I remember, the King James Version.

If you are a preacher and reading this, is it not true that, no matter what version we use in our reading, study, and use, when we get in the pulpit and find ourselves quoting scripture from memory - a verse here and a verse there - we revert back to our childhood and youth and speak in KJV terms? Those are the verses that sail, that flow, that move rhythmically off one's tongue. The KJV is beautiful but difficult. And it is difficult but beautiful. Either way, this treasure from 1611 will continue to be around a very long time.

789

If you were to ask me what, in my mind, is the greatest book on preaching ever written, I might be able to name a dozen candidates: anything by Fred Craddock, and Tom Long, and Eugene Lowry, and Thomas Troeger, and Phillips Brooks, and Calvin Miller, and Henry Ward Beecher, and Gardner Taylor. I have learned from every book on the subject I ever read, and still buy all I can on preaching. I am looking now at a book on my desk that I consider a classic - so well written, so beautifully formed, so powerfully presented - that I turn to it often. It is Peter Taylor Forsyth's <u>Positive Preaching and the Modern Mind</u>, (Eerdmans,

1964, with earlier printings in England in 1907, 1909, and 1949). I purchased it in 1969 while living in Fort Worth, Texas. The price is on the front: $1.95. I could quote endlessly from this great book, but perhaps a few examples will suffice (we will keep male-referenced language as Forsyth wrote it):

"We must all preach to our age, but woe to us if it is our age we preach, and only hold up the mirror to the time." p. 5

"It is not cheer that we need but salvation; not help but rescue; not a stimulus but a change; not tonics but life." p. 38

"The one great preacher in history, I would contend, is the Church. And the first business of the individual preacher is to enable the Church to preach." p. 53

"Preaching is not simply pastoral visitation on a large scale." p. 59

"The preacher is not there to astonish people with the unheard of; he is there to revive in them what they have long heard." p. 62

"What makes the Church is not Christ as its founder but Christ as its tenant, as its life, as its power, the Christ living in the faith of its members in general, and of its ministers in particular." p. 63

"Preaching is 'the organized Hallelujah of an ordered community.'" p. 64

"When a man is entrusted with the pastoral care of a Church from its pulpit he accepts, along with the normality of the Scripture, the obligations, limitations, and reserves of the pastoral commission. He that sweareth by the altar sweareth also by that which is upon the altar: and he abuses his position if he simply unload upon his charge certain startling views by way of relief to his own egoist conscience." P. 69

"A Christianity of short sermons is a Christianity of short fibre." p. 75

"You are there (in the pulpit) not simply to speak what people care to hear but also to make them care for what you must speak." p. 94

"I am afraid that, for the general public, religion has become associated with the small and negligible side of the soul. Nowhere has mediocrity its chance as it has in religion. Nowhere has the gossipy side of life such scope. Nowhere has quackery of every kind such a field and such a harvest." p. 116

790

I think it was Emerson who went to see Thoreau, who was in jail, and asked, "What are you doing in there?" To which Thoreau replied, "What are you doing out there?" So much has been accomplished by people in jail or prison, some long-lasting, valuable achievements, mostly in written form. Dietrich Bonhoeffer, the great German theologian and preacher, was imprisoned by the Nazis during World War II. In fact, he would not come out alive. His writings were later published in a book called <u>Letters and Papers from Prison</u>. Martin Luther King found himself in a Birmingham, Alabama, jail during the civil rights conflicts of the 1950s and 1960s, and he wrote a historic "Letter from a Birmingham Jail." The Apostle Paul landed in jail and wrote to the church in Philippi while incarcerated. It was in that letter he wrote, "Rejoice in the Lord always" (4:4). A bit later in the same letter he penned these words, "I have learned,, in whatever state I am, to be content" (4:11). Words of wisdom, experience, and praise have flowed from the pens of some heroes of the faith who were behind bars, and we are thankful for their insight.

791

Sign outside a Memphis church telling it like it is:

HELP WANTED
APPLY INSIDE

792

A highway sign advertising a store where old comic books and magazines are available:

WE HAVE ISSUES

793

If you stand at the North Pole, there is only one direction you can go: South. Whichever way you turn, left or right, or behind or in front, it is still the same. One step this way or that, and you will be going South.

This thought has occurred to me with the transition from one U.S. administration to another. Some are scared the new folks will go "left." "Left" this and "left" that seems to be the cry. Hey, if an administration has been on the far right throughout its lifetime, any different action or decision the new leaders take will be "left." You can't go any farther right. And what is "left" to folks who are worried might really be "moderate" or even "center-right" - but compared to the place where we have been the past eight years it is "left."

794

My worst funeral experience - ever - happened sometime back in the late 70s or early 80s. I lived in Burleson, Texas, and some distant relative whom I had never met died up in Iowa City, Texas, somewhere north of Wichita Falls or thereabouts. It was a three-hour drive, at least. I don't know how the family got my name. Evidently other relatives who were ministers could not be there so they got me to help in the service. At that time of the month I had no cash. A trip to the bank would have been futile as there was none there, either. But I did have a MasterCard, or whatever it was called then. So I could get gas for my car if needed. I started mid-morning and planned to get there around noon for a 1:30 service. I figured I would get there just in time for the meal that somebody would be providing at the church, and folks would say, "Come on in; grab a plate!" I got to the church, and I was pretty hungry by that time. Inside the church were people, none of whom spoke to me. No one was eating because there was no food and no sign that there would be some any time soon. I tracked down the funeral director who gave me necessary information about the service. I believe a local pastor was to participate, as well. I seem to recall it was my duty to bring the message. Trouble was, I did not know the deceased, had never heard of him until a day or two ago, and vaguely understood the family connection: the son of my granddaddy's half brother. Same last name as all my mother's side of the family: Estes. The deceased had a nickname that somebody told me everybody in town knew him by. He was the public address announcer for local high school football games, well known in the community, a non-church person. Turns out none of the family attended church. I tried to preach a sermon on behalf of someone I did not know and whose nickname in the course of the message I promptly forgot. The whole thing was weird. I felt totally out of place.

After the service I rode with the funeral director to the cemetery, not far away. On the way, he asked, "Has anybody given you an honorarium yet?" I replied, "No." I could have added that not a single member of the family of the deceased said a word to me. He said, "The funeral home will send you a check within the next few days." That meant no cash to have on hand going back home. I didn't stay around very long after the burial service and was soon on my way back to Burleson, at least three hours away. Now it was the middle of the afternoon. I had not eaten since a cup of coffee early in the morning. I had no cash, but surely my trusty MasterCard would buy me a meal somewhere. Would you believe that whatever restaurants were open along that often long and lonely stretch of road did not take credit cards, or at least did not take MasterCard? I was seven o'clock getting home and very hungry. It had not been a good day.

795

Sign outside a corner grocery store:

> ON BEHALF OF OUR CUSTOMERS
> WE OPEN ON TIME.
> ON BEHALF OF OURSELVES
> WE CLOSE ON TIME.
>
> Open 8:00 A.M.
> Close 6:00 P.M.

796

I heard this story decades ago: Three hard-of-hearing old men were sitting on a park bench. One commented on the weather: "It is windy." The second replied, "I thought it was Thursday." The third answered, "I'm thirsty too; let's go get a drink."

797

The highlight of the year for the Program of Alternate Studies of the Cumberland Presbyterian Church is the annual Summer Extension School held on the campus of Bethel College in McKenzie, Tennessee, every July. The school consists of three five-day schools (Blocks). Those attending may go one, two, or three Blocks, often depending on time allowed away from work, courses needed, or personal choice. Some students go only one Block, others go two. And possibly one-third attend all three Blocks for a total of fifteen days of early morning to late night class attendance, worship, and fellowship. After attending all three Blocks, some persons are mentally, physically, and spiritually exhausted. Reactions from two past students may say it all. Just as Alfonso Marquez is quoted earlier in this book on this subject, another great quote comes from George Sprague, then a PAS student from

Kentucky. He testified, "One day I was so tired I tried to start my car with my dorm room key." While the Apostle Paul advised against "growing weary in well-doing" (Galatians 6:9), sometimes folks just "grow weary" and that's the way it is.

798

The Cumberland Presbyterian Church is a denomination with small churches. While there are large congregations, "large" for us is anything over 100 members. We have a few with 1,000 or more members, and several with 500 or more, but still the average active membership is around 50, maybe fewer than that. There are hundreds of churches with fewer than 50 members, including some below 25. This is true for most denominations although we hear of the mega-churches and other larger congregations more often than the smaller churches. Thomas H. Campbell, my father, had a heart for the small church. Whenever he was invited to preach in one of them, almost invariably his sermon would be taken from Luke 12:32: "Fear not, little flock, for it is your Father's good pleasure to give you the kingdom." A lot of very small churches are alive and vibrant, with an authentic witness in the community. Sometimes, the main thing they need is encouragement. That would be the message he would bring to a small congregation

799

This was posted on the refrigerator door of some friends:

DOGS HAVE MASTERS
CATS HAVE SUPPORT STAFF

800

The novelist Thomas Wolfe took four years to write one of his books and still was not finished. Finally the editor practically tore the manuscript from his hands. Even then, it took another year of work to come up with the finished product. Merrill Abbey in his 1964 book from Abingdon Press, Living Doctrine in a Vital Pulpit, reminds us preachers that we don't have four years between productions. We have seven days. Therefore we need dependable methods in order to be ready each week.

Chapter 801-850

"No Wasted Words"

801

In writing and speaking we so-called writers and speakers waste words. We use too many big words and too many adverbs and adjectives, especially in writing, when that is not the way we talk. Consider this example of how we might economize on words. Somebody asks about a river. I can say, "The river is <u>incomprehensively</u> wide." That is six syllables. Too much. Then I can say, "The river is <u>unbelievably</u> wide." That is five syllables. Still too much. Then I can say, "The river is <u>tremendously</u> wide." That is four syllables. Still too long. How about this? "The river is <u>terribly</u> wide." That is just three syllables. I'm sorry. Still too long a word. Then this, maybe? "The river is <u>very</u> wide." That's only two syllables. That should work. I'm sorry. Still too long. Then maybe this: "The river is <u>too</u> wide." Guess what. Still too much. Here is your better way: "The river is wide." How wide is that river? "Listen, that river is wiiiiiiide."

802

You have probably heard that there are three kinds of people in this world, those that are good at math, and those that aren't.

803

Preaching is sort of like radio. Words are important. Many of us remember radio shows like "Fibber McGee and Molly." We could sit in our living rooms and listen to that show and "see" what was happening. Although the actors were reading from a script and standing at their respective microphones, and the sound effects man was doing his part, still we could "see" the terrible, and predictable, crash when somebody would - despite Molly's warnings - open the hall closet door and things would fall out onto the floor with a big bang. And we could "see" Jack Benny on his show. The paper boy would come to collect the monthly 75 cents and Jack would say, "Just a minute." Then we would "see" him walk through one door and shut it behind him, then through another door and shut it behind him, all the time "seeing" him walk farther and farther down to his vault where he kept his money, the distance and darkness being more pronounced. Far, far down in the nether regions of his house, Jack would open his vault. We could "see" him turning the knob to the right combination. We could "see" him take out 75 cents, and then we could "see" him start that long walk back up to the front door where the paper boy waited. We "saw" Sergeant Preston of the Yukon" and his trusty dog, "On King, on you huskies!" And we "saw" Matt Dillon in "Gunsmoke." We knew he was tall. He sounded tall. To us he was tall. He was played by William Conrad, a short, rotund man almost as wide as tall, who later played "Cannon" on his own television detective show.

In preaching we have words at our disposal. We use words to draw and paint pictures. We tell stories. We try to help our listeners "see" what we are talking about. That is, of course, how we talk. "Do you understand what I am saying?" "Yes, I see now what you are saying," is our reply. Much of our preaching is an attempt to persuade and help listeners to "see" what we are trying to say.

ೞଓೞଓೞଓೞଓೞଓೞଓೞଓೞଓೞଓೞଓ

804

As I confessed earlier in this book, I am resistant to change. Political candidates run promising to bring "change." Church leaders say we need "change." Economists say we are living in an era of "change." Even the Christian faith meddles in that sort of thing: "You are going to have to 'change' your ways!" Doesn't anybody remember that in one of our most sacred hymns, "Abide With Me," one of the lines tells it like it is? Second verse: "Change and decay in all around I see…" The two are negatives we must combat. See what I mean? The only "change" I need or want is the "change" I get back when I put a twenty-dollar bill down while paying $7.87 for lunch. I join that long line of nay-sayers in history who looked with suspicion on a particular so-called musical instrument that was too big, too cumbersome, too complicated, and had a strange sound. The piano, common sense said, would never make it as a popular musical standard. Or consider the computer age. I would have joined others- if I could have found their e-mail address or the fax number - and protested all these new "thingamojigs" and "jibbertyswitches" that others called computers. It was simply too much. Stay with the tried and true typewriter, white out, and mimeograph machine (I just thought I would add the last). Or take the structure of the Cumberland Presbyterian Church. Years ago there was the General Assembly Planning Committee. But then in 1971 along came this special report by an outside consultant and the church moved to have a General Assembly Council and corresponding GA

Executive Committee. I was against that change. Later when the church decided to move away from the GA Executive Committee (The General Council had been discarded earlier), I was against the next thing believing that the GA Executive Committee was doing a good job. However, since I was the Moderator and had to name the Task Force to work up a new plan, I entered into the process. In 1993 a new entity called The General Assembly Council was born, and, although I thought the old GA Executive Committee was just fine, I went along. In 2006 the church decided to abandon the GA Council and naturally I was against that action, and was certainly against any and all proposals to alter the present course because I was of the opinion that the GA Council was doing its job well. Thus, the GA Ministry Council came into being, without my support. Not that I ever had a vote, for I was not a commissioner (delegate) to any of the meetings of the General Assembly that considered the change. I did write a small opinion paper on the issue and had a chance to distribute it to a committee at the General Assembly in 2007, although they said, "You can bring it and distribute it, but you cannot talk to us." I believe you may have a quick view of my opinions about "change." Where am I in all of this? It is like a train with a caboose. Thank goodness for cabooses. As the train for "change" is pulling out and speeding up, I manage to catch hold of the last rail on the caboose and get dragged along until I am able to hop aboard. Now, while we are on this tirade, let me tell you another dangerous word: <u>Progress</u>. But that's another item, maybe in my next book.

805

One author quoted another author so I will follow that example. The quote is an outstanding statement on the church. Frank G. Honeycutt in his book, <u>Preaching to Skeptics and Seekers</u> (Abingdon, 2001, p. 161) quoted from a book by Douglas John Hall entitled <u>Why Christian? For Those on the Edge of Faith</u> (Augsburg Fortress, 1992, p. 123). Here is Dr. Hall's look at the church:

"There is no such thing as a 'perfect' church, and the people who go about looking for such an ideal are bound to be disappointed. The Christian gospel isn't about the perfect church, it's about the perfect love of God, which none of us deserves, and from which we all fall short. The church is not a little bit of the world that has finally fixed up, righted. In a real way, the only thing that distinguishes church and world is that the church knows something about the world that it doesn't usually know about itself: that it is greatly loved."

806

Dr. Honeycutt in his book (see #805 above) mentions a song from a country band from Texas called the Lounge Lizards. The title of the song is "Jesus Loves Me, But He Can't Stand You." (p.155)

807

In a pastorate in my early years our church was in the suburbs and many of our members lived in the suburbs. City buses did not go to the suburbs. I heard one of our members say he was helping in a community effort to keep the buses from coming out to the suburbs. He was clear about the purpose of the move to prevent the city's rapid transit system from extending that far. It was so that the "riff-raff" and the poor and the other "scary" people might not move out there. It might lower housing values. Some of their children would be in the area schools. All sorts of reasons. I don't think the city ever expanded its transit service that far. What was my role as a pastor in that regard? I did and said nothing. Perhaps I should have done or said something.

808

I have become a fan of Martha Stewart. As a television hostess who helped homemakers cook and plant their gardens and tend to their flowers and use closet space wisely, she was an icon, as they say, in the business. Then she was tried and convicted of, I think, insider trading. Personally I always felt she got a raw deal in this, and others, men, especially, got off pretty much free and unpunished. Nevertheless, she went to prison for several months. She may have had private moments of depression, sadness, even shame. However, it is reported that even in prison she was a positive help to other inmates in helping them with their lives and relationships and hopes for the future. When she had served her time some thought she might be washed up and the work she had previously done would wilt away. But instead she picked right up with just about everything and continued with her profitable worldwide business that included a magazine, contracts with major stores, and her television shows. And she did this with a great spirit and attitude. The feeling seemed to be: I'm moving on. I will look ahead. I seem to recall she even went on shows like Letterman and talked about her experiences in prison. She was convicted. Martha Stewart paid the price. And now she is moving on. Sounds pretty good to me.

809

As a pastor I have had the privilege of welcoming persons into my study or office for what one might call counseling. I considered it more of a pastoral conversation that might include some counseling. It is always better when persons come of their own free will. One of the most awkward occasions was when a teenage boy in the church came to my office. His mother had made the appointment for him. He had been in some kind of trouble and, in general, seemed sort of rebellious. His mother thought a visit with the pastor might help. He arrived and sat down. And said nothing. I tried to start the conversation. Still nothing. Questions came from me and he answered with a yes or a no. He was obviously there against his will. I was keenly aware of that fact. I seem to recall that I openly acknowledged that I knew he was there against his will. Nothing was accomplished. I did learn from this - or experienced the reinforcement of what I think I already knew - that persons "sent" to talk to somebody against their will are not likely to be helped or be open to counsel. I really felt for the young teenager and told him I was as uncomfortable as he was. I once heard a minister say, "When you see a turtle on a stump, you know somebody put him there." I knew somebody put this young man there, and the results were negative.

810

Don't you think that every older generation believes that the one they grew up in was simpler, more orderly, and less dangerous than the present time? For one thing, progress (that dreaded word) has been swift and relentless over the years. We have to run to catch up. In addition, probably everyone tends to be nostalgic and exaggerate the previous generation's simplicity and orderliness. The farther away in years we get from childhood and youth the more we idealize those times. The Cumberland Presbyterian

Church was born out of the Great Revival of 1800. I recall reading something from around 1825 that lamented the lost zeal of previous times, just twenty five years earlier. God can help us to appreciate the past, learn from it, put it in perspective, and put our energies into living in the present. The hymn "A Charge to Keep I Have" (written by Charles Wesley) has this verse: "To serve the present age, My calling to fulfill; O may it all my powers engage to do my Master's will!" There are three verses in the hymnal I am using. This verse is the only one that ends with an exclamation point! Don't lament the present. Live it. Live now!

811

One item of the past that I wish would return is the simple, easy grocery aisle. You wanted Pringles Potato Chips, you went down the appropriate aisle and there they were. But now you have to search hard to find the "Original Pringles Potato Chips." You will, in your search, come upon Cheese Flavored, Bar-Be-Cue Flavored, Vinegar Flavored, Onion and Sour Cream Flavored, and, I exaggerate here, Chocolate Flavored, to name only a few. Hidden among all this stuff will be the "Original" Pringles. Or consider the breakfast cereal aisle. No, don't. It is too painful. All I want is Post Toasties. Or all I want is Raisin Bran. Good luck. You think Baskin-Robbins has a monopoly on flavors. Re-think that proposition. I know there is occasionally a decrying of the preponderance of denominations in church life. Well, I have a proposal to make. Let's first straighten out our grocery aisles before we get on with the churches.

812

There may be a place out there where people are trained to say such things as I will mention. A person does or says something mean or hurtful and you confront the individual. That person responds by saying, "I'm sorry you feel that way." Believe me, that is no apology. The individual speaking is trying to put the onus back onto the person who was hurt or offended: "I'm sorry you feel that way." What is <u>not</u> said is, "I'm sorry I said it or did it." In fact, it becomes no apology at all. Just the other day, some public official in one of our states uttered slanderous things about a national personality. If not libelous, the accusations were very close to being so. When confronted, the slanderer said, about the person being insulted, "I am sorry she feels that way." Nothing could be further from an apology than that. How about saying this: "I am deeply sorry for the things I said and sorry that I hurt and offended her." Now that's better.

813

In the book <u>The Hemingses of Monticello</u>, by Annette Gordon-Reed (W. W. Norton and Company, 2008, p. 100), I read where Thomas Jefferson as a young lawyer argued before a judge and lost the case. He was so discouraged and embarrassed over the loss, that he paid his client instead of accepting any payment from the one he represented! Do not. I repeat: Do <u>not</u> let this idea get out into the church. How many times have we preachers completely bombed, said nothing worth remembering, and brought embarrassment to God and the church? And, deep down, we knew that, whatever the honorarium or salary, <u>we</u> should pay <u>them</u> (the church) instead of the other way around. Forget you read this. Please. You did not see it here.

814

I don't know to whom to give credit for the following. It was found among the papers and poems and clippings our late Grandmother Grace Barefoot Estes ("Nanny Estes", Margaret Estes Campbell's mother and the mother of six other Estes children) left behind. There is no doubt that she lived this poem, with its acknowledged temptations and valiant goals. Here is "A Prayer As We Grow Older." Capitalized words are as they appear in the clipping.

> Dear Lord,
> keep me from the fatal habit of thinking
> that I must say something on every subject
> and on every occasion.
> Release me from craving to straighten out everybody's affairs.
> MAKE me thoughtful but not moody,
> helpful but not bossy.
> With my vast stores of endless wisdom,
> it seems a pity not to use it at all,
> but Thou knowest, Lord,
> that I want a few friends at the end.
> KEEP my mind from the recital of endless details,
> and give me wings to get to the point.
> SEAL my lips on my aches and pains.
> They are increasing every day,
> and my love for rehearsing them
> is becoming sweeter as the years go by.

I DARE not ask for grace to enjoy the tales of others,
but give me the patience to listen.
I DARE not ask for improved memory
but a growing humility and lessening of sureness
when my memory seems to clash with the memory of others.
TEACH me that glorious lesson that occasionally I may be mistaken.
GIVE me the ability to see things in unexpected places,
and talents in unexpected people,
and give me the grace to tell them so.
AMEN.

815

Henry Montes, a member of one of the churches I serve in northern Mississippi, had applied to be a member of the Gideons and was filling out the appropriate forms. One Sunday morning a few minutes before the worship service he had some papers I as his pastor was asked to sign. I didn't have anything to write with so he loaned me his pen. I signed everything and we moved immediately into the service. At its conclusion, after just about everybody had left the church building, Henry stayed behind. As I was also getting ready to leave, he still lingered. I had experienced moments like this in my long ministry. This usually meant a person had a serious question, or a concern, or an issue that needed concentrated attention. In this case it no doubt meant that Henry wanted to talk further about his ministry in the Gideons and how that might impact the congregation, community, and world. This would be his first venture into something like this and, knowing of my vast and varied experience as a pastor, preacher, teacher, and counselor, he knew he could come to me for pastoral and theological counsel and advice. I quickly shifted gears from the service just ended and focused on Henry and his concerns that would no doubt come up as we stood and talked. Now I could give my whole mind and heart to Henry's concerns - theological or personal. He spoke first, "You have my pen." "Oh," I replied, 'I forgot." He had, in fact, been awarded that pen the night before at a company dinner for outstanding achievement. He wanted his pen back. Another great moment in my vast and varied ministry.

On having an inflated sense of importance

816

Ulysses S. Grant was a great Civil War general and a good man. His presidency left much to be desired, largely because he trusted in too many people who had self-interest ahead of national interest. His personal memoir, written during a serious illness and published, largely through the influence of publicity generated by his friend Mark Twain, is considered one of the greatest military histories ever written. Grant, from all indications, was not musically inclined. Thomas Jefferson was known to hum or sing as he went about his work at Monticello. He also played the violin as did, later, his sons. Harry Truman and Richard Nixon were pretty good at the piano. Bill Clinton played a mean saxophone. He sang tenor in the Baptist church choir in Little Rock when he was governor of Arkansas. During his presidency he sang in the choir at Camp David on the Sundays he was there. A former chaplain at Camp David said the choir met for rehearsal in the middle of the week and, since Clinton could not be there for that, the director would place a copy of the Sunday morning anthem in the pew rack where the presidential family would be sitting. When the time came for the special music, Clinton would rise and come forward with the rest of the choir and would "sight-read" the sheet music and sing with the others. But Grant evidently did not play an instrument nor did he sing. When someone inquired as to whether he knew any songs, he answered, "Yes, I know two songs. One is 'Yankee Doodle' and the other isn't."

817

A former staff member in the Justice Department who blew the whistle on the wiretapping of American citizens during the George W. Bush administration, was asked if he thought those responsible for this and other crimes should be prosecuted. He said yes. He said that some will say, "All that is past. We need to move ahead." His reply: "I was a prosecutor for several years. Every crime I tried happened in the past. All crimes that are prosecuted have been in the past," said Thomas Tamm.

818

I heard a minister/counselor on the radio talking about grief, hard times, loneliness, and loss during the Christmas season. She said it was good to talk to others and to be honest about what bothers and burdens us. Then she said, "Share, but don't compare."

819

A prominent, convenient parking place at the Cumberland Presbyterian Church of Germantown, Tennessee, has this sign:

>RESERVED FOR THE
>SUNDAY SCHOOL
>BIBLE TRIVIA
>CHAMPION

820

Reverend James E. Clarke was a pivotal figure in Cumberland Presbyterian history as the nineteenth century turned into the twentieth, a little over a hundred years ago. First as a pastor in a church in Russellville, Kentucky, and later at another in Nashville, Tennessee, and then as editor of The Cumberland Presbyterian, the official magazine of the denomination, he was influential in the church. Early on in talks about union with the Presbyterian Church USA he was against the idea. Later he was for it and as editor closed down the pages of the magazine to those opposed to union. Therefore, he "went with the union" of 1906, when the Cumberland Presbyterian Church voted to merge with the Presbyterian Church USA. Those who stayed in the Cumberland denomination had a long, uphill climb to bring the church back to anything close to what it was and then to exceed its previous accomplishments. James Clarke later published his autobiography. In it he referred occasionally to the Cumberland Presbyterians, his former church. In A Life Testimony (no publication date, but probably sometime in the 1920s) he had some nice things to say about his former denomination (as opposed to some harsh words of criticism in the magazine to those who decided to perpetuate the church after 1906). He defended those former Cumberlands now in the PCUSA denomination. There was a controversy brewing in the larger church and people were wondering how the newest ministers and members of the church were going to respond to certain issues.

Clarke refers to himself in his book as "he" throughout. So in pages 42 and 43 he wrote:

"At the most critical General Assembly (of the PCUSA) he was called into an important but informal conference which wanted help in changing the attitude of the commissioners from his part of the country. He told them that most Cumberland Presbyterians needed no changing; that liberty of belief was the demand that brought the Cumberland Presbyterian Church into existence, and led to their much earlier revision of the Confession; that they had always emphasized a vital spiritual life, rather than the details of a creed; that they had never had a heresy trial in their history; that when other churches divided on Civil War issues they remained as one church, though on both sides of the line, and that the paper which they read (of which Clarke was editor) had always sought to develop spiritual vitality, rather than dogmatic rigidity."

It makes you kind of proud to read the above, if you have Cumberland Presbyterian ties of any kind, or know somebody who does.

821

Pontius Pilate gets "bad press" most of the time from us Christians, and well he should. It doesn't help his standing that when Jesus was brought before him by the crowd, all this high official could say about Jesus was, "I find no fault in this man" (Luke 23:4). Nothing positive about Jesus. No good things to say. Just, "I find no fault in this man." Years ago I read that the Coptic Church (in Egypt perhaps??) proclaimed Pontius Pilate to be a saint largely on the basis of this statement: "I find no fault in this man." Sadly, we sometimes use the same reasoning about things. "Well, I didn't think there was anything wrong in doing this or that, or saying this or that." There probably were few if any parts of the consideration that were <u>right</u> but at least we found nothing wrong. Is that the highest standard or can we do better?

822

The more I read up on Cumberland Presbyterian history, the more I learn of the achievements and "firsts" that so many accomplished. In a collection of biographies of ministers of the denomination who lived during the early nineteenth century, Richard Beard wrote of one Jacob Lindley (1774-1857). I learned in reading this portion of Beard's work (pp. 228-237) that Reverend Mr. Lindley, just a few years before coming into the Cumberland Presbyterian Church was a Presbyterian who founded and became the first president of Ohio University in Athens, Ohio (<u>The Writings of Richard Beard</u>, Matthew Gore, editor, Boardman Books, Ellendale, Tennessee, 2007). There undoubtedly is more history to learn. For example, I read in a little book entitled <u>Our</u>

Senior Soldiers (Cumberland Presbyterian Board of Publication, Nashville, Tennessee, 1915, pp. 64-67) that one of our nineteenth-century and early twentieth-century ministers, J. L. Goodnight, was president of West Virginia University in Morgantown from 1895 to 1897. While there he brought the school to university status and doubled its student enrollment. He then became president of Lincoln University in Illinois, a Cumberland Presbyterian-related school. Among his other accomplishments were several pastorates including Waynesburg, Pennsylvania; Covington, Kentucky; and Nashville, Tennessee; as well as attendance at the Pan-Presbyterian Alliance at Belfast, Ireland in 1884. He graduated from Cumberland University in Lebanon, Tennessee, and later did postgraduate work in the University of Edinburgh as well as Jena University in Germany, He was Stated Clerk of the General Assembly from 1907 to his death in 1914. These are some of the interesting facts learned while reading Cumberland Presbyterian history.

823

You sometimes run across some interesting sentences in your casual reading. The legendary scholar, Alexander Cruden, compiled Cruden's Concordance (Philadelphia, Toronto: The John C. Winston Company, 1949), a valuable source, for over two hundred and fifty years, for tracking down Bible verses and key words in the Old Testament and New Testament. In the Preface, the publishers tell of the author's life and work. One paragraph has the following:

"Its author, Alexander Cruden, was born in 1701 at Aberdeen, where he was educated at the grammar school and Marischal College. He was intended for the Presbyterian ministry, but ill-health, which for a time affected his mind, led him to take up teaching at the age of twenty-one." What? Say that again! "Ill-health, which for a time affected his mind, led him to take up teaching..." I always thought it worked the other way around, from teaching to preaching, when your mind was "affected"!

824

I was the new pastor of the new church just starting on Fort Worth's south side, just at the city limits. We wanted to publish news of the church fellowship that had been going for about a year by the time I arrived in May of 1965. So that summer I began to place different articles in a small town suburban paper called The Everman Times. We were meeting in a borrowed Methodist Church in Everman, just two or three miles from where we would build in Fort Worth. As we got closer to moving into our new facilities, I continued the articles and at the same time visited in the different housing developments in the area. In early 1966 (we would occupy our new facilities in late February) I had an article plus my picture in the Everman paper. I was knocking on doors, ringing doorbells, speaking to people all around. The day that people got their Everman paper in the mail, I was out there going from street to street again. I rang the doorbell of a family and the wife/mother answered. As she opened the door and I told her who I was and what I was representing, she let out something between a cry and a scream. It turns out that just as I rang the doorbell she was finishing reading the most recent article that had my picture beside it. And now the very one - yours truly - in the picture stood at the door. Talk about perfect timing! As it developed, she (the daughter of a Cumberland Presbyterian minister, by the way) and her husband and two children joined that church. He became one of our early elders and the entire family was active. I will not dignify this story by suggesting that, for her, in that moment, the word became flesh.

825

The Bank of Rogersville, in Missouri, was advertising on the radio. They said: "Other banks have Branches but we have Roots in this town."

826

Our grandmother on our mother's side, Grace Barefoot Estes, went into a nursing home at her own request around the age of 85 and stayed for about ten years until her death. She was a "people person" as they describe individuals these days. She almost immediately met just about everybody, started leading the Bible study group, and, in general, livened up the place. Our mother, her oldest child, tells us that when "Nanny" went to the nursing home the meals left a little to be desired, especially the cornbread. When Nanny complained more than once about it, the staff invited her to the kitchen to show the folks there how to make good cornbread, which she did, and henceforth that portion of the meals was much better. Sometimes you just have to speak up.

827

Missouri is the "Show-Me" state, as just about everybody knows. I have been privileged to be a member of Missouri Presbytery of the Cumberland Presbyterian Church for almost a decade and a half. What a lot of people do not know is that there were several characters in the Bible that were from Missouri. Consider Moses, who in Exodus 33:18, said to God, "Show me thy glory." In John 20:25, we have another from Missouri. After the resurrection most of the disciples were gathered together and the risen Lord met them. However, Thomas was not present. When later his colleagues tried to tell him about their wonderful experience, he replied, "Unless I see in his hands the print of the nails, and place my hands in his side, I will not believe." In other words: "Show me!" And I have no doubt but what the writer of the Letter of James was from Missouri. The entire letter is, in effect, saying, "Show me." Show me your faith by your works. I have heard you talk over and over and over about your faith. Do you have any good deeds or sacrificial service to "show" for it? "Show me."

828

Funeral processions always pose some interesting situations, especially as cars are pulling into the cemetery. More than once, I have conducted a graveside service where all the family is gathered together and several friends are there, too, but the cars are still streaming in. Do we wait or go on? The funeral director and I check glances and, seemingly, at the right time, the brief burial ceremony takes place. However, even at that time, some folks are just getting out of their cars and others are still parking their cars a very long walk from the gathering. Evidently this is not a new problem. Upon the death of Thomas Jefferson, only a graveside service was planned. He would be buried on the grounds of his beloved Monticello, which was situated at the top of a mountain. This meant that people coming up from Charlottesville and other places would have a very long walk. There was a misunderstanding, and some conflict, among family members and the minister as to when to start the service. A small group was present from the town, but others were on their way, it was reported. Some wanted to wait for the others. Some wanted to go ahead. It was decided to proceed with the service. The book <u>Twilight at Monticello: The Final Years of Thomas Jefferson</u>, by Alan Pell Crawford (Random House, 2008), p. 245, tells the story. The service was read, the coffin was lowered into the ground, and the grave was filled up. Then the family returned to the house. "The townspeople (those who had gotten there in time for the service) started back down the mountain, where they met the official procession, about fifteen hundred strong, trudging through the rain. 'They were sorely disappointed,' a participant said, 'and in some cases angered' to learn that the ceremonies were over. One young man who had arrived in time to witness the burial, one whose sensibility was so unlike Jefferson's as to signal the passing of one age and the dawn of another, was a morbidly sensitive seventeen-year-old student from Richmond who entertained his fellows with satirical verse. This was Edgar Allan Poe."

829

I read of a new classification for some church members. It was in the newsletter of the First Cumberland Presbyterian Church of Knoxville, Tennessee. The new label that could be put beside some names is "FBP." That means For Burial Purposes. The newsletter asked, "Are you a member of First Church in name only?" Unfortunately, we all have seen instances where a person's obituary mentions membership in a certain church when for decades no one ever saw that person at church. This was surely an occasion for being classified as "FBP."

830

Earth Day is almost forty years old. I was in the Kansas City area in the spring of 1970 for a wedding and heard about it on the radio. This was the first year of such an observance. The announcer took this a bit further when he said, "Since this is Earth Day, take a Clod to lunch." I have had several invitations to lunch on Earth Day.

831

A prominent, nationally-known minister who received much publicity when called on to be one of the ministers to lead prayer at the January, 2009, inauguration of Barack Obama, once listed two reasons for a wife to leave a marriage. They were Adultery and Abandonment. I don't know why he left out another: Abuse.

832

Ronald Reagan coined a phrase regarding U.S. relations with other countries on nuclear arms reduction agreements and other high voltage issues that involved treaties, understandings, or joint resolutions: "Trust, then verify." On a much lower scale, I have been doing that for years. As a minister and worship leader, I have every week prepared an order of worship and selected the hymns. When looking up a particular musical selection in the index, I would see that it was on page 75, or page 153, or some other. But that has never been enough: I must turn to page 75, or page 153, or some other, to verify that such is the case. I don't know why but I have felt the need to practice that routine and make sure that what the index says is true. It just makes me feel better. But I do trust you, never forget. Later I will verify, if you don't mind.

833

What do we do if peace breaks out? It can be exhilarating for some, exasperating for others. This is what happened in World War I around Christmas time. In a book entitled Silent Night: The Story of the World War I Christmas Truce (The Free Press, New York and other locations, 2001), author Stanley Weintraub tells of a time when German, British, French, and Belgian soldiers dropped their arms to bury their dead, as was the custom. But they also serenaded each other with Christmas carols on Christmas Eve, and broke bread, exchanged addresses, and played soccer. This was most frustrating and aggravating to the generals on both sides. The soldiers were ordered back to their trenches with mandates to shoot to kill, but they aimed their guns to the sky harmlessly. It is very frustrating when peace breaks out. We are not used to that. We must demonize and dehumanize the "enemy" - this makes killing them easier and less of a burden on the conscience. And, by all means, do not get to know them personally.

834

Lay leaders of churches might flinch at the following, but there may be some truth to the thought. A pastor visited with another pastor and told his story. The first had served a congregation for a number of years, and, so far as known, nothing had changed and no problems had arisen. But, almost out of the blue, there arose within the church the drive to see the pastor leave. What went wrong? What was the matter? When confronted, some of the lay leaders said, "Well, the pastor isn't doing this, and the pastor isn't doing that, and is doing too much of this and not enough of that, and visits these but does not visit those," and so on, and so forth. The second pastor, upon hearing of these developments, gave an analogy. "Let us suppose a person has a car and with each passing year the car, while one year older, does a very good job. Six, seven, eight years pass, and the car is still doing just fine. But, almost out of the blue, the owner decides there is a need for a new car. Feeling that way, the owner subsequently dreams up a rationale for such a conclusion. The arm rest on the driver's side is not all that secure. The steering wheel is slick and sometimes my hands get sweaty. The air conditioning seems slow to start working. The heater works too fast and it gets hot quickly in the car. The color of the exterior leaves something to be desired. Even a new muffler doesn't seem to work well at all. The front seats do not adjust all that well for different drivers any more. The radio has too much static at times. And so on, and so forth." Which is to say, when people decide there is a need for a change, no amount of reasoning or logic or even a look at evidence to the contrary matters. The change will take place. And when it is time for a new car, it is time for a new car, regardless of how well the current vehicle is doing. The same with pastors.

835

I think congregations want several things from their preachers when sermons are given each Sunday. Two of them are <u>structure</u> and <u>clarity</u>. As to structure, it is always helpful if the minister early on says, "First," and then follows that with a section of the sermon, and later, "Second," with some more of the message, and, possibly, "Third," and so it would go. By the way, stopping at "Third" might well be the best plan. However, if you are like I am, if you hear "First," you feel like there will be a "Second," and if there is not you wait and wait and wait in vain. You begin to say to yourself: "The preacher has spent twenty-five minutes on 'First' and where in the world is 'Second' or did I miss something?" Your greatest fear is that if it takes twenty five minutes for "First" we are going to be here all day and into the night. If you are preaching, and you say "First," for heaven's sake, come forth - eventually - with a "Second" and possibly a "Third." Otherwise, don't make such promises. As to clarity, small words, short sentences, few adjectives, and fewer adverbs will contribute to that goal, as well as simple ideas and easy-to-understand concepts. Abstractions should be few. Concrete examples should be many. Your congregation will be grateful.

836

I am always needing a better resume' just for the principle of the thing. I have one more thing my references can say about me: "He has been around the block." In August of 2008 I spent almost a week in the home of Sid and Lita Swindle in Tampa, Florida. I was there to teach some Cumberland Presbyterian-related courses to their pastor, Mike Laperche, who was serving Christ Cumberland Presbyterian Church in suburban Lutz. After a day or two when others drove me around, the Swindles thought it was time for me to launch out on my own. Sid gave specific directions on how to get out of the neighborhood and onto the main highway. "You go out the driveway, drive in front of the house, turn left on the next street, and then head straight for the highway that leads to Lutz," he said. He gave me the keys to the van, and I got in. I backed out of the driveway, onto the street in front of the house. He was in the front yard helping to get me on the right track, but I did not pay heed as he was waving me to turn left and I instead turned right. I therefore drove in the opposite direction. I turned right at the first opportunity, then right at the next opportunity, because nothing looked right. When I turned right a third time, I drove in front of a house that looked familiar and there was a man in the front yard waving at me. "I think I know him," I said to myself. "He looks familiar." It was Sid. I had gone around the block. He then waved me toward the left turn and this time I watched him and followed his directions. However, this does add to my resume'. It can now be said when somebody asks about Tom Campbell, "I know him. Listen. Let me tell you. He's been around the block."

837

Some of the fuss over women preachers and elders and teachers in churches has faded, but a few churches still make restrictions on this, if not total prohibitions against women holding positions of responsibility in churches. The phobia and fear and irrational thoughts that create these kinds of roadblocks to Christian service for all people are not new. One of my favorite stories of a man who had real problems with women in society was Abimelech of Old Testament fame. In Judges, chapter 9, there was a battle going on. Abimelech led some armed forces into Thebez and tried to overpower the people. There was a tower in the city, so the story goes, "and all the people fled to it, all the men and women, and shut themselves in; and they went to the roof of the tower." Here comes the real story now. "And Abimelech came to the tower, and fought against it, and drew near to the door of the tower to burn it with fire. And a certain woman threw an upper millstone upon

Abimelech's head, and crushed his skull. Then he called hastily to the young man his armor-bearer, and said to him, 'Draw your sword and kill me, lest men say of me, "A woman killed him."' And his young man thrust him through, and he died" (Joshua 9:51-54). I don't blame Abimelech. Imagine the writing on his headstone at the cemetery: "Killed by a woman." Just think of the embarrassment, the humiliation, the mockery. Even in anticipation of death and the hereafter, he could not come to terms with this item.

838

Lending a book to somebody else is a gracious gesture, but can have negative results. The owner may never get the book back. I have been eager for friends or students to read certain books and have handed them over as <u>temporary</u> reading material. only to have to wait a very long time to retrieve it or, worse, never to possess it again and find that the transaction was <u>permanent</u>. I have sinned on the other side, too. A minister once gave some one-word advice about lending books: "Don't." In an old book on my shelf - the book once belonged to the late E. Thach Shauf, a renowned Cumberland Presbyterian minister, some of whose books were given to Memphis Theological Seminary, whose library staff offered a few to folks at cut rates - are these words inside the front cover:

> "This book, if borrowed by a friend,
> Right welcome shall he be.
> To read, to study, not to lend,
> But to return to me.
>
> Not that imparted knowledge doth
> Diminish learning's store,
> But books I find, if often lent,
> Return to me no more."

839

I once heard of a church-related college where in one of the Bible classes the professor at the beginning of the class each day would have a different student read a portion of scripture and lead in the morning prayer. It so happened that on a certain day one young man was supposed to give a report on a book he was supposed to have read but had not. So not having his assignment ready, he volunteered to do the scripture reading and prayer. His selection was Psalm 119... which has 176 verses!!!

840

When weddings or other special programs are held in church sanctuaries, sometimes the pulpit is moved, as are the communion table, and the baptismal font. Fortunately, in most cases, when the service or program is over, those items are returned to their rightful places. I fear that some would move the pulpit out and never return it if they had their way. This seems to speak to the lessening importance of preaching in some minds. Or it might mean that preaching takes place, but the pulpit as furniture is "in the way." Or it could be a way of saying that, since our pastor doesn't stand behind a pulpit anyway, even when it is there, we may as well take it from the scene. It could also mean a diminished understanding and appreciation of worship and its elements. With any of these reasons there is cause for concern. The sermon is not performance. It is not part of a show. It is to be delivered from the sacred desk called the pulpit as the one behind it proclaims the message of God as specifically presented in a particular scriptural text. The focus should not be on the preacher as much as on the message. The one proclaiming the message should not even be tempted to strut around the stage or make a big thing of "connecting" with the people by avoiding or removing the pulpit. A few complaints are heard every now and then about the placement of the pulpit, how high it is. It is elevated so the people can see the preacher. When the preacher wanders around the stage or podium area they are likely not to be able to do that.

841

A vivid description of the pulpit's place in the sanctuary in one person's view is seen in Moby Dick, by Herman Melville (Boston: L. C. Page & Company, Publishers, 1892), pp. 40-42. The "Whaleman's Chapel," near the sea, was where whalers and their families worshiped. Melville writes: "Like most old-fashioned pulpits, it was a very lofty one, and since a regular stairs to such a height would, by its long angle with the floor, seriously contract the already small areas of the chapel, the architect, it seemed, had acted upon the hint of Father Mapple (the preacher), and finished the pulpit without stairs, substituting a perpendicular side ladder, like those used in mounting a ship from a boat at sea." The preacher climbed the rope ladder and, upon reaching the pulpit, pulled the rope up after him.

Melville goes on: "Can it be that by that act of physical isolation, (Father Mapple) signifies his spiritual withdrawal for the time from all outward worldly ties and connections?"

In fact, the pulpit area, Melville continues, is like a ship. "Its panelled front was in the likeness of a ship's bluff bows, and the Holy Bible rested on a projecting piece of scroll work, fashioned after a ship's fiddle-headed beak.

"What could be more full of meaning? for the pulpit is ever this earth's foremost part; all the rest comes in its rear; the pulpit leads the world. From thence it is the storm of God's quick wrath is first descried, and the bow must bear the earliest brunt. From thence it is the God of breezes fair or foul is first invoked for favourable winds. Yes, the world's a ship on its passage out, and not a voyage complete; and the pulpit is its prow."

842

The next chapter in <u>Moby Dick</u> gives the sermon Father Mapple preached. It was about Jonah. The message begins this way: "Shipmates, this book containing only four chapters, four yarns, is one of the small strands in the mighty cable of the Scriptures. Yet what depths of the soul does Jonah's deep sea-line sound! What a pregnant lesson to us is this prophet! What a noble thing is that canticle in the fish's belly!" It gets even better than that as one reads along. It is a powerful sermon about Jonah's attempted escape from the call of God and his sojourn in the ship with others as well as his adventures in the belly of the fish. One would not go wrong in reading this sermon in a morning worship service, giving full credit, of course, to Herman Melville and urging listeners to read it for themselves. Would that I (and all of us preachers) could preach with "Father Mapple-power!"

843

A county sheriff in one of our states - as with all such sheriffs in the state - received money each year to feed inmates in his jail. The law says whatever money is not needed for food, the sheriff gets to keep, no questions asked. He withheld good and plentiful food from the inmates. They were skinny, hungry, and helpless to do anything about it until lawyers got hold of the case. A lawsuit was filed against the sheriff. Over a period of two years, the sheriff had accumulated for himself over $200,000 of unused food money while withholding nourishing meals from those incarcerated in his county jail. The judge sentenced the sheriff to one night in the jail and the sheriff promised to do better. There is no report on what the sheriff's meals in the jail consisted of while he was locked up.

This raises some serious questions about us preachers. What kind of nourishment are we providing for our flocks? Do our sermon-meals consist of dependable, enriching, and nourishing spiritual food, or do we serve instead some gospel-lite, easily-thrown-together so-called spiritual food that leaves our listeners malnourished when the sermon is over? God gives us an abundance of spiritual food to share with others. How well do we do in the feeding of the sheep?

844

I was getting started with Calvin Miller's latest book which is entitled <u>Preaching: The Art of Narrative Exposition</u> (Baker Books, 2006), when on page 19 I came upon a quote from the late Malcolm Muggeridge from his essay entitled <u>Fourth Temptation of Christ</u>. Muggeridge alleged that Jesus's fourth temptation was thirty minutes of prime-time television.

845

Humility is an elusive trait in some preachers. Remember that once a week people stream by and shake the ministerial hand and compliment (sincere or not) the one who just proclaimed the message from the raised pulpit. I have often wondered how hard it is for those to stay humble whose bus or outdoor sign or stationery says "_____ Evangelistic Association" or "_____Christian Ministries" or "_____ _____ World Outreach, Inc." with their name filling in the blank. More than a few television ministries announce the name of the preacher and not the name of the congregation in their publicity. Thank goodness I am humble... and PROUD OF IT!!!

846

Many churches have "greeters" and they are good at their job. I trust this does not let other church members off the hook, for they, too, are the unofficial "greeters" for the church. Anyway, I rejoice to see that a church where I formerly served as pastor has its official "greeters." I am glad they have found the key to doing that at that rather large church. We didn't manage to have them when I was there, although, fortunately, there were many great people who took it upon themselves to make sure first-time visitors, and other visitors, were made to feel welcome and had help in finding classrooms, restrooms, and the nursery. What am I talking about? The problem, in my mind, was that the church facility has thirteen entrances. Count 'em! Thirteen entrances! Where should we have placed our "greeters"? I never could figure out a way to contribute to that discussion. Regarding the sanctuary, there are only three entrances, so perhaps these days the "greeters" linger around that area most of the time.

847

Somewhere I read that the work of a pastor is both "very public and very private." So it is. We are called to proclaim the good news, from the rooftops, if necessary, but also commissioned to maintain confidentiality in our personal conversations with persons. We preach our sermons before multitudes, well, maybe just crowds, well, more likely several people, fully remembering that we prepared for that public proclamation in the quiet solitude of office or study. We are "people of the community" who are to meet and greet people easily and naturally, but are prone to desire aloneness just as much as crowds as we contemplate life and death and other concerns. We are "people-people" but also, supposedly, people of prayer. Most of the time we can deal with these distinctions. My greatest, my absolute greatest, regrets in ministry are those moments (rare, but still painful) when I have betrayed a confidence, either inadvertently or by mistake or some other reason. When these blunders have occurred, I feel myself to be a total failure in the ministry. Nothing is more sacred than confidentiality. We preachers are public persons, but we are also private persons, and what we hear in private is not for public consumption. We should never cross that line.

848

Sign in front of a facility housing a congregation of the Church of the Nazarene in Clarksville, Tennessee:

> KEEP THE FAITH
> BUT NOT FROM OTHERS

849

It depends on what part of the Bible you are reading, as well as the conditions under which the words were written, as well as the attitude of the writer (in the following cases, the prophet), as well as the spirit of the times, as well as the context. Two glaring contrasts, to illustrate the above, are in the Old Testament books Isaiah and Micah, on the one hand, and Joel in the other.

Isaiah 2:4 says, "He shall judge between the nations, and shall arbitrate for many peoples; they shall beat their swords into plowshares, and their spears into pruning hooks; nation shall not lift up sword against nation, neither shall they learn war any more." The book of the prophet Micah says exactly the same thing, but follows it with: "But they shall all sit under their own vines and under their own fig trees, and no one shall make them afraid; for the mouth of the Lord of hosts has spoken."

The prophet Joel, however, saw it differently. He envisioned a world where things were just the opposite. Joel 3:10 says, "Proclaim this among the nations: Prepare war, stir up the warriors. Let all the soldiers draw near, let them come up. Beat your plowshares into swords, and your pruning hooks into spears; let the weakling say, 'I am a warrior.'"

850

Contrasting approaches, such as the above, occur today. Dr. Fred Craddock's first book on preaching was entitled As One Without Authority (Abingdon, 1971, 1974, 1979). It introduced forcefully the idea of inductive preaching, among other good things. Later, another homiletics professor, wrote a book entitled As One With Authority (Bristol Books, 1989). As I read the latter, I felt throughout that this was an almost blatant attempt to put down, and almost belittle, the former. One day in the Kansas City airport I came upon still another homiletics professor. He said he had read both books. I asked him about the latter while also expressing my opinion that it was too much of an unspoken, yet obvious, criticism of the former. The latter, written toward the end of the career of that author, was, in the words of the one I met in the airport, "a terrible benediction" to an otherwise distinguished preaching and teaching career.

Chapter 851-892

"The Kitchen Sink and the Adding Machine"

851

Besides the traditional ways of accepting a request to fulfill some assignment, such as "Yes," or "I accept," one could employ the following, learned (and used) over the years:

"As the kitchen sink once said, 'I am at your disposal.'"

"As the adding machine once said, 'You can count on me.'"

༄༅༄༅༄༅༄༅༄༅༄༅༄༅༄༅༄༅༄༅

852

The scriptures wisely leave a lot to our imaginations. What is left unsaid becomes as important as what is said. Take, for example, the book of Jonah, the end of Chapter 2. Jonah has run away from the call of God, has boarded a ship, has been thrown into the sea, has been swallowed by a big fish, and has prayed a fervent prayer while inside the belly of the fish. There follow these words in 2:10: "Then the Lord spoke to the fish, and it spewed Jonah out upon the dry land."

Think about that. This man who has been inside the belly of a fish, with stomach acid and digestive juices and different food particles floating around, is "spewed out upon the dry land." It looks to me like the fish could have had enough courtesy and forethought to "spew" Jonah out in the water so he could wash off. But, no, he vomited him up onto the dry land - sand, dirt, more sand, more dirt - so that now Jonah, with all the sticky, smelly stuff from the fish's stomach on him, now wallows in the dirt and sand and it all gets mixed up and icky and smelly and filthy and dirty and absolutely terrible. Jonah smells to high heaven in all four directions and no one can stand to come close to him until he washes himself off. Then comes Chapter 3.

Chapter 3 of the Book of Jonah starts out this way: "The word of the Lord came to Jonah a second time." Question: Do you figure the Lord waited until Jonah got rinsed off or did "the word of the Lord" come to him right then and there amid the sand and the dirt and the worst stench ever? We don't know. The Lord, I am sure, was so determined to get to Jonah and give him that second chance that it probably did not make any difference. However, it is safe to assume, I think, that before Jonah set out for Nineveh he took a bath. A long, hot bath. Twice. Maybe three times, for good measure.

853

I got my come-uppance one time and it taught me a lesson. I was talking with a woman who was grieving because the only child of her and her husband, a daughter, had left her husband after several years of marriage. It was a shock to everyone. The woman was telling me about it and talking very animatedly as she was very upset. Then I replied, "I know how you feel." To which she answered sharply, "No, you don't." And she was right. I didn't know how she felt.

854

My younger brother Paul, many years ago, told me strongly and definitely that he wasn't going to be a "yes man" anymore.

He said, "Ask me if I have quit being a 'yes man.'"

"Have you quit being a 'yes man'?"

"Yes."

855

Sign outside of a United Methodist Church in Memphis:

> LIFE IS A JOURNEY
> LET FAITH BE YOUR GUIDE

856

Richard Stoll Armstrong, a minister in the Presbyterian Church (USA), taught evangelism at Princeton Theological Seminary and wrote several books on the subject. A notable quotation out of <u>The Pastor-Evangelist in the Parish</u> (Westminster John Knox Press, 1990, p. 206) is the following: "A distinction has to be made between the offense of the gospel and the offensiveness of the witness." On that same page Armstrong wrote: "The integrity of the witness has nothing to do with the authority of the scriptures, but it has much to do with the credibility of the witness." Another connection I have with Richard Armstrong is that, as a loyal fan of the Baltimore Orioles, I learned that before entering the ministry, he was the public relations director of that baseball team. On our first trip to Baltimore to see the Orioles, back in 1991, Linda and I stayed in the home of old friends Barry and Judy Baker of Newark, Delaware, just about sixty miles from Baltimore. The day before we arrived at their house, they had gone to an evangelism workshop at their local Presbyterian church. Their leader? Dick Armstrong. In informal conversations they mentioned we were coming up and would go over to see the Orioles. Dr. Armstrong responded excitedly (they said) and told of his earlier employment by the team. Later at a missions/evangelism conference in the Memphis area where he was one of the guest leaders, he and I had chances to talk in detail about our common baseball interests.

857

William Sloane Coffin was a distinguished minister who, as chaplain at Yale University, and later as pastor of the famed Riverside Church in New York City, was noted for his powerful sermons. After his death, Westminster John Knox Press published The Collected Sermons of William Sloane Coffin: The Riverside Years, Volume I (Randy Wilson Coffin, 2008). He had a knack for succinct, probing sentences, such as the following, chosen almost at random out of the book:

"Duty calls only when gratitude fails to prompt." P. 355

"Preachers should be explorers as well as pulpit pounders. The energy which abounds in many preachers, that glandular energy which so frequently is mistaken for the Holy Spirit - such energy is no substitute for wisdom." P. 356

"From Paul to Fosdick, all the great preachers of the Christian church have tried to engage the hearts and to inform the minds of their hearers. They have tried to link love with learning, piety with intellect, knowing that aroused but uninformed Christians are as dangerous as quack physicians." P. 356

"There is no smaller package in all the world than that of a man all wrapped up in himself." p. 405

858

The modern telephone system is remarkable. Phone booths and, therefore, pay phones, are just about obsolete. Now, in some instances, people can see each other as they talk. They can drive in their cars and push buttons that help them "be on the phone."

Cell phones once were rare. Now they are plentiful. It looks like everybody has one. I remember in the 1950s when we had party lines. The Campbells and the Bakers shared one. We were 20-W and they were 20-J. If we wanted to make a call and picked up the phone and heard voices, we quickly hung up and waited awhile. And vice versa. However, one time we experienced what might have been one of the first "conference calls." My 20-W and Barry Baker's 20-J, by advance planning, got on the phone after one of us called Billy Webb, who lived down the street. We were juniors in high school and were going to sing as a trio at a banquet that evening. We practiced over the phone. While this may not have been the first "conference call" in McKenzie, Tennessee, I'm guessing it was the first "conference song."

859

Julius Caesar ("I came, I saw, I conquered.") has nothing on church business meetings. We are sometimes just like him. How? General Assembly, Presbytery, Conference, Diocese, Regional, and Association meetings (the previous words cover several denominations) consider committee or board reports and then act on them. Usually, the motion is to "concur in the report and adopt its recommendations." So part of our work is to "concur" in the report - agree with it, approve it. We "concur." So a delegate reporting back to home base about a very agreeable meeting could honestly say, "I came, I saw, I concurred." Eat your heart out, Julius! I'm sorry. It just had to be told.

860

Do you occasionally feel intimidated by what the Bible says? For example, those reports about "the voice of the Lord" leave me floundering. Old Testament and New Testament alike speak of "the voice of the Lord." I am here to announce that I have never heard the voice of the Lord, if by that you mean the verbal intonations we normally associate with "voice." A person reading about this in the Bible might have a sense of being "left out" because of not having had that experience. Does the frequent mentioning of it in the Bible mean that the "voice of the Lord" was literally out there in those days? Why is it not now? When CNN was in its early stages, it needed someone to announce, periodically, the name of the network. Those in charge chose the great actor James Earl Jones. He inquired as to what they had in mind, and they replied, "Well, just be the voice of God." I can't think of anyone in the world who could come any closer to our pre-conceived notions of how that might sound than James Earl Jones, when he would proclaim, "THIS... IS CNN!"

But what about the issue of hearing the voice of the Lord? The answer: We hear with our hearts, not our ears. There may be some folks who have heard God with their ears. Some of them are on the third floor of your closest psychiatric hospital. Others who have taken too much medication might tell you that, too. In fact, there might be some, in very bad shape, who say they hear many voices, and inform you THEY are the voice of the Lord!

But we listen with our hearts.

861

Sign outside a small church near Cullman, Alabama, that admits to having limited financial resources:

> OUR PARKING LOT IS GRAVEL
> BUT OUR FAITH IS SOLID

862

Sherry Warren grew up Baptist, is still a member of the Baptist church, and has been playing the piano for her northern Mississippi congregation for over forty years. Across the street is a small Presbyterian church where I have been preaching at 9:00 every Sunday morning for twelve years and counting. Because of the early Presbyterian service and the 11:00 Baptist service, Sherry plays for both churches and has been helping the Presbyterians for a long time. A few months ago she had heart surgery and as my wife and I visited with her one day in the hospital we met some of her Baptist friends. Sherry cut to the chase. She introduced us this way: "This is the Presbyterian pastor and his wife. Presbyterians sing all the verses." I guess that just about summarizes most of the major differences between the two denominations, don't you think?

863

Childhood and youth memories keep coming back. Our family had a television set, but we also had bedtimes, and sometimes the two collided. At bedtime, at the end of the program we were watching, our mother would tell us to turn off the TV and go to bed and if there was some hesitation on our part she would come and stand in front of it and say it one more time. Then, as the credits were rolling, she would turn the thing off. We would be whining and complaining with words like, "I want to see who the Assistant Director was," or, "You didn't let us see who the Makeup Artist was!" Anything to stay up a little longer.

864

A sign outside a church in West Tennessee:

> MANY PEOPLE POSSESS MUCH
> BUT HAVE LITTLE

865

Another act of good sportsmanship occurred the other night. A high school basketball game would be missing one player whose mother had died the previous day. Therefore, he would not be listed on the program. However, as the second half started, he showed up, dressed out and ready to play. His coach put him in and when that happened the referees called a technical foul on the team because the player's name was not on the eligibility list. The coach for the other team even objected to the technical and did not want his team to shoot the required two free throws, and in fact insisted on letting the boy play. But the officials had to go by the book. When they would not relent, the coach relented, and now needed one of his players to shoot the free throws. One young man volunteered. He stepped to the free throw line and on both shots simply bounced the ball forward, intentionally missing (by a mile) his free throws. The crowd gave a standing ovation. Sportsmanship lives. Say it stronger: humanity, goodness, and courtesy are alive and well.

866

Self-image is important. Sometimes we need someone else to help us on that. On more than one occasion I have been in the audience when a certain nationally known speaker on evangelism and church life has stood before us. His greetings were always this way, and they always caught us off guard: "Good morning, saints!" and we would respond with a hearty "Good morning!!!!" Then, "Good morning, sinners!" And we would mumble in a volume much, much lower, "Good morning." His first greeting was glorious. His second was blunt and humbling and brought us down to earth. When I heard the first, I felt great. When I heard the second I wanted to scream out, "Now wait just a minute! Hold it right there!" Like I said, we sometimes need help on our self-image.

867

What is it with people who leave a basketball game (or any other athletic contest) before it is over? In basketball, it doesn't seem to matter what the score is, who is ahead and how much, or how intense the game has been. With about three minutes to go, out they go. You can see a stream of people heading for the exits full-steam ahead. Are they leaving early to beat the traffic? Do they plan to hear the rest of the game on the radio? I have no pity or sympathy for them when the game goes into overtime, then two overtimes, then three. By that time they are home - and missing out on a great game! Hey! I like to stay until it is over, and then sit there a while longer while everybody else is leaving. That way I can contemplate what just happened in the contest, ponder on what it will mean for the future of the world, such as world peace, and wait until most of the crowd is gone. When we lived in the Knoxville, Tennessee, area, a ministerial colleague who was an avid University of Tennessee men's basketball fan had season tickets. And, as you could guess, he and his wife left at exactly three minutes to go, no matter what. It was hard to get tickets and so my wife and I usually attended only if someone let us use theirs. So it was that my colleague offered us two tickets for a particular game. I knew of his propensity for exiting early. When I accepted, I asked, "Do we have to leave with three minutes to go?" He graciously replied, "No." It's not over until it's over. Stay to the bitter, or better, end. See it through.

868

We were traveling from Memphis to Pontotoc, Mississippi, on a spring Saturday night. We would stay in a motel in order to rise early and attend the Algoma community Easter sunrise service the next morning. On the way down we had the radio on and were listening to an NCAA men's basketball tournament game. The contest involved Illinois and Arizona. Two items caused me to turn the radio off the farther we got from Memphis, First, the station was fading out. We could barely hear anything the more we traveled away from the city. Second, with three minutes to go in the game, Arizona was leading Illinois by 15 points, so it looked hopeless for the Fighting Illini. I turned the radio off and really didn't think anything else about it. We checked into our motel room and flipped on the television to ESPN. "Stay tuned for highlights of one of the greatest comebacks in NCAA history," said the announcer. That raised some interest for me, but still it did not register. When the commercials were over and SportsCenter was back on, and I was now paying attention, the highlights of the Arizona-Illinois game, especially the last three minutes, were featured. You guessed it. Illinois, down by 15 with three minutes go, had come back, miraculously forced it into overtime, and won the game. It's not over until it's over. Stay to the bitter, or better, end.

869

I received some homework assignments from one of our PAS classes. The student had found a mentor in his region and was reporting on the development of that relationship. The two of them had become "fishing buddies." The older minister's advice was to "keep your boat at all costs." He also said that "you would be a better preacher if you fished more." The young pastor wrote that the advice from his older, more experienced mentor at first did not sound right but now was beginning to make sense. I don't fish and I don't own a boat, but I admire and respect those ministers who do. A lot of good thinking can take place out there on the river. I'm guessing that sometimes the greatest interruptions may come when one actually catches a fish. It takes a lot of time, I surmise, to handle things after you catch a fish, and your thinking processes have now been disturbed. I am sure, though, that the interruptions are easily handled and one can get on with one's quiet time and helpful meditations.

870

I thought somebody was going to be out a whole lot of money the other day. For some strange reason the Memphis Theological Seminary-owned car I drive as Director of the Program of Alternate Studies had a seatbelt problem. On the driver's side the thing would not fasten. The thingamajig would not go into the whatchamacallit. I tried and tried, but it would not go. I was afraid to push too hard for fear it might go and then I couldn't get out. So for a full day I pulled my seat belt all the way across the hump in the middle of the seat and fastened it to the thing on the passenger's side. I felt fairly secure, but I knew this had to change. I was afraid of money, big money, that I or the school would be out in getting fixed what was obviously broken. I walked over to the office of the Facilities Department of the Seminary and described my plight. One of the men of the staff walked with me back to my car parked in my spot in the parking lot. He opened the door and looked in and worked with it for a while. Soon he emerged holding a penny. It had fallen into the opening where the seat belt was supposed to click. No problem! No charge! No trouble! Thank goodness. Thank God. Thank the Facilities Department. What I thought was a great big problem was little at most, and really not a problem at all. Sometimes our personal or family problems experience similar outcomes. Years ago when we lived in Burleson, Texas, our television went out, and we knew we did not have a lot of money to get it fixed. We went at least a month without watching any television, trying to accumulate enough money to fix the TV set, maybe. Finally we called a TV repair man and he came out and looked it over. Turns out all it needed was a little tube. Total cost: $7.00. Sometimes it is the small things that look or feel like big things that bother us the most.

871

Pastors can learn from other pastors. Churches can learn from other churches. I read where a pastor and some lay leaders of a church were going to visit one of our large, growing churches over a weekend to see that church "in action." There is no doubt that this can be a learning event and the group can come away with a host of great ideas that might go well back home. But a word of caution is in order, and I am sure the group of visitors would agree already: You can't go back to your own church and duplicate what another church does. Every situation is unique. What "works" in one setting may not in another. And, on a reverse note, you may be able to do some great things in your own church that those you are visiting cannot do in their context.

The trouble comes when, for instance, a pastor, on witnessing the miraculous happenings at the place visited returns home and throws it all out there and expects the local folks to "buy into" the entire set of ideas that were picked up. The pastor with unreasonable expectations might grow impatient with the people if they hesitate or express some reservations about some suggestions shipped in from another place. Then the pastor might complain that the home folks "are not following my leadership."

A growing acceptance and use of "contemporary worship" in our churches may be a case in point. This style of worship seems to be picking up in popularity, but it may serve a pastor well to remember that the 30-member or 130-member congregation being served may not have the music leadership, or the interest, or the desire to embark on such a new journey. What the pastor wants, in this regard, may not be what the congregation wants or needs. And, of course, the reverse could be true. The pastor might be an old curmudgeon, like the present writer, and adhere to "traditional worship" at all costs while the people are eager to move on to other styles. That pastor is just as much out of touch. So there, I think I've helped.

872

Some old friends of mine, long-time Cumberland Presbyterian ministers, have for years been making annual trips to Arkansas to fish on the White River. I think they stay around a week or ten days in a cabin near the river. They fish a lot, but they also relax on the porch of the cabin and enjoy eating and talking. While out on the river they have come across such well known persons as Garrison Keillor of "Prairie Home Companion" fame as well as the nationally known Lutheran preacher, Oswald Hoffmann. The widely accepted "title" for their sojourn - which we friends back this way, and they, too, give it - is the "White River Bible Conference." This great tradition among these half a dozen or so ministers has thrived through the years. These guys know how to relax.

873

A bumper sticker on a car here in Memphis describes the state of being of many people in the area and around the world:

> I HAVE DISCOVERED MY
> INNER ELVIS

874

Because of our much traveling, three persons on the Memphis Theological Seminary campus drive Seminary-owned cars: the President, the Director of Advancement, and the PAS Director, who is yours truly. In the spring of 2008 my car needed some repair work. When it came back, I noticed that I now had a front license plate. It had one word in very big letters: "E L V I S." It had these words in smaller letters surrounding the name: "A Tribute to ELVIS. Long Live the Songs of the King." While I noticed it almost immediately I said nothing for a few days, thinking that someone at the repair shop put it on the car. However, one of the Facilities people at the Seminary was talking to me a little later and with a smile said that the license plate was in an old closet on campus that also harbored other old license plates and, to play a joke, the Facilities folks placed it on the front of my car, I said, "Keep it on." A month or two later, it was decided PAS needed a new car and I requested that the front license plate be transferred to that automobile. So now I drive around the country with "E L V I S" on the front and running interference. The tag itself is gold, gaudy, ostentatious, tacky, rather ugly, and probably glows in the dark. Just right for my car. It's great. I did check with higher authorities of the Seminary. No one objects. A few family members may question the wisdom or good sense of it all, but they are kind enough to refrain from saying anything about it.

875

Sunday is - supposedly - a day of rest. Say that to a pastor's family - or just about any other family - as they get ready to go to church. Talk about panic! Talk about chaos! Our girls were very young and their mother and I were trying to get them to get ready to go on a Sunday morning. Instead, they were running around and having a good time, laughing and yelling and being happy. Their father - yours truly - tried vainly to instill in them some sense of obligation mixed with Christian responsibility as to why they should get dressed. I may have said something like, "Quit that laughing!" To which our youngest, Kristen, probably age six or seven, at the time, said, "Oh yeah, I forgot; this is Sunday. We are not supposed to be happy on Sunday." Ouch, ouch, and more ouch. Sunday a day of rest? You are at the church pretty much all day, it seems. You come home late Sunday night dragging and bedraggled. I recall that my main time of "rest" was somewhere between 9:00 and 10:30 on a Sunday evening. The week was over, so to speak. It would start up again on Monday. But for these ninety minutes, I will rest, I told myself. Did you know or have you noticed that the word REST when two more of the letter S are added can be jumbled up so that the letters spell STRESS?

876

I am going to have to be more helpful with new students here on the campus of Memphis Theological Seminary. My office is upstairs in the "second building," Cumberland Hall. At the bottom of the stairs there are some easy chairs where students sometimes lounge as they wait for their next class. More than once as I have descended the stairs and have seen three or four sitting there, I have said, "They let me come down every three months." There may or may not be a twitter of laughter, mostly not, emanating from the easy chairs. In a Directors' meeting we were informed that a special committee would be working to provide more written information that would be more "student-friendly" so that those new to the school would feel more at home as early as possible. So I guess I have to be truthful about how often they let me come down. I told all this to my fellow Directors in that meeting and a few wise guys at the other end suggested it should have been every four months, but they would settle for two.

In "Days of our Lives," on daytime TV, Dr. Tom Horton and his wife Alice had two sons, Bill and Mickey. After the show had been going about two years, or so it seems, one day there descended from upstairs another young man. As he walked down the stairs, family members said something like, "Oh, hi, Tommy." This was the first time viewers knew there was a son named Tommy and this was the way he was introduced. Had he been locked in a bedroom upstairs for these two years? Now he appears and family members take it casually. Where has he been these two years? Well, it was so confusing to the daughter of Tom and Alice, that she fell in love with Tommy well before she knew Tommy was her brother. When the news of their brother-sister connection was presented to her, she was so heartbroken she became a nun and entered a monastery, or other church-related establishment where nuns go. So that is where I got the nerve and the go-ahead to make my announcement as I descended the stairs of Cumberland Hall.

877

In a biography of Edgar Allan Poe, I read where he was prone to criticize other poets, even to the point of accusing them of plagiarism, the most famous being Henry Wadsworth Longfellow and James Russell Lowell, two of his contemporaries. Poe had his problems with drinking, depression, anger, loneliness, and a host of other issues. Sometimes he felt he had to strike out at somebody. But putting somebody else down just dragged him down.

(From Poe: A Life Cut Short, by Peter Ackroyd (Talese/Doubleday, 2008) pp. 124-129

878

Abraham Lincoln's contacts with the Cumberland Presbyterian Church are the stuff of legend in the denomination. They were few in number, but significant. One of them is recorded in a recent biography entitled A. Lincoln, by Ronald C. White, Jr. Abe's first love was Ann Rutledge. However, she died as a teenager on August 25, 1835, probably of typhoid fever. "Her uncle, John M. Cameron, a Cumberland Presbyterian minister, preached her funeral sermon," reports the author on pages 100-101 (Random House, 2008).

879

Every church - large or small, city or country, new or old - is fragile. Even the best organized, best financed, best led, and most committed congregation is fragile. Churches have been split over strong-willed people's insistence on their own way, over differences among well-meaning people about a pastor, over whether to build on and assume debt or not build on and risk becoming stagnant in a growing community. These reasons and a host of others demonstrate that a church is fragile. Paul said it best in 2 Corinthians 4:7: "We have this treasure in earthen vessels." I suspect he was talking about the treasure of the Christian gospel entrusted to us. Perhaps he could also have meant the family. Paul could have also been referring to the human soul, carried around in a fragile, breakable human body. Or he might have meant a group of churches, such as a denomination. All fragile. All treasures, but in human constructions and therefore always subject to breakage. This is all the more reason for being tender and kind to one another, forgiving of one another, and, amid strong convictions rightly held, honoring other viewpoints.

880

Part of the following is true. Really, all but the last part. Our three girls were born in 1966, 1968, and 1970, all election years. Linda told me later she would no longer accept the nomination and if elected would not serve. In those days you did not know whether it was a boy or a girl until the event happened. The first was a girl, Kelly Lynne. The second was a girl, Kimberly Kaye. As I stood out in the hall awaiting the news on the third child - back then fathers, thank goodness, did not go into the labor room - I broke out into a cold sweat: I panicked. What if this one is a boy? I will have to start setting a good example. And we will have to buy some boys' clothes! But, praise God, it was another girl, Kristen Lee. In gratitude, we thought about re-naming our girls after those three great women in the 23rd Psalm: Shirley, Goodness, and Mercy. Since then they have been "following me all the days of my life" - and I love it.

881

This just came to me. It's about us humans. The reader can decide whether it came by "inspiration" or not. A poem by Thomas D. Campbell, with apologies to Ogden Nash.

OUR EARS

Our ears make us look silly.
What can we say about 'em?
The only thing that's sillier
Is how we'd look without 'em.

882

I remember reading about Ralph Nader, the burr under the skin of corporate America. His first real splash was his book <u>Unsafe At Any Speed</u>. It was about a certain make of car that one of the major automobile companies had manufactured and sold, but that was later proven to be hazardous to drive. He later became an advocate for consumers and usually took many of the least popular, but often appropriate, positions politically and environmentally. As he told his life story he said that as a child his family never sent him to his room when the grownups started visiting. They, in fact, encouraged him to stay, and as he listened his life was being shaped as a person who would speak out for the "little guy." His parents and other adults would discuss many of the concerns in which Ralph later became involved.

When I read the story of Ralph Nader, I recalled with gratitude that I was never "sent to my room" either. At our house in McKenzie, Tennessee, the site of Bethel College and the Cumberland Presbyterian Theological Seminary (now Memphis Theological Seminary in Memphis, Tennessee) there would be visitors - ministers in the church, college and seminary students and families, and visiting lecturers for ministers' conferences (Julian Price Love of Louisville Presbyterian Theological Seminary, for one). I may have chosen not to stay in the room but I was never told to leave. Naturally I listened a lot and learned a lot. I came to love and appreciate the church as my parents did, and to love and appreciate other leaders in the church. To this day, I still remember Ralph Nader's account of his childhood in this regard.

883

Somewhere, I don't remember where, I read a scholar's analysis of faith in the Bible. He suggested at least three kinds. First, there is Reflective Faith. I can now look back and see how God was involved in events in my life. While they were occurring I did not give it much thought, but now in retrospect I can understand, and appreciate, God's activity in my life. A second look at faith might be The Book of James Faith. There the writer, who has obviously heard a lot about faith from different people, is rather impatient. He has heard testimonies on how people love Jesus, how they could not live without faith, how grace has played a big part in their lives. But the writer of James is from Missouri, the "Show Me State." He wants action. "Show me your faith by your works" seems to be the theme. Faith must be followed by deeds of mercy, acts of service to others, and self-sacrifice. No more talk only; now action is needed. Yet a third kind of faith can be called Abraham Faith. This is following the example of Abraham of old, who "went out not knowing where he was going," who was called of God to "go from your father's house" into the unknown, led of God. Some of us choose this kind of faith; others have it thrust on us. This Abraham Faith is based on belief and trust in God, and to walk with God into the darkness of uncertainty and danger is a challenging and even rewarding way to live. We have lived by and been blessed by all three kinds of faith. Somehow the Abraham Faith may be the most challenging.

884

While I was their pastor, she came to Sunday school and worship every Sunday; he hardly ever did. It wasn't long after I resigned to take another church position that I began to read in the newsletter that he was on this committee and that task force, and that he soon was elected as an elder. Another family was absent from church activities all the time I served that congregation. They never "darkened the door," as the phrase goes. Within weeks after my departure, I read in that church's newsletter that the family was active and highly involved in church life. Talk to any pastor anywhere, and you will probably hear the same story as I have told about two different pastorates in my years as a minister. There are people you just can't reach, or who do not respond to your ministry. And then, when you leave and another pastor comes in, lo and behold, they are right there - joining the church, singing in the choir, teaching a class, serving as elders on the church session, participating in a work day. You could not establish a relationship but somebody else could. And you are grateful.

The reverse may be true when you enter a new pastorate. You hope so. You hope that if the previous pastor was unable to make an impact on a particular life or family, you might. No one can reach everybody and no one person can appeal to everybody in a positive way. We all have strengths and weaknesses.

885

I was talking with a fellow Cumberland Presbyterian minister and we were lamenting that some ministers and churches do not participate in the life of the denomination - nor do they support it - as we think they should. Then I made an off-hand remark: "We are connected, but not connectional." The first is the way we are constitutionally. The second is dependent on our attitude. In the first, we are connected in that ministers belong to a Presbytery and are required to attend the meetings. Churches have elders and are required to send an elder to the regular meetings of the Presbytery. Most presbyteries require that churches pay their presbyterial "dues" to keep programs like camping programs going and to undergird the work of the stated clerk of the presbytery. It is presbyteries that ordain ministers, whether we like it or not. It is presbyteries that approve and dissolve pastoral relationships. These things are pretty much required. We are connected.

However, to be connectional goes even farther and has to do more with spirit and attitude and priorities. For example, strictly on the financial side, all churches are requested and urged to give one-tenth, a tithe, of their regular offerings to Our United Outreach, something similar to United Way in a community. Our United Outreach (OUO) is used to support denominational programs nationally and worldwide, such as our children's home, our seminary, our national and global mission projects, stewardship education, denominational youth and children's work, the historical archives, and so many other programs. A lot of churches give a tithe, but many do not. And size doesn't matter. Many of our smaller churches are faithful and heroic in sending one-tenth of their regular offerings each month to OUO. Some of our larger churches send a mere pittance, if that much. One congregation has an annual income of over one million dollars. They give less than $10,000 each year to OUO. Still, our churches do rather well.

In 2007, 700 churches (there are almost 900 churches in all) gave $2,600,000 to support the denomination's many areas of mission, service, compassion, education, and stewardship.

More than the financial part would be the attitude of being connectional in promoting and being enthusiastic about what our church does nationally and worldwide. We do much more together than any one congregation can do alone. We can celebrate the fact that we are hand in hand and arm in arm with thousands of Cumberland Presbyterians around the world by our mutual participation in prayers, in service, and in financial giving.

886

Inspired by #881 above and the poem entitled "Our Ears" I have gone further and written something else about us:

THE HUMAN FOOT

The human foot is ugly
There is no way around it
We cover it with socks and shoes
But still we have to pound it

On the pavement, on the road
In the town and city
And when the day is over we
Look down on it with pity.

What to think and what to do
As we lie down to sleep now?
Ugly as the foot may be
It's something we will keep now.

887

When we moved to the big city of Memphis and needed dental or medical or other such professional help I turned to the Yellow Pages. You never know how fortunate or unfortunate you may be. First, I leafed through the book to find a dentist. The location of one particular dentist was reasonably close so I chose him. I needed some crowns and perhaps a filling or two. I do not recall exactly what all was needed. I was a bit disappointed that their office music, while the crowns were being inserted, did not play, "Crown Him With Many Crowns." I got over that slight because something else caught my eye and ear. The dentist was almost always yelling at his assistant. It was an impatient, almost angry, yell. I noticed something else: Every time I went back for more work or a checkup there would be a different assistant, and once or twice an entirely new staff. When finally the work was completed - and I had to return a couple of times so he could make some corrections in his work - I was relieved. I was very much relieved to be out of there. A couple of years later, a woman bled to death in his dental chair because he did not take the right precautions during dental surgery. Later the state board brought him up on charges and he lost his dental license.

My second experience with finding professional help in the Yellow Pages was entirely different. From 1984 on I would have periodic inflammation of one eye. In the fall of 1994, after we moved to Memphis, it became much worse. I leafed through the Yellow Pages and found an eye specialist. From the first visit satisfaction has been excellent. That malady has been and is being treated. A few years later the same doctor removed cataracts from both eyes in two separate trips.

You take your chances as you deal with "unknowns" out there.

888

I imagine that churches seeking pastors go through some of the same horrors and joys as are mentioned in #887 above. Prospective pastors can send in impressive (and true) resumes, can sit down for equally impressive interviews, and can generally win over the search committee. And then, upon entering onto the task at hand they can fail to measure up to the promise shown earlier. On the other hand, someone not so impressive, and certainly not flashy or exciting, can make a mediocre impression and, if given a chance, can later emerge as an outstanding pastor and preacher and leader in the church. Many churches (and this is the right way to do it) ask for and receive Personal Information Forms (PIFs) on different ministers, and it is sort of like looking through the Yellow Pages. You take your chances.

Of course, prospective pastors have similar experiences on the other side. A church that looks good on paper, in interviews, and in visits, and makes good promises, may not come through and may indeed be a disappointment. The pastor went there on what turned out to be false promises or at least unrealistic expectations. This happens occasionally.

889

I go to the dentist as seldom as possible. This is in keeping with my religion: I am an "orthodox coward." However, in every place we have lived I have eventually had to choose one. In Lexington, Kentucky, just down the street from where we lived, was a dentist. I chose him. I made a few trips there. I remember he - like others before and after - instructed me on how to brush my teeth. It's not "up-down-up-down." It is "up-up-up" and "down-down-down." I was, according to the Lexington dentist, brushing too hard. He said, "Remember, you are not cleaning the deck of a battleship." Those memorable words have stayed with me for these twenty-five years.

I suppose his advice could be carried to church problems. A simple problem may not need the full force of pastoral or lay leadership that involves official action. It may need only a mild suggestion. Those things that appear to be imposing might on second glance turn out to need light touches instead of aggressive confrontations.

890

In college I took a course called General Psychology. Interesting. The next year there was another course: Adolescent Psychology. VERY interesting. I learned a lot. However, my strongest reaction was: Where was this course when I needed it five or six years earlier, back in high school? If I had known what this class taught me WHEN ADOLESCENCE WAS HAPPENING, I could have maneuvered through life a whole lot easier. But no, they wait until you have stumbled through the darkness and uncertainty of that time in your life - and then they tell you later what all of that meant. Truth be told, we usually don't have the time or inclination to study or evaluate events while they are happening anyway. It is after the fact, after the dust has settled, that we can look back and understand.

891

I was the middle of three brothers (still am). Older brother Sam (Sammy then) could say things and I would believe every word, no questions asked. He especially had a way to end arguments, coming forth with something wise and indisputable. For example, when we would be arguing and I was complaining that he had changed his mind on something, he would say, "Wise people change their minds; fools never do." That was it. That was enough for me. Conflict over. End of subject. On another matter: he was born in Tennessee and I in Texas, so we had a running debate on which state was the better. He said Tennessee; I said Texas. He was a Tennessee Volunteers fan and I was a Texas Longhorns fan. Then Sam would stop all debate with another wise saying, surely one of the most authoritative statements I had ever heard up to that time: "Tennessee has more people per square mile than Texas." What a concept! What keen insight! What wisdom! What was he talking about? It didn't matter. It sounded so good and so smart and so... well, authoritative. Younger brother Paul had two big brothers. Just think of the wisdom we imparted to him!

892

"Enoch walked with God." So reads Genesis 5:24. I read something the other day that jolted my mind and brought joy and reassurance. Whoever the modern writer was added this important thought: "And God walked with Enoch." Enoch walked with God. And God walked with Enoch. Yes.

893

As I think back on it now, I am ashamed of my words, but at the time they seemed appropriate. I was at a church conference in south Texas. Different denominations were represented. Our small group gathered in a circle and we were asked to say our names and tell something about ourselves. I got just a little irritated when, as we went around, two and then three and then four people introduced themselves and said to this effect: "I am fluent in two (or three or four) languages." It was as if they were trying to outdo one another in showing bi- or tri-lingual superiority. So, when they got to me - and this is embarrassing now - I had had it up to here with that. I told my name and where I lived and then said, "I can remain silent in twelve languages, and I am working on my thirteenth." As I recall, no one commented on that. Perhaps they thought I was serious. They all seemed so serious through it all.

894

A bumper sticker had this wise advice:

MORE WAG

LESS BARK

895

I was on "drugs" once just as one of our PAS students said he was, mentioned earlier in this book. My wife "drug" me to the car and we went to the mall. Then she "drug" me to the men's store where there was a sale on suits. She thought I should buy three suits. I told her I had a good one at home and it "suited" me just fine. So I tried them on and we bought three suits. The sign said they were "On Sale" but you couldn't prove it by me; the total looked mighty high in my eyes.

I preach at two little churches in Mississippi. Two Sundays after this giant purchase we arrived at our 9:00 A.M. church on a Sunday morning and I took a coat off the hanger and started to put it on. It was then I noticed this new coat still had the tag on it. That wasn't so bad. I could cut the tag off. However, I remembered that this was the suit I wore LAST Sunday and nobody mentioned seeing the tag! I felt like Minnie Pearl and her hat. So I announced the blunder to the church folks at both the 9:00 congregation and the 11:00 congregation. Nobody confessed to noticing anything the previous Sunday. Church folks are some of the best around. They are so kind.

896

My old friend Herbert Blumenthal reminds me that I told this story years ago: As a little boy I was misbehaving, acting badly. My mother sent me upstairs to my room. "Don't come back down until you have learned how to act." I went upstairs and, a few minutes later came halfway down the stairs and called out, "Mother." She appeared at the bottom of the stairs. "How about this?" I asked. "To be... or not to be, that is the question." I got the answer when she pointed me back upstairs.

897

A ministerial colleague was visiting in my office and we were discussing the length of this book you are reading. I said I didn't know when to stop. He looked around at the books on my shelf and said, "I imagine that many of these authors didn't say everything they would have liked to have said." That reminded me that movies shown to the public are something like an hour and a half long, but many more hours were filmed with much left "on the cutting floor." Sermons are the same. Preachers have twenty to twenty five minutes to tell the story, make the point, seek to inspire. They will say less than they know about a text. They will leave unsaid some very nice Christian things. A great amount of sermon preparation is deciding what not to say. So it should have been with this book. But I just kept on and on and on and on, world without end, Amen. And that is where I should leave it, with an Amen. Thanks for reading it.

The author and his wife, Linda, in San Francisco.

Dudley and Joyce Condron. (He provided the illustrations.)

Herbert and Wanda Blumenthal with the Taj Mahal in the background.

Thomas H. and Margaret Campbell, parents of the author.

Theodore and Mary Kathryn Coleman, parents of Linda Campbell.

Three brothers and a sister with their mother, Margaret Campbell, on the occasion of Margaret's 90th birthday.
Back Row: Paul, Tom, and Sam.
Front Row: Jo Nell and Margaret.

Dr. Campbell (center above) and the ministers in Korea where classes were conducted.

Dr. Campbell with co-teacher, Young Kim.

The Campbell girls in the mid-seventies.
From left: Kelly, Kim, Kristen, children of Tom and Linda Campbell.

McKenzie, TN, Little League All-Star Team, June 1950.
The author is in the front row, fourth from the left. Herbert Blumenthal next to him, third from the left.

Two churches where the author served as pastor.

St. Luke, Fort Worth, Texas.

Beaver Creek, Knoxville, Tennessee.

The administration building at Bethel University, McKenzie, Tennessee. The Cumberland Presbyterian Theological Seminary was on this campus until 1964, when it moved to Memphis, Tennessee, and was named Memphis Theological Seminary of the Cumberland Presbyterian Church.

The Program of Alternate Studies of the Cumberland Presbyterian Church meeting on the campus of Bethel College, July 2002. The school is now Bethel University.

The Campbell girls 2006. Left to right: Kristen, Kim, Kelly.

The McKenzie, Tennessee, High School Class of 1957 at their 50th anniversary reunion. The author (back row, far left) and Billy Webb (back row, far right) were co-captains and seniors on the boy's basketball team that went 23-8 and won the district championship. Managers for the team were Barry Baker (top row, fourth from the left) and Herbert Blumenthal (not pictured).

www.ingramcontent.com/pod-product-compliance
Lightning Source LLC
Chambersburg PA
CBHW071103230426
43666CB00009B/1811